JAINA YOGA

LALA SUNDAR LAL JAIN
RESEARCH SERIES

VOLUME I

JAINA YOGA

A SURVEY OF THE MEDIAEVAL ŚRĀVAKĀCĀRAS

R. WILLIAMS

MOTILAL BANARSIDASS PUBLISHERS
PRIVATE LIMITED • DELHI

First Edition: Oxford, 1963
First MLBD Reprint: Delhi, 1983
Reprint: Delhi, 1991, 1998
By arrangement with Oxford University Press

ISBN: 81-208-0775-8

MOTILAL BANARSIDASS

41 U.A. Bungalow Road, Jawahar Nagar, Delhi 110 007
8 Mahalaxmi Chamber, Warden Road, Mumbai 400 026
120 Royapettah High Road, Mylapore, Chennai 600 004
Sanas Plaza, Subhash Nagar, Pune 411 002
16 St. Mark's Road, Bangalore 560 001
8 Camac Street, Calcutta 700 017
Ashok Rajpath, Patna 800 004
Chowk, Varanasi 221 001

PRINTED IN INDIA

BY JAINENDRA PRAKASH JAIN AT SHRI JAINENDRA PRESS,
A-45 NARAINA INDUSTRIAL AREA, PHASE I, NEW DELHI 110 028
AND PUBLISHED BY NARENDRA PRAKASH JAIN FOR
MOTILAL BANARSIDASS PUBLISHERS PRIVATE LIMITED,
BUNGALOW ROAD, DELHI 110 007

PREFACE

THE work here presented is an attempt to examine the contents of the principal Jaina *śrāvakācāras*. As these texts are not well known and often not easily accessible, some information about their authors has also been given and a few excerpts, designed to show the extent to which one writer depends on another, have been included in an appendix.

It will be noted that, to avoid confusion, all technical terms employed have been given in Sanskrit even in cases where an original Prakrit form has been falsely sanskritized.

A certain amount of repetition has been imposed by the plan of the work, and it can only be hoped that this has been kept to a minimum.

I should like to express my gratitude to Professor W. Schubring, who very kindly lent me his own copy of the *Śrāvaka-prajñapti*, the basic Śvetāmbara text on *śrāvakācāra*, when he learned that I was unable to procure the work from any other source.

Finally I wish to acknowledge the generous assistance provided by the authorities of the School of Oriental and African Studies who have included this book in the London Oriental Series and met the full cost of its publication.

CONTENTS

INTRODUCTION

When Hemacandra gave to his treatise on the rules of conduct for laymen and ascetics the name of *Yoga-śāstra* he intended to convey that it covered the whole religious striving—what in Western terms might be rendered as a walking in righteousness all the days of one's life. Though he may have chosen this title in order to stimulate the interest of his royal patron, who appears to have been attached to yogic practices, it is normal Śvetāmbara usage to equate the term *yoga* with the *ratna-traya*, that combination of right belief, right knowledge, and right conduct on which the practice of Jainism is based. It is to a consideration of *śrāvaka-dharma* or *śrāvakācara*, the corpus of rules which have been elaborated to regulate the daily life of a layman, that this survey will be restricted.

The term *śrāvakācāra*, current among the Digambaras but unknown, it would seem, to the Śvetāmbaras, serves both as a general name for the topic and as a title for individual expositions designed to serve as breviaries for the householder and composed on parallel lines to the *yaty-ācāras* which explain the duties of monks. These treatises though to some extent they form a counterpart to the Hindu *dharma-śāstras* do not embrace as wide a range of contents. For *śrāvakācāra* the Digambaras also employ the synonym *upāsakā-dhyāyana*, which is their name for the lost *aṅga* corresponding to the Śvetāmbara *Upāsaka-daśāḥ*. According to the *Ṣaṭ-khaṇḍāgama*[1] this dealt with the eleven *pratimās*, the conferment of the *vratas*, and the proper way of carrying them out. A later account[2] of the lost *aṅgas* expands this enumeration and includes in the subject-matter the *pratimās*, *dāna*, *pūjā*, *saṅgha-sevā*, *vrata*, *guṇa*, *śīla*, and *kriyā*: in view of the ambivalence of some of these terms the delimitation remains imprecise. *Śrāvaka*, *upāsaka*, *śramaṇopāsaka*, *gṛhin*, *sāgāra*, *deśa-saṃyamin*, *deśa-virata*, *śrāddha* (this last a purely Śvetāmbara usage) are amongst the names applied indifferently, at least in the mediaeval period, to the lay disciple whose partial or limited vows of good conduct form the subject of the *śrāvakācāras*.

[1] Vol. i, p. 102. [2] *Aṅga-prajñapti* of Śubhacandra, pp. 44–46.

The term mediaeval is purely one of convenience, for Jaina history may usefully be separated into three divisions. To the early period—the dark age covering the first millennium—belong the whole of the Śvetāmbara canon and such fundamental Digambara works as the *Prābhṛtas* of Kundakunda and the *Tattvārtha-sūtra*. The middle, or mediaeval, period extending from the fifth to the end of the thirteenth century is the most important historically and sees the greatest achievements in art and literature. Jaina groups and individuals in various parts of western and southern India are found exerting at times considerable influence on political developments, until the renaissance of Śaivism (especially in the form of Vīraśaivism) in the south and the expansion of Islam in the north shatter the flourishing Jaina communities. The fourteenth century is the great divide. From then on Jainism is on the defensive, and its adherents having lost access to the sources of power are relegated to the role of a scattered minority, no longer proselytizing, and increasingly identified with certain narrow social groups. This modern period is therefore, by comparison with the past, an age of decadence.

The *śrāvakācāras* are not the only, nor indeed the best, source of information on the lay life. Clearly their authors, who for the mediaeval period seem all, except Āśādhara, to have been monks, have not portrayed society as it existed but rather as they would have wished to see it, so that this survey may be said to be concerned in a sense with theory rather than with reality. Like the Hindu *dharma-śāstras* these treatises present a one-sided view but in them it is the idealized figure of the *muni* and not of the brahmin that occupies the centre of the stage. The rich and varied *kathā* literature, however artificial and shackled by convention it may be, can add much to complete the picture whilst the epigraphical evidence remains still largely unexploited.

Though less voluminous than the treatises devoted to the monastic life the *śrāvakācāras* are still sufficiently numerous to make it difficult to cover their contents within a reasonable compass, even allowing for the fact that many have never been published or, even if printed, are not accessible in Europe. It was therefore decided to exclude all works in Tamil and Kanarese and to limit the scope of this survey to writings in Sanskrit and Prakrit. The very extensive literature in Hindi and Gujarati belongs in any event to the modern period. If therefore the relatively small number of texts surveyed is taken into consideration the generalizations may seem at times too categoric and any conclusions reached are bound to rest on incomplete evidence.

This survey then is an attempt to describe the contents of the mediaeval *śrāvakācāras* including also the three *aśvāsas* from Somadeva's *Yaśastilaka* which are often collectively referred to as an *upāsakādhyayana* and the three *parvans* from Jinasena's *Ādi-purāṇa* which describe the *kriyās* or ceremonies marking the stages of progress in the lay and monastic life: in view of the esteem which they enjoy in the Digambara tradition it would have been impossible to omit these. On the other hand, with works such as the *Dharma-bindu*, *Cāritra-sāra*, *Yoga-śāstra*, and *Dharmāmṛta* which treat of both the lay and the monastic life, only the sections relevant to the former have been taken into consideration. Nor are all the actual contents of the *śrāvakācāras* suitable for inclusion. The epitomes of the *tattvas* or *padārthas*, the basic dogmas of Jainism, prefixed by certain writers to their treatises offer, for example, no material that is not easily available elsewhere. The refutations of doctrines regarded as forms of *mithyātva* or false belief, though of intrinsic interest, are not germane to this survey: in general they are directed against the *nāstikas* (with whom the Jainas are at great pains not to be confused), the Buddhists, or the Śaivas, no attention being devoted to the Vaiṣṇavas. Other excursions from the main theme are the heterogeneous items of information on topics as remote, for example, as *stena-śāstra* which are to be found in the Śvetāmbara commentaries and the technical instructions for the building of temples and fashioning of images.

It might be desirable in a study of this kind to concentrate on a fixed point in time and it may be objected that the period covered by the survey—eight centuries—is too long to permit of any cohesion of treatment. In fact three-quarters of the works considered belong to the eleventh and twelfth centuries. If any one book is to be taken as a standard it must be the *Yoga-śāstra*, the general plan of which has moreover been followed in deciding the sequence of the contents, which, following the Jaina pattern, have been arranged by numerical categories. No other religion has been so obsessed by the hallucination of numbers and any description which failed to take account of this unprepossessing presentation would not be faithful. For some aspects of Jaina practice in which there have been considerable innovations such as the *yātrā*, where the mediaeval texts do not offer sufficient material, works subsequent to A.D. 1300 have been drawn on for supplementary information.

Before discussing certain points which arise from the survey it would perhaps be desirable to note how far the subject of *śrāvakācāra* has attracted attention in the past. Weber touched on it in the course of his researches into the Jaina canon but the earliest attempt to produce an edition of a relevant text seems to have been made by Windisch when he published the first four *prakāśas* of the *Yoga-śāstra*; in the absence of the commentary his translation was naturally, at that stage, often speculative and sometimes wide of the mark. On the other hand, Hoernle's edition of the *Upāsakadaśāḥ* included Abhayadeva's commentary and his renderings of text and commentary are still in the main valid. Jacobi's edition of the *Tattvārtha-sūtra*[1] made that fundamental work available with translation, but the section of it devoted to *śrāvakācāra*—the seventh *adhyāya*—is a small and relatively unimportant part of the whole. Ernst Leumann's researches into the *Āvaśyaka* literature were of relevance to the lay doctrine by the light which they threw on the Śvetāmbara and Digambara liturgy. The two best general works on Jainism—*Der Jainismus* by H. von Glasenapp and *Die Lehre der Jainas* by W. Schubring—are not concerned to a very great extent with the *śrāvakācāra*. The former dealt mainly with the contemporary scene; the latter covered the subject as far as it figures in the canonical literature with his usual masterly concision and impeccable scholarship.

There was in Italy during the early years of this century a very great interest in Jaina and Middle Indian studies as the names of Tessitori, Pulle, Pavolini, Ballini, Belloni-Filippi, and Suali bear witness. Suali in particular, in his edition of the *Dharma-bindu* in the *Giornale Asiatico*, unhappily never continued beyond the fourth *adhyāya*, offered one of the most successful translations of a Sanskrit text into a European language, a version in which elegance and poetical felicity of style are matched by the author's mastery of his subject. With the text and translation are included an introduction and a commentary, based on that of Municandra, which together give a good idea of the classical Śvetāmbara *śrāvakācāra* doctrine. Belloni-Filippi, in the same periodical, embarked on an

[1] H. Jacobi, 'Eine Jaina Dogmatik', *ZDMG* lx (1906), pp. 287–325 and 512–55.

edition and translation of the *Yoga-śāstra* which did not progress very far.

In India in the twenties and thirties a group of Digambara propagandists headed by Jagmandarlal Jaini and Champat Ray Jain produced in the *Bibliotheca Jainica* editions of works such as the *Ratna-karaṇḍa* and the *Puruṣārtha-siddhy-upāya*, coupling them with English translations of no high merit in which a modern interpretation often disfigures the sense of the original. The same objection applies to the pamphlets on the lay doctrine compiled by Champat Ray Jain and others. They belong rather with the voluminous ethical literature which issues so freely from the presses in Hindi and Gujarati.

Whilst in Śvetāmbara circles no great attention seems to have been devoted to the study of the older *śrāvakācāra* treatises there is a small body of work done by scholars, all Digambaras, that cannot be ignored. In particular from Nāthurām Premī, Jugalkiśor Mukhtār, and Hīralāl Jain have come a number of contributions of significance written in Hindi and for the most part scattered over periodicals or incorporated in introductions to texts. Premī's essays, mainly drawn from the *Jaina Hitaishi*, have been reprinted in book form under the title *Jaina sāhitya aur itihās* and provide a mine of information, always cautious, always accurate, on a multiplicity of Jaina and mainly Digambara themes including that of the layman's duties. Hīralāl Jain has prefaced his edition of the *Vasunandi-śrāvakācāra* by an introduction which is, in effect, the first monograph on *śrāvakācāra* in any language though limited to Digambara sources. Jugalkiśor Mukhtār, who in an early publication, *Grantha parīkṣā*, had discussed the spurious *śrāvakācāras* current in Digambara milieux, has more recently assembled in the introduction to the *Purātana Jaina-vākya-sūci* much information on the chronology of Jaina writers. A. N. Upadhye, who writes in English, has lately dealt with the subject in the admirable introduction to his edition of the *Dvādaśānuprekṣā*. Another very recent work is the translation of the *Sarvārtha-siddhi* commentary by S. A. Jain, who has made a remarkably successful rendering of a difficult subject. A sociological study, the *Jaina Community* of V. Sangave, contains much of interest on the *śrāvakācāra*; its value would have been higher had the author gone to the original sources instead of relying on such unsure guides as Mrs. Stevenson.

Though Hindi or Gujarati or, in a few cases, English translations exist for a number of the works which form the subject of this survey, only three of these are of sufficient quality to be utilizable without reference to the text. These are Suali's version of the *Dharma-bindu*, S. A. Jain's version of the *Sarvārtha-siddhi*, and the admirable *Yaśastilaka and Indian Culture* of K. K. Handiqui; this last might well serve as a prototype for similar studies of other classical works. It is not a translation, but all passages of significance in the original are so accurately rendered and clearly commented that recourse to the text can be avoided.

The traditional distinction between the code of behaviour for the householder, the *śrāvakācāra*, and that for the monk, the *yaty-ācāra*, is a fundamental one. Initially the lay estate was admitted by the Jina only in deference to human frailty and was regarded in theory as a stage of preparation for the ascetic life. In the early period of Jainism the *śrāvakācāra* was therefore of minimal importance, and as it has grown progressively in significance various expedients have had to be adopted to make up for the silence of the canonical texts. The corpus of the lay doctrine is in fact a creation of the mediaeval period. The *Upāsaka-daśāḥ* supplied the framework of the *vratas*, each with its five typical *aticāras* or infractions, and the *pratimās*. Though the notion that these *aticāras* were intended only as examples[1] is familiar to the older Śvetāmbara *ācāryas*, they soon became, in practice, the basis of a complete moral code. The *Āvaśyaka* literature gave the details of the necessary duties which are obligatory on the layman as well as on the monk, and, doubtless because some practices belong at the same time to several categories—the *sāmāyika*, which is both *vrata*, *pratimā*, and *āvaśyaka*, is a case in point—and because in some of them the ascetic is assimilated temporarily to the position of a monk, the transference to the lay life of rules originally intended for the community of monks was facilitated. This process of adaptation was developed on a wide scale and contributed notably to the building up of the vast edifice of the temple ritual. An expanding tradition of sacred legends such as those which under the appellation of *purāṇas* have been fashioned by the Digambaras into the shape of a scripture helped to lend authority to innovations in practice as when the name of Kṛṣṇa Vāsudeva is invoked as the

[1] See, for example, Abhayadeva's remarks on UD i. 55.

originator of the *dvādaśāvarta-vandanaka.*[1] A similar purpose was achieved by the conferment of a quasi-canonical authority on famous *pūrvācāryas*; an example is the use of the phrase *iti Haribhadra-sūri-matam.*[2] The Digambaras, who by not admitting the authenticity of the extant canon have to some extent rejected the servitudes of tradition, have not hesitated before a conscious rationalization of the texts: this is true notably of the *Tattvārtha-sūtra* and the *Ratna-karaṇḍa.* Local usage or customary law, the *deśācāra*, though accorded no mandatory force, has always been admitted as a guide wherever there is no conflict with Jaina doctrine and more particularly in the modern period has been increasingly incorporated in the *śrāvakācāra.* An extreme instance of this process would be the sanctification of the *arka-vivāha* in the seventeenth-century *Traivarṇikācāra.* At all times the building up of the *śrāvakācāra* has been assisted by the polyvalence of certain terms and by the habit, widespread among the commentators, of arbitrarily treating words or phrases as *upalakṣaṇas*—symbols or examples of wider categories: and again and again the word *ādi* is inserted by the commentators in places where the text offers no justification for it. The methods used in constructing the *śrāvakācāra* have their analogies elsewhere: it is with rather similar exiguous resources that the Christian and Moslem exegetes raised their elaborate edifices of morality.

In the presentation of the *śrāvakācāra* the original pattern, Digambara as well as Śvetāmbara, seems to have been a description of *samyaktva* and the twelve *vratas* followed by a sketch of the ritual and incorporating miscellaneous injunctions that cannot be brought under the head of any particular vow. Hemacandra, drawing on ideas to be found in the *Dharma-bindu*, introduced the concept of the *dina-caryā* as a device for describing the *āvaśyakas* and prefaced his discussion of the *vratas* by a delineation of the thirty-five *śrāvaka-guṇas*. Both of these devices served as models for later *śrāvakācāras*: treatises like the *Śrāddha-dina-kṛtya* and *Śrāddha-vidhi* are based on a description of the day's ritual duties into which are inserted, under no very orderly arrangement, the moral precepts of the creed; whilst the more popular, discursive pattern of the *śrāvaka-guṇas*, embodying the qualities of the ideal layman, is adopted in the *Śrāddha-guṇa-vivaraṇa.* The Digambaras have often chosen a framework in which the essential

[1] YŚ iii. 130 (p. 679). [2] PS v. 277.

divisions are furnished by the *pratimās*, the *vratas* being treated under the second *pratimā*; or, less commonly, they have preferred a schema based on the categories of *pakṣa* (favourable inclination to the doctrine), *niṣṭhā* (performance of the *pratimās*), and *sādhana* (completion of one's life by ritual suicide). In general they have given only a perfunctory treatment of the *āvaśyakas*, esteeming them to belong rather to the province of *yaty-ācāra*.

Perhaps because they disclaim the continuity of tradition the Digambaras seem to have felt more keenly than the Śvetāmbaras the need to concretize and systematize the lay doctrine, and, in attempting a more logical presentation of the creed, they have effaced more than one discrepancy. It is basically this fact which has made it impossible to accept the same ascription for the *Śrāvaka-prajñapti* and for the *Tattvārtha-sūtra*, which from the angle of *śrāvakācāra* is a wholly Digambara text. Ordinarily in any conflict of usage between the two sects, except in the practice of ascetic nudity, the Digambaras appear in the position of innovators, and it is precisely because they have largely jettisoned the deadwood of an earlier age that their testimony is of greater value for the conditions of the mediaeval period. Fidelity to tradition has meant that while much valuable material lies embedded in the Śvetāmbara commentaries the precise dating of any passage is very difficult since whole sections are handed on from one writer to another until, when all relevance to the contemporary scene has been lost, they are tacitly dropped, to risk being resurrected by some learned reformer like Yaśovijaya in a later age. From the religious angle a more serious handicap has been the oversubtilization of the exegesis of the *vratas*. *Syādvāda* logic has been pressed into service to determine the exact nature of each *bhaṅga* and *aticāra* but the niceties of calculation have weakened the compulsive force of moral commandments and ethical principles. For this reason probably, the Śvetāmbaras in their later *śrāvakācāras* abandoned the framework of the *vratas*.

Jaina writers have shown a quite remarkable aptitude for the subtle handling of words evidenced by such achievements as the Jaina version of the *Megha-dūta*. The polyvalence of certain expressions even within the limits of the same text is often disconcerting: *guṇa* in particular is greatly overworked and so are *kriyā* and *karman*. Indeed one is led to wonder whether the double meanings given to many words and their formal identity with Hindu terms may not be voluntary. Examples of such coincidences (with the Jaina meanings noted in parenthesis) are: *śiva (mokṣa)*, *liṅga* (the monk's symbols such as the *rajo-haraṇa*), *guṇa-traya* (the *ratna-traya*), *paśupati* (the *Jina*), *mahā-deva* (the Jina) whilst on the other hand the word Digambara itself can be an epithet of Śiva. It may be that such resemblances were intended to render Jaina doctrines attractive to Śaivas or that a Śaiva persecution made it desirable to give to certain Jaina texts an innocuous aspect. Certainly the Jainas's concept of *asatya* would make it easy for them to adopt an attitude similar to that of those Shiite sectarians who in the early days of Islam maintained an outward conformity by concealing their real beliefs under forms of words.

Two aspects of Jainism have been overstressed in most descriptions: the negative formulation of the creed and the absence of change in its history. In the last resort every moral code rests, like the Christian decalogue, on prohibitions; but even in Jainism each *anuvrata* has its positive as well as its negative aspect, *ahiṃsā* can be reformulated as *dayā*, active compassion for all living beings. If Jainism has never challenged the constituted order of society, it has essayed to permeate it with the spirit of compassion but because human beings are actuated by self-interest it has pointed out to them the lower motives for doing good. Merit may be rewarded at any of three levels: by fortune in this life, by an auspicious reincarnation in the *deva-loka* or in a *bhoga-bhūmi*, and by release from the cycle of existence. In popular Jainism where the second aim rates as high as the third it becomes as important to build up a good karma (which is not in harmony with the creed) as to destroy all karma.

The changelessness of Jainism is no more than a myth. Admittedly there have been no spectacular changes in basic assumptions such as there were, for example, in Mahāyāna Buddhism. At most there have been variations in emphasis. Had Jainism, as at one time must have seemed possible, become a majority religion in southern India something akin to a Digambara Mahāyāna might, with continuing favourable circumstances, have emerged. But all that can be detected today are the traces of aborted developments: thus in the *Ratna-karaṇḍa* the *devādhideva* is apostrophized as the annihilator of Kāmadeva who seems from the context cast for the role of the Buddhist Māra. But whilst the dogma remains strikingly firm the ritual changes and assumes an astonishing complexity and richness of symbolism. From implying merely the feeding of religious mendicants the duty of *dāna* comes to mean the provision of rich ecclesiastical endowments and, amongst the Śvetāmbaras, the monk is no longer, except in theory, a homeless wanderer. It is recognized that he needs comfort, shelter, warmth to enable him to concentrate on study. The *yātrā* ceases to be a mere promenading of the idols through the city on a festival day and comes to denote an organized convoy going on pilgrimage to distant sacred places. And all the time more and more stress is being laid on the individual's duties to the community.

The Jaina religion is a *tīrtha*, a way of progress through life, and whilst the *yaty-ācāra* teaches the individual how to organize his own salvation the aim of *śrāvakācāra* is to ensure that an environment is created in which the ascetic may be able to travel the road of *mokṣa*. It must therefore be concerned with the community as well as with the individual and if the right people—the *bhavyas*—are to be attracted to the right *tīrtha* missionary efforts are necessary. Jainism welcomes the like-minded even if they do not outwardly profess its beliefs, and relies very much on the force of examples: a whole chapter of the *Dharma-bindu* is devoted to the need to cultivate those qualities in a person which are susceptible of encouraging respect for his beliefs in the community.

However, the essential change in Jainism during the mediaeval period is its transformation from a philosophy, a *darśana*, to a religion. All the new trends are in one sense or another movements towards a fuller way of life. One of the most important of these is that of which Jinasena is the chosen exponent. The *kriyās* or ceremonies listed in the *Ādi-purāṇa* are the principal expression of a religion adapted to a *kṣatriya* concept of society. Most striking is the prominence given to the *upanayana* or initiation rite which, like the monastic *dīkṣā*, is described as a second birth. This and other imitations of Hinduism are decked with a certain external Jaina symbolism. However contrary the sanctification of marriage may be to the dictates of reason a religion that disdains such aid can with difficulty achieve a hold on the masses. An elaborate wedding ceremonial, again patterned on Hindu models, is therefore presented in the *Ādi-purāṇa*. Apart from this there is barely a mention of marriage in the *śrāvakācāras* except for a recapitulation of the eight forms recorded in the Hindu *dharma-śāstras*. Some of these, such as the *gandharva-vivāha*, are, as Āśādhara notes, directly contrary to the tenets of Jainism.

If this metamorphosis from a *darśana* to a religion is slowly taking place the rites continue to be no more than an elaborate apparatus of symbolism designed to enable the worshipper the better to concentrate on pious meditation. Jinasena admits the utility of a Jaina brahmin or *kṣullaka* for the performance of certain *kriyās* but no professional ministrants are needed to officiate in the temple. When even the *garbha-gṛha*, the inner sanctuary, conceals no sacred mystery each man has the right to remain his own priest. That role cannot belong to the monk who by his very vocation is restricted to the position of a passive witness. Certain *āvaśyakas* —*pratikramaṇa*, *ālocanā*, *pratyākhyāna*—are best performed before him but even there his presence is not essential for like the Jina, now for ever absent in the euphory of his perfection but portrayed in the image, the monk too may be symbolically represented (by the *sthāpanācārya*). His one duty (if this term may be used) towards the layman is to instruct him in the sacred doctrine on which he remains the unchallengeable authority.

The polarity of householder and ascetic is indeed one of the most characteristic features of the Jaina structure. The layman has the obligation to cherish his family, the monk must sever all ties with them. The layman is enjoined to perform *dravya-pūjā*: not only does he offer fruits and flowers and sweetmeats but he cleans the image, and if he has skill in music and dancing (accomplishments which when put to any other use are regarded as undesirable and indeed harmful) he should display it; the monk on the other hand may offer only mental praise. Even if the tradition provides that as little water as possible should be used, the householder must still bathe frequently, but in theory at least the ascetic should never bathe. The monk—the Digambara monk—should be naked but the layman has to be decently clad, and for all religious ceremonies must wear at least two pieces of cloth. This antithesis of the partial and the complete vows disappears to some extent in some of the *āvaśyaka* rites where the layman is assimilated to the ascetic but in general it may be said that where the monk is excessive, since his life is the negation of compromise, moderation must be the key-note of existence for the householder whose life is rooted in compromise.

In his every action the householder is beset by the unintentional evil which he provokes in his daily work. As a *deśa-virata*, one whose gaze is only half averted from the sensual world, he must always be on his guard, apprehensive of sin. As the *śrāvaka-guṇas* portray him he works hard, conforms to conventions, obeys constituted authority, leads a frugal and unostentatious life, and carefully calculates the consequences of every step he takes. This conception of the lay life which follows logically from the dogmas of the creed is assuredly the main factor responsible for the close association, so often noted, of Jainism with the middle-class trading community. Such a conclusion is very far from the view[1] which, falsifying the picture of its origins, regards it as tailor-made for the *bourgeoisie*. Agriculture, India's basic occupation, has never been reckoned among the forbidden callings though various restrictions on its practice have been introduced on the basis of the *ahiṃsā-vrata* and commerce, medicine, astrology, and administration have all been recognized as licit. Some Digambaras like Jinasena and Cāmuṇḍarāya have even legislated for a *kṣatriya* society. Not all Jainas are merchants but many merchants happen to be Jainas because the qualities highlighted in the ideal layman are also those which generally contribute to success in business, and so a creed of complete otherworldliness has offered a background for the successfully worldly.[2]

The differences which separate Jainism from Hinduism and Buddhism, the other two religions which India has given to the world, are largely differences of emphasis for all have built from common material. *Ahiṃsā*, for example, is preponderant in, but not peculiar to, Jainism: it is extolled even in such Hindu texts as the *Manu-smṛti* (which Hemacandra[3] stigmatizes as a *hiṃsā-śāstra*) but it is the central position and pervading character of *ahiṃsā* that separate the Jaina ethic sharply from Hinduism as well as from Islam and Christianity.

Resemblances to Christianity are of course no more than the fortuitous result of a common ascetic ideology, but the question may be raised whether Moslem influence may not at certain points during the mediaeval period have touched Jaina practice. A clear answer is hard to give but some developments which cannot be traced back to an early date have possibly been stimulated, if not

[1] Such as that in effect taken by W. Ruben in *Einführung in die Indienkunde*.
[2] A European parallel might be found in the history of the Quakers.
[3] YŚ ii. 35.

originated, by Islamic contacts. The wide extension of the category of the *āśātanās*—the activities that are unfitting or indecent in a temple—if, on the one hand, it is evidence of an epoch when religious observance had grown weak, also reveals a notion of the sanctity of the physical edifice which is more evocative of Moslem *barakah* than of any traditional Jaina attitude. Ratnaśekhara's picture[1] of a pilgrim caravan making its way to Śatruñjaya bears less resemblance to any Hindu pilgrimage than to the *ḥajj*, the example of which may have contributed to the spectacular development of what seems once to have been a mere variant of the *yātrā* or religious festival. Similarly, when Medhāvin[2] proclaims that the essence of Jainism lies in the conviction that 'there is no *deva* but the Jina' it is difficult to believe that he was unacquainted with the Moslem profession of faith. But such likenesses are few and unimportant, and the only evidence for them comes from very late writers.

The interaction of Buddhism and Jainism dates from the very beginning of their history and lies largely outside the scope of this work though throughout the mediaeval period the two communities must have been in constant contact as the recurring references to Buddhism as the principal form of *mithyātva* attest. It, however, might be noted that some Sanskrit Buddhist texts show curious similarities of terminology with the Jaina *śrāvakācāras* in the discussion of the layman's duties.

Hindu influences are at work throughout Jaina history though the Digambaras are significantly affected by them at an earlier date than the Śvetāmbaras. The main line of hinduization runs through Jinasena, Cāmuṇḍarāya, and Āśādhara. On the basis of the Hindu *saṃskāras* an ambitious fabric of Jaina *kriyās* was set up and at the same time *mantras* intruded more and more into the continually enriched ritual, yogic techniques were adopted and, as the quotations from such works as the *Manu-smṛti*, the *Vātsyāyana-kāma-sūtra*, and the Āyurvedic texts show, Hindu *śāstras* gained wider currency. In the case of the Śvetāmbara community the opening up of new and wider horizons was largely the work of Hemacandra.

Earlier Jainism had relegated to the *deśācāra* all aspects of human activity not specifically covered by the traditional literature and had tacitly admitted non-Jaina practices provided that they

[1] *Śrāddha-vidhi*, p. 123*b*. [2] Śr (M) iv. 29.

were not in blatant conflict with its principles. Even the *Kali-kāla-sarvajña* himself is content to say that where the religious law is silent the *deśācāra* should prevail.[1] It is in fact only with the close of the mediaeval period that come the great inroads of Hinduism which completely reverse this attitude, and that elements contrary to the spirit of the religion are incorporated into the practice.[2] Above all, the characteristic of the latest phase of Jainism is that what was once regarded as optional comes to be expounded as obligatory.

It has already been noted that the early Jainism showed no concern with the *rites de passage*. Though an abundant literature is devoted to ritual suicide it is difficult to detect any reference to funeral customs or again to *sūtaka* before the fifteenth century. Marriage remained a question of regional usage at least until Jinasena prescribed a ceremony based on the Hindu fire ritual and the earliest Śvetāmbara work to deal in detail with this subject seems to have been the *Ācāra-dinakara*. But the immemorial usage of Hindu neighbours must at all times have coloured the individual Jaina's life. Though only very late texts enjoin the use of cow's urine for purification, a chance statement, repeated by the commentators in explaining the *brahma-vrata*, attests the importance attached to it in ordinary custom. The general validity of the menstruation taboo is nowhere alluded to, but is attested by Devendra's casual reference to the story of a woman who brought on herself an evil reincarnation by making the *Jina-pūjā* whilst in a state of ritual impurity. Against the formal denial of attachment to loved ones the family reasserts its rights and the begetting of a son, recommended already by Āśādhara, becomes a duty in the late texts. Early Jainism knows no rules for eating, for bathing, for excretion save those which are designed to avoid destruction of life, and none at all for copulation, which theoretically should not take place, but the late *śrāvakācāras* take over from Hinduism minute instructions on these points. *Pūjā*, which initially has little importance because it does not affect the survival of the Jaina religion as such, comes to be given a greater significance than *dāna*, which is essential since without it the monks could not live. Of all late accretions from Hinduism, however, the most striking is the introduction of *śrāddha* or *pitṛ-tarpana*, condemned in the classical *śrāvakācāras* as a regrettable form of *mithyātva*.

[1] YŚ ii. 49. [2] See Jugalkiśor Mukhtār, *Grantha Parīkṣā*, pp. 99–118.

Parallel with the phenomenon of hinduization goes that of sanskritization. Māhārāṣṭrī Prakrit, though long a dead language, was, in the mediaeval period, largely used by the Śvetāmbaras with whom it had replaced another dead language, the Ardhamāgadhī of the canon, both for ornate *kāvyas* in prose and verse and for scientific exposition. It is possible that its use was favoured by certain *gacchas* whilst others preferred Sanskrit but in any event, as treatises like Yaśodeva's *Pañcāśaka-cūrṇī* show, Haribhadra's innovation in writing commentaries on the sacred texts in Sanskrit was very far from dealing it a fatal blow. Hemacandra, however, though he wrote a grammar of Prakrit and himself composed a *kāvya* to illustrate its rules, virtually put an end to its use by spreading Sanskrit culture in Jaina circles, and within a century of his death it had ceased to be adopted except for the composition of skeleton verses on which, as in the case of the *Śrāddha-vidhi* of Ratnaśekhara, a prose treatise could be draped. With the Digambaras the linguistic situation is less clear. Sanskrit had come into general use at an earlier date, but from time to time works were still written in Prakrit, perhaps again in particular milieux. As with the Śvetāmbaras, however, the end of the mediaeval period seems to mark the final limit of its utilization.

BIBLIOGRAPHY

A. SANSKRIT AND PRAKRIT TEXTS USED IN THE PREPARATION OF THIS SURVEY[1]

Amitagati: Śrāvakācāra (Anantakīrti Digambara Jaina Granthamālā, no. 2). Bombay, 1922. Śr (A)

—— 'Subhāṣita-ratna-sandoha', edited with translation by R. Schmidt in *ZDMG* lix. 61.

Amṛtacandra: Puruṣārtha-siddhy-upāya (Rāyacandra Jaina Śāstramālā). Bombay, 1905. PASU

Āśādhara: Sāgāra-dharmāmṛta (Māṇikacandra Digambara Jaina Granthamālā, no. 2). Bombay, 1917. SDhA

—— Anagāra-dharmāmṛta (Māṇikacandra Digambara Jaina Granthamālā, no. 14). Bombay, 1919.

Āvaśyaka-sūtra with commentary of Haribhadra (Āgamodaya Samiti Siddhānta Saṃgraha, no. 1). Bombay, 1916. Āv (H)

Āvaśyaka-sūtra with Cūrṇī (Ṛṣabhadeva Keśarīmala Jaina Śvetāmbara Saṃsthā). Ratlam, 1929. Āv Cū

Cāmuṇḍarāya: Caritra-sāra (Māṇikacandra Digambara Jaina Granthamālā, no. 9). Bombay, 1917. CS

Cāritrasundara: Ācāropadeśa. Ahmedabad, 1925. ĀU

Devagupta: Nava-pada-prakaraṇa with Laghu-vṛtti (Devacandra Lālabhāī Jaina Pustakoddhāra, no. 68). Bombay, 1926. NPP

Devasena: Bhāva-saṃgraha in Bhāva-saṃgrahādi (Māṇikacandra Digambara Jaina Granthamālā, no. 20). Bombay, 1922. BhS (D)

Devendra: Śrāddha-dina-kṛtya (Ṛṣabhadeva Keśarīmala Jaina Śvetāmbara Saṃsthā). Ratlam, 1937. ŚrDK

—— Bhāṣya-traya (Ātmānanda Grantha-ratna-mālā, no. 15). Bhavnagar, 1912.

—— Caitya-vandana-bhāṣya with Saṅghācāra-vṛtti. Surat, 1938. CVBh

Guṇabhūṣaṇa: Śravakācāra. Surat, 1925.

Haribhadra: Śrāvaka-dharma-pañcāśaka with Cūrṇī of Yaśodeva (Devacandra Lālabhai Jaina Pustakoddhāra, no. 102). 1952. P (Y)

—— Pañcāśaka with commentary of Abhayadeva (Ṛṣabhadeva Keśarīmala Jaina Śvetāmbara Saṃsthā). Ratlam, 1941.

[1] The symbols on the right indicate the abbreviations used in the footnotes.

Haribhadra: Abhayadeva's commentary on the Śrāvaka-dharma-pañcāśaka is quoted as P (A)
and the text of the individual Pañcāśakas as:
Śrāvaka-dharma-pañcāśaka P (ŚrDh)
Vandana-vidhāna-pañcāśaka P (Vandana)
Pūjā-vidhāna-pañcāśaka P Pūjā)
Yātrā-vidhi-pañcāśaka P (Yātrā)
Śramaṇopāsaka-pratimā-pañcāśaka P (ŚrUP)

—— Dharma-bindu, edited with translation by L. Suali in *GSAI* xxi (1908), 224–90. DhB

—— Dharma-bindu with commentary of Municandra (Āgamodaya Samiti). Bombay, 1924.

—— Lalita-vistara commentary on Caitya-vandana-sūtra (Devacandra Lālabhāī Jaina Pustakoddhāra, no. 29). Bombay, 1915. LV

Hemacandra: Yoga-śāstra (Bibliotheca Indica, no. 172). Calcutta, 1907–21. YŚ

Jinadatta: Caitya-vandana-kulaka (Jinadatta Sūri Prācīna Pustakoddhāra, no. 11). Bombay, 1920.

Jinamaṇḍana: Śrāddha-guṇa-vivaraṇa (Ātmānanda Grantha-ratna-mālā, no. 29). Bhavnagar, 1914. ŚrGuV

Jinasena: Ādi-purāṇa (Jñānapīṭha Mūrtidevī Jaina Granthamālā, no. 9). Benares, 1951. MP

Kārttikeya: Dvādaśānuprekṣā, ed. by A. N. Upadhye. Bombay, 1960. KA

Kundakunda: Cāritra-prābhṛta in Ṣaṭ-prābhṛtādi-saṃgraha (Māṇikacandra Digambara Jaina Granthamālā, no. 17). Bombay, 1920.

Mānavijaya: Dharma-saṃgraha with commentary of Yaśovijaya (Devacandra Lālabhāī Jaina Pustakoddhāra, no. 26). Bombay, 1915.

Medhāvin: Śrāvakācāra Dharma-saṃgraha-śrāvakācāra. Benares, 1910. Śr (M)

Nemicandra: Pravacana-sāroddhāra (Devacandra Lālabhāī Jaina Pustakoddhāra, nos. 58, 64). Bombay, 1922–6. PS

Padmanandin: Dharma-rasāyana in Siddhānta-sārādi-saṃgraha (Māṇikacandra Digambara Jaina Granthamala, no. 21). Bombay, 1922.

—— Śrāvakācāra. Belgaum, 1911.

Pūjā-prakaraṇa in Tattvārtha-sūtra (Bibliotheca Indica, no. 159). Calcutta, 1903–5.

Rājamalla: Lāṭī-saṃhitā (Māṇikacandra Digambara Jaina Granthamālā, no. 26). Bombay, 1927.

Ratna-sāra or Rayaṇa-sāra ascribed to Kundakunda, ed. Jñānasāgara. Calcutta, 1934.

Ratnaśekhara: Śrāddha-vidhi (Ātmānanda Grantha-ratna-mālā, no. 48). Bhavnagar, 1917.

Sakalakīrti: Praśnottara-śrāvakācāra. Surat, 1927.

Samantabhadra: Ratna-karaṇḍa-śrāvakācāra with commentary of Prabhācandra (Māṇikacandra Digambara Jaina Granthamālā, no. 24). Bombay, 1926. RK

Śānti Sūri: Dharma-ratna-prakaraṇa (Ātmānanda Grantha-ratna-mālā, no. 30). Bhavnagar, 1913. DhRP

Śivakoṭi: Ratna-mālā in Siddhānta-sārādi-saṃgraha (Māṇikacandra Digambara Jaina Granthamālā, no. 21). Bombay, 1922.

Somadeva: Yaśastilaka (Kāvya-mālā, no. 70). Bombay, 1901–3.

References to this work are quoted from:

K. K. Handiqui: Yaśastilaka and Indian Culture (Jīvarāja Jaina Granthamālā, no. 2). Sholapur, 1949. Handiqui

Somasena: Traivarṇikācāra, ed. by Pannalāl Sonī. Bombay, 1925. TrA

Śrāddha-pratikramaṇa-sūtra with Vandāru-vṛtti of Devendra (Devacandra Lālabhāī Jaina Pustakoddhāra, no. 8). Bombay, 1912.

Śrāddha-pratikramaṇa-sūtra with commentary of Ratnaśekhara (Devacandra Lālabhāī Jaina Pustakoddhāra, no. 48). Bombay, 1919.

Śrāvaka-dharma-dohaka (or Sāvaya-dhamma-dohā), ed. by Hiralal Jain (Karanja Jain Series, no. 2). Karanja, 1932. Doha

Umasvāmin: Tattvārtha-sūtra with Sarvārtha-siddhi of Pūjyapāda (Jñānapīṭha Mūrtidevī Jaina Granthamālā, no. 13). Benares, 1955. T (P)

—— Reality: an English translation of the Sarvārtha-siddhi, by S. A. Jain (Vīraśāsana Saṅgha). Calcutta, 1960.

—— Tattvārtha-sūtra with commentary of Siddhasena (Devacandra Lālabhāī Jaina Pustakoddhāra, no. 76). Bombay, 1930. T (S)

Umāsvāti: Śrāvaka-prajñapti. Bombay, 1905. ŚrPr

Vāmadeva: Bhāva-saṃgraha in Bhāva-saṃgrahādi (Māṇikacandra Digambara Jaina Granthamālā, no. 20). Bombay, 1922. BhS (V)

Vardhamāna: Ācāra-dinakara (Kharatara Gaccha Granthamālā, no. 2). Bombay, 1923. ADK

Vasunandin: Śrāvakācāra, ed. by Hiralal Jain (Jñānapīṭha Mūrtidevī Jaina Granthamālā, Prakrit series, no. 3). Śr (V)

Upāsaka-daśāḥ with commentary of Abhayadeva, ed. with trans. by Hoernle, (Bibliotheca Indica, no. 105). Calcutta, 1890. UD

B. OTHER WORKS AND ARTICLES

F. Belloni-Filippi: Yoga-çāstra in *GSAI* xxi (1908).

G. K. Bruhn: Śīlāṅkas Cauppaṇṇamahāpurisacariya (Alt- und Neu-Indische Studien, no. 8). Hamburg, 1954.

G. Bühler: Über das Leben des Jaina-Mönches Hemacandra, Vienna, 1889.

M. B. Desai: Jaina sāhitya no itihās. Bombay, 1927.

H. von Glasenapp: Der Jainismus. Berlin, 1925.

H. Jacobi: Samarāicca Kahā (Bibliotheca Indica, no. 169). Calcutta, 1908–26.

Jagdish Chandra Jain: Life in Ancient India. Bombay, 1947.

Jagmandarlal Jaini: Outlines of Jainism. Cambridge, 1940.

Jinavijaya Muni: Haribhadra Sūri kā samaya-nirṇaya in *Jaina Sāhitya Saṃśodhaka*, Part I.

P. V. Kane: History of Dharmaśāstra. Bombay, 1930–58.

K. von Kamptz: Über die vom Sterbefasten handelnden älteren Paiṇṇa des Jaina-Kanons. Hamburg, 1929.

W. Kirfel: Symbolik des Hinduismus und des Jinismus. Stuttgart, 1959.

—— and L. Hilgenberg: Übersetzung von Aṣṭāṅgahṛdaya. Leiden, 1941.

J. Klatt: Specimen of a Literary-Bibliographical Jaina-Onomasticon. Leipzig, 1892.

J. F. Kohl: Pflanzen mit gemeinsamen Körper in *Zeitschrift für Ethnologie*, Bd. 78/1 (1953).

—— Einige Bemerkungen zur Zahlensymbolik und zum Animismus im botanischen System des Jaina-Kanon in Studia Indologica, pp. 125–35. Bonn, 1955.

E. Leumann: Übersicht über die Āvaśyaka-Literatur. Hamburg, 1934.

J. J. Meyer: Trilogie altindischer Mächte und Feste der Vegetation. Zürich, 1937.

Jugalkiśor Mukhtār: Grantha-parīkṣā. Bombay, 1917.

—— Purātana Jaina vākyasūci (Vira Sevā Mandira Granthamālā, no. 5). Sarsawa, 1950.

Nāthurām Premī: Jaina sāhitya aur itihās. Bombay, 1942.

J. Przyluski: La Grande Déesse. Paris, 1950.

V. A. Sangave: Jaina Community. Bombay, 1959.

W. Schubring: Die Lehre der Jainas. Berlin, 1935.

—— Kundakunda echt und unecht in *ZDMG* cvii (1957), pp. 554–74.

—— Das Mahanisīha-Sutta (Abh. d. Preuss. Akad. d. Wiss., Berlin, 1918).

M. N. Srinivas: Marriage and Family in Mysore. Bombay, 1942.

H. D. Velankar: Jina-ratna-kośa. Poona, 1944.

E. Windisch: Yoga-śāstra in ZDMG xxviii (1874), pp. 185–262.

M. Winternitz: History of Indian Literature, vol. ii. Buddhist and Jaina Literature. Calcutta, 1933.

THE AUTHORS—ŚVETĀMBARA SAMPRADĀYA[1]

Umāsvāti	Śrāvaka-prajñapti	5th century (?)
Haribhadra Virahāṅka	Pañcāśaka	*ob.* 529 (?)
Haribhadra Yākinī-putra	Dharma-bindu	*c.* 750
,, ,,	Lalita-vistarā	,,
,, ,,	Āvaśyaka commentary	,,
Siddhasena Gaṇin	Tattvārtha-sūtra commentary	9th century (?)
Dhanapāla	Śrāvaka-vidhi	*c.* 970
Devagupta	Nava-pada-prakaraṇa with commentary	1016
Śānti Sūri	Dharma-ratna-prakaraṇa	*ob.* 1040
Abhayadeva	Upāsaka-daśāḥ commentary	1061
,,	Pañcāśaka commentary	1068
Nemicandra	Pravacana-sāroddhāra	11th century (?)
Municandra	Dharma-bindu commentary	*ob.* 1122 (?)
Yaśodeva	Pañcāśaka commentary	1116
Hemacandra	Yoga-śāstra	1089–1172
Siddhasena Sūri	Pravacana-sāroddhāra commentary	1185
Devendra	Śrāddha-dina-kṛtya	*ob.* 1270
,,	Vandāru-vṛtti commentary	,,
,,	Bhāṣya-traya	,,
Dharmaghoṣa	Śrāddha-jita-kalpa	,,
,,	Saṅghācāra	*c.* 1270
Jinadatta	Caitya-vandana-kulaka	*c.* 1300
	Pūjā-prakaraṇa	14th century (?)
Jinadatta	Viveka-vilāsa	14th century (?)
Vardhamāna	Ācāra-dinakara	1411
Cāritrasundara	Ācāropadeśa	1430
Jinamaṇḍana	Śrāddha-guṇa-śreṇi-saṃgraha	1441
Ratnaśekhara	Śrāddha-vidhi	1450
Yaśovijaya	Dharma-saṃgraha commentary	1624–88

Umāsvāti

Amongst the works usually ascribed to Umāsvāti the Vācaka at least three have a bearing on the *śrāvakācāra*: the *Tattvārtha-sūtra*,

[1] The chronology here, and still more in the Digambara *sampradāya*, is often uncertain, and all that has been attempted in this list is to establish rather hesitantly the sequence of the authors.

the *Śrāvaka-prajñapti*, and the *Pūjā-prakaraṇa*. The last-named is patently spurious and need not concern us here: it will be discussed in its proper place in the chronological sequence; and there is equally convincing internal evidence that the *Śrāvaka-prajñapti* cannot be by the same hand as the famous *Sūtra*.

Consider first the seventh *adhyāya* of the *Tattvārtha-sūtra*, the only section devoted—and that only in part—to the lay life. Here the Śvetāmbara and Digambara recensions do not differ except in the numbering, as *sūtras* 4 to 8, which are missing from the Śvetāmbara version, have in fact been transferred to the *bhāṣya*.[1] Yet the text as accepted by the Śvetāmbaras shows some curious features. First, in *sūtra* 18 it is specified that the layman, before he can take the *vratas*, must be devoid of the three *śalyas*; elsewhere this condition is only laid down in the Digambara *śrāvakācāras*, indeed the term does not seem to find a mention in Śvetāmbara texts. Secondly, the sequence of the *vratas* in *sūtra* 21 does not follow the model of the *Upāsaka-daśāḥ* which is rigidly observed in the Śvetāmbara tradition and, by making the *desāvakāśika-vrata* follow the *dig-vrata*, violates the principle by which practices of brief duration repeated at intervals are confined to the category of the *śikṣā-vratas*. Thirdly, in *sūtra* 24 the term *śīla* is used in a sense, normal in Digambara works but not elsewhere admitted by the Śvetāmbaras, to designate the *guṇa-vratas* and *śikṣā-vratas*. Fourthly, for the *satya-*, *bhogopabhoga-*, *anartha-daṇḍa-*, *poṣadhopavāsa-*, and *sallekhanā-vratas* the *aticāras* listed diverge markedly from the schema of the Śvetāmbara texts, which, apart from the *Dharma-bindu*, adhere unvaryingly to the *Upāsaka-daśāḥ* pattern until the time of Hemacandra. Fifthly, the information supplementary to the *vratas* is limited to a couple of *sūtras* (38 and 39) emphasizing the importance of *dāna*, no mention at all being made of the *āvaśyakas*, which are given very extensive treatment in all the Śvetāmbara *śrāvakācāras*. As the *vratas* and their *aticāras* represent the nucleus of the whole lay doctrine any variation in their presentation must be of considerable significance; and for these reasons the *Tattvārtha-sūtra* cannot, from the point of view of the *śrāvakācāra*, be regarded as a Śvetāmbara work.

The *Śrāvaka-prajñapti*,[2] on the contrary, is a typically Śvetām-

[1] The *bhāṣya*, which is markedly Śvetāmbara in tone, is considered by that sect to have been written by Umāsvāti himself.

[2] There is, incidentally, a reference to a *Sāvaga-paṇṇatti* in the *Vasudeva-hiṇḍi* (p. 185).

bara production, in style and content very closely related to the *Pañcāśakas*: its treatment of the *vratas* is exactly in accord with that of the *Upāsaka-daśāḥ*, and it deals extensively with the *āvaśyakas*. When the text was published in 1905 the editor, Keshavlal Premchand, in a brief introduction in Sanskrit, discussed whether the work should be attributed to Haribhadra, to Umāsvāti the Vācaka, or to some other Umāsvāti. In support of the first hypothesis he cited two rather ambiguous passages, one of them drawn from Abhayadeva's commentary on the *Pañcāśakas*.[1] However, in another quotation from the same work Umāsvāti is described as the author of the *Śrāvaka-prajñapti*, and the assertion is repeated by Municandra in his commentary on the *Dharma-bindu*, and at a much later date by Yaśovijaya in the *Dharma-saṃgraha*. More striking is an explanation by Yaśodeva,[2] in his commentary on the *Śrāvaka-dharma-pañcāśaka*, of the reasons which prompted Haribhadra to compose his treatise when Umāsvāti had already written the basic text on the subject, from which it is not unreasonable to infer that the *Śrāvaka-prajñapti* was already regarded by the Śvetāmbaras as the first compilation exclusively devoted to *śrāvakācāra*. That Haribhadra was the author of the work seems excluded by this evidence, though certain of its verses are in fact found repeated in the *Pūjā-pañcāśaka*.[3]

It may well be that the shared ascription of the *Tattvārtha-sūtra* and the *Śrāvaka-prajñapti* results from a confusion of name (the use by the Śvetāmbaras of the form Umāsvāti when the Digambaras prefer Umāsvāmin lends added probability to the hypothesis[4]) and that there in fact existed a Śvetāmbara *ācārya* named Umāsvāti to whom the *Tattvārtha-sūtra*, when it had already acquired general fame as an exposition of the doctrine, came also to be attributed. In any event the two works are incontestably of different authorship, and it may be added that the development of the *śrāvakācāra* is only understandable if the *Tattvārtha-sūtra* is regarded as belonging originally to the Digambaras.

The *Śrāvaka-prajñapti* is written in Prakrit and runs to some 400 verses. It contains a brief exposition of certain Jaina doctrines,

[1] I am unable to trace any of these quotations.

[2] P (Y) 1 (p. 2).

[3] In fact ŚrPr 345 = P (Pūjā) 41; ŚrPr 348 = P (Pūjā) 44, ŚrPr 349 = P (Pūjā) 45.

[4] I have adopted the form Umāsvāti for the author of the *Śrāvaka-prajñapti* and the form Umāsvāmin for the author of the *Tattvārtha-sūtra*.

particularly the nature of *jīva* and *karman*; a description of *samyaktva* and its *aticāras*; a fairly lengthy analysis and refutation of arguments commonly advanced by opponents of *ahiṃsā*; a list of the twelve *vratas* and their *aticāras* with particular attention to the *sāmāyika*; a summary of the ritual of *pūjā* and *caitya-vandana* with an indication of the *dina-caryā*,[1] the ideal pattern for each day's life; a description of *sallekhanā*; and a final exordium on the attainment of *mokṣa*. If the anteriority of this work to the *Pañcāśakas* is taken as established it cannot be held to be later than the fifth century. Printed with the text is the Sanskrit commentary of Haribhadra, large sections of which, in particular those dealing with the *aticāras* of the *vratas*, are identical with the corresponding passages of his *Āvaśyaka* commentary.

Haribhadra Virahāṅka

It was in 1919 that Muni Jinavijayajī, in a paper read to the First All-India Oriental Conference in Poona, showed that certain works ascribed to Haribhadra Sūri must, because of the authors quoted and the views expressed in them, be subsequent to the year 529 in which the most commonly accepted Jaina tradition places his death.[2] Further arguments in support of a later date were to be drawn from Muni Kalyāṇavijaya's introduction to the *Dharma-saṃgrahaṇi*, and the conclusions were reviewed and confirmed by Jacobi in his introduction to the *Samarāicca-kahā*, published in 1926. In all this there was a tacit assumption that the whole of the literary production ascribed to Haribhadra was the work of one man, although already, much earlier, Klatt had noted the existence of several authors of that name.[3]

Amongst the writings attributed to Haribhadra there are a number which are concerned with *śrāvakācāra*, notably the *Dharma-bindu*, the *Pañcāśakas*, and the commentaries on the *Āvaśyaka*, the *Śrāvaka-prajñapti*, and the *Caitya-vandana-sūtra*. As a commentator is always to some extent limited by his text it

[1] In the present study I have generalized the use of this convenient term employed by Hemacandra (YŚ iii. 122).

[2] See Muni Jinavijaya, *Haribhadra Sūri kā samaya-nirṇaya* in *Jaina Śāhitya Saṃśodhaka*, pt. i, and for a summary of the arguments about Haribhadra's date Winternitz, *History of Indian Literature*, ii. 479.

[3] Klatt, *Specimen of a Literary-Bibliographical Jaina-Onomasticon*, pp. 5, 8.

will be preferable to take a look at the first two, which are original works. They show differences as considerable as those which were apparent between the *Tattvārtha-sūtra* and the *Śrāvaka-prajñapti*. In the first place whilst the *Śrāvaka-dharma-pañcāśaka* is indistinguishable from the *Śrāvaka-prajñapti* in its rigid adherence to the Śvetambara tradition of reproducing the *vratas* and their *aticāras*, the *Dharma-bindu* follows for the *satya-*, *bhogopabhoga-*, *anartha-daṇḍa-*, and *poṣadhopavāsa-vratas* (the *sallekhanā-vrata* is not treated in the *śrāvakācāra* section of this work) the model of the *Tattvārtha-sūtra*, except that for the third *aticāra* of the *satya-vrata* the form *sva-dāra-mantra-bheda* is preferred to *sākāra-mantra-bheda*.[1] However, the more logical Śvetāmbara sequence of *guṇa-vratas* and *śikṣā-vratas* is followed. At the same time there are indications in the *Dharma-bindu* that its author had access to a much wider Sanskrit culture than is shown by the writer of the *Pañcāśakas*, whose outlook seems bounded by Jaina tradition. Like the *Tattvārtha-sūtra* the *Dharma-bindu* is written in *sūtra* style whilst the *Pañcāśakas* are composed in Prakrit verses that appear perceptibly archaic when compared, for example, with the *Dhūrtākhyāna*, another Prakrit work attributed to Haribhadra.

If we examine the legends associated with the life of Haribhadra as they are recounted by various writers all separated from the period in which he is held to have lived by very considerable intervals of time, these are seen to centre around two incidents: that he was converted to Jainism because he was impressed by the superior knowledge of the nun Yākinī Mahattarā, and that he was afflicted by remorse because he had provoked the death of certain Buddhists who had murdered his two nephews. With the second legend is associated the figure of 1,400 or 1,444—both are familiar round numbers in Jainism—given as the total of the works he is supposed to have written, as well as the use of the word *viraha* as an *aṅka* in the concluding verses of his works; and there is a reminiscence of the former in the colophon sometimes found: *kṛtir iyaṃ Sitāmbarācāryasya Jinabhaṭṭa-nigadānusāriṇo Yākinī-mahattarā-sūnor Haribhadrasya*. It would not then seem unreasonable to suggest that the works bearing this colophon may belong to one writer of the name of Haribhadra and those signed with the *aṅka* to another. Of course the wide currency of the colourful narrative

[1] Haribhadra's avoidance of the *Tattvārtha-sūtra* variant seems to confirm the supposition that this may have been originally a textual corruption.

by which the *aṅka* is explained, and the ease with which terminal verses can be manufactured by a copyist for a prose treatise will have made it not unlikely that the *aṅka* may in some cases be spurious; at any rate by its nature it is peculiarly susceptible of being forged.

If we examine from this angle the texts under discussion, the printed editions of the *Lalita-vistarā*, *Āvaśyaka*, and *Śrāvaka-prajñapti* commentaries are all seen to have colophons basically identical with the specimen just given. (So too has the Prakrit *Dhūrtākhyāna*.) Each *Pañcāśaka*, on the other hand, shows in its concluding verse the *aṅka*. These short treatises of approximately, but not always, exactly fifty verses are all written in a rather archaic Māhārāṣṭrī Prakrit which, particularly in the occurrence of particles which are said to be merely *pāda-pūraṇas* and in the use of the cases, confronts the commentators with problems which they can only answer by the phrase *prākṛta-śailatvāt*. The language contrasts markedly with the conventional Māhārāṣṭrī of the *Dhūrtākhyāna*. The verses have clearly an essentially mnemonic value and are designed to be studied with the aid of a commentary: indeed without it they are often unintelligible. Nothing in them suggests acquaintance with non-Jaina milieux. On the other hand the three commentaries in Sanskrit give evidence of a very wide and not purely Jaina erudition. It is of particular interest to note in the *Āvaśyaka* commentary the treatment of the *aticāras* of those *vratas* for which the *Tattvārtha-sūtra* has introduced innovations. These are interpreted on conventional Śvetāmbara lines except for the explanation of the third *aticāra* of the *bhogopabhoga-vrata*: *apakvauṣadhi* where a variant reading (*pāṭhāntara*) *sacitta-sammiśrāhāra* is noted. Admittedly the text is undeviatingly traditional, but that is no reason for supposing that the authorship of the commentary is different from that of the *Dharma-bindu*. Yet the *Dharma-bindu*, as printed, has no colophon but, on the contrary, a concluding verse with the *aṅka* which must therefore here be assumed to be spurious.

What, then, I would here suggest is that the revised dating of Haribhadra (A.D. 750) introduced by Muni Jinavijaya should be assumed only for that Haribhadra who is, *inter alia*, the author of the three commentaries mentioned, the *Dharma-bindu*, and the *Dhūrtākhyāna*, and that for works written in archaic Māhārāṣṭrī and bearing the *aṅka* the Jaina tradition that he died in 529 should be retained.[1] On this basis the *Pañcāśakas* would belong to the beginning of the sixth century A.D.

Something has already been said to indicate their characteristic peculiarities. In the printed edition they are nineteen in number, the first ten of them relating to the lay life. Of these the most important for the *śrāvakācāra* are the *śrāvaka-dharma-*, *vandana-vidhāna-*, *pūjā-vidhāna-*, *stava-vidhi-*, *yātrā-vidhi-*, and *śramaṇopāsaka-pratimā-pañcāśakas.*

Siddhasena Gaṇin

Apart from the concise *bhāṣya* which by the Śvetāmbaraṣ is said to be the work of Umāsvāti himself but which must, if the *Tattvārtha-sūtra* is Digambara, be by another hand, the best-known Śvetāmbara commentary on the *Tattvārtha-sūtra* is that of Siddhasena Gaṇin. This author, who is distinct from the more celebrated Siddhasena Divākara and the much later Siddhasena Sūri who wrote the commentary on the *Pravacana-sāroddhāra*, records in his colophon that his guru was Bhāsvāmin and his guru's guru Siṃhasūra, pupil himself of Dinna Gaṇin, but these details offer no secure basis for dating. Reference is made in the *vyākhyā* to certain other works and if the Dharmakīrti author of the *Pramāṇa-viniścaya* mentioned is the Buddhist writer of the seventh century, Siddhasena cannot well be much earlier than A.D. 800.[2] In numerous passages there is an identity of phraseology in the discussion of the *aticāras* of the *vratas* between the *Tattvārtha-sūtra-vyākhyā* and Haribhadra's *Āvaśyaka-vṛtti*,[3] so striking that it seems almost inevitable that one must have borrowed from the other: it would seem that Siddhasena was the borrower.

Haribhadra Yākinī-putra

If we accept the existence of two major figures of the name of Haribhadra it is to the second, whose date was fixed by Jinavijaya

[1] An exhaustive study of all works attributed to Haribhadra could confirm or invalidate this hypothesis. Only a few of them are available in good editions and the overall picture is very confused. Thus verses 1–2 and 78–120 of the work published under the title *Śrāvaka-vidhi-prakaraṇa* are identical with verses 1–2 and 8–50 of the *Śrāvaka-dharma-pañcāśaka*. It would probably be found that the appellation Haribhadra embraces more than the two authors distinguished above. One fact seems certain: that the *Dharma-bindu* and the *Pañcāśakas* cannot be by the same hand.

[2] See T (S), vol. ii, Introduction, p. 63, and ABORI xiii. 335.

[3] See Appendix.

at *circa* A.D. 750, that belong the *Dharma-bindu* and the *Śrāvaka-prajñapti*, *Āvaśyaka*, and *Caitya-vandana-sūtra* commentaries.

The *Dharma-bindu* is a compilation of rules of conduct both for the layman and the ascetic, written, in evident imitation of the *Tattvārtha-sūtra*, in Sanskrit *sūtras* clearer and more elegant than those of its prototype. Only the first three *adhyāyas* are relevant to the *śrāvakācāra*. The first draws a picture of the ideal layman by listing the qualities which should enter into his make-up: though the term is not used these represent in effect the earliest traceable enumeration of what Hemacandra calls the *śrāvaka-guṇas*. The second *adhyāya* deals with methods of expounding the *dharma*, both by precept and example, and is clear evidence that Jainism was still a proselytizing religion. The third *adhyāya* is in itself a *śrāvakācāra* in miniature from which nothing essential is omitted. The exposition of *samyaktva* and the *vratas* and their *aticāras* is followed by a picture of the daily round of life from dawn to dusk which provides a framework in which to include *dāna* and *pūjā* and the six *āvaśyakas*. This section offers in brief compass an example of the *dina-caryā* which was later taken as a model for *śrāvakācāras* of the type of the *Śrāddha-dina-kṛtya*. As has already been noted Haribhadra follows the *Tattvārtha-sūtra* in his delineation of the *vratas* and their *aticāras*; whilst for the *āvaśyakas* and other daily duties his pattern is the *Śrāvaka-prajñapti*.

DHANAPALA

This compiler of a short Prakrit verse treatise on the lay life, the *Śrāvaka-vidhi*, is presumably to be identified with the author of the *Tilaka-mañjarī* and the *Ṛsabha-pañcāśaka*, who flourished about A.D. 970.[1]

DEVAGUPTA

Devagupta, a *sūri* of the Upakeśa Gaccha, pupil of Kakka Ācārya, and known as Jinacandra Gaṇin before his *dīkṣā*, tells us that, although the *śrāvaka-dharma* has been expounded in many ways by the *ācāryas* of old, his *Nava-pada-prakaraṇa* is the first attempt to present it by treating *samyaktva*, *mithyātva*, and the *vratas* each from nine angles.[2] These are: the nature of the *vrata*

[1] Winternitz, op. cit., pp. 534, 553. The text of the *Śrāvaka-vidhi* was not accessible to me.

[2] NPP 137 (p. 61*b*).

(*yādṛg bhūta*); the varieties of it (*bheda*); how it comes into existence (*yathā jāyate*); the evil arising from neglecting it (*doṣa*); the good arising from carrying it out (*guṇa*); the striving to be made (*yatanā*); its *aticāras*; its *bhaṅgas*; and the themes of meditation on it (*bhāvanā*).[1] The subject-matter can only with difficulty be accommodated to this strait jacket and it is open to doubt if Devagupta was successful in his innovation. To explain his text, written in rather crabbed Prakrit verse, the author himself composed a Sanskrit commentary, the *Laghu-vṛtti*, completed in *saṃvat* 1073. There is another, much more extensive, commentary composed in *saṃvat* 1165 by Yaśodeva, whose identity with the author of the commentary on the *Śrāvaka-dharma-pañcāśaka*[2] cannot be excluded. Devagupta himself is also the author of the *Nava-tattva-prakaraṇa*, and is said to have written a commentary on the *Tattvārtha sūtra*.

Śānti Sūri

Śānti Sūri of the Candrakula Gaccha, who is said to have died in A.D. 1040, was the author of the *Sīra-vicāra* and of the *Dharma-ratna-prakaraṇa*, a Prakrit verse tract on the qualities of the ideal layman and the ideal monk, which is of interest primarily as the earliest literary source for the 21 *śrāvaka-guṇas*. These, together with the six types of *bhāva-śrāvaka*, are described in the first 77 stanzas whilst the remaining 68 are devoted to the delineation of the *bhāva-sādhu*.

The Sanskrit *vṛtti*, printed with the text and attributed on the title-page to Śānti Sūri himself, is stated by Schubring[3] to be by Devendra. Commentaries both by Śānti Sūri and by Devendra are mentioned as existing in manuscript.[4]

Abhayadeva

Abhayadeva, a *sūri* of the Candrakula Gaccha, was a very celebrated commentator on the canon. Both his *vivaraṇa* on the *Upāsaka-daśāḥ* in *saṃvat* 1117[5] and his *Pañcāśaka-vṛtti* in *saṃvat*

[1] NPP 2.

[2] Thus Yaśodeva, in his *Pañcāśaka* commentary, quotes not only verses from the *Nava-pada-prakaraṇa* but a large number of otherwise unidentified verses which are found in Devagupta's *Laghu-vṛtti*.

[3] See Schubring, *Die Lehre der Jainas*, p. 223.

[4] Velankar, *Jina-ratna-kośa*, p. 191.

[5] Ibid., p. 55.

1124[1] cover the field of *śrāvakācāra*. Older works utilized by him include the *Śrāvaka-prajñapti*, the commentaries of Haribhadra, and the *Nava-pada-prakaraṇa*.

Nemicandra

Nemicandra, pupil of Āmradeva, pupil of Jinabhadra, is distinct from the other Nemicandra, author of the *vṛtti* on the *Uttarādhyāyana-sūtra*, who before *dīkṣā* was called Devendra Gaṇin.[2] His *Pravacana-sāroddhāra* is a Prakrit verse compendium of Jaina philosophy, ethics, and ritual set out as far as possible in the form of numerical apothegms. Some of these, such as the lists of *abhakṣyas* and *ananta-kāyas*, are of considerable importance for the development of the *śrāvakācāra*. In a compendium of this kind much will certainly have been borrowed and the fact that one of the verses on the *ananta-kāyas* is quoted by Abhayadeva in his commentary on the *Śrāvaka-dharma-pañcāśaka* is without significance as Nemicandra has quoted them from an earlier source. It is of more interest that the verses on the twenty-one *śrāvaka-guṇas* have been incorporated in the text of the *Pravacana-sāroddhāra* as this would show that Nemicandra is not at any rate earlier than Śānti Sūri unless the latter had taken them over ready-made from another writer. It is difficult therefore to give more than a vague approximation of the author's date. He is not later than the twelfth century, as the commentary by Siddhasena Sūri was completed in *saṃvat* 1242,[3] and he may well be considerably earlier. He mentions in verse 470 a Candra Sūri, who cannot be the *ācārya* who wrote a commentary on the *Āvaśyaka-sūtra* in A.D. 1165,[4] but may be the same as the author of a *Munisuvrata-caritra*.

Municandra

Nothing seems to be known with certainty of the author of the commentary on the *Dharma-bindu*. According to Weber he died in A.D. 1122. He may or may not be identical with the author of a Prakrit *Gāthā-kośa* and a *Ratna-traya-kulaka* or with the fortieth *ācārya* in Klatt's list of the Tapā Gaccha.[5]

Yaśodeva

Yaśodeva, of the Candrakula Gaccha—his guru was Candra

[1] Velankar, *Jina-ratna-kosa*, p. 231. [2] Ibid., p. 271. [3] Ibid., p. 272.
[4] Winternitz, op. cit., p. 496. [5] Suali in GSAI xxi (1908), 232.

Sūri and his guru's guru Vīra Gaṇin—completed his *cūrṇī* on the first three *Pañcāśakas*, only the first of which has been published, in *saṃvat* 1172.[1] This commentary is of special interest because it is written in Prakrit (a very clear Māhārāṣṭrī prose), and because though the author is careful to say that he has followed Abhayadeva in his interpretation of the text[2] he has in fact given much additional information derived from earlier sources. He also composed in 1180 a *vṛtti* on the *Pākṣika-sūtra* and is perhaps identical with the author of the *Bṛhad-vṛtti* on the *Nava-pada-prakaraṇa*.[3]

HEMACANDRA

The *Kali-kāla-sarvajña*, as this remarkable man was even in his lifetime styled, though he lacked perhaps the originality of mind of Haribhadra Yākinī-putra, surpassed him in the range of his knowledge. There was scarcely a branch of literature or science as then known to which he did not contribute, and his influence both on his contemporaries and on the whole subsequent history of Śvetāmbara Jainism and through Āśādhara to some extent even on the Digambaras can scarcely be overestimated. It may reasonably be suggested that as a poet he overrated himself but he wrote excellent Sanskrit prose, only slightly tinged with peculiarities that are sometimes described as Jaina but might with more propriety be regarded as characteristic of Gujarat. To a greater degree than any other Jaina writer he had a gift for the marshalling of facts and for clear and orderly exposition.

By birth a Gujarati and a member of a merchant caste he played a prominent role in the politics of his homeland and for this reason perhaps the facts of his long life (A.D. 1089–1172) are fairly well documented: as they can be found in Bühler's narrative,[4] it would be superfluous to go into them here.

His main contribution to *śrāvakācāra* is to be found in the *Yoga-śāstra*, or *Adhyātmopaniṣad*, an encyclopedic compilation on the duties of laymen and ascetics of which only the first three *prakāśas* are here of relevance. The substance of the work lies less in the text, which, written apparently in obedience to the fashion of the day in verse, serves only as an outline, than in the commentary. This is easy to read, rich in facts, and supported by quotations from the

[1] P (Y), p. 158.
[2] P (Y), p. 1.
[3] P (Y), *Upodghāta*, pp. 11–13.
[4] Bühler, *Über das Leben des Jaina-Mönches Hemacandra*, Vienna, 1889.

most diverse sources. It is only to be regretted that, except when citing from other works of his own composition, Hemacandra rarely names his sources, but it is clear that he made extensive use of the *Śrāvaka-prajñapti*, the *Pañcāśakas* with Abhayadeva's commentaries, the *Dharma-bindu*, and Siddhasena's commentary on the *Tattvārtha-sūtra*. The *Yoga-śāstra* belongs to the close of his life, having been written about 1160.

The first *prakāśa* of the work evokes certain general principles of Jainism and sets forth the thirty-five *śrāvaka-guṇas*. The second *prakāśa* discusses *samyaktva*, its *guṇas* and *aticāras* (1–17); condemning animal sacrifices, extols the virtues of *ahiṃsā* (18–49); and outlines the nature of the other four *aṇu-vratas*. The third *prakāśa* begins by explaining the *guṇa-vratas* (including under the *bhogopabhoga-vrata* such topics as *rātri-bhojana* and all that the Digambaras would understand by the *mūla-guṇas*) and *śikṣā-vratas* (1–88); and then goes on to list the *aticāras* of the twelve *vratas* (89–119), and to inculcate the necessity of *dāna* (119–21). Verses 122–30, covered by a commentary of over a hundred pages, portray a typical day in the life of a *mahā-śrāvaka*, thereby affording an opportunity for a detailed treatment of the six *āvaśyakas* and the *pūjā*; subjects of meditation for sleepless nights are given in verses 131–47; and the remaining six verses are given over to a description of *sallekhanā*.

In view of its very full picture of the life of a layman in twelfth-century Gujarat it is unfortunate that no translation of the work in a western language exists. Windisch attempted a rendering with his *editio princeps* of the first four *adhyāyas*[1] but this suffered from the handicap that his manuscript contained only the verses without the commentary. For the commencement of the work there is a full translation of text and commentary by Belloni-Filippi in an Italian periodical[2] but its publication was soon abandoned. Nor does a satisfactory edition of the complete text exist, since that which was published in the *Bibliotheca Indica* has remained unfinished.

Siddhasena Sūri

Little is known of this *ācārya*, author also of a *Padmaprabha-caritra*. His exhaustive commentary on the *Pravacana-sāroddhāra* is

[1] ZDMG 28. [2] GSAI xxi. 122–222 (1908).

dated A.D. 1185.[1] The sections dealing with the *vratas* and their *aticāras* have been borrowed with scarcely any changes in phraseology from the *Yoga-śāstra*, written only a quarter of a century earlier.

Devendra

For the medieval period the last major work on *śrāvakācāra* is the *Śrāddha-dina-kṛtya* of Devendra, a *sūri* of the Tapā Gaccha and pupil of Jagaccandra Sūri, who is said to have died at Malwa in A.D. 1270.[2] The text consists of 342 verses in conventional Māhārāṣṭrī Prakrit and is divided into eight *prastāvas*. On this framework the author has constructed his own voluminous Sanskrit commentary, in bulk largely made up of illustrative stories. The pattern is that of the *dina-caryā*, the duties of a Jaina layman being outlined first for the day and then for the fortnight, the month, and the year, so that the main emphasis is on the *āvaśyakas*, the *pūjā*, and the individual's obligations to the community. The *vratas* and their *aticāras* are covered by Devendra's own commentary—the *Vandāru-vṛtti*—on the *Pratikramaṇa-sūtra*, which he has incorporated into the *Śrāddha-dina-kṛtya*. He has also treated certain elements of the ritual separately in the Prakrit *bhāṣya-traya*.

Devendra quotes from the *Śrāvaka-prajñapti*, the *Pañcāśakas*, the *Nava-pada-prakaraṇa*, and the *Dharma-ratna-prakaraṇa*. His treatment of the *vratas* and their *aticāras* is in accordance with the orthodox Śvetāmbara tradition and shows no trace of the innovations made by Haribhadra and Hemacandra, but it is difficult to believe that he was not acquainted with the *Yoga-śāstra* and not indebted to it for the general plan of his work. Like almost all Jaina writers subsequent to Hemacandra, he shows by his references to such works as the *Manu-smṛti* and the *Vātsyāyana-kāma-sūtra*[3] that he was open to the general currents of Sanskrit culture.

Dharmaghoṣa

This *sūri* of the Tapā Gaccha, the pupil and successor of Devendra, is often known by the name of Dharmakīrti, which was his prior to *dīkṣā*.[4] He is the author of a Prakrit *Śrāddha-jita-kalpa* in 141 verses conceived as a sort of appendix to the *Jita-kalpa-sūtra*,[5]

[1] PS: *Upodghāta*, p. 5*b*.
[2] ŚrDK, pt. ii, p. 95.
[3] Schubring, *Die Lehre der Jainas*, p. 181.
[4] Winternitz, op. cit., p. 591.
[5] Velankar, op. cit., p. 126.

and of the *Saṅghācāra* commentary on the *Caitya-vandana-bhāṣya* of his master Devendra. This latter work is stated to be not later than *saṃvat* 1327.[1]

JINADATTA

Jinadatta Sūri of the Kharatara Gaccha, who would seem to belong to the thirteenth century A.D., wrote a *Caitya-vandana-kulaka* in Prakrit verse on which, in *saṃvat* 1383, Jinakuśala of the same *gaccha* composed a voluminous Sanskrit commentary consisting mainly of illustrative stories.[2]

THE PŪJĀ-PRAKARAṆA

This twenty-verse Sanskrit tract on the *pūjā*, which has been fathered on Umāsvāti, is quoted *in extenso* in the fifteenth-century *Śrāddha-vidhi* of Ratnaśekhara. However, there is no mention of it in the *Śrāddha-dina-kṛtya* of Devendra although these two works cover the same topics and use largely the same sources. It might not be unreasonable therefore to infer that its date lies somewhere between them. In view of the constant development of the ritual it is to be expected that endeavours should be made to give to innovations a spurious veneer of antiquity. Whether this tract is excerpted from, or older than, the *Viveka-vilāsa* is not clear.

JINADATTA

The *Viveka-vilāsa*, a Sanskrit verse manual constructed on the *dina-caryā* pattern and permeated with accretions from Hinduism, has sometimes been ascribed to the thirteenth century and may be later.[3] Fifteen verses from it[4] are found also in the *Pūjā-prakaraṇa*. In any event it cannot be the work of the Jinadatta Sūri who wrote the *Caitya-vandana-kulaka*. Jugalkiśor Mukhtār has shown that with the addition of some introductory verses and a false colophon it circulates among Digambaras under the name of the *Kundakunda-śrāvakācāra*.[5]

Its contents include elaborate rules for eating and drinking and for excretion, bathing, and sleeping, some general principles of

[1] Velankar, op. cit., p. 126.

[2] Ibid., p. 124.

[3] It is quoted by Jinamaṇḍana in the *Śrāddha-guṇa-vivaraṇa*, by Ratnaśekhara in the *Śrāddha-vidhi* (p. 46*b*), and by Yaśovijaya in the *Dharma-saṃgraha* (pt. i, p. 126*b*).

[4] *Viveka-vilāsa*, i. 85–97

[5] Mukhtār, *Grantha-parīkṣā*, pp. 26–45.

nīti, a list of the *lakṣaṇas* or lucky marks of men and women, some remarks on the technique of yoga, and a long description of remedies for snakebite.

VARDHAMĀNA

This *sūri* of the Kharatara Gaccha composed an *Ācāra-dinakara* which, owing apparently to a confusion of the author with an earlier namesake, has been falsely ascribed to the eleventh century. This Sanskrit prose treatise on the *kriyās* or *saṃskāras* appropriate to the various phases of life, both lay and monastic, seems to have been the first Śvetāmbara work of its kind, but from the fact that the author quotes from Hemacandra's *Yoga-śāstra*[1] and because the details, for example, of the *pūjā*, show a very developed stage,[2] an early date is impossible. Although the ceremonies noticed in the *Ācāra-dinakara* are very different from the fifty-three *kriyās* of the *Ādi-purāṇa* it seems impossible that these latter were completely unknown to Vardhamāna. Nāthurām Premī[3] had already noted that the work could not be as old as was supposed (he suggested *saṃvat* 1500), and a recent writer in fact gives its date of compilation as *saṃvat* 1468.[4]

CĀRITRASUNDARA

Cāritrasundara Gaṇin, pupil of Ratnasiṃha, composed the *Ācāropadeśa*, a rather brief metrical *śrāvakācāra* in six *adhyāyas*, in *saṃvat* 1487.[5] It has enjoyed considerable popularity but offers little of interest except in its details of the *pūjā*. The writer is presumably to be identified with the author of an elaborate allegorical *dūta-kāvya*, the *Śīla-dūta*, dated A.D. 1420.[6]

JINAMAṆḌANA

Jinamaṇḍana Gaṇin was a pupil of Somasundara Sūri of the Tapā Gaccha. He completed his *Śrāddha-guṇa-vivaraṇa*, more correctly styled, it would seem, the *Śrāddha-guṇa-śreṇi-saṃgraha*, in *saṃvat* 1498 in the town of Aṇahilapaṭṭana in Gujarat.[7]

[1] ADK, p. 43*a*.

[2] e.g. the description of the twenty-one *snapanas* required for the *pratiṣṭhā* ritual (ADK, pp. 152–5).

[3] Premī, *Jaina sāhitya aur itihās*, p. 561.

[4] V. A. Sangave, *Jaina Community*, p. 267.

[5] Velankar, op. cit., p. 25.

[6] Winternitz, op. cit., p. 574.

[7] ŚrGuV: *prastāvanā*, p. 2.

This Sanskrit prose composition on the thirty-five *śrāvaka-guṇas* is remarkable both for the author's erudition and for the many curious details from Jaina tradition which he preserves. At the same time he displays great familiarity with Hindu sources.

Ratnaśekhara

Certain details of the life of this *ācārya* of the Tapā Gaccha are available. Born in *saṃvat* 1452, ordained in 1463, and elevated to the dignity of *sūri* in 1502, he died in 1517.[1] His writings—the *Ācāra-pradīpa* (1516), the *Śrāddha-vidhi* (1506), and the commentary on the *Śrāddha-pratikramaṇa-sutra* (1496)—are among the best productions of an age of decadence and show his familiarity with the canon and with the works of Hemacandra and Devendra, though traces of increasing hinduization are everywhere apparent.

The *Śrāddha-vidhi* preserves the fiction of a metrical composition by its framework of seventeen Prakrit *gāthās* divided into six *prakāśas*, but these are manifestly only a peg on which to hang a vast Sanskrit prose treatise which imitates in its general outlines the *Śrāddha-dina-kṛtya*. It might even be described as an adaptation of this work to contemporary conditions. Similarly the *Pratikramaṇa* commentary represents a more extensive version of Devendra's *Vandāru-vṛtti*.

Yaśovijaya

Of the extensive literature on *śrāvakācāra* surviving from the sixteenth and seventeenth centuries only one work will retain our attention. In A.D. 1681 Mānavijaya wrote a *Dharma-saṃgraha* in Sanskrit verses apparently designed to serve as a vehicle for the comprehensive prose commentary of Yaśovijaya. This great reformer, who lived from 1624 to 1688, sought to regenerate his age by a return to the teachings of the canon and had probably a better command of the whole range of Jaina literature than any man since Hemacandra. In his commentary, modelled on the *Yoga-śāstra*, which he quotes repeatedly, but as only one of many sources, he has shown an extraordinary sureness of touch in rejecting the non-Jaina elements which had invaded the writings of predecessors like Ratnaśekhara.

[1] *Śrāddha-vidhi: upodghāta*, p. 4*a*.

THE AUTHORS—DIGAMBARA SAMPRADĀYA

Kundakunda	Cāritra-prābhṛta	2nd century (?)
Umāsvāmin	Tattvārtha-sūtra	3rd century (?)
Kārttikeya	Dvādaśānuprekṣā	4th century (?)
Samantabhadra	Ratna-karaṇḍa-śrāvakācāra	*c.* 450 (?)
Pūjyapāda	Sarvārtha-siddhi	6th century (?)
	Ratna-sāra	8th century (?)
Jinasena	Ādi-purāṇa	late 9th century
Devasena	Bhāva-saṃgraha	early 10th century
Somadeva	Yaśas-tilaka	959
Amitagati	Subhāṣita-ratna-sandoha	993
,,	Śrāvakācāra	
Cāmuṇḍarāya	Cāritra-sāra	*c.* 1000
Amṛtacandra	Puruṣārtha-siddhy-upāya	11th century
	Śrāvaka-dharma-dohaka	11th century (?)
Vasunandin	Śrāvakācāra	*c.* 1100
Padmanandin	Dharma-rasāyana	12th century (?)
Āśādhara	Sāgāra-dharmāmṛta	1240
Māghanandin	Śrāvakācāra	*c.* 1260
Guṇabhūṣaṇa	Śrāvakācāra	*c.* 1300 (?)
Padmanandin	Śrāvakācāra	15th century (?)
Vāmadeva	Bhāva-saṃgraha	15th century (?)
Sakalakīrti	Praśnottara-śrāvakācāra	15th century
Medhāvin	Dharma-saṃgraha-śrāvakācāra	1504
Brahmanemidatta	Dharma-pīyuṣa-śrāvakācāra	*c.* 1530
Rājamalla	Lāṭī-saṃhitā	1584
Śivakoṭi	Ratna-mālā	17th century (?)
Somasena	Traivarṇikācāra	1610

Kundakunda

Amongst the many works attributed to Kundakunda two are of some relevance to the *śrāvakācāra*. The summary of the rules of right conduct given in the *Cāritra-prābhṛta* devotes a few verses to the lay life, listing, *inter alia*, the twelve *vratas*. The *Ratna-sāra* in view of some of its contents is best ascribed to a considerably later period.

Much has been written on the date of Kundakunda but to little result. The tradition of the Digambara *paṭṭāvalīs* places him in the first century A.D.[1] It is noteworthy that all the works ascribed to him are in Prakrit. Upadhye has placed him in the second century.[2]

Umāsvāmin

Since Jacobi's[3] edition and translation at the end of last century the *Tattvārtha-sūtra*, the most authoritative exposition of Jaina doctrine, regarded even by the Śvetāmbaras with a veneration scarcely less than that accorded to the canon has been too well known to need description. Only the seventh *adhyāya* is concerned with the lay life.[4] Umāsvāmin's date remains uncertain; according to the Digambara tradition he lived between 135 and 219.

The reasons which have led me to regard, from the aspect of *śrāvākācāra*, the *Tattvārtha-sūtra* as a purely Digambara work have been noted above.

Kārttikeya

About a hundred verses (302 to 391 in the printed edition) of the *Dvādaśānuprekṣā* or *Dharma-bhāvanā* of Kārttikeya are devoted, as part of the *dharmānuprekṣā*, to a brief consideration of the lay life; they cover the topics of *samyaktva*, the twelve *vratas* (without any indication of the *aticāras*), *sallekhanā*, and the *pratimās*.

The dating of Kārttikeya presents considerable difficulties. Upadhye[2] would put him later than Yogindu and Pūjyapāda, somewhere between the sixth and thirteenth centuries in fact. Jugalkiśor Mukhtar[5] rejects the arguments on which this view is based and regards Kārttikeya as much nearer Umāsvāmin in date. The special eulogy of those *tīrthaṅkaras* who were said to have been *kumāra-śramaṇas* would also suggest for him that Kārttikeya, too, had taken the monastic initiation whilst still a boy, whilst certain other points such as the general use of the title *svāmi* with his name would lead to the belief that he belonged to south India.

[1] Winternitz, op. cit., p. 476.

[2] Upadhye, Introduction to KA, pp. 67–70.

[3] ZDMG lx (1906), 287 ff., 512 ff.

[4] Mukhtār has pointed out that there exists a spurious *Umāsvāmi-śrāvakācāra* which is no more than a haphazard assemblage of didactic verses for laymen, taken from Śvetāmbara as well as Digambara sources (see *Grantha-parīkṣā*, pp. 1–25).

[5] See Mukhtār, *Purātana Jaina-vākya sūci: prastāvana*, pp. 22–27, for a general summary of these arguments.

SAMANTABHADRA

The *Ratna-karaṇḍa-śrāvakācāra* of Samantabhadra would appear to be the earliest Digambara work devoted exclusively to the exposition of the rules of conduct for a layman. It is divided into five *paricchedas*, the first of which deals with *samyag-darśana*, the second with *samyag-jñāna*, the third with the *aṇu-vratas* and *guṇa-vratas*, the fourth with the *śikṣā-vratas*, and the fifth with *sallekhanā* and the *pratimās*. Like Umāsvāmin Samantabhadra has been responsible for many innovations in the *śrāvakācāra* doctrine and, to an even greater extent, he has rationalized the *aticāras* of the *vratas* and given them a more universal content. Even the change in the designation of the last *vrata* (*vaiyāvṛttya* for *atithi-saṃvibhāga*) is an indication of his attitude. Many of his alterations have been rejected by almost all his successors but this notwithstanding, his influence has been far-reaching and whenever the term *Svāmi* is used alone it is to Samantabhadra that reference is made.

Many legends attach to his life but little can be said of it with certainty. He would seem to have been a native of the Tamil land and to have belonged to a *kṣatriya* family.[1] It seems difficult to assert with Hiralal Jain that the *Ratna-karaṇḍa* is based on the *Tattvārtha-sūtra*, the *Dvādaśānuprekṣā*, and the *Darśana-prābhṛta* of Kundakunda:[2] at the most it may be stated that in the development of the *śrāvakācāra* doctrine it would seem to be posterior to Kārttikeya's work. Widely differing figures are given for Samantabhadra's date. An ancient tradition puts him as early as the second century;[3] equally it has been conjectured that he flourished in the first half of the eighth century[4] which would seem to be too late a date, if only because of the extreme veneration with which he was regarded already in Jinasena's time. Mukhtār, after an exhaustive study of all available evidence, would go no further than to suggest somewhere between the first and fifth centuries A.D.[5] Arbitrarily the present writer has accepted the upper limit—*circa* A.D. 450—as a probable date.

PŪJYAPĀDA

One of the oldest and probably the most authoritative of the commentaries on the *Tattvārtha-sūtra* is Pūjyapāda's *Sarvārtha-*

[1] RK: *prākkathan*, pp. 4–15.
[2] Śr (V): *prastāvanā*, p. 45.
[3] RK: *prākkathan*, p. 115.
[4] See Winternitz, op. cit., p. 580.
[5] RK: *prākkathan*, p. 196.

siddhi. Pūjyapāda, or Devanandin, who again, it seems, belonged to south India, was also the author of a *Jainendra-vyākaraṇa* in which, unless as is sometimes held this name is merely fictitious, mention is made of Samantabhadra, who must therefore be anterior to him in date.[1] On the faith of epigraphical evidence Mukhtār would place Pūjyapāda in the second half of the fifth century,[2] and this view is accepted by the editor of the *Sarvārtha-siddhi*. Winternitz assumed that he lived before Samantabhadra and placed him between the fifth and the seventh centuries.[3]

There is in existence also a *śrāvakācāra* ascribed to Pūjyapāda.

The Ratna-sāra

Many doubts exist on the authenticity of the attribution of this work to Kundakunda and both Schubring[4] and Jugalkiśor Mukhtār[5] have expressed the opinion that the text in its present form cannot be as old as that. This little Prakrit verse tract on the *ratna-traya* contains at least one verse—that which refers to the fifty-three *kriyās*—of considerable interest for the development of the *śrāvakācāra*.

Jinasena

The *Mahā-purāṇa*, one of the most ambitious productions of Digambara Jainism, is composed of the *Ādi-purāṇa* and the *Uttara-purāṇa*. The first forty-two *parvans* of the former were written by Jinasena, whose guru was Vīrasena of the Sena Saṅgha, and the rest of the work was completed by his pupil Guṇabhadra. Both enjoyed the patronage of the Rāṣṭrakūṭa kings and the date of termination of this epic—A.D. 897—has been recorded.[6] Like the *Māhā-bhārata*, which it was designed to rival, it includes many digressions of an edifying character and parvans 38, 39, and 40 are often regarded as constituting a *śrāvakācāra* in their own right. They are mainly devoted to a description of the fifty-three *kriyās* or ceremonies which mark the stages in a man's life both as layman and ascetic and furnish the only extant description of these

[1] Mukhtār, op. cit., pp. 150–3.
[2] Phūlcandra Siddhānta Śastri in T (P) *Prastāvanā*, pp. 94–96.
[3] Winternitz, op. cit., p. 478.
[4] Schubring, *Kundakunda echt und unecht*, p. 568.
[5] Mukhtār, op. cit., p. 15.
[6] Winternitz, op. cit., pp. 497–9.

which can pretend to any antiquity. Jinasena's views have been held in especial reverence by all succeeding Digambara writers.[1]

Somadeva

The *Yaśas-tilaka* of Somadeva is in fact a *campū*, a romance partly in verse, partly in prose, written in 959 at Gangadhārā near the modern Dharwar in the territory of the Rāṣṭrakūṭa kings.[2] Little is known of the author's life except that he belonged to the Deva Saṅgha, and his influence on later writers apart from Āśādhara is not very marked. The narrative of the *Yaśas-tilaka* does not run through the whole work: the sixth, seventh, and eighth books together constitute an excursus on the *śrāvakācāra* which is often referred to as Somadeva's *Upāsakādhyāyana*. This covers *samyaktva*, the twelve *vratas*—for the five *aṇu-vratas* illustrative stories are given—and *sallekhanā*. The section dealing with the *sāmāyika* contains an exhaustive treatment of *dhyāna*, and numerous hymns and verses on the *anuprekṣās* are included. Somadeva differs from other Jaina *ācāryas* in not adhering strictly to the figure of five *aticāras* for each *vrata* and by his often very personal contributions to the *śrāvakācārā* such as the introduction of the four categories of truth and falsehood or of the five classes of persons entitled to maintenance by the faithful. He is noteworthy, too, for the extent to which he is permeated by Vedāntist concepts.

Devasena

There are good grounds for assuming, as is usually done, that the *Bhāva-saṃgraha* and the *Darśana-sāra* are by the same hand. Now the latter is clearly stated to have been written in the temple of Pārśvanātha at Dhārā in *saṃvat* 990, and since the author strongly condemns all other sects as heretical he would appear to have belonged to the Mūla Saṅgha. The *Bhāva-saṃgraha* may then be dated in the first half of the tenth century A.D.[3]

This work—in Prakrit verse—gives a description of the fourteen *guṇa-sthānas*. The *śrāvakācāra* section is contained in verses 350–

[1] It is for this reason, doubtless, that his name has been attached to a strongly hinduized compilation on the layman's duties known as the *Trivarṇācāra* of Jinasena. Mukhtār has characterized this work as a blatant forgery of quite recent date. See *Grantha-parīkṣā*, pp. 46 ff.

[2] Handiqui, p. 4.

[3] Mukhtār, *Purātana Jaina-vākya sūci*, pp. 59–61.

599, which describe the fifth *guṇa-sthāna*: after a brief summary of the *vratas* and *mūla-guṇas*, *dhyāna*, *pūjā*, and *dāna* are described in detail. The main emphasis is on the amassing of *puṇya* and the performance of *pūjā* and *dāna*; and, as in other *śrāvakācāras* of a popular type, it is on the joys of the *deva-loka* and the *bhoga-bhūmis* rather than on *mokṣa* that stress is laid.

The Śrāvaka-dharma-dohaka

When he edited this anonymous Apabhraṃśa text Hiralal Jain,[1] after eliminating Yogīndradeva as a possible author, proposed its ascription to Devasena and listed a number of parallels between this work and the *Bhāva-saṃgraha*. Mukhtār[2] is reluctant to accept this view and it is possible that the editor himself would no longer uphold it. The passages selected for comparison offer in fact little more than recurrences of certain clichés common in Jaina writings. On the other hand the description of the various forms of *pūjā* and results to be achieved by each of them differs considerably in the two works. If this Apabhramśa work does not then belong to Devasena it might well be a century or so later than Hiralal Jain suggests, for its enumeration of the *abhakṣyas* seems to be more fully developed than that of Amitagati while it appears strange that its author should be the only writer before Vasunandin to mention the two divisions of the eleventh *pratimā*. Śrutasāgara, in his commentary on the *Ṣaṭ-prābhṛta*, quotes eight verses from this work, which he ascribes to Lakṣmīcandra.[3]

The *Śrāvaka-dharma-dohaka* is a compilation in some 200 Apabhraṃśa *dohās*, giving in summarized form an account of the *pratimās*, the *mūla-guṇas*, the *vratas*, *dāna*, *vinaya*, *vaiyāvṛttya*, and *pūjā*.

Cāmuṇḍarāya

The Cāmuṇḍarāya who wrote the *Cāritra-sāra* is, according to Winternitz,[4] distinct from the minister and general of the Gaṅga king Rācamalla (*saṃvat* 1032–41) at whose instance the *Gommaṭa-sāra* was composed. This other Cāmuṇḍarāya had also, however, followed the active life of a soldier before becoming a monk but nothing more seems to be known of him.

[1] Doha, *Bhūmikā*, pp. 9–19.
[2] Mukhtār, *Purātana Jaina-vākya sūci*, pp. 59–61.
[3] Velankar, op. cit., p. 394.
[4] Winternitz, op. cit., p. 587.

The *Cāritra-sāra* is a work which has received less than its due: Hiralal Jain does not even mention it in his survey of the Digambara *śrāvakācāras*. It is an admirably concise exposition of both the *śrāvakācāra* and the *yaty-ācāra* (about a quarter only of the contents being devoted to the former), written in clear and elegant Sanskrit prose. The arrangement is by *pratimās*; and the *vratas*, with their *aticāras* and adequate explanations of these, are given under the second *pratimā*. For the *aticāras* Cāmuṇḍarāya follows closely Pūjyapāda's commentary on the *Tattvārtha-sūtra*, often retaining his exact wording; as a model he has evidently preferred it to Samantabhadra's *Ratna-karaṇḍa* though his familiarity with this work is evident from the very striking division of the *pāpopadeśa* category of *anartha-daṇḍa* into four types, and from the listing of the *bhogas*, which should be avoided, into five classes. Though not mentioned by name the *mūla-guṇas* are in fact discussed after the *vratas*. *Rātri-bhojana* is held to be the sixth *aṇuvrata*. After the *pratimās* comes a description of the sixteen *bhāvanās* (for which again the author is heavily indebted to Pūjyapāda) and, by way of appendix, an account of the *sallekhanā* ritual. Many topics normally included in a *śrāvakācāra*, for example, the *āvaśyakas*, and, under the head of *dhyāna* the *anuprekṣās*, are relegated to the *yaty-ācāra* section.

Cāmuṇḍarāya is clearly very close to Jinasena (from whose *Ādi-purāna* he quotes) in his affiliations. He notes the four Jaina *āśramas*, the third of which, the *vānaprastha*, is equated with the status of the layman in the eleventh *pratimā*. Like Jinasena he is very open to Hindu influences and in fact quotes from the *Manu-smṛti*.[1]

Amitagati

Amitagati, pupil of Mādhavasena, was an *ācārya* of the Māthura Saṅgha, a branch of the Kāṣṭhā Saṅgha.[2] Munj and Sindhul are mentioned in his works and accordingly it is suggested he belonged to the literary school of Munj.[3] His *Subhāṣita-ratnasandoha* was composed in *saṃvat* 1050 and his commentary on the *Pañca-saṃgraha* in *saṃvat* 1073[3] so that his *śrāvakācāra* may well be dated within the first quarter of the eleventh century A.D.

It is an extensive and comprehensive work, in Sanskrit verse, the

[1] *Manu-smṛti*, v. 55.
[2] Premī, op. cit., p. 172.
[3] Premī, op. cit., pp. 176–7.

first *pariccheda* of which is devoted to the praise of the *dharma*, the second to *samyaktva* and its opposite, *mithyātva*, the third to an explanation of the seven *tattvas*, and the fourth to a refutation of Buddhists, *nāstikas*, and other heterodox sects. The fifth *pariccheda* begins the *śrāvakācāra* proper with a discussion of the *mūla-guṇas* (this actual designation is not, however, employed), the sixth and seventh are devoted to the twelve *vratas* and their *aticāras* and to *sallekhanā* and the *pratimās*, the eighth to the six *āvaśyakas*, and the ninth, tenth, and eleventh to the topic of *dāna*. *Pūjā* and the seven *vyasanas* are covered in the twelfth, *vinaya*, *vaiyāvṛttya*, and *svādhyāya* in the thirteenth, the *anuprekṣās* in the fourteenth, and *dhyāna* in the fifteenth *paricchedas*. It is only in the case of the *pūjā* that the details are surprisingly exiguous. Amitagati's treatise does not seem to bear a specially close relation to any earlier work.

In another poem, the *Subhāṣita-ratna-sandoha*, he touched on similar subjects. The whole of *pariccheda* XXXI of this work is devoted to the basic vows of the layman and the interdictions of the *mūla-guṇas* are covered in *paricchedas* XX, XXI, and XXII. The Sanskrit style of both poems is characterized by a conspicuous preference for recondite grammatical forms.

AMṚTACANDRA

Nothing at all is known of the life of this *ācārya*. On the faith of a Digambara *paṭṭāvalī* quoted in Peterson's eighteenth report it had been accepted—by Nāthurām Premī[1] in his edition of the *Puruṣārtha-siddhy-upāya* and by Winternitz[2]—that Amṛtacandra was alive in A.D. 904. Upadhye,[3] in his introduction to the *Pravacana-sāra*, placed him somewhere between 800 and 1100 but Nāthurām Premī,[4] in a later article, suggested that his date must lie between 1000 and 1250, the upper limit being given by the year of compilation of the *Sāgāra-dharmāmṛta* in which he is quoted. Premī has also noted that in this commentary Amṛtacandra is twice referred to as *ṭhakkura*, a title that is usually given to the people of Rajagharana.[5]

In its outward form the *Puruṣārtha-siddhy-upāya* is a *śrāvakācāra* like so many others: after a short introduction giving certain basic

[1] PASU: *prastāvanā*, p. 4. [2] Winternitz, op. cit., p. 561.

[3] *Pravacana-sāra*, ed. by A. N. Upadhye, p. 101.

[4] Premī, op. cit., p. 458. This article was originally published in the *Jaina Hitaiṣī* in 1920. [5] See Premī, op. cit., p. 457.

principles of Jainism it discusses the *ratna-traya*, the twelve *vratas* and *sallekhanā* with their *aticāras*, and *tapas* and the *pariṣahas* (from its position in the text *a-rātri-bhojana* would appear to be considered the sixth *aṇu-vrata* though it is not given this designation). It is in the spirit that animates it that the work differs from all others of its kind. In rather harsh verse Amṛtacandra sings the praises of *ahiṃsā* with the fervour of a mystic, always stressing his theme that all the evil man can do is in some sense an expression of *hiṃsā*. The only other writer who at all approaches him in this singlemindedness is Amitagati.

VASUNANDIN

Again of this author really nothing is known. Several *ācāryas* of this name are recorded but it seems safe to say that the same man composed the *Śrāvakācāra* and the *Pratiṣṭhā-sāra-saṃgraha* as well as the *Ācāra-vṛtti* commentary on the *Mūlācāra*. This commentary quotes Amitagati, and for this reason and because Vasunandin himself is quoted in the *Sāgāra-dharmāmṛta* commentary Nāthurām Premī[1] and Jugalkiśor Mukhtār[2] agree in placing him somewhere between A.D. 1050 and 1200. Hiralal Jain is prepared to situate him—more precisely—in the second half of the eleventh century since his guru's guru, Nayanandin, would seem to be identical with the author of the Apabhraṃśa *Sudarśana-carita*, composed in *saṃvat* 1100.[3]

The *Śrāvakācāra* or, as it is sometimes called, *Upāsakādhyāyana* of Vasunandin in Prakrit verse is based on the *pratimā* framework which allows for a description under the first *pratimā* of the seven *vyasanas* and of the misfortunes of the *jīva* in the four *gatis*, and, under the second *pratimā*, of the twelve *vratas*. The *vratas* are given rather anomalously—they do not include *sāmāyika* and *poṣadhōpavāsa*, which are treated only as *pratimās*—and without any indication of the *aticāras*. The two phases of the eleventh *pratimā* are noted. After the *pratimās* follow miscellaneous topics: *rātri-bhojana*, *vinaya*, *vaiyāvṛttya*, *pūjā*, and *dhyāna*, and the work concludes with a panegyric of the monk's life. It has been shown that Vasunandin used Devasena's *Bhāva-saṃgraha* and it is probable that he was familiar with Amitagati's *Śrāvakācāra*.[4]

[1] See Premī, op. cit., p. 457.
[2] See Mukhtār, *Purātana Jaina-vākya sūci*, p. 100.
[3] See Śr (V): *prastāvanā*, pp. 18–19.
[4] See Śr (V): *prastāvanā*, p. 41.

Padmanandin

The name of the author of the *Dharma-rasāyana*, a short verse tract in Prakrit on the four *gatis*, is given as Padmanandin, who cannot be identical with the writer of the *Śrāvakācāra*. Of Jaina lay doctrine it gives little more than the twelve *vratas* and is unusual in replacing *ahiṃsā* as the first *aṇu-vrata* by 'the non-killing of animals for sacrifice'. Such a formulation is not met with in any other text surveyed here but is found in the *Varāṅga-carita* of Jaṭila.[1] The *Dharma-rasāyana*, which may be as old as the eleventh or twelfth century (though the use of Prakrit does not necessarily imply this), has some verses on the sufferings of the *jīva* in hell which are written with considerable verve.

Āśādhara

The author of the *Sāgāra-dharmāmṛta* is a very much less shadowy figure for he has given considerable information about himself and his writings in his *praśastis*, and on the basis of these Nāthurām Premī has reconstructed his life. Born about *saṃvat* 1235, he belonged to the Bagheravāla *jāti* one of the most important *vaiśya jātis* of Rajputana, and members of his family held appointments under the rulers of Dhārā, then a considerable centre of learning, whither they had moved from Māṇḍalgaṛh (Mewār) after the conquest of Delhi by Shihāb al-Dīn Ghorī in *saṃvat* 1249. He subsequently lived for thirty-five years at Nālachā. Though later writers sometimes call him *sūri*, he remained, according to Premī till his death—he was still alive and writing in *saṃvat* 1300—a layman (perhaps at its close a *kṣullaka*).[2] In the course of a life devoted, it would seem, to the promotion of his religion,[3] he did not hesitate to criticize and admonish the monks, as witness the verse:[4]

> *paṇḍitair bhraṣṭa-cāritrair baṭharaiś ca tapo-dhanaiḥ*
> *śāsanam jina-candrasya nirmalam malinī-kṛtam*

Āśādhara's erudition is remarkable, perhaps as comprehensive as that of the *Kali-kāla-sarvajña*: he lacked only Hemacandra's capacity to present his rich material in clear and orderly fashion. Yet, more than any other writer considered here, he possessed the

[1] *Varāṅga-carita*, xv. 106.
[2] Premī, op. cit., pp. 130–1.
[3] *Jina-dharmodayārthaṃ yo Nalakacchapure 'vasat* is the phrase used in the *praśasti*.
[4] Premī, op. cit., p. 131.

temperament and habits of a scholar. Wherever he has discerned differences of opinion between the *ācāryas* of old he has noted whatever he felt to be of importance, carefully indicating his sources. Thus he cites Samantabhadra ('the Svāmi'),[1] Jinasena, Cāmuṇḍarāya, Somadeva, Amitagati, Amṛtacandra, and Vasunandin, often affording, as we have seen, valuable indications for dating them. But he did not confine himself to Digambara sources; in fact on many points, particularly on the *aticāras* of the *vratas*, he transcribed whole passages from the *Yoga-śāstra*.[2] Hemacandra is not mentioned by name but the phrase '*Sitāmbarācārya*'[3] nearly always refers to him.

In this readiness to use Śvetāmbara writings he may have been showing the same catholicity of outlook that in a later age animated Yaśovijaya in his attempts to reconcile the two sects; but it cannot be left out of account that, although he belonged to the Mūla Saṅgha, he may also have been the inheritor of a Yāpanīya tradition. Amongst his surviving works there is a commentary on the *Bhagavatī Ārādhanā*, which, as Premī[4] has shown, may well have been a Yāpanīya production (its most important commentator certainly belonged to that sect). It is particularly in the section on *sallekhanā*, to which Āśādhara attaches a quite special importance, that the influence of the *Bhagavatī Ārādhanā* on the *Sāgāra-dharmāmṛta* is apparent. Many of the topics discussed in this work figure in no other Digambara *śrāvakācāra* save that of Medhāvin, who, as we shall see, belonged to the same *sampradāya*: the mention of *sthūla-hiṃsā* and *sūkṣma-hiṃsā*, the distinction of *aticāra* and *bhaṅga*; the tabulation of the *aticāras* of the *brahma-vrata* that may be committed by women; the catalogue of the fifteen forbidden callings; the notation of the *kumārī-go-bhū* classification of *satya*; the reference to the harming of *vāyu-kāyas* and *ap-kāyas* under *anartha-daṇḍa*; and the description of the *dina-caryā*, the ideal daily round for the layman. All these have their analogies in the generality of Śvetāmbara works, and though some may be direct borrowings from Hemacandra—the *dina-caryā* is a case in point—others may stem from an earlier tradition. More significant from the angle of possible Yāpanīya affiliations is the description of the rite of *sallekhanā* when performed by women for whom nudity is then authorized.[5]

[1] SDhA iv. 64. [2] See Appendix. [3] SDhA v. 23.
[4] Premī, op. cit., pp. 31–32. [5] SDhA viii. 38.

The list of Āśādhara's works as given by him in his *praśastis* is a long one but many of those mentioned seem to have disappeared completely. Apart from some short *kāvyas* and a number of commentaries they include writings on logic, on ayurvedic medicine, on the technique of yoga, and on various elements of the Jaina ritual such as the *pūjā*.[1] But the most important extant works are the *Sāgāra-dharmāmṛta* and *Anāgāra-dharmāmṛta*, which are conceived on exactly parallel lines and together form a complete manual of the secular and the monastic life. The metrical text is amplified by a prose commentary which in both cases bears the name *Bhavya-kumuda-candrikā*.

The *Sāgāra-dharmāmṛta*, which alone concerns us here, was completed in *saṃvat* 1296 and its commentary three years later. The plan of the work rests on the division into the three stages through which the *śrāvaka* should pursue his spiritual progress: *pākṣika*, *naiṣṭhika*, and *sādhaka*. The first two *adhyāyas* are concerned with the *pākṣika* stage, the next five with the *naiṣṭhika*, and the last with the *sādhaka*. The first *adhyāya* is taken up with a consideration of *samyaktva* and with definitions of a number of terms, mentioning incidentally the *śrāvaka-guṇas*. The second lists the *mūla-guṇas* (noting the divergent interpretations of other *ācāryas*) and then deals in detail with *pūjā* and *dāna* (including marriage, which is regarded as *kanyā-dāna*). As is made clear later these terms have a different meaning for the *pākṣika* and for the *naiṣṭhika*. With the third *adhyāya* begins the consideration of the *pratimās*; and this chapter is in fact taken up by a condemnation of the seven *vyasanas* and ancillary *vyasanas*, which must be eschewed before the first *pratimā* is attained. The next two *adhyāyas* cover the twelve *vratas* and their *aticāras*, the sixth is devoted to the *dina-caryā*, and the seventh delineates the remaining *pratimās*, culminating in the final stage with its divisions into *kṣullaka* and *ailaka*. The last *adhyāya* prescribes how the *sādhaka* is to terminate his earthly existence by the rite of *sallekhanā*.

Māghanandin

This *ācārya*, pupil of Kumudacandra, was the author of a *Śrāvakācāra* in Sanskrit and of other works in Kannada: he belongs to *circa* A.D. 1260.[2]

[1] See Premī, op. cit., pp. 134–7.

[2] Premī, Introduction to *Siddhanta-sārādi-saṃgraha*, p. 23. This *Śrāvakācāra* does not appear to have been published.

Guṇabhūṣaṇa

The date of this author is very uncertain. The upper limit is furnished by the date of the manuscript on which the printed edition of the work is based—*saṃvat* 1526.[1] At the same time he must be at least later than Vasunandin for, as Hiralal Jain[2] has shown, very many of his verses are no more than paraphrases of the Prakrit *gāthās* of Vasunandin's text. The editor of the *Guṇabhūṣaṇa-śrāvakācāra* hazards a conjecture that it may have been written in the fourteenth-century *saṃvat*.[1] In view of its indebtedness to Vasunandin the importance of this work is not very great.

Padmanandin

The author of the *Dharma-rasāyana* is distinct from the Padmanandin to whom a brief metrical *Śrāvakācāra* in Sanskrit is ascribed. The contents of this latter work suggest that is not likely to be later than the fourteenth or fifteenth century.

Vāmadeva

Vāmadeva, pupil of Lakṣmīcandra of the Mūla Saṅgha and a *kāyastha* by caste, is the author of the *Bhāva-saṃgraha*, a Sanskrit metrical treatise covering the same themes as Devasena's work of the same name. He quotes from the *Jina-saṃhitā*, so that if this is the *Jina-saṃhitā* of Ekasandhi, who belongs to the fourteenth-century *saṃvat*, he must be later than A.D. 1350.[3]

The lay doctrine is covered in verses 441–619, which deal with the fifth *guṇa-sthāna*. The topics treated include the *pratimās*, the *mūla-guṇas*, the *vratas*, *pūjā*, *dāna* and, very summarily, the *āvayakas*. Nāthurām Premī, in his introduction to the text, is perhaps rather unjust to the author whose work he characterizes as a mere paraphrase of Devasena,[3] when in fact it contains many original elements.

Sakalakīrti

The *Dharma-praśnottara* or *Praśnottara-śrāvakācāra* of Sakalakīrti is an extremely voluminous verse *śrāvakācāra* treatise in twenty-four *sargas* in the form of question and answer. It is a

1 *Prastāvanā*, p. 3.
2 He records these parallels in the footnotes to his edition of the Śr (V).
3 BhS (V): *Bhūmikā*, p. 7.

humdrum composition mainly consisting of longwinded narratives: for the details of the *vratas* the author slavishly follows Samantabhadra.

Sakalakīrti is supposed to have died in A.D. 1464[1] but, to judge from style and contents, a date considerably later might more easily have been conjectured. Winternitz,[1] however, accepts the ascription of this *śrāvakācāra* to the fifteenth century.

MEDHĀVIN

The author of the *Dharma-saṃgraha-śrāvakācāra* tells us in his *praśasti* that Paṇḍita Mīha, a *kṣullaka* living at Hīsarapura and a pupil of Jinacandra Muni, commenced this work during the reign of Firūz Khān of Nagpur and that he, Medhāvin, also a native of Hīsarapura, completed it in *saṃvat* 1561, basing it on the writings of Samantabhadra, Vasunandin, and Āśādhara.[2] It might have been better had he dwelt more on his debt to Āśādhara, to whose *sampradāya* he evidently belongs, for many of the Śvetāmbara features, such as the *kumārī-go-bhū* classification and the picture of the *dina-caryā*, not found in other Digambara works reappear in Medhāvin and his treatment of *sallekhanā* is exactly parallel.

The *Dharma-saṃgraha*, which, according to the author, contains exactly 1,440 verses, is divided into ten *adhikāras*, the first three of which describe the Jina's *samavasaraṇa*. These have been published separately under the title of the *Samavasarana-darpaṇa*.[3] The rest of the work follows exactly the arrangement of the *Sāgāra-dharmāmṛta* and differs from it only in certain passages that reflect increasing hinduization such as the differentiation of touchable and untouchable *śūdras*[4] or new external influences such as the passage in which the author is concerned to justify the worship of images.[5]

BRAHMANEMIDATTA

A *Dharma-pīyūṣa-śrāvakācāra*[6] in four *adhyāyas* was composed by Brahmanemidatta, who also wrote a *Śrīpāla-carita* (A.D. 1528) and an *Ārādhanā-kathā-kośa* (1530).[7]

1 Winternitz, op. cit., p. 592.
2 Śr (M), pp. 327–8.
3 Schubring, *Die Lehre der Jainas*, p. 210.
4 Śr (M) ix. 233.
5 Śr (M) ix. 38.
6 This work was not accessible to me and in fact does not seem to have been published.
7 Winternitz, op. cit., p. 544.

Rājamalla

The *Lāṭī-saṃhitā*, a Sanskrit verse treatise on *śrāvakācāra* written by Rājamalla Kavi at Vairāṭ, which was part of the Mogul empire, in *saṃvat* 1641, opens with a panegyric of Akbar and his dynasty. In seven *sargas* it treats the *mūla-guṇas*, *samyaktva*, the *pratimās*, and the *vratas*, the last-named being defined by quotations from the *Tattvārtha-sūtra*. It is important in the Digambara tradition as the first work to use the terms *ailaka* and *kṣullaka*[1] in their modern sense and to treat of the *bhoga-patni* and *dharma-patni*.[2]

Śivakoṭi

The *Ratna-mālā* of Śivakoṭi is a short verse tract on *śrāvakācāra* of little importance and only noticed here because its author has sometimes been confused with the author of the *Bhagavatī Ārādhanā*. Premī[3] suggests that it is modern; it may belong to the seventeenth century.

Somasena

The *Traivarṇikācāra*, an extensive Sanskrit metrical treatise in thirteen *adhyāyas*, composed by Somasena in A.D. 1610, is of particular interest for its picture of a very hinduized Jaina community in the Kannada country in the early seventeenth century. It advocates many practices which in Jugalkiśor Mukhtār's[4] definition are contrary to Jainism. In scope it goes very much beyond the limits of other *śrāvakācāras* and contains a considerable amount of information on the Jaina law of personal status.[5]

[1] *Lāṭī-saṃhitā*, vii. 55.
[2] Ibid. ii. 178–83.
[3] *Siddhānta-sārādi-saṃgraha: nivedan*, pp. 22–23.
[4] See Mukhtār, *Grantha-parīksā*, pp. 98 ff.
[5] Extracts from it were published by Champat Ray Jain in *Jaina Law*, Arrah, 1916.

THE RATNA-TRAYA

THE Jaina religion, the *dharma*, which leads to release from the cycle of transmigration, is made up of right belief (*samyag-dṛṣṭi*, *samyaktva*), right knowledge (*samyag-jñāna*), and right conduct (*samyak-cāritra*), which together constitute the *ratna-traya* or three gems,[1] sometimes also called the *guṇa-traya*.

As *samyag-dṛṣṭi* implies faith in the dogmas of the religion and *samyag-jñāna* accurate knowledge of those dogmas, many writers, especially among the Digambaras, have found it desirable to preface to their *śrāvakācāras* a more or less extensive summary of Jaina doctrine, particularly of the nature of *jīva* and *karman*. Thus, for example, Somadeva,[2] Amitagati,[3] and Vasunandin[4] commence their treatises by a discussion of the seven *tattvas* or *padārthas*, the basic subjects of belief. More thoroughly treated in other works, these may be left out of account here as of no direct relevance to the practical aspects of the *śrāvakācāra*, but a few categories to which reference is frequently made in the exposition of the *vratas* are worth listing:

Thus there are nine 'matrices of the doctrine' (*pravacana-mātṛ*), consisting of three forms of self-control (*gupti*):

(1) curbing of activity of speech (*vāg-gupti*);
(2) curbing of activity of body (*kāya-gupti*);
(3) curbing of activity of mind (*mano-gupti*):

and five rules of conduct (*samiti*):

(1) care in walking (*īryā-samiti*);
(2) care in speaking (*bhāṣā-samiti*);
(3) care in accepting alms (*eṣana-samiti*);
(4) care in taking up and setting down (*ādāna-nikṣepa-samiti*);
(5) care in excreting (*utsarga-samiti*).

Of the many complex and sometimes highly artificial divisions conceived for the category of *jīva*, two are commonly used:

[1] RK i. 3. [2] Handiqui, pp. 246–52. [3] Śr (A) iii.
[4] Śr (V) 1–47.

The six *jīva-nikāyas* (the first five of which are collectively styled *sthāvara-jīvas*) are:

(1) earth bodies (*pṛthvī-kāya*);
(2) water bodies (*ap-kāya*);
(3) fire bodies (*tejaḥ-kāya*);
(4) wind bodies (*vāyu-kāya*);
(5) plant bodies (*vanaspati-kāya*) which may be either *sādhāraṇa* or *pratyeka*;
(6) bodies with the power of movement (*trasa-kāya*).

The nine *jīvas* are:

(1) with one sense organ (*ekendriya pṛthvī-kāya*);
(2) ,, ,, ,, (*ekendriya ap-kāya*);
(3) ,, ,, ,, (*ekendriya tejaḥ-kāya*);
(4) ,, ,, ,, (*ekendriya vāyu-kāya*);
(5) ,, ,, ,, (*ekendriya vanaspati-kāya*);
(6) with two sense organs (*dvīndriya*);
(7) with three sense organs (*trīndriya*);
(8) with four sense organs (*caturindriya*);
(9) with five sense organs (*pañcendriya*).

There are four passions (*kaṣaya*):

(1) anger (*krodha*);
(2) pride (*māna*);
(3) deceit (*māyā*);
(4) greed (*lobha*);

and nine quasi-passions (*akaṣaya, no-kaṣaya*):

(1) laughter (*hāsya*);
(2) liking (*rati*);
(3) disliking (*arati*);
(4) sorrow (*śoka*);
(5) fear (*bhaya*);
(6) disgust (*jugupsā*);
(7) male sex urge (*puṃ-veda*);
(8) female sex urge (*strī-veda*);
(9) androgyne sex urge (*napuṃsaka-veda*).

Most of these recur again in the category of the *pāpa-sthānas* or occasions of sin.

On the road to liberation from *karman* fourteen stages or *guṇa-sthānas* are counted of which the fifth is that of the Jaina layman. This *deśa-virati-guṇa-sthāna* sometimes gives occasion, in works devoted to the *guṇa-sthānas*, for an exposition of the *śravakācāra*.

For the Digambaras *śrāvakācāra* belongs to a division of their substitute canon or *catur-veda* which they term *caraṇānuyoga* covering works on moral conduct and religious duties. Such treatises are therefore mainly concerned with the third *ratna*: *samyag-cāritra*. This varies according to whether it applies to the monastic life (*yaty-ācāra*) or the lay life (*śrāvakācāra*). Amṛtacandra[1] characterizes the former as the complete, and the latter as the partial, abstinence from *hiṃsā*. The lay life represents, in effect, a compromise expressed originally in the imposition of twelve *vratas* defining the householder's *samyag-cāritra*, and for each of these the *Upāsaka-daśāḥ* cited five typical offences.

Samyaktva has in a sense, by the Śvetāmbaras as well as by the Digambaras, been assimilated to the status of a *vrata* and fitted with an apparatus of five infractions or *aticāras* which, absent from the canon, are found enumerated at least as early as the *Tattvārtha-sūtra*;[2] and in fact a discussion of *samyaktva* comes to be an essential element of any work devoted to the lay life.

The word *dharma* is interpreted 'as that which puts the soul in the place of salvation' (*ātmānam mukti-sthāne dhatte*) or 'that which sustains beings in the cycle of transmigration' (*saṃsāra-sthāne prāṇino dharate*).[3] There are two *dharmas* or rules of conduct, one applicable to the monk's and the other to the layman's life. The latter is defined by Cāmuṇḍarāya[4] as the successive attainment of the eleven *pratimās*.

The *Tattvārtha-sūtra*[5] had laid down the monk's *dharma* to consist of ten elements, in the main, abstract virtues:

(1) forbearance (*kṣamā*);
(2) humility (*mārdava*);
(3) uprightness (*ārjava*);
(4) desirelessness (*śauca*);
(5) truthfulness (*satya*);
(6) self-discipline (*saṃyama*);
(7) self-mortification (*tapas*);

[1] PASU 40. [2] T (P) vii. 23. [3] CS, p. 2. [4] RK i. 3.
[5] T (S) ix. 7. See Schubring, *Die Lehre der Jainas*, pp. 192–3.

(8) renunciation (*tyāga*);
(9) poverty (*ākiñcanya*);
(10) celibacy (*brahmacarya*).

The elements of this tenfold ascetic *dharma* are sometimes transferred, not always appropriately, to the lay life;[1] but more generally the layman's *dharma* is said to consist of four elements:[2]

(1) almsgiving (*dāna*);
(2) virtue (*śīla*);
(3) ascetic practices (*tapas*);
(4) spiritual attitude (*bhāva*).

The word *śīla* is often ambiguous: here it would seem to mean the maintenance of all the *vratas*.[3] There is a slight variation in the four elements of *dharma* as defined by Āśādhara:[4]

(1) *dāna*;
(2) *śīla*;
(3) *upavāsa* (this is equivalent to *tapas*, which in practice means 'fasting');
(4) *pūjā*.

[1] e.g. *Padmanandi-śrāvakācāra*, 59.
[2] e.g. ĀU vi. 3.
[3] Śr (A) xii. 41.
[4] SDhA vii. 39.

CATEGORIES OF SRĀVAKAS

VARIOUS etymologies are given for this, the commonest term used to designate a layman. The *śrāvaka* is one who listens (*śṛṇoti*), or one who has recourse to faith (*śraddhālutāṃ śrāti*), or one whose sins flow away from him (*śravanti yasya pāpāni*).[1] With the *nāma*, *sthāpanā*, *dravya*, *bhāva* category we find:[2]

(i) *nāma-śrāvaka*—one who is a Jaina in name only, just as a poor slave may bear the appellation of a god;
(ii) *sthāpanā-śrāvaka*—the statue of a layman;
(iii) *dravya-śrāvaka*—one who carries out the rites obligatory for a Jaina but who is empty of spirituality;
(iv) *bhāva-śrāvaka*—a believing Jaina.

Amongst the Digambaras Cāmuṇḍarāya[3] has taken over the Hindu concept of the four *āśramas*, which, following Jinasena,[4] he terms *brahmacārin*, *gṛhastha*, *vānaprastha*, and *bhikṣu*.

1. The *brahmacārin* may be:[5]

(i) *upanaya-brahmacārin*—the young student who after the *upanayana* ceremony studies the *āgama* before entry into the household life;
(ii) *avalamba-brahmacārin*—one who passes a novitiate as a monk studying the *āgama* in the *kṣullaka* stage but then goes back to the household life;
(iii) *adīkṣā-brahmacārin*—one who studies the *āgama* without taking orders or wearing the monk's garb, but adheres to the household life;
(iv) *gūḍha-brahmacārin*—one who becomes a boy ascetic (*kumāra-śramaṇa*) but later abandons this higher ideal for the household life either of his own volition or owing to pressure from a ruler or from relatives or because of *parīṣahas*;
(v) *naiṣṭhika-brahmacārin*—a man who begs his food, wears a red or white loincloth and the sacred thread on his chest, and has his hair shaven save for a top-knot.

[1] *Śrāddha-vidhi*, p. 33*b*. [2] DhRP 32. [3] CS, p. 20.
[4] MP xxxix. 152. [5] CS, pp. 20–21.

All of these are pledged to continence but all save the last (who is what in later times is called a *kṣullaka*, a layman in the *eleventh pratimā*) may later marry.

2. The *gṛhastha* may belong to the:[1]

(i) *jāti-kṣatriya*—i.e. brahmins, *kṣatriyas*, *vaiśyas*, and *śūdras*;
(ii) *tīrtha-kṣatriya*—who are of various kinds according to the way of their life.

3. The *vānaprastha*[2] is one who has not taken the vow of nudity but wears one piece of cloth and engages in moderate asceticism. (This would perhaps correspond to the *ailaka* layman of later times.)

4. *The bhikṣu* may be:[2]

(i) *anagāra*—an ordinary monk;
(ii) *yati*—a monk who has already begun to ascend the spiritual ladder;
(iii) *muni*—a monk who possesses supernatural knowledge (*avadhi-*, *manaḥ-paryaya-*, and *kevala-jñāna*);
(iv) *ṛṣi*—a monk who has attained to divine powers (*ṛddhi*).

According to Medhāvin (fifteenth century) the *vānaprastha*—here equivalent to a *kṣullaka*—is also styled *apavāda-liṅgin* and the *bhikṣu utsarga-liṅgin*.[3]

These classifications cannot be taken to be representative of any works except those of the school of Jinasena and the definitions of terms like *muni* have no relevance in a normal Jaina context. Even the word *bhikṣu*[4] is commonly used by the Digambaras to describe a layman in the eleventh *pratimā*; but some Śvetāmbaras employ it as a designation for an ordinary Jaina monk[5] whilst for others again it means a Buddhist,[6] as opposed to a Jaina, ascetic.

Some Digambaras, Āśādhara,[7] and Medhāvin, for example,[8] have a threefold division of the *śrāvaka* and on this their expositions of the doctrine are based:

(i) *pākṣika*—a layman who has an inclination (*pakṣa*) towards *ahiṃsā*. He possesses *samyaktva* and practises the *mūla-guṇas* and the *aṇu-vratas* and is assiduous in performing the *pūjā*;

[1] CS, p. 21.
[2] CS, p. 22.
[3] Śr (M) ix. 280.
[4] e.g. by Somadeva.
[5] e.g. Haribhadra Yākinī-putra.
[6] e.g. in the commentary of DhRP 21.
[7] SDhA i. 19–20.
[8] Śr (M) v. 1–8.

(ii) *naiṣṭhika*[1]—one who pursues his path upwards through the *pratimās* till he reaches the eleventh. At this culminating point (*niṣṭhā*) he quits the household life and practises the tenfold *dharma* of the ascetic. It would seem that if he backslides he is down-graded to the state of a *pākṣika*:[2]

(iii) *sādhaka*—one who concludes (*sādhayati*) his human incarnation in a final purification of the self by carrying out *sallekhanā*.

Āśādhara, who repeats Cāmuṇḍarāya's categories of *brahmacārins*[3] and the list of the four *āśramas*, also gives a classification of the *śrāvaka* based on his progress through the *pratimās*:[4]

(i) least satisfactory (*jaghanya*)—first to sixth *pratimās*—*gṛhin*;
(ii) next best (*madhyama*)—seventh to ninth *pratimās*—*varṇin*;
(iii) best (*uttama* or *utkṛṣṭa*)—tenth and eleventh *pratimās*—*bhikṣuka*.

This is based on a similar grouping by Somadeva, who calls the *varṇin* a *brahmacārin*.

[1] Is in fact equivalent to a *naiṣṭhika-brahmacārin* and to what is later called a *kṣullaka*.
[2] SDhA iii. 4.
[3] SDhA vii. 19–20.
[4] SDhA iii. 2–3.

CATEGORIES OF FOOD

THE descriptions of the *poṣadhopavāsa* and of the forms of *pratyākhyāna* are not intelligible without an explanation of the classifications of what may be eaten or drunk. Prohibited foods (*abhakṣyas*) are discussed separately elsewhere.

In the first place there are the fourfold aliments (*caturvidhāhāra*):[1]

1. *aśana*—all that is swallowed: grains and pulses of all kinds, particularly the staple, boiled rice. Forbidden foods falling under this head include meat and the tuberous vegetables, which are condemned as *ananta-kāyas*. Dairy products are also sometimes covered by this designation.

2. *pāna*—all that is drunk: water, milk, the juice of fruits such as grapes and tamarinds, and the water in which rice or barley or other cereals have been boiled, particularly rice-gruel (*kāñjika* or *sauvīra*). Prohibited under this head are alcohol and the liquid from meat.

3. *khādima*—all that is chewed or nibbled: fruits and nuts such as mangoes, dates, almonds and coconuts, dairy products, sugar and molasses, and various cakes and sweetmeats. *Abhakṣyas* coming into this category include honey and the *udumbara* fruits.

4. *svādima*—all that is tasted or serves as a relish: pepper, cumin seeds, myrobalans, ginger, herbs such as basil, and betel. Sugar-cane, molasses, and honey are also sometimes put into this category. More surprisingly toothpicks (*dantavana*) are covered by this designation.

There is another classification of food—or rather of certain articles of food—into ten *vikṛtis*:[2]

(1) *kṣīra*—milk, which may be of five kinds according to whether it comes from the cow, buffalo, goat, sheep, or camel;

(2) *dadhi*—curds
(3) *navanīta*—butter
(4) *ghṛta*—ghee
} these may be from cow's, buffalo's, goat's or sheep's milk, but not from camel's milk;

[1] Śr (A) vi. 96, 97; PS 207, 211.

[2] YŚ iii. 130 (pp. 707–8); PS 217–21.

(5) *taila*—oil, which may be of four kinds: sesamum, flax (*atasī*), mustard, and saffron (*kusumbha*). Other oils are not for consumption as food but are used for preparing plaster or for sticking;

(6) *guḍa*—molasses;

(7) *madya*—alcohol, which may be of two kinds: from sugar-cane juice or from the fermentation of grain;

(8) *madhu*—honey, which may be of three kinds; made by bees (*bhrāmara*), by flies (*makṣikā*), or by *kuttiya*;[1]

(9) *māṃsa*—meat, which again is said to be of three kinds: of birds, beasts or fishes; sometimes, however, this threefold division is explained as skin, meat, and blood.

(10) *avagāhima*—the term is difficult to translate: it is the product which results from cooking rice in a pan filled with ghee or oil; after the third cooking in the oil there is no further production of *avagāhima* and the rice cooked will be *nirvikṛtika*.

Food is also distinguished by four flavours or *rasas*:[2]

(1) *go-rasa*—milk flavour comprising ghee, butter, and curds;
(2) *ikṣu-rasa*—sugar flavour including molasses and honey;
(3) *phala-rasa*—fruit flavour covering fruits such as mangoes;
(4) *dhānya-rasa*—cereal flavour comprising oil and rice-gruel.

The essential idea of a *vikṛti* seems to be that of a foodstuff that has changed its nature owing to a process of cooking or to bacteriological action. In the conventional interpretation of the commentators it is 'that by which tongue and mind are perverted.'[2]

The expression *ācāmāmla* deserves a special mention. This is a sanskritization of the Prakrit which is also rendered as *āyāmāmla* and *ācāmla*. It consists of grain or pulses cooked only in water with a sour flavouring (*āmla-rasa*).

[1] No satisfactory explanation of this word (the enumeration goes back to the *Sthānāṅga-sūtra*) seems to have been given.

[2] SDhA v. 35.

SAMYAKTVA AND MITHYĀTVA

Samyaktva or *samyagdṛṣṭi*, in the translation generally used: 'right belief', is defined by Pūjyapāda and Cāmuṇḍarāya as 'faith in the path to final liberation indicated by the Jina'.[1] Other Digambaras such as Samantabhadra, Somadeva, and Vasunandin describe it with greater precision as faith in the three articles of belief:[2] *āpta* (the Jina), *āgama* (the scriptures), and *padārtha* or *tattva* (the dogmas). Others again prefer to visualize it from the negative angle as the absence of twenty-five blemishes (*dṛg-doṣas*) generally held to be the eight *madas*, the three *mūḍhatās*, the six *anāyatanas*, and the eight *doṣas*. These blemishes are carried to a higher total in some works such as the *Ratnasāra*, which adds to the above list the seven *bhayas* or types of fear, the five *aticāras*, and the seven vices or *vyasanas*. For the Śvetāmbaras from the *Pañcāśakas*[3] onwards *samyaktva* means faith in the truths enunciated by the Tīrthaṅkara. Hemacandra[4] calls it 'faith in the right *deva*, the right guru, and the right *dharma*'.

The subject of *samyaktva* is too vast and too imprecise to lend itself readily to numerical categorization and there is considerable confusion and overlapping in the lists of qualities and defects conceived to describe it. Here are some of the categories used by different *ācāryas*, Digambara and Śvetāmbara:

Liṅga	*Guṇa*	*Bhūṣaṇa*	*Aṅga*	*Doṣa*	*Aticāra*
saṃvega	saṃvega	sthairya	niḥśaṅka	śaṅka	śaṅka
śama	upaśama	kauśala	niḥkāṅkṣā	kāṅkṣā	kāṅkṣā
nirveda	nirveda	tīrtha-sevā	nirvicikitsā	vicikitsā	vicikitsā
āstikya	bhakti	bhakti	amūḍha-dṛṣṭi	mūḍha-dṛṣṭi	para-pāṣaṇḍi-praśaṃsā
anukampā	anukampā	prabhāvanā	prabhāvanā	aprabhāvanā	para-pāṣaṇḍi-saṃstava
	nindā		upagūhana	anupagūhana	
	garhā		sthiti-karaṇa	asthiti-karaṇa	
	vātsalya		vātsalya	avātsalya	

Of these categories, *liṅga* and *bhūṣaṇa* belong to Hemacandra, the former being known also to Āśādhara and the latter to Devagupta though not under those names: *aṅga*, *doṣa*, and *guṇa* seem to be

[1] CS, p. 2. [2] Śr (V) 4. [3] P (Śr Dh) 3. [4] YŚ ii. 2.

purely Digambara concepts, the first named being common to almost all the writers in the field; whilst the *aticāras* ranged symmetrically alongside those of the *vratas* are given in nearly all the texts Digambara and Śvetāmbara. The *doṣas* are of course merely the negations of the *aṅgas*. It will be convenient to treat first the category *guṇa*.

(i) Spiritual craving (*saṃvega*). Pūjyapāda[1] has defined this as the ever-present fear of the cycle of transmigration. Hemacandra[2] characterizes it more positively as the desire for *mokṣa* arising from the realization that the pleasures of gods and men are, in the last resort, unsatisfying. Amitagati[3] calls it unwavering attachment to *deva*, *guru*, and *dharma*. For Āśādhara[4] it is fear of the unstable *saṃsāra* which brings sickness and sorrow and sudden calamity.

(ii) Tranquillity (*śama*, *upaśama*). This is taken to imply the stilling of the *kaṣāyas*.[5]

(iii) Disgust (*nirveda*). This is the loathing induced in a man of right faith by contact with the world and its miseries: he will have known the world and found it evil. But, continues Hemacandra,[6] others hold *saṃvega* to mean disgust with mundane existence and *nirveda* desire for final release. Amitagati[7] understands by *nirveda* the distaste for sensual pleasures.

(iv) Devotion (*bhakti*). By Hemacandra this is placed among the five *bhūṣaṇas* of *samyaktva* and is best considered there. Amitagati[8] understands by it 'devotion to Jina and guru'.

(v) Compassion (*anukampā*). This Hemacandra[9] defines as the desire to eliminate suffering: in this compassion for those in misery no partiality may be shown, for even a tiger will manifest affection for its own offspring. In its material aspect this virtue takes the form of practical steps to remedy suffering where one has the power and in its non-material aspect it expresses itself in tenderness of heart. It is, as Āśādhara[10] stresses, the root of the whole sacred doctrine.

(vi) Remorse (*nindā*). This is the remorse felt by a pious man when for the sake of wife or son or brother or friend he has committed some act inspired by passion or hate.[11]

(vii) Repentance (*garhā*). This is the repentance expressed in

[1] T (P) vii. 12.
[2] YŚ ii. 15 (p. 181).
[3] Śr (A) ii. 74.
[4] SDhA i. 4.
[5] YŚ ii. 15 (p. 180).
[6] Ibid. (p. 182).
[7] Śr (A) ii. 75.
[8] Ibid. 79.
[9] YŚ ii. 15 (p. 182).
[10] SDhA i. 4.
[11] Śr (A) ii. 76.

the form of *ālocanā* made in the presence of a guru for faults committed under the influence of passion and hate.[1] The interpretation of this as of the preceding *guṇa* depends on Amitagati as the other *ācāryas* do not explain these terms.

(viii) Loving kindness (*vātsalya*) This belongs also to the category of the *aṅgas*.

The above eight *guṇas* are listed by Cāmuṇḍarāya, Amitagati, and Vasunandin.

Hemacandra lists five *liṅgas*[2] of *samyaktva*, four of which find a place also in the Digambara category of *guṇas*. The remaining element *āstikya* is explained as the acceptance of the Jaina doctrine as the veritable creed even in the presence of other opinions.

The *aṅgas* of *samyaktva* are noted by Pūjyapāda, Samantabhadra, Cāmuṇḍarāya, Somadeva, and Amṛtacandra:

(i) Freedom from fear (*niḥśaṅka*). This meaning is preferred by Samantabhadra,[3] who sees in it a determination 'rigid as the temper of steel' to follow the path of righteousness, and by Camuṇḍarāya, who lists the seven types of fear (*bhaya*):[4]

- (i) fear of this world (*iha-loka*);
- (ii) fear of the next world (*para-loka*);
- (iii) fear of sickness (*vyādhi*);
- (iv) fear of death (*maraṇa*);
- (v) fear of being without protection (*agupti*);
- (vi) fear of being without defence (*atrāṇa*);
- (vii) fear of something unexpected (*akasmika*).

Amṛtacandra,[5] however, prefers to interpret *niḥśaṅka* as freedom from doubt about the truths proclaimed by the Jina. Somadeva[6] offers both explanations: doubt, in his view, would mean an inability to choose between one doctrine and another, one vow and another, and one divinity and another.

(ii) Desirelessness (*niḥkāṅkṣā*). For Samantabhadra[7] this means the absence of desire for pleasure which is finite, sinful, and attended by sorrows. Camuṇḍarāya and Amṛtacandra[8] interpret it either as lack of craving for the enjoyment of sensual pleasures in this or in a subsequent life, or else as absence of interest in false creeds. Somadeva[9] elaborates the same explanations remarking that

[1] Śr (A) ii. 77. [2] YŚ ii. 15. [3] RK i. 11.
[4] CS, p. 2. [5] PASU 23. [6] Handiqui, p. 259.
[7] RK i. 12. [8] PASU 14. [9] Handiqui, p. 259.

to exchange *samyaktva* for the joys of the world is like bartering a ruby for buttermilk.

(iii) Overcoming of repugnance (*nirvicikitsā*, *nirjugupsā*). Samantabhadra[1] holds this to imply the love of virtue without disgust for the body which is impure by nature but sanctified by the *ratna-traya*. For Amṛtacandra[2] it means the victory over a person's natural repugnance for whatever is physically nauseating like excrement, or productive of discomfort like heat and cold, hunger and thirst. Cāmuṇḍarāya[3] explains this *aṅga* as the removal of the false concept that the body is pure by comprehending the nature of its impurity; or else as the absence of the regrettable idea that such and such a doctrine of the Jaina religion is inappropriate and horrifying whilst another doctrine is in every way admirable. For Somadeva[4] *nirvicikitsā* means that there must be no hesitation in the practice of *vaiyāvṛttya*.

(iv) Unswerving orthodoxy (*amūḍha-dṛṣṭi*). This is the refusal to approve in thought, word, or deed the path of wrong belief,[5] in other words the rejection of *mithyātva*.

(v) Good works (*prabhāvanā*). This is also a *bhūṣaṇa* and will be dealt with as such.

(vi) Edification (*upagūhana*, *upabṛmhana*). Samantabhadra[6] defines as the removal of any reproach levelled at the Jaina by ignorant people unable to follow the vows. Cāmuṇḍarāya and Amṛtacandra[7] understand by it the development of one's religious faith by cultivating forbearance (*kṣamā*) and the other nine elements of *dharma*. At the same time faults committed by co-religionists should, as far as lies within one's power, be concealed, 'as a mother conceals the failings of her children',[8] But the Jaina religion will not be sullied by one unworthy adherent any more than a pool of water will be fouled by one dead frog.[9]

(vii) Strengthening in the faith (*sthiti-karaṇa*). Samantabhadra[10] defines this as the reaffirmation in the faith, by intelligent men full of *vātsalya*, of those who are lapsing from right views and right conduct, whether their wavering is due to a faulty acquaintance with the creed or to external causes. This *aṅga* is virtually equivalent to the *sthairya-bhūṣaṇa* of Hemacandra.

[1] RK i. 13.
[2] PASU 15.
[3] CS, p. 3.
[4] Handiqui, p. 259.
[5] RK i. 14.
[6] RK i. 15.
[7] PASU 27.
[8] Handiqui, p. 260.
[9] Ibid., p. 261.
[10] RK i. 16.

(viii) Loving kindness (*vātsalya*). This Samantabhadra[1] defines as unfeigned and wholehearted assistance to members of one's community. Cāmuṇḍarāya[2] calls it 'unfeigned affection for the fourfold Jaina community, like that of a cow for its calf, as a result of attachment to the sacred doctrine'. Somadeva[3] connects with this *aṅga* the qualities of *vaiyāvṛttya*, *vinaya*, and *bhakti*. *Vinaya* comprises veneration for all who are deserving of respect, and *bhakti* devotion to the Jina, the gurus, and the scriptures. As the concept denoted by *vaiyāvrttya*, or sometimes by *vātsalya*, is so important in the Jaina community it deserves separate consideration.

Hemacandra has listed five *bhūṣaṇas*[4] of *samyaktva*:

(i) Firmness (*sthairya*). This means strengthening the faith of anyone who is wavering in the Jaina creed or maintaining one's own faith firmly despite the success of adherents of other religions.

(ii) Conversancy with the Jaina doctrine (*Jina-śāsane kauśala*). This *bhūṣaṇa* is self-explanatory.

(iii) Frequentation of the *tīrthas* (*tīrtha-sevā*). The term *tīrtha* is to be explained either in a material sense as the places of birth, consecration, enlightenment, and *nirvāṇa* of the Jinas or in a transferred sense as the fourfold Jaina community.

(iv) Devotion (*bhakti*). This according to Hemacandra can take two forms: *vinaya* and *vaiyāvṛttya*. The former is expressed in an eightfold *upacāra* like that accorded to an *atithi* in the ritual of *dāna*.

(v) Good works (*prabhāvanā*). This term covers anything done to spread the Jaina faith and increase the consideration in which it is held. For Somadeva[5] this may take the form of the practice of almsgiving, celebration of festivals, setting up of images, or building of temples. The glory of the Jina's teaching, says Samantabhadra,[6] is to be illuminated by removing the darkness of ignorance. *Prabhāvanā* for Amṛtacandra[7] would be expressed in almsgiving, feats of asceticism, *pūjā*, and study. Hemacandra[8] distinguishes several types of persons (*prabhāvakas*) who are responsible for this *bhūṣaṇa*: experts in the Jaina canon, reciters of religious stories, debaters, astrologers, those who practise religious

[1] RK i. 17. [2] CS, p. 3. [3] Handiqui, p. 262.
[4] YŚ ii. 16. [5] Handiqui, p. 261. [6] RK i. 18.
[7] PASU 30. [8] YŚ ii. 16 (p. 185).

asceticism, those who are learned in the sciences, and those who are conversant with magic spells.

The *aticāras* of *samyaktva* may virtually, if the fourth and fifth of them which are closely related are merged together, be equated with the first four *doṣas*. Both *aticāraṣ* and *doṣas* represent the negation of the *aṅgas*. Pūjyapāda[1] holds that it is in any event unnecessary to have eight *aticāras* corresponding to the eight *aṅgas* as the fourth and fifth—*para-pāṣaṇḍi-praśaṃsā* and *para-pāṣaṇḍi-saṃstava*—are elastic and comprehensive. Here, first, then, are the *aticāras*:

(i) Doubt (*śaṅka*). Siddhasena Gaṇin and Haribhadra[2] consider this to be doubt in respect of the *padārthas* of the Jaina creed; this may be either partial when, for example, one *padārtha* is called in question, or total when the whole structure of Jaina belief is challenged. Total doubt (*sarva-viṣaya-śaṅka*) is virtually the same as *mithyātva*. This interpretation of *śaṅka* as 'doubt' is given by all writers, Śvetāmbara and Digambara.

(ii) Desire (*kāṅkṣā*). This again, like the preceding *aticāra*, will tarnish *samyaktva* but not eradicate it. It is generally held to imply a hankering for other doctrines than Jainism, for one particular one if it is partial and for all in general if it is total.[3] Such a desire may be provoked by hearing that the Buddhists, for example, put no restriction on eating and drinking or bathing or easy living. It is wrong—in fact it amounts to a *nidāna*—to cherish such purely material desires as to be handsome, or to have many sons, or to be reborn as a king, seeing in them a recompense for adherence to the right faith.

(iii) Repulsion (*vicikitsā*). Two interpretations of this are given by the Śvetāmbaras[4] from Siddhasena Gaṇin onwards: either it means hesitation or doubt about the value of the results of various human activities (not about the tenets of Jainism as in the case of the first *aticāra*); or else it means repugnance for the bodies of Jaina ascetics because these are evil-smelling owing to the accumulation of filth and sweat on their unwashed limbs. What hinders them from bathing in water that has been rendered sterile, people ask, oblivious of the fact that a monk must insist on the impurity of the body.

[1] T (P) vii. 23.
[2] YŚ ii. 17 (p. 187).
[3] Ibid. (pp. 187–8).
[4] Ibid. (p. 189).

(iv) Admiration of adherents of other creeds (*para-pāṣaṇḍi-praśaṃsā*).

(v) Praise of adherents of other creeds (*para-pāṣaṇḍi-saṃstava*).

The distinction between the fourth and fifth *aticāras* seems artificial. As has been noted they both have for antonym the *aṅga* of *amūḍha-dṛṣṭi* and in fact Somadeva[1] couples them together under the designation of *anya-ślāghā* or *mūḍhatā*. With that exception the Digambaras (for example, Cāmuṇḍarāya)[2] define *praśaṃsā* as 'praise expressed in the mind' and *saṃstava* as 'praise expressed in words'. The Śvetāmbaras[3] interpret *praśaṃsā* as 'praise' and *saṃstava* as 'acquaintance'. Siddhasena Gaṇin,[4] however, prefers the Digambara explanation.

For many writers these two *aticāras* give an occasion to describe and criticize the false beliefs of other sects—180 varieties of *kriya-vādins*, 84 of *akriya-vādins*, 67 of *ajñānikas*, and 32 of *vainayikas* are listed—particularly the Buddhists and Śaivas.[5]

As was mentioned at the beginning the *aticāras* and *doṣas* are not the only blemishes of *samyaktva*. The six *anāyatanas* or non-abodes (sc. of right belief[6]) appear to be a purely Digambara category:

(i) false divinities (*ku-deva*);
(ii) false ascetics (*ku-liṅgin*);
(iii) false scriptures (*ku-śāstras*);
(iv) worship of false divinities (*ku-deva-sevā*);
(v) worship of false ascetics (*ku-liṅgi-sevā*);
(vi) worship of false scriptures (*ku-śāstra-sevā*).

Together these *anāyatanas* amount to *mithyātva*—the direct opposite of *samyaktva*—which is defined by Hemacandra[7] as belief in false divinities, false gurus, and false scriptures.

For the Śvetāmbaras *mithyātva* may be of five types:[8]

(i) *ābhigrahika*—the attitude of those whose horizon is limited to their own scriptures which they are able to defend in discussion;

(ii) *anābhigrahika*—the attitude of simple people who imagine that equal respect is to be shown to all gods, teachers, and creeds;

[1] Handiqui, p. 258.
[2] CS, p. 4.
[3] YŚ ii. 17 (p. 189).
[4] T (S) vii. 19 (p. 102).
[5] Ibid. (pp. 100–2).
[6] Handiqui, p. 257.
[7] YŚ ii. 3.
[8] NPP 4.

(iii) *ābhiniveśika*—the attitude of those who, like Jamāli, possess the faculty of discernment but deformed by some evil preconception (*abhiniveśa*);
(iv) *sāṃśayika*—a state of uncertainty or hesitation between various viewpoints;
(v) *anābhogika*—the innate state of false belief typical of living organisms which have not attained to a higher stage of development.

The Digambaras prefer a division into three types:[1]

(i) *agṛhīta*—an inherent, non-acquired quality found even in the lowest stages of living organisms;
(ii) *gṛhīta*—an attitude acquired, for example, by birth in a family which professes a false creed;
(iii) *sāṃśayika*—an attitude of indecision as in the previous list.

Or else a sevenfold category:[2]

(i) *ekāntika*—the absolute attitude as, for example, the belief that the *jīva* perishes;
(ii) *sāṃśayika*—the attitude of uncertainty about the right faith as in the previous lists;
(iii) *vainayika*—the view that all gods, gurus, and scriptures are alike;
(iv) *gṛhīta*—the attitude of acquired habit like the leather-worker's dog which gnaws hides;
(v) *viparīta*—the view that what is true is false and vice versa;
(vi) *naisargika*—the inherent false belief of creatures devoid of consciousness which, like a blind man, cannot discern fair from foul. This is equivalent to the *agṛhita* of the previous list, or the *anābhogika* of the first list;
(vii) *mūḍha-dṛṣṭi*—the false belief where the divinity, the guru, and the *dharma* are sullied by passion and violence.

This *mūḍha-dṛṣṭi* which is more properly one of the *doṣas* of *samyaktva* is presented in a more detailed form in the category of the three *mūḍhatās* or foolish ideas relating to the divinity, to the teacher and to worldly life. These seem to be listed only by the Digambaras but Hemacandra and other Śvetāmbaras find the same opportunity for criticizing the superstitions of other religions

[1] SDhA i. 5. [2] Śr (A) ii. 1–13.

when they discuss the nature of the *ku-deva*, *ku-guru*, and *ku-śāstra*.

(i) *Devatā-mūḍhatā*. It is a misconception of the nature of the divinity, says Samantabhadra,[1] to worship *devas* stained with passion and hate in order to obtain a boon. Hemacandra[2] characterizes the *ku-devas* or *a-devas* as addicted to women (symbolizing *rāga*), weapons (symbolizing *dveṣa*), and rosaries (symbolizing *moha*), and accustomed to inflict punishments or grant boons. All these attributes are inappropriate to the Jina who is devoid of passion, hate, and delusion. The deities that take pleasure in dancing, music, and theatrical performances cannot offer their votaries any lasting good.[3] In this connexion Hemacandra delivers a long attack on Hindu religion condemning particularly the worship of the sacred cow.

(ii) *Pāṣaṇḍi-mūḍhatā*. Samantabhadra[4] defines this as the praise of false ascetics who are engaged in worldly occupations, who have not divested themselves of possessions, and who are guilty of *hiṃsā*. By false gurus Hemacandra[5] understands those who lust after women, gold, lands, and houses, who do not refrain from the consumption of meat, honey, alcohol, and *ananta-kāyas*, who do not keep vows of chastity but are attached to wives and children, and who preach false doctrines.

(iii) *Loka-mūḍhatā*. As such worldly foolishness Samantabhadra[6] instances the bathing in rivers or in the ocean, the making of heaps of stones or sand, the throwing oneself from a precipice, and the entering into fire. Equally senseless are such customs as the use of the *pañca-gavya* and the adoration of trees, stones, gems, and other material objects.[7]

Among the twenty-five *dṛg-doṣas* mentioned earlier occur the eight *madas*[8] or forms of vainglory:

(i) pride in one's knowledge (*jñāna*);
(ii) pride in one's worship (*pūjā*);
(iii) pride of family (*kula*);[9]
(vi) pride of caste (*jāti*);[9]
(v) pride in one's strength (*bala*);

[1] RK i. 23. [2] YŚ ii. 6. [3] YŚ ii. 7.
[4] RK i. 24. [5] YŚ ii. 9. [6] RK i. 12.
[7] YŚ iv. 102. [8] RK i. 25.
[9] Perhaps better translated following Jinasena (MP xxxix. 85) 'paternal ancestry' and 'maternal ancestry'.

(vi) pride in one's wealth (*ṛddhi*);
(vii) pride in one's ascetic practices (*tapas*);
(viii) pride in one's beauty (*vapus*).

Various classifications of *samyaktva* are given particularly by the Digambara *ācāryas*, the most widespread being the threefold division into *kṣayika*, *aupaśamika*, and *kṣayaupaśamika* varieties which depend on the extent to which karmic matter has been removed from the *jīva*.[1]

Closely associated with *samyaktva* is the category of the three *śalyas* which the Digambara writers[2] generally define before discussing the *vratas*. These are the harmful stimuli or 'stings' which distract the person who has attained to right belief:

(i) deceit (*māyā*);
(ii) hankering for worldly pleasures and fame (*nidāna*);
(iii) false belief (*mithyātva*).

And, unless he rids himself of these *śalyas*, he cannot properly observe the *vratas*. The Śvetāmbaras do not seem to employ the term *śalya* in this sense but Abhayadeva, in his commentary on the *Upāsaka-daśāḥ*,[3] quotes a verse in which the *śalyas* seem to be equated with the *aticāras* of *samyaktva*.

THE MŪLA-GUṆAS

PROBABLY no term of Jainism is used to cover so many different categories as the word *guṇa*. The *mūla-guṇas* for the Śvetāmbaras[4] mean generally the five *aṇu-vratas* (though sometimes a single *mūla-guṇa—ahiṃsā* is mentioned) whilst the *guṇa-vratas* and *śikṣā-vratas* together make up the *uttara-guṇas*. The Digambaras, however, apply the name *mūla-guṇa*[5] to a category of interdictions which must be respected if even the first stage on the ladder of the *pratimās* is to be attained. Similar concepts are not foreign to Śvetāmbara Jainism but they are not displayed with the same prominence nor is the designation *mūla-guṇa* ever applied to them.

[1] Handiqui, p. 255.
[2] T (P) vii. 18.
[3] UD i. 70 (p. 26): *saṅk-āi-salla*.
[4] YŚ iii. 130 (p. 696).
[5] Āśādhara opposes the *mūla-guṇas* as a category to the *agra-guṇas* by which he understands the twelve *vratas* (SDhA iii. 7–8). A similar term reappears in Medhāvin, who speaks of the *agra-pada* (Śr (M) v. 4).

The following table will show the variations that occur among Digambara writers in determining these *mūla-guṇas*:

	AMṚTACANDRA	SAMANTABHADRA	JINASENA	ĀŚĀDHARA
	Amitagati,[1] *Āśādhara Śrāvaka-dharma-doha, Devasena, Medhāvin, Sakalakīrti, Rājamalla, Somasena*	*Śivakoṭi*	*Cāmuṇḍarāya Somadeva Āśādhara*	
(1)				āpta-nuti
(2)				dayā
(3)	udumbara-pañcaka-virati (1–5)	aṇu-vrata-pañcaka (1–5)	aṇu-vrata-pañcaka (1–5)	jala-galana
(4)				a-rātri-bhojana
(5)				udumbara-pañcaka-virati
(6)	māṃsa-virati	māṃsa-virati	māṃsa-virati	māṃsa-virati
(7)	madya-virati	madya-virati	madya-virati	madya-virati
(8)	madhu-virati	madhu-virati	dyuta-virati	madhu-virati

In the sense given to the term by the Digambaras there is no canonical authority for the *mūla-guṇas* and for this reason it is all the more important to determine which enumeration of them is likely to have been the original one. The *Ratna-karaṇḍa*[2] is the oldest text under review to mention this category. But as has been noticed elsewhere Samantabhadra is responsible for many innovations in the *śrāvakācāra*, and the same observation can be made with equal appropriateness about Jinasena. Yet it seems difficult to believe that, had Samantabhadra's version been the original one, the *aṇu-vratas* as *mūla-guṇas* would have been replaced by the *udumbaras* in other lists, least of all by a writer like Amṛtacandra whose work is the direct antithesis of the popular *śrāvakācāras*. And if the *aṇu-vrata-pañcaka* wears a new look in comparison with the *udumbara-pañcaka-virati* Jinasena's version in which *dyūta* is linked with *māṃsa* and *madya* has even more unmistakably the air of having been refurbished. In this context it is perhaps not irrelevant to note that Āśādhara,[3] who offers

[1] Amitagati, who does not employ the actual term *mūla-guṇas*, adds a ninth element: *a-rātri-bhojana* (Śr (A) v. 1).

[2] RK iii. 20.

[3] SDhA ii. 2–3.

three variant enumerations of the *mūla-guṇas* clearly prefers that of Amṛtacandra.

If this last list is examined more closely the impression of its authenticity is confirmed. The apparently disparate elements—the five *udumbara* fruits and three forbidden *vikṛtis*: meat, alcohol, and honey—from which abstention is enjoined have one aspect in common: they are all used as offerings to the spirits of the ancestors. Now of all Hindu customs that which has met with the keenest reprobation from Jainism has been the custom of *śrāddha* and the offering of sacrifices to the *pitṛs*.[1] That *śrāddha* in an innocuous form has been accepted by Jains in modern times in no way invalidates this contention; even a work as late as Vāmadeva's *Bhāva-saṃgraha* can declare that those who propitiate the *pitṛs* with meat consume their own *gotra*.[2]

The cult of the ancestors is linked, as Meyer[3] has shown, with the worship of fertility spirits including the Great Mother, and since the bee is believed to incarnate the *pitṛs* honey is used as an offering to them. Przyluski[4] has noted the epithet *Aditi madhu-kaśa* 'she whose whip is of honey' because honey is held to be, among all foodstuffs, that which gives the most vigour. For Amitagati, in the *Subhāṣita-ratna-saṃdoha*,[5] the common characteristic of meat, alcohol, and honey is their aphrodisiac quality. The *udumbaras*, perhaps because they live long and have nutritive fruits, perhaps because of their milky latex, have been identified with the source of all fertility, and possibly owing to the ceaseless rustling of their leaves have been regarded as homes of the spirits of the dead.[6]

In Jaina number magic there is often an interplay between the groups of five and the groups of four (and its multiples); thus the five *aṇu-vratas* are made up to a total of twelve by the addition of the *guṇa-vratas* and *śikṣā-vratas*. It may be that originally the Digambaras had inherited a tradition—a tradition, perhaps, in which the designations alone had survived—of twelve *uttara-guṇas* (which were the *vratas*) and five (later transformed into eight) *mūla-guṇas*. For a religion, at that date essentially missionary, the

[1] Note, for example, YŚ ii. 47 for the whole argument of the *Dharma-rasāyana*.
[2] BhS (V) 443.
[3] Meyer, *Trilogie altindischer Mächte und Feste der vegetation*, Pt. iii, pp. 77 ff.
[4] Przyluski, *La Grande déesse*, p. 30.
[5] *Subhāṣita-ratna-saṃdoha*, xxi. 13; xxii. 18; xx. 24.
[6] Przyluski, op. cit., p. 80.

first step before a layman could assume the *vratas* would be for him unambiguously to reject the cult of the ancestors by a religious interdiction of the offerings most commonly associated with that cult.

The *udumbaras* are the fruits of five trees of the genus *Ficus*:

(i) umbara, udumbara—*Ficus glomerata* Roxb.;
(ii) vaṭa, nyagrodha—*Ficus bengalensis*;
(iii) pippala, aśvattha—*Ficus religiosa* Linn.;
(iv) plakṣa—*Ficus infectoria* Roxb.;
(v) kakombari, guphala—*Ficus oppositifolia* Willd.

In the older texts the *udumbaras* are not *ananta-kāyas* though the sixteenth-century Digambara Rājamalla[1] says explicitly that the word *udumbara* is the symbolic representation (*upalakṣaṇa*) for the *sādhāraṇa* plants. The reason for not eating them is that they are full of innumerable tiny insects and of invisible living organisms, the epithet *kṛmi-kulākula* which is often applied to meat being used of them.[2] A pious man, Hemacandra[3] says, should avoid them even if he is hungry and unable to obtain any other food. Sometimes the *trasa-jīvas* are said to be present only in the moist fruits but even the eating of the dried fruits is sinful because of the *rāga* involved.[4]

In the *Śrāvaka-dharma-pañcāśaka* the *udumbaras* are coupled with the *atyaṅgas* and the *ananta-kāyas* in the interdictions covered by the *bhogopabhoga-vrata*; if the *atyaṅgas* mean the *ma-kāras* there is here a virtual equivalence with the *mūla-guṇas* but there seems to be no absolute ban on eating the *udumbaras* until the layman reaches the stage of the *sacitta-tyāga-pratimā*.[5] Similarly Siddhasena,[6] discussing the *aticāras* of the *bhogopabhoga-vrata*, cites as examples of *sacitta-sambaddhāhāra* the consuming of jujubes or *udumbara* fruits because large numbers of seeds are swallowed. By the time of Devagupta[7] the attitude towards the *udumbaras* has become clearer: the second *guṇa-vrata* is defined as limiting the use of clothes, unguents, and other items of personal expenditure and as banning the three *ma-kāras* (*māṃsa*, *madhu*, *madya*) and the five *udumbaras*; and in Hemacandra this eightfold ban is given an

[1] *Lāṭī-saṃhitā*, ii. 79.

[2] This phrase, one of the commonest of all Jaina clichés, is also found in Bhartṛhari's *Nīti-śataka*.

[3] YŚ iii. 42–43.

[4] PASU 73.

[5] P (ŚrUP) 24.

[6] T (S) vii. 30.

[7] NPP 75.

importance almost equivalent to that of the *mūla-guṇas* in Digambara texts.[1]

The eating of meat and drinking of alcohol are also catalogued among the seven *vyasanas* and a confusion, deliberate or involuntary, of *vyasanas* and *mūla-guṇas* is doubtless responsible for Jinasena's[2] mention of gambling (*dyūta*) and for the enumeration found in a late writer, Vāmadeva,[3] who obtains a figure of eight *mūla-guṇas* by reckoning together abstention from the *udumbara* pentad, the *ma-kāra* triad, *rātri-bhojana*, whoring, adultery, theft, and gambling with *jīva-dayā* (compassion for living beings).

Meat, alcohol, honey, and butter (which too is an *abhakṣya* though not coming under the interdictions imposed by the *mūla-guṇas*) are *vikṛtis*—the four harmful *vikṛtis*. The eating of meat is, above all, a sin against compassion and the guilt belongs not only to the actual slaughterer but to anybody who buys or sells, cooks or carves, or gives or eats meat as in fact the Hindu *dharma-śāstras* confirm. To eat meat is to acknowledge vultures, wolves, and tigers as one's gurus. Some people, continues Hemacandra (alluding to the *śrāddha*),[4] not only eat meat themselves but offer it to the *devas* and *pitṛs*.

The Digambaras tend to emphasize the sharp distinction between eating meat which contains *trasa-jīvas* and fruits or corn in which there are present only *sthāvara-jīvas*.[5] Even where a bull or buffalo has not been slaughtered but has died a natural death the consumption of its flesh involves the destruction of the minute living organisms (*nigodas*) that have found refuge there and these continue to come into existence in meat either raw or cooked or in process of cooking so that very great *hiṃsā* is caused even by touching a piece of it. The eating of meat, says Āśādhara,[6] increases the lusts of the flesh and keeps a man wandering in the *saṃsāra*.

While some writers tend to stress the pernicious effects of alcohol in befuddling the mind of the drinker others are more concerned with the inevitable *hiṃsā* involved in the process of fermentation. Thus Somadeva[7] and Āśādhara[8] refer to the immense number of *jīvas* transformed into a drop of alcohol and the former adds that sometimes in the cycle of transmigration beings are metamorphosed into wine to bemuse the minds of men.

[1] YŚ iii. 8–43.
[2] MP xxxix. 8.
[3] BhS (V) 448.
[4] YŚ iii. 29–31.
[5] PASU 65–68.
[6] SDhA ii. 8.
[7] Handiqui, p. 262.
[8] SDhA ii. 4.

Honey is condemned by Somadeva[1] because 'it is pressed out of the young eggs in the womb of bees and resembles the embryo in the first stage of its growth'. To provide but a single drop, says Amṛtacandra,[2] bees have to be killed and even if they have been driven by some artifice from the comb or if the honey has dripped down of itself *hiṃsā* will still occur since other living creatures find their way into it. This same honey is unclean because it is derived from the vomit or spittle of insects and even though it may possess medicinal properties it will still lead to hell. Hemacandra[3] mentions especially the use of honey in the Śaivite *deva-snāna*, and the false idea that it is holy. No doubt because of the traditional method of honey-gathering which involves the destruction of the hive by smoking out the bees it has become a proverbial saying that he who eats honey takes on himself the sin of burning seven villages.[4]

THE VRATAS

FIVE *aṇu-vratas*, three *guṇa-vratas*, and four *śikṣā-vratas*, making a total of twelve, are listed in the *Upāsaka-daśāḥ*, together with the supplementary, and by its nature non-obligatory, *sallekhanā-vrata*. Except for one text of minor importance the mediaeval *ācāryas* show no hesitations in the enumeration of the *aṇu-vratas*, but the *guṇa-vratas* and *śikṣā-vratas* to which the Digambaras give the collective designation of *śīlas*, vary considerably in their sequence, certain elements, generally the *deśāvakāśika-vrata* which is by its nature susceptible of being confounded with the *dig-vrata*, being at times eliminated to allow of the inclusion of *sallekhanā* among the *śikṣā-vratas*. The *aṇu-vratas* are of course closely parallel to the *mahā-vratas* of an ascetic; and it is therefore not surprising that some writers have imitated the *Daśa-vaikālika-sūtra* which counts a sixth *mahā-vrata*—that of *a-rātri-bhojana*—in the *aṇu-vratas*. In fact this sixth *aṇu-vrata* is noted by Cāmuṇḍarāya[5] (and at a later date by Sakalakīrti) though no list of five *aticāras* seems ever to have been devised for it.[6]

The *aṇu-vratas* are: *ahiṃsā*, *satya*, *asteya*, *brahma*, and *aparigraha*. The *Dharma-rasāyana* is alone in substituting for the first of these the prohibition of killing living creatures for sacrifice to

1 Handiqui, p. 263. 2 PASU 70. 3 YŚ iii. 41.
4 Śr (A) v. 28. 5 CS, p. 7.
6 Other writers such as Vīranandin in his treatise on the monastic life, the *Ācāra-sāra*, count *a-rātri-bhojana* as an additional *mahā-vrata*.

the gods (*devatā-nimittam a-jīva-maraṇa*), the *ahiṃsā-vrata* itself being relegated to a place among the *guṇa-vratas*.

The variations in the *guṇa-vratas* and *śikṣā-vratas* can best be shown in tabular form:

GUṆA-VRATAS

Śvetāmbaras	dig-vrata	bhogopabhoga	anartha-daṇḍa
Tattvārtha-sūtra			
Cāmuṇḍarāya			
Amṛtacandra			
Somadeva	dig-vrata	deśāvakāśika	anartha-daṇḍa
Amitagati			
Rājamalla			
Vāmadeva			
Vasunandin			
Samantabhadra			
Āśādhara			
Medhāvin			
Sakalakīrti			
Somasena	dig-vrata	anartha-daṇḍa	bhogopabhoga
Kārttikeya			
Kundakunda			
Devasena			
Śivakoṭi			
Padmanandin[1]	anartha-daṇḍa	ahiṃsā	bhogopabhoga

ŚIKṢĀ-VRATAS

Śvetāmbaras	sāmāyika	deśāvakāśika	poṣadhopavasa	dāna
Tattvārtha-sūtra				
Cāmuṇḍarāya				
Amṛtacandra				
Amitagati	sāmāyika	poṣadhopavāsa	bhogopabhoga	dāna
Somadeva				
Vāmadeva				
Rājamalla				
Samantabhadra				
Āśādhara				
Medhāvin	deśāvakāśika	sāmāyika	poṣadhopavāsa	dāna
Sakalakīrti				
Somasena				
Kārttikeya	sāmāyika	poṣadhopavāsa	dāna	deśāvakāśika
Kundakunda				
Devasena	sāmāyika	poṣadhopavāsa	dāna	sallekhanā
Śivakoṭi				
Padmanandin				
Vasunandin	bhoga	upabhoga	dāna	sallekhanā

Certain points are made clear by a glance at these tables. It has

[1] In this and the following tables the author of the *Dharma-rasāyana* is meant.

been remarked that the *guṇa-vratas* are additional vows, special cases in fact of the *aṇu-vratas*, whilst the *śikṣā-vratas* refer to spiritual exercises. The Śvetāmbaras, even those among them who follow the *Tattvārtha-sūtra* in some interpretations, insist on the designations *guṇa-vrata* and *śikṣā-vrata* and have also, as is logical, retained the sequence which leaves these two types of vows distinct. The Digambaras who follow the *Tattvārtha-sūtra* have blurred this distinction by making the *deśāvakāśika-vrata* follow the *dig-vrata* to which it is related in content, the *bhogopabhoga-vrata* being inserted immediately before the *dāna-vrata* probably because of resemblances in the *aticāras*. Another Digambara current stemming from Samantabhadra agrees with the Śvetāmbara tradition except in the one minor detail that it transposes the *sāmāyika-* and *deśāvakāśika-vratas*. (Kārttikeya puts the *deśāvakāśika-* after the *dāna-vrata*.) Kundakunda, Devasena, and one or two others suppress the *deśāvakāśika-vrata* altogether and give *sallekhanā* twelfth place on the list. Vasunandin, who follows the *Tattvārtha-sūtra* for the order of the *guṇa-vratas*, eliminates the *sāmāyika-* and *poṣadhopavāsa-vratas* altogether probably because the same subjects are treated as *pratimās* and creates in their place a *bhoga-vrata* and an *upabhoga-vrata*.

It is possible to discern in the treatment of the *vratas* and their *aticāras* a number of different traditions which it is of importance to note:

1. The orthodox Śvetāmbara tradition rigidly faithful to the *Upāsaka-daśāh*.
2. Another Śvetāmbara tradition that owes its origin to Haribhadra, who was considerably influenced by the *Tattvārtha-sūtra*. This includes Hemacandra and the seventeenth-century Yaśovijaya.
3. The Digambara tradition based on the *Tattvārtha-sūtra*.
4. Another Digambara tradition going back to Samantabhadra, who compiled completely new lists of *aticāras* for some *vratas*. He is followed by Sakalakīrti and Somasena.
5. One significant writer—Somadeva—who alone has not respected the tradition of five *aticāras* for each *vrata*.

The following table will show in detail how the *aticāras* are treated by them.

[1] The designations of the *aticāras* vary considerably from writer to writer. I have preferred to use, wherever possible, those given in the *Upāsaka-daśāḥ*.

AHIṂSĀ-VRATA

All	bandha	vadha	chavi-ccheda	ati-bhārāropaṇa	bhakta-pāna-vyavaccheda

SATYA-VRATA

Śvetāmbaras except	sahasābhyākhyāna	raho'bhyākhyāna	sva-dāra-mantra-bheda	mṛśopadeśa	kūṭa-lekha-karaṇa
Hemacandra, Mānavijaya and	sahasābhyākhyāna	guhya-bhāṣaṇa	viśvasta-mantra-bheda	mṛśopadeśa	kūṭa-lekha-karaṇa
Haribhadra	nyāsāpahāra	raho'bhyākhyāna	sva-dāra-mantra-bheda	mṛśopadeśa	kūṭa-lekha-karaṇa
Tattvārtha-sūtra, Cāmuṇḍarāya, Amṛtacandra, Āśādhara, Medhāvin, Sakalakīrti, Rājamalla	nyāsāpahāra	raho'bhyākhyāna	sākāra-mantra-bheda	mṛśopadeśa	kūṭa-lekha-karaṇa
Samantabhadra, Somasena	nyāsāpahāra	raho'bhyākhyāna	paiśunya	parivāda	kūṭa-lekha-karaṇa
Amitagati	nyāsāpahāra	guhya-bhāṣaṇa, paiśunya	mantra-bheda	mṛśopadeśa	kūṭa-lekha-karaṇa
Somadeva	mūḍha-sākṣi-padokti	paiśunya	mantra-bheda	parivāda	kūṭa-lekha-karaṇa

ASTEYA-VRATA

All except Somadeva	stenāhṛtādāna	stena-prayoga	viruddha-rājyātikrama	kūṭa-tula-kūṭa-māna	tat-pratirūpaka-vyavahāra
Somadeva	stenāhṛtādāna	stena-karman	vigrahe saṃgraho 'rthasya	pautava-nyūnatā	pautavādhikya

BRAHMA-VRATA

All except	itvara-parigṛhītā-gamana	a-parigṛhītā-gamana	anaṅga-krīḍā	para-vivāha-karaṇa	kāma-bhoga-tīvrābhilāṣa
Āśādhara, Samantabhadra, Sakalakīrti, Somasena	itvarikā-gamana	viṭatva	anaṅga-krīḍā	para-vivāha-karaṇa	kāma-bhoga-tīvrābhilāṣa
Somadeva	parastrī-gamana	—	anaṅga-krīḍā	para-vivāha-karaṇa	kāma-bhoga-tīvrābhilāṣa

APARIGRAHA-VRATA

All except	kṣetra-vastu	hiraṇya-suvarṇa	dhana-dhānya	dvipada-catuṣpada	kupya
Somadeva	kṣetra-vastu	śayanāsana	dhana-dhānya	dvipada-catuṣpada	kupya
Samantabhadra, Sakaiakīrti	ati-vahana	ati-saṃgraha	ati-vismaya	ati-lobha	ati-bhārāropana

DIG-VRATA

All	ūrdhva-dig-atikrama	adho-dig-atikrama	tiryag-dig-atikrama	kṣetra-vṛddhi	smṛty-antardhāna

BHOGOPABHOGA-VRATA

Śvetāmbaras except	sacittāhāra	sacitta-pratibaddhāhāra	apakvauṣadhi	duṣpakvauṣadhi	tucchauṣadhi
Haribhadra Hemacandra Mānavijaya and Digambaras except	sacittāhāra	sacitta-pratibaddhāhāra	sacitta-sammiśrāhāra	duṣpakvauṣadhi	abhiṣava
Somadeva	niṣiddhāhāra	jantu-sambaddhāhāra	jantu-sammiśrāhāra	duṣpakvauṣadhi	avīkṣitāhāra
Samantabhadra Sakalakīrti	viṣayānupekṣā	viṣayānusmṛti	viṣayātitṛṣā	viṣayātilaulya	viṣayānubhava

ANARTHA-DAṆḌA-VRATA

Śvetāmbaras except	kandarpa	kautkucya	maukharya	saṃyuktādhikaraṇa	upabhoga-paribhogātireka
Haribhadra and Digambaras except	kandarpa	kautkucya	maukharya	asamīkṣyādhikaraṇa	upabhoga-paribhogātireka
Samantabhadra Sakalakīrti Somasena	kandarpa	kautkucya	maukharya	asamīkṣyādhikaraṇa	ati-prasādhana
Somadeva	vañcana-pravartana	ārambha-pravartana	hiṃsā-pravartana	bhārādhikya	ati-kleśa

SĀMĀYIKA-VRATA

All	mano-duṣpraṇidhāna	vag-duṣpraṇidhāna	kāya-duṣpraṇidhāna	smṛty-akaraṇa	anavasthita-karaṇa

DEŚĀVAKĀŚIKA-VRATA

All	ānayana-prayoga	preṣya-prayoga	śabdānupāta	rūpānupāta	bahya-pudgala-prakṣepa

POṢADHOPAVĀSA-VRATA

Śvetāmbaras except	apratilekhita-śayyā	apratilekhita-sthaṇḍila	apramārjita-śayyā	apramārjita-sthaṇḍila	samyag ananupālana
Haribhadra Hemacandra Mānavijaya and Digambaras except	apratyupeksitā-pramārjitotsarga	apratyupekṣitā-pramārjitādāna-nikṣepa	apratyupekṣitā-pramārjita-saṃstāra	anādara	smṛty-anupasthā-pana
Somadeva	anavekṣā	apratilekhana	duṣkarmārambha	durmanaskāra	āvaśyaka-virati

DĀNA-VRATA

All except	sacitta-nikṣepa	sacitta-pidhāna	kālātikrama	para-vyapadeśa	matsaritā
Samantabhadra Sakalakīrti	sacitta-nikṣepa	sacitta-pidhāna	kālātikrama	anādara	matsaritā

SALLEKHANĀ-VRATA

Śvetāmbaras	iha-lokāśaṃsa	para-lokāśaṃsa	jivitāśaṃsa	maranāśaṃsa	kāma-bhogāśaṃsa
Digambaras	sukhānubandha	mitrānurāga	jivitāśaṃsa	maranāśaṃsa	nidāna
except Samantabhadra	bhaya	mitra-smṛti	jivitāśaṃsa	maranāśaṃsa	nidāna

SAMYAKTVA

All	śaṅka	kāṅkṣā	vicikitsā	para-pāṣaṇḍi-praśaṃsā	para-pāṣaṇḍi-saṃstava

The *aticāras* given in the *Upāsaka-daśāḥ* are specifically described as 'typical'[1] (*peyāla*), but though Abhayadeva[2] draws attention to this in his commentary on the *sūtra* pointing out that the set of five infractions attached to each *vrata* is not a restrictive definition (*avadhāraṇa*) but a symbolic indication (*upalakṣaṇa*) of other similar offences, little heed has been in practice paid to this and the Digambaras in particular seem to regard the *aticāras* as furnishing the detailed draft of a moral code.

With the exception of Āśādhara, who has here borrowed from Hemacandra, the Digambaras do not appear to take into account the distinction of *bhaṅga* and *aticāra*, which has led many Śvetāmbara *ācāryas* into a tangle of sophistry. Whilst an *aticāra* according to Abhayadeva[3] is a lapse from the vow, due, for example, to lack of understanding of it, any conscious and flagrant infraction constitutes a *bhaṅga*. Abhayadeva admits he is unable to understand the distinction of *bhaṅga* and *aticāra* in the *Āvaśyaka-ṭīkā* but his own definition is hardly satisfactory. In practice a *bhaṅga* is held to be a complete negation of the *vrata* (for example, the outright refusal to give alms is a *bhaṅga* of the *dāna-vrata*) whilst an *aticāra* is an offence against the *vrata* in which the vow is partly kept and partly infringed or, as this might be expressed in over-simplified terms, an *aticāra* is half a *bhaṅga*. But other types of transgression, intermediate between *bhaṅga* and *aticāra* and involving more subtle differentiations, are also mentioned in the discussion of *pratikramaṇa* and *ālocanā*: such, for example, are the *khaṇḍita* and *virādhana*. An *aticāra*, it is considered, may occur when an offence is palliated by ignorance, or when it is carried out through the agency of a third party, or when an evil intention is cherished but not put into effect, or when the spirit but not the letter of an injunction is contravened. It would seem that on this theme of *bhaṅga* and *aticāra* the Śvetāmbara *ācāryas* are the prisoners of a traditional exegesis which constrains them to contortions of casuistry alien to the very ideas they have set forth in other places.

To the same type of intellectual hair-splitting belong the computations of the possible number of *bhaṅgas* of a *vrata* of which some examples are given under the *ahiṃsā-vrata*. It is enough to explain here that any *bhaṅga* may be committed in speech, in body,

[1] See Schubring, *Die Lehre des Jainas*, p. 188.
[2] UD i. 56 (p. 21).
[3] UD i. 56 (pp. 21–22).

or in mind (these are collectively referred to as the *pada-traya*), the offender may himself be guilty of the act (when it is *kṛta*), may cause it to be done (when it is *kārita*), or may approve of its being done (when it is *anumata*); together the resulting nine possibilities make up what the Digambaras call the *nava-koṭi*. There are also three possible stages in the commission of the offence: preparation (*saṃrambha*), inception (*samārambha*), and execution (*ārambha*).

Where *aticāras* of a *vrata* are given (for some Digambaras do not note any) they are always, except in a few cases in the *Yaśastilaka*, five in number. Five is also the number of the *aṇu-vratas* themselves (except where *arātri-bhojana* is recognized as a *vrata*) Abhayadeva[1] explains that they are five, and not four like the *mahā-vratas* in the times of the twenty-two earlier *tīrthaṅkaras*, because Śailaka-rājā accepted the *śrāvaka-dharma* in the guise of five *aṇu-vratas* and seven other *vratas* in the presence of Sthāpatyaputra, the pupil of Neminātha. The same writer explains the term *aṇu-vrata* as meaning either a vow that is 'minor' (*aṇu*) in comparison with the major vows (*mahā-vratas*) or the vow of a person who is 'minor', that is of secondary importance, in comparison with an ascetic, or (in the form of *anu-vrata*) as a vow expounded subsequently to the *mahā-vratas*.

THE AHIṂSĀ-VRATA

By all the Jaina *ācāryas*, except by the author of the rather aberrant and isolated *Dharma-rasāyana*, the *ahiṃsā-vrata* is recognized as the first of the *aṇu-vratas* and even in that work where it is relegated to second place among the *guṇa-vratas* its position is taken by a specialized variant of non-violence—the refusal to kill animals in sacrifice to the gods.[2] This primacy of *ahiṃsā* lies at the very root of Jainism: *daya mūlu dhamm'-aṅghivaha* as the *Śrāvaka-dharma-dohaka*[3] says; and the instinct is sound which leads Amṛtacandra to explain every other *vrata* as but a restatement in different terms of the content of the first.

Amongst the Digambaras it is Amṛtacandra,[4] and next to him Amitagati,[5] who have devoted most attention to refuting argue ments commonly advanced in the world in criticism of absolute

[1] P (ŚrDh) 7.
[2] *Dharma-rasāyana*, 143.
[3] Doha 40.
[4] PASU 79–89.
[5] Śr (A) vi. 33–44.

ahiṃsā. They point out that it is wrong to kill destructive creatures —and by this lions, tigers, snakes, and scorpions, and similar dangerous animals and insects are intended—in the belief that by so doing other living creatures will be saved from death or injury. Slaughter for the purpose of extirpating evil is as senseless as cutting down a tree with an axe in order to make it grow. Since destructive creatures when slain go to a fate of great misery those who inflict such misery on them will inevitably incur great guilt. It is equally contrary to the concepts of true religion to destroy creatures that are in a state of wretchedness on the assumption that they will be out of their misery when dead, for of necessity they will be reborn in another incarnation where their plight may be yet worse. Vigorously to be combatted is the teaching of those who maintain that a good disciple should cut off the head of his preceptor when through constant practice of religion he has achieved a mental state which will assure him a happy reincarnation; for it is fallacious to imagine that since the attainment of happiness is difficult the blissful if killed will remain blissful. To claim that the religious life stems from the gods and therefore to them all things are to be offered, or to assert that there is no fault in slaughtering goats or other animals to satisfy the duties of hospitality, are other untenable points of view. The contention that it is better to kill one higher animal than to destroy a very great number of lower forms of life is refuted by the explanation that the carcass will inevitably be full of minute organisms called *nigodas*. For this reason perhaps, too, it is forbidden to kill oneself in order to offer one's body as food for the starving.

Amṛtacandra is concerned on these issues mainly with the refutation of other creeds, but in ordinary life the commonest problem to present itself in the application of the doctrine of *ahiṃsā* would probably be whether or not it is licit to kill a destructive animal, and in fact the question is put and answered by a number of writers including Āśādhara[1] and Hemacandra. Hemacandra[2] in fact is the only mediaeval Śvetāmbara authority on *śrāvakācāra* to treat at length of the wider issues of *ahiṃsā*, though at an earlier epoch they had been discussed in the *Śrāvaka-prajñapti*.

The nature of the layman's *ahiṃsā-vrata* depends on the distinction between *sūkṣma-hiṃsā*, the taking of life in any form,

[1] SDhA iv. 6–22. [2] YŚ ii. 22–49.

abstention from which is obligatory for the ascetic, and *sthūla-hiṃsā*, the destruction of the higher forms of life from *dvīndriyas* upwards, which is forbidden to all Jainas. The layman is also enjoined to avoid as far as possible the killing of *ekendriyas* and the useless destruction of *sthāvara-jīvas*. The objection is sometimes raised that since the monk has renounced *hiṃsā*, whether *kṛta*, *kārita*, or *anumata*, he should not instruct the layman to maintain only *sthūla-hiṃsā* since this amounts to an implicit assent to the killing of *ekendriyas*. To elucidate the monk's attitude a parable[1] is narrated.

The wives of a certain king obtained permission from their husbands to leave the women's quarters and visit the city by night. To ensure that they could do so unmolested he gave order that all the men of the city should be outside the walls by dusk. However, the six sons of a merchant were detained by some business in their counting-house and failed to leave. They were arrested and condemned to death. Their father besought the king for pardon but was only able to obtain the release of the youngest one by a reasoned plea to the ruler. Here the sons who are executed are the *jīva-nikāyas*, the father is the *sādhu*, and his plea is his exposition of the *dharma* at the time that the layman takes the *aṇu-vratas*. He knows that the *śrāvaka* will not spare the lives of all living beings and so he attempts to save at least some of them.

Hiṃsā may be either inherent in an occupation (*ārambha-ja*) or intentional (*saṅkalpa-ja*), in other words, unrelated to the occupation (*anārambha-ja*). Offences against the *vrata* may be either conscious (*sārthaka*) or fortuitous (*anarthaka*), and in the former case they may be committed with due care and attention (*sāpekṣa*) or carelessly *nirapekṣa*.[2] These distinctions are sometimes known as *bhedas*.

Hiṃsā does not depend on acts alone: the *vrata* will be broken merely by the absence of compassion shown when a man allows himself to be carried away by anger. A distinction can therefore be made between *bhāva-hiṃsā* (the intention to hurt) and *dravya-hiṃsā* (the actual hurt).[3]

The *aticāras* of this *vrata* are given in the same form by Śvetāmbaras and Digambaras:

(i) keeping in captivity (*bandha*);

[1] See Haribhadra's comm. on ŚrPr 115 or Municandra's comm. on DhB iii. 16. [2] NPP 22. [3] T (S) vii. 8 (p. 64).

(ii) beating (*vadha*);
(iii) mutilating (*chavi-ccheda*);
(iv) overloading (*ati-bhārāropaṇa*);
(v) depriving of food and drink (*bhakta-pāna-vyavaccheda*).

(i) Bandha. This according to Haribhadra[1] applies to the tying up or keeping in captivity of men or beasts. Siddhasena Gaṇin[2] stresses that this is very often utterly wanton as when ants, or other insects, are tied for amusement. It may, however, be quite legitimate when an unruly child, or slave, or servant has to be corrected or when horses, cattle, buffaloes, or elephants are kept for domestic use. The general view seems to be that such action—and this applies to the other contraventions of this *vrata*—ranks as an *aticāra* when done in anger. This is stressed by Hemacandra,[3] who defines *bandha* as 'the restraining of cattle by ropes and withies or the restraining of one's children for the sake of correcting them'. The tying should be done with consideration (*sāpekṣa*), the rope being knotted loosely so that it can be easily slipped in case of fire. Āśādhara[4] follows Hemacandra in his explanation but notes also that it is licit to bind a thief or other intruder who may have entered one's home. Pūjyapāda and Cāmuṇḍarāya[5] state simply that *bandha* means fastening with a rope to a block or post in such a way as to restrict freedom of movement from place to place. This and the following *aticāras* they appear to take as referring only to animals.

(ii) Vadha.[6] Haribhadra[7] explains this as 'thrashing with whips'. When occasion arises, says Siddhasena Gaṇin,[8] a pious layman may administer a whipping to a person or animal in his charge with due consideration for age and avoiding any vital spot; pulling the ears or slapping is also permissible. The consensus of later opinion is perhaps best expressed by Devendra[9] when he says that it is merciless flogging that constitutes the *aticāra*. The Digambaras define *vadha* as 'the beating of living creatures with rods, whips, or withies'.

[1] Āv (H), p. 820*a*.
[2] T (S) vii. 20.
[3] YŚ iii. 90 (p. 547).
[4] SDhA iv. 16.
[5] CS, p. 5.
[6] This *aticāra* has sometimes erroneously been rendered as 'killing'.
[7] Āv (H), p. 819*b*.
[8] T (S) vii. 20.
[9] SrDK, pt. ii, p. 84.

(iii) CHAVI-CCHEDA.[1] For Haribhadra[2] this implies 'cutting the body with swords and other sharp instruments'. The word *chavi* is in fact variously interpreted as 'body' or 'skin'. The *Tattvārtha-bhāṣya* introduces[3] here the idea of purposeless cutting of the bark of trees and Siddhasena Gaṇin extends this to the wounding of *ap-kāyas* by cutting ice or of *pṛthvī-kāyas* by disturbing the ground, offences which later are usually found under the *anartha-daṇḍa-vrata*. But, as he notes, this *aticāra* applies rather to branding and ear-piercing or to methods of punishment used to intimidate criminals such as cutting off the nose and ears, or fingers and thumbs. Such *chavi-ccheda* is of course merciless and devoid of consideration (*nirapekṣa*) but it ceases to be an *aticāra* when it is done with due care (*sāpekṣa*), for example, in lancing a boil. Hemacandra[4] mentions as an instance of beneficent *chavi-ccheda* opening the swollen leg of a person suffering from elephantiasis (*pāda-valmīka*). For the Digambaras[5] this *aticāra* implies the mutilation of the ears, or nose, or other organs of the body.

(iv) ATI-BHĀRĀROPAṆA. Haribhadra[6] understands by this the loading on to the back, or shoulders, or head of an animal or human being of an excessive weight of goods such as betel nuts. Siddhasena Gaṇin[3] comments that a Jaina ought not to make his living by *bhāṭaka-karman* or *śakaṭa-karman* which are forbidden trades, but, if unable to do otherwise, he should load his oxen or other beasts of burden with a load rather below the maximum that they can bear and unyoke them during the heat of the day, giving them food and water; whilst human beings should not be expected to carry more than they can take without undue effort. Pūjyapāda and Camuṇḍarāya[5] define this *aticāra* as the loading on oxen or other animals, out of greed, of a burden greater than they can bear.

(v) BHAKTA-PĀNA-VYAVACCHEDA. Siddhasena Gaṇin[3] says that the stinting of food or water to man or beast without cause is always to be avoided. For the moral good of undisciplined children or the physical good of fever patients it is, however, admissible when done with due care. The Digambaras understand this *aticāra* to mean 'provoking the suffering of hunger or thirst in animals for any reason.[5]

[1] In Jaina jurisprudence *chavi-ccheda* is one of the seven forms of *daṇḍa-nīti*; it covers any mutilation inflicted in punishment of a crime. See *Arhan-nīti*, ii. 2.

[2] Āv (H), p. 819*b*.

[3] T (S) vii. 20.

[4] YŚ iii. 90 (p. 547).

[5] CS, p. 5.

[6] Āv (H), p. 819*b*.

'How can there be any *aticāra* of the *ahiṃsā-vrata* which is designed to express a renunciation of killing if in fact no killing has taken place?'[1] This question is often raised by the Śvetāmbara *ācāryas*, only to be answered at once by the explanation that where the intention to hurt or kill arises under the influence of anger and other passions there is *bhāva-hiṃsā*. Even if there is no *dravya-hiṃsā* or physical injury the *vrata* will have been infringed by the putting away of compassion. In a phrase of Amṛtacandra[2] *hiṃsā* exists wherever *rāga* and *dveṣa* occur even though no creature perishes. A mere thought in an angry man's mind is *hiṃsā*: once delivered to the empire of his passions he destroys himself even if he destroys no other living being. Conversely where a person of pure life, for example, a *sādhu* practising *īryā-samiti*, inadvertently extinguishes the life of a *jīva* he does not bind on himself further karma. *Aticāras* of the layman's *ahiṃsā-vrata* therefore occur when the vow is broken in spirit (*antar-vṛttyā*) through anger but kept in the letter (*bahir-vṛttyā*), for example, when an animal is beaten mercilessly but recovers owing to its natural strength.[3]

Many writers are preoccupied by the calculation of the number of ways in which the *vrata* can be broken. Thus for Amitagati[4] a *bhaṅga* may be *kṛta*, *kārita*, or *anumata*, may be committed in speech, in body, or in mind, may refer to the stages of *saṃrambha*, *samārambha*, or *ārambha* and may belong to any one of the four *kaṣāyas*: *krodha*, *māna*, *māyā*, or *lobha*: from this computation, which is that of the *Tattvārtha-sūtra*, he derives a total of 108 forms of *hiṃsā*. Devagupta[5] reckons 243 *bhaṅgas* of the *ahiṃsā-vrata*: *kṛta*, *kārita*, or *anumata*, in speech, in body, or in mind, committed against the nine categories of *jīvas* in past, present, or future time. Hemacandra[6] prefers a more complex calculation: each offence may be committed in speech, in body, in mind, in speech and body together, in speech and mind together, in mind and body together, or in speech, body, and mind together, and each may be *kṛta*, *kārita*, *anumata*, *kṛta-kārita*, *kṛtānumata*, *kāritānumata*, or *kṛta-kāritānumata*; and the variants which result may occur in past, present, or future time, giving a possible total of 147 *bhaṅgas*. It seems idle to follow the *ācāryas* into the network of these theoretical speculations, and though they are applied to many injunctions of

[1] UD i. 45 (p. 7). [2] PASU 41–48. [3] ŚrDK, pt. ii, p. 84.
[4] Śr (A) vi. 12–13. [5] NPP 21. [6] YŚ ii. 18 (p. 192).

the Jaina creed, and recur with increasing frequency in the later texts in tabulated form, no further allusion will be made to them in the present study.

The content of the *ahiṃsā-vrata* is much wider than the *aticāras* indicate, though many subjects which are treated under this head by early writers are later held to fall within the province of the *anartha-daṇḍa-vrata* and the *bhogopabhoga-vrata*. The *Śrāvaka-prajñapti*[1] records that the practice of *ahiṃsā* implies the straining of water through a cloth and the use of grain that is free from weevils. Siddhasena Gaṇin[2] mentions the ban on the consumption of meat, alcohol, and honey as forming part of the *ahiṃsā-vrata*. Somadeva,[3] too, includes under it the obligation to avoid unstrained water, *abhakṣyas*, *ananta-kāyas*, and *rātri-bhojana*. Āśādhara,[4] who notes that the lay estate cannot exist without activity (*ārambha*) or activity without killing, deals especially under the *ahiṃsā-vrata* with eating by night and meat-eating.

It is the eating of meat and the sacrifice of animals that provoke Hemacandra[5] to an attack on the *hiṃsā-śāstra* as he calls the *Manusmṛti*. It is, he says, a hideous distortion of reality to pretend that animals have come into existence to be offered to the divinities for the prosperity of the world and that the *jīvas* inhabiting them will be reborn as divine beings. Those who perform such sacrifices will go to the lowest hell, and even a wretched atheist, a *cārvaka*, will have a better destiny than the hypocrites who preach a *dharma* of cruelty. That men abandon the *dharma* of compassion for this repellent creed is evidence of the evil of the age. If sacrificial victims really went to an abode of bliss why should not one kill one's parents in the sacrifice? How can figures like Śiva, Skandha, Viṣṇu, or Yama, who are represented with terrible weapons, be adored as divinities? Like many other Jaina writers, Hemacandra quotes the famous verse:

> *savve jīvā vi icchanti jīvium na marijjiuṃ*
> *tamhā pāṇi-vahaṃ ghoraṃ nigganthā vajjayanti naṃ*[6]

'Killing horrifies because all beings wish to live and not to be slain.' It would here be well to stress that *ahiṃsā* is not something negative; it is another aspect of *dayā*—compassion—in Hemacandra's

[1] ŚrPr 259. [2] T (S) vii. 8. [3] Handiqui, p. 264.
[4] SDhA iv. 12. [5] YŚ ii. 33–49.
[6] *Daśa-vaikālika-sūtra, gāthā*, 219.

words 'the beneficent mother of all beings', 'the elixir for those who wander in suffering through the ocean of reincarnation'. This positive *ahiṃsā* is expressed in the form of *karuṇa-dāna* or *abhaya-dāna*, the giving of protection to all living creatures.

For Somadeva,[1] who emphasizes this positive aspect, *ahiṃsā* as in the *Tattvārtha-sūtra*[2] is compounded of *maitrī*—the non-infliction of suffering, *pramoda*—affection combined with respect for the virtuous, *kāruṇya*—charity to help the needy, and *mādhyasthya*—a state of equanimity without attraction or repulsion in regard to those who are devoid of virtues. Evil, he says, cannot dwell in a man crowned with the halo of compassion for this quality is more efficacious than the practice of all ceremonies.

THE SATYA-VRATA

THE term *satya* has been given such a wide connotation here that it is scarcely possible to render it merely as 'truth'. Its specifically Jaina interpretation was already apparent to Pūjyapāda as his commentary on the *Tattvārtha-sūtra*[3] shows. In fact the amplitude of this *vrata* has been concisely expressed by Vasunandin[4] as the abstention from untruth spoken out of passion or hate, and from truth, too if it provokes the destruction of a living being.

From the earliest times certain divisions or delimitations of *satya* have been established in the texts. The most primitive (dating from the older *Āvaśyaka* literature) takes the following form (based on the gifts most commonly mentioned):

(i) untruth relating to a girl (*kanyālīka*), e.g. saying that a girl is or is not a virgin;
(ii) untruth relating to a cow (*gav-alīka*), e.g. saying that a cow gives much milk or little milk;
(iii) untruth relating to land (*bhūmy-alīka*), e.g. saying that a piece of land belongs to oneself or belongs to another person;
(iv) untruth told for the sake of making away with a pledge (*nyāsa-haraṇa*), e.g. falsely denying that gold or other valuables have been entrusted to one;
(v) bearing false witness (*kūṭa-sākṣya*).

[1] Handiqui, p. 264. [2] T (P) vii. 11. [3] Ibid. 14.
[4] Śr (V) 209.

The above classification is that of the *Pañcāśaka*[1] but it is given without perceptible variation in all Śvetāmbara works, from the *Śrāvaka-prajñapti* onwards, that treat of the *vratas*. Āśādhara[2] borrows it from Hemacandra but is not followed by any other Digambara writer except Medhāvin, who mentions only the first three categories. It should be noted that in all cases these three forms of *asatya* are interpreted as *upalakṣaṇas* or symbolic examples so that they cover any false statements made in reference to human beings (*kanyālīka*), animals (*gav-alīka*), or inanimate objects (*bhūmy-alīka*).

Another classification which bears the stamp of the logicians divides *asatya* into the following categories:[3]

(i) denial of what is (*bhūta-nihnava* or *sad-alapana*), e.g. 'there is no *ātman*'; 'there is no *pāpa*'; 'there is no *puṇya*'; or 'Devadatta is not here' (when in fact he is present);

(ii) assertion of what is not (*asad-udbhāvana* or *abhūtodbhāvana*), e.g. 'the *ātman* is immanent' (*sarvagata*), or 'the *ātman* is of the size of a grain of millet or rice' or 'the pot is there' (when in fact it is not there);

(iii) representation of something in a form other than its real form (*arthāntara* or *viparīta*), e.g. describing a cow as a horse or saying, as do the Buddhists, that the *ātman* is non-eternal or, as do the Sāṅkhyas, that it is eternal;

(iv) reprehensible speech (*nindya*)—in Hemacandra's terminology *garhita*—which is again subdivided into:

  (*a*) speech that is tactlessly hurtful (*apriya*) as, for example, in alluding to a person's physical deformity. Nothing should be said to cause embarrassment, anxiety, or unhappiness to others;

  (*b*) speech that is insulting (*garhya*)—in Hemacandra *ākrośa-rūpa*—or inspired by malice or mockery, e.g. calling someone a bastard;[4]

  (*c*) speech in which encouragement to harmful actions is given (*sāvadya*). This would include not only advice to steal or to kill but even an injunction such as 'plough the fields'.

[1] P (ŚrDh) 11. [2] SDhA iv. 39.
[3] Śr (A) vi. 49–54; PASU 91–98.
[4] YŚ ii. 57; textually *yathā are bāndhakineya ity ādi*.

The foregoing classification is given not only by the Digambaras Amitagati and Amṛtacandra but also in the *Yoga-śāstra* where the treatment goes back directly to Siddhasena's commentary on the *Tattvārtha-sūtra*[1] and indeed to the Śvetāmbara *Bhāṣya*. The three types of *nindya* speech (styled *garhita* in the *Bhāṣya*) are, in corresponding order, *paiśūnya-yukta*, *pāruṣya-yukta*, and *hiṃsā-yukta*.

Since in general it would seem that in numerical presentations the tetrads are older than the pentads, the fivefold classification set out in the *Nava-pada-prakaraṇa*[2] and repeated by Yaśodeva[3] in his commentary on the *Pañcāśaka* is probably a later development. On the authority of a Prakrit verse quoted this is given as: (i) *abhūtodbhavana*, (ii) *bhūta-nihnava*, (iii) *viparīta*, (iv) *garhya*, (v) *sāvadya*.

Āśādhara[4] too has five categories but he has arrived at them by suppressing the *sāvadya* class, doubtless from a feeling that it was unnecessary because identical with the *pāpopadeśa* division of *anarthadaṇḍa*. With that exception he has faithfully followed Hemacandra's enumeration.

Somadeva[5] gives another fourfold division of *satya* and *asatya*:

(i) *satya-satya*—what is wholly true, the exact reproduction of facts;
(ii) *asatya-satya*—a statement part true, part false in which the falsehood predominates, e.g. weave the cloth, (where it would be more accurate to say weave the yarn);
(iii) *satyāsatya*—again a statement part true, part false, but with truth predominating, e.g. promising to give something within a fortnight and giving it only after a month or a year;
(iv) *asatyāsatya*—what is wholly false, e.g. promising to give something which it is not within one's power to give.

Āśādhara[6] incorporates this rather casuistic analysis into his *śrāvakācāra* but no other writer appears to have noted it. In conformity with the usage of the world the first three are permissible but the fourth is always to be avoided.

For the five *aticāras* the older Śvetāmbara authorities maintain unchanged the list of the *Upāsaka-daśāḥ*:

(i) sudden calumniating (*sahasābhyākhyāna*);
(ii) secret calumniating (*raho'bhyākhyāna*);

[1] T (S) vii. 9. [2] NPP 30. [3] P (Y) 11.
[4] SDhA iv. 44. [5] Handiqui, p. 265. [6] SDhA iv. 40–43.

(iii) divulging the confidences of one's wife (*sva-dāra-mantra-bheda*);
(iv) spreading of false information (*mṛśopadeśa*);
(v) false statements expressed in writing (*kūṭa-lekha-karaṇa*).

However, even here, there are some divergencies in interpretation. The oldest Digambara list, that of the *Tattvārtha-sūtra*,[1] varies *sva-dāra-mantra-bheda* to *sākāra-mantra-bheda* (at its origin probably no more than a textual corruption), omits *sahasābhyākhyāna*, and from the primitive categories of *asatya* borrows *nyāsāpahāra*, assigning to it the vacant space in the *aticāra* pentad. This pattern is followed by Amṛtacandra,[2] Cāmuṇḍarāya, and Āśādhara and, one may add, by Amitagati[3] though there is some blurring of the distinction between the second and third infractions called by him 'revealing of secret actions' (*prakāśanā guhya-viceṣṭitānām*) and 'divulging the confidences of others' (*para-mantra-bheda*). Haribhadra, in the *Dharma-bindu*,[4] has kept the original Śvetāmbara version except for the replacement of *sahasābhyākhyāna* by *nyāsāpahāra*. Hemacandra[5] on the contrary has preferred to retain *sahasābhyākhyāna*; he recognizes *raho'bhyākhyāna* as a variant reading for this and fills its place in the list by *guhya-bhāṣaṇa* whilst for *sva-dāra-mantra-bheda* he gives *viśvasta-mantra-bheda*. In other words, for the second and third *aticāras*, he is in exact agreement with Amitagati. Samantabhadra[6] follows the *Tāttvārtha-sūtra* but for *sākāra-mantra-bheda* and *mṛśopadeśa* he has *paiśunya* and *parivāda* (for his commentator Prabhācandra the use of these terms does not change the meaning). For this *aṇu-vrata* as for others, Somadeva's[7] list of *aticāras* is the most aberrant: *mudhā-sākṣi-padōkti* (false witness), *mantra-bheda* (revealing of confidences), *paiśunya*, *parivāda*, and *kūṭa-lekhana*. It is clear therefore that for him *paiśunya* cannot have the sense that Prabhācandra gives to it or it would be tautological. It would probably be more correct to give to it its everyday meaning of 'calumny' and to *parivāda* that of 'reproach'. Yet it must be pointed out in support of Prabhācandra's explanation that Amitagati in the *Subhāṣita-ratna-saṃdoha* uses the term *paiśunya* to describe what in his *Śrāvakācāra* he calls *prakāśanā guhya-viceṣṭitānām* and that Siddhasena Gaṇin[8] equates *paiśunya* with what is *apriya*.

[1] T (P) vii. 25. [2] PASU 184. [3] Śr (A) vii. 4.
[4] DhB iii. 27. [5] YŚ iii. 91. [6] RK iii. 10.
[7] Handiqui, p. 265. [8] T (S) vii. 9 (p. 74).

The interpretation of these various *aticāras* even when they bear the same designation shows considerable variations:

(i) SAHASĀBHYĀKHYĀNA. Haribhadra,[1] quoting the *Āvaśyaka Cūrṇī*, defines this as imputing to someone without due reflection a non-existent fault, such as saying, 'You are a thief, you are an adulterer'. There is a danger that the victim might be killed or otherwise punished for this if the calumny were overheard by an ill-intentioned person. According to a Prakrit verse[2] quoted anonymously by Abhayadeva and again by Hemacandra this transgression is a *bhaṅga* when spoken intentionally in the knowledge that it is untrue and an *aticāra* in other circumstances.

(ii) RAHO'BHYĀKHYĀNA. In the traditional Śvetāmbara interpretation, that of the *Āvaśyaka Cūrṇī* and Haribhadra,[3] the example cited for this *aticāra* is to say: 'They are discussing an act directed against the king'; the consequences for the persons thus calumniated are obvious. But already Siddhasena Gaṇin[4] had given an explanation drawn from the *sva-dāra-mantra-bheda aticāra*. In his view this offence is committed if, for example, an older woman is told that her husband is in love with a young girl or if a younger woman is given to understand that her husband is infatuated with a more mature rival, or if a man is informed that his wife denigrates him, saying that he is a lecherous brute (*kāma-gardabha*). Such allegations made by way of gibes constitute *aticāras*, but if there is a conscious evil intent (*abhiniveśa*) underlying them they are *bhaṅgas*.

(iii) SVA-DĀRA-MANTRA-BHEDA. Haribhadra[5] defines this as the divulging to others of what has been said by one's wife in confidence under special circumstances. His explanation is followed by successive Śvetāmbara authorities. Yaśodeva[6] takes the word *dāra* as an *upalakṣaṇa* to include 'friends' and Hemacandra[7] goes further, designating this *aticāra* as *viśvasta-mantra-bheda*. The gravity of this transgression, as is pointed out from the *Āvaśyaka Cūrṇī* onwards, lies in the fact that it might bring about the death of the wife (or friend) through shame. Because of this evil potentiality there is in it an element of *bhaṅga* and at the same time, if it is true, an element of *abhaṅga* so that it can properly

[1] Āv (H), p. 821*b*. [2] P (ŚrDh)12. [3] Āv (H), p. 821*b*.
[4] T (S) vii. 21 (p. 105). [5] Āv (H), p. 821*b*.
[6] P (Y) 11 (p. 60). [7] YŚ iii. 91.

be classed as an *aticāra*. Siddhasena Sūri[1] notes that in this offence a fact which ought not to be revealed is divulged by a person concerned and not, as in the preceding one, by a third party.

(iv) MṚŚOPADEŚA. This is explained by Siddhasena Gaṇin[2] as 'words that may cause suffering to others' such as 'Let the camels and donkeys be loaded' or 'Let the slaves be beaten'. On the basis of the *Bhāṣya* he gives also as an alternative interpretation 'showing someone how to get the better of someone else in a dispute'. Both ideas are adopted by Hemacandra[3] but the second is preferred by the other Śvetāmbara texts from the *Āvaśyaka Cūrṇī* onwards. From 'instruction in methods of deceit' this *aticāra* is extended to cover the encouragement of the study of texts mainly concerned with falsehood. Devendra,[4] however, narrows it down to 'teaching the use of unknown *mantras* and herbs'. The conventional Digambara view, exemplified by Pūjyapāda and Cāmuṇḍarāya,[5] understands by this *aticāra* the giving of advice which would be prejudicial to the attainment of *mokṣa* or to rebirth in the *deva-loka*. Āśādhara[6] offers in addition to this the choice of the first two explanations favoured by Hemacandra. If the commentator Prabhācandra is to be trusted the *parivāda* of the *Ratna-karaṇḍa*[7] is to be understood as *mṛśopadeśa*.

(v) KŪṬA-LEKHA-KARĀṆA. Haribhadra,[8] and in general the Śvetāmbara writers, understand by this the counterfeiting of another person's seal, or stamp, or the use of such a seal with a false text, but Siddhasena Gaṇin[9] more specifically relates it to the false writing of symbols on birch bark. The Digambara definition is 'alleging in writing with intent to deceive that what was not in fact said or done by someone was said or done by him'.[10] Āśādhara[11] notes both the Śvetāmbara and Digambara versions. Abhayadeva,[12] Hemacandra, and others say that this offence, though a flagrant breach of truth, is an *aticāra* and not a *bhaṅga* because the *vrata* in its literal sense applies to the speaking, and not to the writing, of *asatya*.

NYĀSĀPAHĀRA. The *Tattvārtha-bhāṣya*[13] defines this as 'the taking of a pledge deposited by another person and forgotten'.

[1] PrSU, p. 72. [2] T (S) vii. 21 (p. 104). [3] YŚ iii. 91.
[4] ŚrDK, pt. ii, p. 87. [5] CS, p. 5. [6] SDhA iv. 45.
[7] RK iii. 10. [8] Āv (H), p. 821*b*. [9] T (S) vii. 21 (p. 105).
[10] CS, p. 5. [11] SDhA iv. 45. [12] P (ŚrDh) 12.
[13] T (S) vii. 21 (p. 105).

Siddhasena Gaṇin expands this by the following example. Suppose someone has deposited in safe custody a sum of five hundred coins but when he comes to collect it, cannot remember whether the figure was five hundred or four hundred. If the holder of the money were to take advantage of that uncertainty to give back only four hundred coins he would be guilty of *nyāsāpahāra*. The same view is taken by Digambara writers.

SĀKĀRA-MANTRA-BHEDA. According to the traditional Digambara interpretation[1] this is the divulging from jealousy or other motives of the secret intention of another person as divined by watching his gestures or facial expression'. The sixteenth-century commentator Prabhācandra applies this definition to the *aticāra*, which Samantabhadra calls *paiśūnya*. Siddhasena, in his commentary on the *Tattvārtha-sūtra*,[2] had explained *paiśunya* as 'breaking up a friendship between two people by revealing what one has learned by studying gestures and expression', and *guhya-bhāṣaṇa* as 'divulging affairs of state'. In the *Bhāṣya* both are associated under the head of *sākāra-mantra-bheda*: Hemacandra in turn groups them as alternative explanations of the *guhya-bhāṣaṇa aticāra*.

In recording the *aticāras* of *sthūlāsatya* the Śvetāmbara texts sometimes note a definition of this, more precise than the general notion that it applies to the layman and not to the ascetic. Thus the *Āvaśyaka Cūrṇi*[3] defines it as 'speech by which great suffering or great hurt is caused to another person or to oneself', whilst *sūkṣmāsatya* is 'inaccurate speech used in play or in jest'; for Haribhadra[4] *sthūlāsatya* must be concerned with significant questions, *sūkṣmāsatya* implying what is trivial.

Positive definitions of *satya* are sometimes given. The *Śrāvaka-prajñapti*,[5] for instance, enjoins that the aim of speech should be the intelligent pursuit of what is best for both worlds and the avoidance of what may cause hurt to others or to oneself or both to others and to oneself. Somadeva[6] considers that in speaking one should aim at measure rather than exaggeration, esteem rather than denigration, and distinction not vulgarity of expression. Amitagati[7] maintains that all such talk as is reprehensible among

1 CS, p. 5.

2 T (S) vii. 21 (p. 106). A *Volksetymologie* is given: *prītiṃ śunayatīti piśunas tadbhāvaḥ paiśunyam*. This will be more easily understood if it is put back into a Prakrit form: *pīiṃ suṇei tti pisuṇo tab-bhāvo pesunnaṃ*.

3 Āv Cū, p. 285.

4 Āv (H) 820*b*.

5 ŚrPr 264.

6 Handiqui, p. 266.

7 Śr (A) vi. 45.

mlecchas, dishonourable to those who seek the religious life, and condemned by the doctors of the church is to be avoided; even truth when it results in suffering, fear, or harmful activity (*ārambha*). Kārttikeya[1] defines the *satya-vrata* as the avoidance of harmful, harsh, cruel, or secret speech and the use of balanced language that gives satisfaction to all living creatures and expresses the sacred truths.

The connexion of *asatya* with *hiṃsā* has been brought out in the discussion of the individual *aticāras*. Amṛtacandra[2] emphasizes that even where this is not apparent all *asatya* contains an element of careless activity (*pramatta-yoga*) which is at the root of *hiṃsā*. However, for this very same reason a sermon on the performance of religious duties even though it seems to come under the head of unpleasing (*apriya*) speech is not *asatya*.

The consequences which may ensue from speaking *asatya* are dwelt on by Hemacandra.[3] A liar may have his tongue and an ear cut off, may be beaten and imprisoned, treated with contumely, and deprived of his possessions. In another incarnation he may be afflicted with dumbness, speech defects, and foetid breath. Wilful calumny in particular is the root of endless miseries. On the other hand, one who always speaks the truth will, so popular belief avers, never be bitten by a serpent.

In the consideration of *asatya* the *abhyākhyāna* infraction has a special importance. It also forms a separate entry in the catalogue of the eighteen *pāpa-sthānas*, and figures among the *āśātanās*.

THE ASTEYA-VRATA

THE Śvetāmbara writers generally preface any discussion of stealing (*steya* or *caurya* or more generally *adattādana*, 'the taking of what has not been given') by fourfold classification of *adatta*:[4]

(i) what is not granted by its owner (*svāmy-adatta*), e.g. gold;
(ii) what is not granted by a living creature (*jīvādatta*), e.g. animal products not given by the slaughtered animal or even a fruit (which has not been given by the *jīva* inhabiting it);

[1] KA 333–4. [2] PASU 99–100. [3] YŚ ii. 53–64. [4] NPP 39.

(iii) what is not granted by the *Tīrthaṅkara* (*Tīrthaṅkarādatta*), e.g. food specially cooked by the householder for the monks (*ādhā-karman*) which, is illicit;
(iv) what is not given to the monks (*gurv-adatta*), e.g. food even though devoid of impurity which is enjoyed without inviting the gurus.

Devagupta, Yaśodeva, Abhayadeva, Hemacandra, Siddhasena Sūri, and Ratnaśekhara, listing the *adattas*, all cite as authority a verse from the *ṭīkā* of the *Praśna-vyākaraṇa*:

> *sāmi-jīvādattam Titthayāreṇaṃ tattheva ya gurūhiṃ*
> *eyaṃ adatta-sarūvaṃ parūviyam āgama-dharehim*

In fact, of course, it is only the first *adatta* with which the *asteya-vrata* is concerned.

Objects which can be stolen are divided in two ways;[1] either as:

(i) animate (*sacitta*) such as salt, horses;
(ii) inanimate (*acitta*) such as gold, silver;
(iii) partly animate, partly inanimate (*ubhaya*);

or as:

(i) two-footed (*dvi-pada*);
(ii) four-footed (*catuṣ-pada*);
(iii) without feet (*apada*).

Such categories, of which other similar specimens will be found under the *aparigraha-vrata*, have no practical importance in the discussion of theft. However, Siddhasena[2] notes these divisions and carefully explains the *Bhāṣya*'s definition of *steya*, 'the taking with intent to steal of objects—even of such things as grass—which are in the possession of others or not given by others', in such a way as to include 'what is reprehended by the scriptures', in effect the *tīrthaṅkarādatta* noted above.

The *aticāras* of this vow are given alike by Śvetāmbaras and Digambaras:

(i) receiving stolen goods (*stenāhṛtādāna*);
(ii) suborning of thieves (*taskara-prayoga*);
(iii) transgressing the limits of a hostile state (*viruddha-rājyātikrama*).

[1] ŚrPr 265; Āv (H), p. 822*b*. [2] T (S) vii. 10 (p. 76).

(iv) using false weights and measures (*kūṭa-tula-kūṭa-māna*);
(v) substitution of inferior commodities (*tat-pratirūpaka-vyavahāra*).

It is only Somadeva's[1] list which shows certain divergencies: *stena-karman* may perhaps be interpreted as equivalent to *stena-prayoga*, and *vigrahe saṃgraho 'rthasya* (accumulation of wealth in war-time) has the merit of being less ambiguous than *viruddha-rajyātikrama*. The last item, *tat-pratirūpaka-vyavahāra*, has been completely omitted but it is possible that the fourth is intended to be split up into two: 'over-weighing' and 'under-weighing', according to whether buying or selling is involved. The Digambaras in general prefer the wording *hīnādhika-mānonmāna* to describe this *aticāra*.

(i) STENĀHṚTĀDĀNA. Siddhasena,[2] following the *Tattvārtha-bhāṣya*, explains this as 'obtaining goods which are the proceeds of a robbery for nothing or at a low price'. For Haribhadra[3] it is 'acquiring cheaply through greed stolen commodities such as saffron from a foreign country'. This explanation is repeated by Devagupta, Abhayadeva, and Yaśodeva. Hemacandra prefers to follow Siddhasena Gaṇin. In the literal terms of the *vrata* this offence is not a *bhaṅga*; on the other hand since the thievish intent is present it is a *bhaṅga*, so that by definition it can be classed as an *aticāra*.[4] Siddhasena Sūri takes an identical view. Amongst the Digambaras Pūjyapāda[5] and Cāmuṇḍarāya consider this offence to mean 'obtaining something stolen from a thief without having employed or prompted him', but Āśādhara prefers to adopt Hemacandra's definition.

(ii) STENA-PRAYOGA. Siddhasena Gaṇin[6] explains this as 'providing thieves with money to ply their trade' and notes that it is wrong to sell implements of burglary. For Haribhadra[7] it means approving or encouraging thieves by saying: 'You steal this.' Abhayadeva and Yaśodeva are of the same opinion. Hemacandra and Siddhasena Sūri leave the choice open between Siddhasena Gaṇin and Haribhadra. Hemacandra, quoting Abhayadeva, pictures the offender as addressing the thieves in these terms: 'Why do you stand idle? If you have no food I will give you to eat. If you find no buyer for your wares I will take them.' Such action is a

[1] Handiqui, p. 265. [2] T (S) vii. 22 (p. 107). [3] Āv (H), p. 823*a*.
[4] YŚ iii. 92. [5] T (P) vii. 27. [6] T (S) vii. 22 (p. 107).
[7] Āv (H), p. 823*a*.

bhaṅga of the vow not to cause theft to be carried out but at the same time not a *bhaṅga* because the instigator does not himself commit theft.[1] In the Digambara view as exemplified by Pūjyapāda[2] and Cāmuṇḍarāya this *aticāra* amounts to the direct or indirect instigation of theft or the expression of approval for it. Once again Āśādhara[3] prefers to follow Hemacandra even to the extent of giving the elaborate details which would seem to belong to a *stena-śāstra*.

(iii) VIRUDDHA-RĀJYĀTIKRAMA. Siddhasena,[4] amplifying the explanation of the *Tattvārtha-bhāṣya*, renders this as 'the acquisition of property in a country which is engaged in hostilities with one's own country since even grass or wood acquired under such circumstances must be regarded as stolen'. For Haribhadra[5] the offence lies merely in the crossing of such a forbidden frontier since the ruler's command is thereby disobeyed. That this would be for the purpose of contraband is implied in Abhayadeva's[6] reference to thievish intent (*caurya-buddhi*). Hemacandra[7] and Siddhasena Sūri are more explicit: they regard the transgression of the forbidden frontier as a form of *svāmy-adatta* which would be of the nature of a *bhaṅga*, and at the same time not a *bhaṅga* because the purpose is to carry out a commercial transaction. Yaśodeva[8] even extends the *aticāra* to cover all trade in one's own country if forbidden by the ruler. The Digambaras Pūjyapāda and Cāmuṇḍarāya[9] have a noticeably different interpretation: 'the obtaining of merchandise by any means other than licit'. Samantabhadra's[10] *vilopa* is given the same definition by Prabhācandra, who then equates it with *viruddha-rājyātikrama* for, as he explains, goods of great value can be acquired with a small outlay under such circumstances.

(iv) KŪṬA-TULA-KŪṬA-MĀNA. Siddhasena,[11] expanding the interpretation of the *Tattvārtha-bhāṣya*, explains this as the use of methods which are fraudulent inasmuch as any deviation from the norm is calculated in one's own favour when buying or selling, or fixing rates of interest. Thus a tenfold or elevenfold rate of interest, which is sometimes practised out of greed, is inequitable (*anyāyya*) and illicit. For Haribhadra[12] the *aticāra* consists in giving short

1 YŚ iii. 92. 2 T (P) vii. 27. 3 SDhA iv. 47.
4 T (S) vii. 22 (p. 107). 5 Āv (H), p. 823*a*.
6 P (ŚrDh) 14. 7 YŚ iii. 92. 8 P (Y) 14.
9 CS, p. 6. 10 RK iii. 12. 11 T (S) vii. 22 (p. 107).
12 Āv (H), p. 823*a*.

measure when selling, and taking an excess when buying. Abhayadeva, Yaśodeva, and Hemacandra accept the same view. Devendra,[1] like Siddhasena Gaṇin, condemns under this head the levying of exorbitant rates of interest. The Digambara definition is extremely precise: 'fraudulent trading in which more is taken for oneself and less given to others when weighing and measuring'.[2]

(v) TAT-PRATIRŪPAKA-VYAVAHĀRA. Siddhasena,[3] following the *Tattvārtha-bhāṣya*, understands this as the counterfeiting of gold, silver, brass, copper, oil, ghee, milk, or curds with materials that resemble them in colour, weight, and other properties, as well as the use of fraudulent devices in trading. As an example of these, it is mentioned that when cattle are stolen the shape of their horns can be changed at will if these are fomented with stewed *kaliṅgi* fruits; otherwise they would be too easily recognizable to be kept or sold. According to Haribhadra[4] this *aticāra* is no more than the adulteration of commodities such as mixing *palañji* with rice, or fat with ghee. Other Śvetāmbara authorities take the same view. Siddhasena Sūri[5] (who gives to this *aticāra* the name of *saḍṛśa-yuti*) and Hemacandra[6] mention amongst other substances mixed with, or substituted for, more valuable ones: *khādira* resin for asafoetida, and urine for oil. Hemacandra considers that this *aticāra* may refer to methods of *vyāji-karaṇa* such as deforming the horns of cattle. For the Digambaras[7] it implies 'fraudulent trading in factitious gold and similar commodities, or more specifically in a later text the *Praśnottara-śrāvakācāra*[8] 'coining false money'; but as on other points here again Āśādhara's views belong with the Śvetāmbaras. Like the preceding *aticāra* this offence can be held to be a *bhaṅga* because people are deprived of their property by false pretences but at the same time not a *bhaṅga* because what is involved is in fact just a commercial transaction.[9]

The transgressions of the *asteya-vrata* discussed above apply, it is clear, more particularly to members of the trading class. But Hemacandra,[9] and with him Āśādhara,[10] raise the point that they may also be committed by the king's ministers and other officials. Thus a vassal ruler (*sāmanta*) who assists an enemy of the king to whom he owes allegiance is guilty of *viruddha-rājyātikrama*.

[1] ŚrDK, pt. ii, p. 91. [2] CS, p. 6. [3] T (S) vii. 22 (p. 108).
[4] Āv (H), p. 823*a*. [5] PSU 273. [6] YŚ iii. 92.
[7] CS, p. 6. [8] *Praśnottara-śrāvakācāra*, xiv. 27.
[9] YŚ iii. 92. [10] SDhA iv. 50.

Officials of the royal treasury are also liable to commit the fourth and fifth *aticāras* in the course of their duties.

Several writers (Abhayadeva, Yaśodeva, Hemacandra) quote a verse from the *Praśna-vyākaraṇa-ṭīkā*:

> *coro corāvago mantī bheya-nnu kāṇaga-kkayī*
> *anna-do thāṇa-do ceva coro satta-viho mao*[1]

According to this popular dictum the category of thief includes the robber, the receiver, the king's minister, the retail trader, the purveyor of food, and the purveyor of office. Another classification of thieves which would appear to have been taken from a *stena-śāstra* is too lengthy to be recorded here.

A distinction of *sthūla-steya* and *sūkṣma-steya* is made in the early Śvetāmbara texts. For Haribhadra,[2] following the *Āvaśyaka Cūrṇi*, the latter implies appropriating trivial objects like rubble from the roadside without asking permission.

For the Digambaras the classical definition of theft is contained in the verse of the *Ratna-karaṇḍa*:[3]

> *nihitaṃ vā patitaṃ vā su-vismṛtaṃ vā parasvam aviśṛṣṭam*
> *na harati yan na ca datte tad-akṛśa-cauryād uparamaṇam*

'not taking the property of others whether pledged or dropped or forgotten unless it has been given'. Cāmuṇḍarāya,[4] taking over this definition, adds 'or if abandoned owing to fear of princes or from some other cause'. Vasunandin[5] and the Śvetāmbara Hemacandra[6] have almost identical verses. Somadeva[7] insists that nothing that belongs to others may be appropriated 'whether in a house or on the highway or on water or in the woods or in the hills'; and his words are echoed by Amitagati:[8] not even a blade of grass is to be taken if it belongs to someone else.

The connexion of theft with *hiṃsā* is brought out by Amitagati:[9] 'whoever takes the possessions of a man takes away his life since they represent his external vital force giving him consolation.' Through the suffering he causes to others the thief is to be classed with the oil-presser, the hunter, the butcher, the cat, and the tiger. From another angle it is contended that *hiṃsā* is a necessary concomitant of theft since it occurs through *pramatta-yoga*.[10]

1 P.(Y) 14 (p. 67). 2 Āv (H), p. 822*b*. 3 RK iii. 11.
4 CS, p. 6. 5 Śr (V) 211. 6 YŚ ii. 66.
7 Handiqui, p. 265. 8 Śr (A) vi. 60. 9 Ibid. 61–63.
10 PASU 104.

There are reminiscences of the *aticāras* in some Digambara works which do not enumerate them: the *Dvādaśānuprekṣā*,[1] for example, describes the *asteya-vrata* in these terms: not buying a valuable article at a low price, being contented with a small profit, not appropriating something that has been forgotten, and not taking the property of others through anger or greed.

Āśādhara[2] extends the scope of the *asteya-vrata* in various ways. Thus when any doubt arises as to whether or not an object belongs to oneself to take it would be to break the vow. Nothing that has not been given is to be appropriated with the exception of property from the succession of a dead relative and of such things as the water of a river or the grass of a meadow which are common property. For example, if a buried hoard is found it must be left alone since, as treasure trove, it is without an owner but belongs to the ruler of the state. A late text, the fifteenth-century *Praśnottara-śrāvakācara*,[3] contains a provision that if a man is unable to leave alone money or other valuables which have been dropped on the ground he should devote them to the performance of *pūjā* in the Jaina temple.

It should be remembered that theft is also one of the seven *vyasanas* and is treated in many Digambara works under that head.

THE BRAHMA-VRATA

VARIOUS preliminary classifications, all summarized in the *Nava-pada-prakaraṇa*, are current. Thus mention is made of twenty-four, ten, and eight divisions of *kāma* all ascribed by Devagupta[4] to the *Dharmārtha-kāmādhyayana* of the *Daśavaikalika-sūtra*; *Brahma* (abstinence from sexual intercourse) is of eighteen kinds, nine relating to celestial females (*vaikriya*) and nine to terrestrial females (*audārika*). *Maithuna* (copulation) is twofold, relating to the *vaikriya* and *audārika* classes and the latter is again divided up into animal and human categories. Under this last head are distinguished: *sva-dāra* (one's own wife or concubine), *para-dāra* (any woman under the authority of another man), and *veśyā* (a prostitute who is considered to have no owner).

[1] KA 335.
[2] SDhA iv. 46–49.
[3] *Praśnottara-śrāvakācāra*, xiv. 6.
[4] NPP 48–50.

Further the standpoint from which the whole subject is treated is only understandable on the basis of three sexes (an assumption common to ancient Hinduism and Buddhism) expressed in Jainism in the theory of the three sex urges (*veda*)—*puṃ*, *strī*, *napuṃsaka*.[1] The triad of male, female, and androgyne seems to conserve memories of an earlier stage of society in which the hermaphrodite was accorded a role of special importance.[2] Mirrored in the grammatical categories of the language it offered a neat response to the desire for schematization.

The *brahma-vrata* differs from all the other vows in its double formulation: positive in the sense of 'contentment with one's own wife' (*sva-dāra-santoṣa*) and negative as 'avoidance of the wives of others' (*a-para-dāra-gamana*). In the former case the translation 'wife' rather than 'wives' or 'women' has been chosen deliberately for reasons that will be apparent later, though in fact the issue of monogamy or polygamy continues to be debated in the texts, despite a social context in which polygamy is the natural prerogative of the well-to-do. Some authorities hold that of the five *aticāras* listed below only the last three can be said to transgress this vow in its negative formulation.

The traditional designations of these *aticāras* are:

(i) intercourse with a woman temporarily taken to wife (*itvara-parigṛhītā-gamana*);
(ii) intercourse with an unmarried woman (*a-parigṛhītā-gamana*);
(iii) love-play (*anaṅga-krīḍā*);
(iv) match-making (*para-vivāha-karaṇa*);
(v) excessive predilection for the pleasures of the senses (*kāma-bhoga-tīvrābhilāṣa*).

For the third and fourth *aticāras* the designations may be said to be invariable and the interpretation substantially the same. Under varying labels two quite separate views on the meaning of the fifth are apparent. Most of the earlier Śvetāmbaras—and it would

[1] The translation 'androgyne' rather than 'neuter' seems to respond best to the usage of the Jaina texts.

[2] Cf. Jean Przyluski, *La Grande Déesse* (Paris, 1950), p. 182: *Entre la Grande Mère et le dieu suprême, père de tous les êtres, on trouve une divinité intermédiaire androgyne. Or le prêtre est semblable au dieu. On ne doit donc pas être surpris de rencontrer à côté de la Vénus hermaphrodite . . . des prêtres bissexués ou supposés tels. . . . Les devins étaient considérés comme des androgynes. Il est possible qu'en théorie tout devin dut être androgyne. . . .*

seem from the wording of the *Upāsaka-daśāḥ* itself that their interpretation is nearer to the intention of the canon—hold that it refers to the pleasures that can be obtained from the eye and ear and the senses of taste, smell, and touch. This is the view offered by Abhayadeva,[1] Devagupta, and Yaśodeva; and it is favoured as an alternative by Municandra. Haribhadra[2] had used it in combination with the second interpretation (favoured by the later Śvetāmbaras and all Digambaras) that the *aticāra* merely refers to excessive venery. It is in the treatment of the first and second *aticāras* that most uncertainty, sometimes provoked by textual variants, prevails. Samantabhadra[3] and Āśādhara are noteworthy as the exponents of an aberrant tradition that fuses these two transgressions into one and inserts in the missing space of the table a totally novel item: *viṭatva* (obscene language).

Naturally the first and second *aticāras* cannot apply to women. To rob a co-wife of a night with the husband that should properly be hers, to make advances to her husband when he has taken a vow of *brahmacarya*, or—though this would more properly be considered a *bhaṅga*—to take a lover are named as offences that may be substituted for them. The distinction of *sva-dāra-santoṣa* and *para-dāra-virati* is of course only valid for men.[4] Except for Āśādhara[5] no Digambara writer makes reference to *aticāras* committed by women.

Siddhasena Gaṇin,[6] in a definition that imposes a harsh precision on ideas in which animistic concepts are fused, classifies *maithuna* as animate (*sa-cetana*) and inanimate (*acetana*):

Sa-cetana: (i) of a man, with a female (celestial, human, or animal);
(ii) of a man, with another man or with an androgyne. This includes masturbation as well as homosexuality;
(iii) masturbation by a woman or use of a plant root as an artificial phallus.

Acetana: (i) of a man, with the statue of a woman (celestial, human, or animal) fashioned in plaster, wood, stone, or leather, or in the form of a painting;

[1] P(A) 16. [2] Āv (H), p. 825*b*. [3] RK iii. 14.
[4] YŚ iii. 94 (p. 558). [5] SDhA iv. 58. [6] T (S) vii. 11 (p. 78).

(ii) with other inanimate objects such as the current of a stream or clay;

(iii) of a woman, with an inanimate phallus of wood or with other artificial devices.

The introduction of the concepts *sa-cetana* and *acetana* into the content of this *aṇu-vrata* seems to be an innovation as it does not appear in the main stream of the Śvetāmbara commentaries, but it recurs among the Digambaras, and Amitagati, for example, refers to females, human, animal, and inanimate.[1]

(i) ITVARA-PARIGṚHITĀ-GAMANA. The first element of the compound raises numerous difficulties. Siddhasena Gaṇin[2] offers two explanations: either *itvarā* (*itvarī*, *itvarikā*) signifies a harlot or else the word is used elliptically for *itvara-kālaṃ*, implying a woman taken for a short time. In any event he regards the *aticāra* as prohibiting intercourse with a prostitute if she is being kept by one man since for a limited period she has ceased to be common property. Haribhadra,[3] too, favours the interpretation 'a kept woman', and Abhayadeva, Yaśodeva, Hemacandra, and Siddhasena Sūri take the same view. This transgression has the character of an *aticāra*, being both a *bhaṅga* because the kept woman, in the mind of her lover, has become his property and been assimilated to the status of a temporary wife, and yet not a *bhaṅga* since she will in fact revert to being a prostitute when her temporary contract expires.[4] Āśādhara,[5] who calls this offence *itvarikā-gamana*, follows closely the explanations of Hemacandra but extends the meaning of *itvarikā* to include any woman who has become 'ownerless' through the loss of her husband and who leads a disorderly life. The parallel offence in Samantabhadra's[6] list seems from Prabhācandra's comment to refer to intercourse with any unchaste woman. For Cāmuṇḍarāya,[7] and presumably for the other Digambara authorities who distinguish this *aticāra* from the next, it refers simply to the frequentation of prostitutes.

(ii) A-PARIGṚHITĀ-GAMANA. For Siddhasena Gaṇin[8] this designation covers intercourse with any 'ownerless' woman whether she be a whore, or a married woman whose husband is absent, or any other woman outside the control of her family. The same acceptation is given to the term by Haribhadra, Abhayadeva,

[1] Śr (A) xii. 77.
[2] T (S) vii. 23 (p. 108).
[3] Āv (H), p. 825*a*.
[4] YŚ iii. 94 (p. 555).
[5] SDhA iv. 58.
[6] RK iii. 14.
[7] CS, p. 6.
[8] T (S) vii. 23 (p. 108).

Yaśodeva, Hemacandra, and Siddhasena Sūri. It is an *aticāra* of *sva-dāra-santoṣa*. A Digambara interpretation is available only from Cāmuṇḍarāya,[1] who holds that this offence is committed with an 'ownerless' woman who is a wanton. Devendra[2] understands by *a-parigṛhītā* 'a widow'.

(iii) ANAṄGA-KRĪḌĀ. Siddhasena Gaṇin's[3] explanation of this seems to overlap with the following *aticāra*. He understands by it a combination of methods to heighten sexual passion: the use of artificial phalli made of wood, leather, clay, and other constituents, caressing the sexual organs, pulling the hair, biting and marking with the nails. Such practices he says, result in disease for the persons who give way to them. Haribhadra's[4] definition is virtually the same: caressing a woman after coitus in order to re-inflame desire, and with Abhayadeva[5] he offers in addition an alternative interpretation: toying (*krīḍā*) with parts of the body—the breasts, loins, armpits or face—other than the sexual organs (literally *an-aṅga* 'not the organ'); Hemacandra and Siddhasena Sūri leave the choice open between this second version and that of Siddhasena Gaṇin. This offence may be regarded as an *aticāra* not a *bhaṅga* because it refers to caresses and love-play, and not to the complete sexual act.[6] The Digambara authorities, including in this case Āśādhara,[7] understand this *aticāra* to include various sexual deviations, particularly fellatio and cunnilinguism.

(iv) KĀMA-BHOGA-TĪVRĀBHILĀṢA. The conventional Śvetāmbara description of this offence visualizes a man who abandons all other thoughts and occupations in order to concentrate his every energy on the satisfaction of his sexual desires, and when his virility fails him has recourse to aphrodisiacs in the hope of attaining the potency of a stallion or bull elephant.[8] Such is the explanation furnished in almost identical language by Siddhasena Gaṇin, Hemacandra, Siddhasena Sūri, and Āśādhara. But as has already been noted this concept does not seem to be the most original. Haribhadra[8] explains that *kāma* means the senses of sight and hearing and *bhoga* those of taste, smell, and touch; the *aticāra* would therefore amount to 'an excessive propensity for the pleasures afforded by the five senses'; but these lead on to the inflaming of passion 'by using the nails or teeth or lotus leaves and

[1] CS, p. 6.
[2] ŚrDK, pt. ii, p. 95.
[3] T (S) vii. 23 (p. 109).
[4] Āv (H), p. 825*a*.
[5] P (A) 16.
[6] YŚ iii. 94.
[7] SDhA iv. 58.
[8] Āv (H), p. 825*b*.

by taking aphrodisiacs or by caressing the woman's pudenda'. This is also the view of Abhayadeva[1] and Yaśodeva, who point out that the vow of *sva-dāra-santoṣa* implies that copulation should never be prolonged once desire is appeased. The vow is sullied if a man seeks to prolong his gratification by the use of aphrodisiacs or of the methods taught in the *kāma-śāstras*.[2] Apart from Āśādhara the Digambaras, who prefer the designation *kāma-tīvrābhiniveśa* (or in Samantabhadra's case *vipula-tṛṣā*), regard the *aticāra* as 'an excessive manifestation of sexual passion.'[3] Devendra[4] understands by this 'lip-biting and other love-play' or else the 84 poses of Vātsyāyana.

(v) PARA-VIVĀHA-KARAṆĀ. Siddhasena Gaṇin,[5] noting that the abstention from this implied in the taking of the *vrata* may seem strange since a householder must of necessity marry off his children, finds an analogy in the duality of the vow itself. A layman promises by *sva-dāra-santoṣa* to abstain from the enjoyment of all women save his own wife; similarly he is to abstain from arranging the marriages of other people's offspring but not of his own. The use of the word *para* implies, says Haribhadra,[6] that he is actuated by a relationship of affection or by desire for the bride-price (*kanyā-phala*). Abhayadeva[7] further comments that the question of bride-price does not arise for a person of right faith whilst an unbeliever will not have taken the vows. However, he must ensure that his own daughters are married off since otherwise they would be led into evil courses. Abhayadeva also notes the view held by some authorities that this *aticāra* implies an obligation to monogamy since it excludes a second marriage (*para-vivāha*) of oneself: in fact the very phrase *sva-dāra-santoṣa* would indicate that to take a second wife implies dissatisfaction with the first.[8] Hemacandra[9] and Siddhasena Sūri, summarizing all the preceding considerations, emphasize that in the case of one's children to marry them represents the lesser of two evils. There is an element of fault in it, but to neglect to do so would be worse still. In general, *para-vivāha-karaṇa* is a *bhaṅga* if one has in mind that its result is copulation, but not a *bhaṅga* if one thinks of it only as a ceremony. Devendra[10] interprets *para* as *parakīya* 'those belonging to others' and so by

[1] P (A) 15.
[2] P (Y) v. 16.
[3] CS, p. 7.
[4] ŚrDK, pt. ii, p. 95.
[5] T (S) vii. 23 (p. 108).
[6] Āv (H), p. 825*b*.
[7] P (A) 16.
[8] Ibid. (p. 26).
[9] YŚ iii. 94 (p. 556).
[10] ŚrDK, pt. ii, p. 95.

definition excludes from the *aticāra* the marrying of one's own children. In this he is in accord with the Digambara tradition as explicitly stated by Pūjyapāda,[1] and implied by Cāmuṇḍarāya. Āśādhara[2] follows the detail of Hemacandra's explanations. The *Āvaśyaka Cūrṇī*[3] has evidently preserved a very ancient tradition when it relates this *aticāra* to beasts as well as to men. Thus to say 'let the bull be released in the *go-dhana*' would be to transgress the *vrata* in the same way as if one said 'let the nubile girl be wedded'. Later writers treat such advice as a contravention of the *anartha-daṇḍa-vrata*.

Siddhasena Gaṇin[4] notes a variant reading for the *Tattvārtha-sūtra* which would lay down the first two *aticāras* to be *itvarikā-gamana* and *parigṛhitāparigṛhitā-gamana*. The former would then apply to intercourse with a low or contemptible woman (*kutsita-saṃkīrṇa-yoṣit*) explained as 'one who is mentally or physically defective or who has entered the religious life'; it is reprehensible because it might incur punishment from the ruler and disparagement from the public. The second *aticāra* would then be 'intercourse with a prostitute or with a married woman separated from her husband'.

There is some uncertainty as to which *aticāras* belong to *sva-dāra-santoṣa* and which to *para-dāra-virati*, though by general agreement the last three are common to both. As to the first two offences, three different opinions[5] prevail:

1. That both are *aticāras* of *sva-dāra-santoṣa* but not of *para-dāra-virati*: this is often referred to as 'Haribhadra Sūri's opinion'.[6]
2. That the first is an *aticāra* only of *para-dāra-virati* and the second only of *sva-dāra-santoṣa*.
3. That both are *aticāras* of *para-dāra-virati* but not of *sva-dāra-santoṣa*. The authority for this is a Prakrit verse quoted in the *Śrāvaka-dharma-pañcāśaka*:

> *para-dara-vajjiṇo pañca honti tinni u sa-dāra-santuṭṭhe*
> *itthīe tinni pañca va bhaṅga-vigappehiṃ aiyārā*

This view, like the first, is at least as old as the *Āvaśyaka Cūrṇī*.[7]

[1] T (P) vii. 28.
[2] SDhA iv. 58.
[3] Āv Cū, pt. ii, p. 292.
[4] T (S) vii. 23 (p. 109).
[5] YŚ iii. 94 (p. 557).
[6] PS 277 (p. 73).
[7] Āv Cū, pt. ii, p. 291.

As has been noted elsewhere, all sexual intercourse is to be condemned. At best, in the words of Yaśodeva,[1] a layman may be permitted, if he cannot resist the sex urge but being fearful of sin (*pāpa-bhīru*) does not wish to be unchaste, to have recourse to a limited use of his own wife. Āśādhara[2] concedes that if he fails to be convinced that meditation and not copulation is the remedy for the disease of lust he may seek such satisfaction. The fever of concupiscence is no more quenched by satisfaction, says Hemacandra,[3] than fire is extinguished by oblations of ghee. The concession may in the general view of the *ācāryas* go further than the use of one's wife and include recourse to prostitutes, but an *anya-strī* (a married woman, or an unmarried girl in the care of her parents) must always be left alone.

Enjoyment of women betakes of the nature of affliction because like fever it brings on thirst, and delirium, and exhaustion of the body. The passionate pleasure of the encounter can give no real satisfaction.[4] Two reasons[5] are alleged as a basis for the condemnation of all carnal contact; that in a moral sense the calm of the soul is disturbed by the increase of the passions of love and hate; and that in a physical sense the sexual act is always accompanied by *hiṃsā*.[6] The second is the expression of a concept which goes back to the canonical texts[7] and on which the Digambaras particularly expatiate, adducing it in support of the contention that a woman cannot attain *mokṣa* in this life. It is held that there are always present in the navel, armpits, and pudenda of a woman myriads of minute living creatures of which large numbers perish during every act of coitus. Thus Amṛtacandra[8] likens the act to the introduction of a heated iron bar into a tube containing grains of sesamum and adds that it has similar destructive results. *Anaṅga-krīḍā* multiplies the risk of *hiṃsā*. The Śvetāmbaras who recognize the possibility of *strī-mukti* do not often touch on this subject, which, however, finds a place in Hemacandra's[9] exposition of the *brahma-vrata*. Concerned as often in other places to seek support for the

[1] P (Y) 15. [2] SDhA iv. 51. [3] YŚ ii. 81.
[4] SDhA iv. 53–54. [5] Ibid. 55.
[6] It is curious to note that Jainism concurs with Christianity in condemning for a very different motivation, all sexual intercourse. Cf. De Sanchez, *De matrimonii sacro sacramento. 'Non desunt ex doctoribus catholicis qui doceant actum conjugalem non posse absque culpa saltem veniali exerceri.'*
[7] See Schubring, *Das Mahānisīha-Sūtta*, p. 70. [8] PASU 108.
[9] YŚ ii. 79.

Jaina concept in outside sources, he quotes Vātsyāyana's *Kāma-sūtra* for the statement that 'tiny worms generated in the blood are to be found in a woman's sexual organs where they produce an itching'.[1] For this apparent attempt at rationalization there would seem to be no justification in the earlier texts.

A distinction is sometimes made between *sthūla-maithuna* and *sūkṣma-maithuna*. According to a definition that comes from a late authority[2] the former is enjoyment of women, human or celestial, in mind, word, or action whilst the latter implies a slight exciting of the sense-organs under the stimulus of desire.

From the oldest stratum of Jainism comes the injunction to avoid, as the *Śrāvaka-prajñapti*[3] puts it, 'the delusive sight of the bodies of women'. Devagupta and his commentator Yaśodeva[4] mention a special *yatanā* or striving for those who seek to perfect the *brahma-vrata*:

> *chann'-aṅga-daṃsaṇe phāsaṇe ya go-mutta-gahaṇa-ku-ssumiṇe*
> *jayaṇā savvattha kare indiya-avaloyaṇe ca tahā*

In other words a man should never stare at, or touch, the sexual organs of a woman or vice versa. Against the background of a pantheistic concept of the universe this interdiction is naturally extended to the animal creation. It is therefore forbidden to stimulate a cow to urinate by rubbing its vagina; the urine should be collected when it is discharged naturally. Again, when a seminal emission occurs during sleep the mind should be concentrated in meditation on the sacred doctrine after recitation of the *pañca-namaskāra*.

Amongst the Digambara writers who do not detail the *aticāras* of the *brahma-vrata* Kārttikeya[5] defines it as 'regarding the wife of another as one's own sister or daughter and realizing that the bodies of women are full of impurity and that beauty and charm can only delude the mind'. For Vasunandin[6] it implies the complete renunciation of *anaṅga-krīḍā* and the abstinence from sexual relations during the *parvan* days. The arrows of Kāmadeva are, he says, fatal to a righteous life.

As will have become evident, the *aticāras* of this *vrata* cover most aspects of sexual deviations. Adultery (*para-dāra*) and fornication

[1] YŚ ii. 80. [2] Ratnaśekhara on *Śrāddha-pratikramaṇa-sūtra*, 15.
[3] ŚrPr 274. [4] P (Y) 17 (p. 72). [5] KA 337–8.
[6] Śr (V) 211.

(*veśyā*) also figure among the seven *vyasanas* and are treated at length under that head in the popular literature. But the offence which incurs the keenest reprobation does not figure in any category. From the earliest days of Jainism there is evident an almost obsessional horror of incest. Thus Haribhadra,[1] repeating the words of the *Āvaśyaka Cūrṇī*, says that if the *brahma-vrata* were not enforced there would be a grave danger of a man having carnal connexion with his mother or sister or daughter through unrestrained lust. A series of cautionary tales to drive home this point are recounted by almost every writer on *śrāvakācāra* and any reference to marriage makes exogamy mandatory.

THE APARIGRAHA-VRATA

THIS vow of non-attachment which alone of the *aṇu-vratas* has no correspondent among the *mahā-vratas* of monks refers both to internal (*abhyantara*) and external (*bahya*) *parigraha*. There are fourteen varieties of the former which are listed by Amṛtacandra,[2] Somadeva, and Āśādhara among the Digambaras and by Siddhasena Gaṇin[3] among the Śvetāmbaras. They are in fact largely irrelevant to the consideration of the *vrata*, but for the sake of completeness will be noted here (they of course comprise the *kaṣāyas* and *no-kaṣāyas*):

(1) false belief (*mithyātva*);
(2) anger (*krodha*);
(3) pride (*māna*);
(4) deceit (*māyā*);
(5) greed (*lobha*);
(6) sense of the absurd (*hāsya*);
(7) pleasure (*rati*);
(8) displeasure, dejection (*arati*);
(9) fear (*bhaya*);
(10) sorrow (*śoka*);
(11) disgust (*jugupsā*);
(12) male sex urge (*puṃ-veda*);
(13) female sex urge (*strī-veda*);
(14) androgyne sex urge (*napuṃsaka-veda*).

It is with the ten or (in the more current enumeration) nine

[1] Āv (H), p. 823*b*. [2] PASU 116. [3] T (S) vii. 24.

external objects of *parigraha* that the vow is concerned. These are:

ŚVETĀMBARA[1]	DIGAMBARA[2]
(1) land (*kṣetra*);	(1) land (*kṣetra*);
(2) houses (*vāstu*);	(2) houses (*vāstu*);
(3) silver (*hiraṇya*);	(3) gold coins (*hiraṇya*);
(4) gold (*suvarṇa*);	(4) gold (*suvarṇa*);
(5) diverse commodities (*dhana*);	(5) livestock (*dhana*);
(6) grain (*dhānya*);	(6) grain (*dhānya*);
(7) servants and birds (*dvipada*);	(7) maidservants (*dāsī*);[3]
(8) livestock (*catuṣpada*);	(8) menservants (*dāsa*);[3]
(9) furniture (*kupya*).	(9) cloth (*kupya*);
	(10) beds (*śayyāsana*).

Detailed classifications of all these types of possessions drawn from the canonical literature are found in almost all the Śvetāmbara authorities[4] and although they seem to have no direct relation with the interpretation of the *vrata* they will be enumerated here. The oldest distinction is that of *sacitta* (animate) and *acitta* (inanimate) objects.[5]

1. Land; this is of three types:

(*a*) *setu-kṣetra*—land irrigated artificially by norias (*araghaṭṭa*) or other means;
(*b*) *ketu-kṣetra*—dry farming land depending on rain;
(*c*) *miśra*—irrigated land which also receives rain.

2. Houses; again of three types:

(*a*) excavated (*khāta*);
(*b*) raised (*ucchrita*);
(*c*) a combination of both (*khātocchrita*).

3. The unanimous testimony of the Śvetāmbara texts interprets *hiraṇya* as 'silver, minted or unminted' and, in fact, the later works from Devendra's *Śrāddha-dina-kṛtya*[6] onwards replace *hiraṇya* by

[1] NPP 58. [2] CS, p. 7.
[3] The translation 'servants' is based on the author's own explanation *bhṛtya-strī-puruṣa-varga* but *dāsa* and *dāsī* are certainly in many instances better trans lated by 'slaves'. See Premī, op. cit., pp. 546–53.
[4] e.g. P (A) 17, 18. [5] e.g. ŚrPr 275. [6] ŚrDK p. 98.

less ambiguous terms. For the Digambara *ācāryas* it seems always to have meant 'coins whether of gold or silver'.

4. There is no hesitation in the interpretation of the word as 'gold', for the Digambaras 'unminted,' for the Śvetāmbaras 'minted or unminted'.

5. The Śvetāmbaras, giving a very broad sense to *dhana*, class it into four categories:[1]

(*a*) What can be counted (*gaṇima*): such as nutmegs (*jāti-phala*), betel nuts (*pūga-phala*);
(*b*) What can be contained (*dharima*): such as saffron (*kuṅkuma*), molasses (*guḍa*);
(*c*) What can be measured (*meya*): such as salt, ghee, oil;
(*d*) What can be divided up (*päricchedya*): such as gems and cloth.

6. There is no unanimity on the number of varieties of *dhānya*: the earlier Śvetāmbaras name seven or eight sorts, Hemacandra and Siddhasena Sūri fix the figure at seventeen, whilst Devendra (and with him later writers such as Ratnaśekhara and Yaśovijaya) prefers a list of twenty-four drawn from the *Daśavaikālika-niryukti*. Here is Hemacandra's list:[2]

(*a*) rice (*vrīhi*);
(*b*) barley (*yava*);
(*c*) lentils (*masūra*);
(*d*) wheat (*godhūma*);
(*e*) the pulse *Phaseolus Mungo* (*mudga*);
(*f*) the pulse *Phaseolus radiatus* (*māṣa*);
(*g*) sesamum (*tila*);
(*h*) the grain *Panicum miliaceum* (*aṇava*);
(*i*) chickpeas (*caṇaka*);
(*j*) Italian millet, *Panicum italicum* (*priyaṅgu*);
(*k*) the grain *Paspalum scrabiculatum* (*kodrava*);
(*l*) hemp (*sana*);
(*m*) a kind of pulse (*kalāya*);
(*n*) the pulse *Dolichos uniflorus* (*kulattha*);
(*o*) the pulse *Phaseolus aconitifolius* (*makuṣṭa*);
(*p*) rice (*śāli*);
(*q*) the pulse *Cajanus indicus* (*āḍhaki*).

7 and 8. *Dvipada* is generally taken to include all the members of the household (wives, slaves, servants) and also domesticated birds such as parrots or peacocks. The oldest texts, for example, the

[1] P (A) 18 (p. 28). [2] YŚ iii. 95.

Āvaśyaka Cūrṇi[1] mention alongside *dvipada* and *catuṣpada* a category of *apada* objects including carts and trees. Carts figure at a much later date in the *dvipada* class of the *Śrāddha-dina-kṛtya*,[2] inappropriately in the context as they cannot be said to propagate themselves.

9. *Kupya* is used by the Śvetāmbaras[3] to mean household chattels (*gṛhopaskāra*) made of iron, copper, brass, tin, lead, earthenware, bamboo, or wood, such as pots and pans, buckets, beds, chairs. It also includes carts and ploughs. The Digambaras[4] seem to understand the expression to mean what might be called luxury goods: sandal (*candana*), silk (*kṣauma*), cotton cloth (*karpāsa*), silk dresses (*kauśeya*).

Ratnaśekhara,[5] who is later than the period we are discussing, recalls a classification of the householder's property from the *Daśavaikālika-niryukti* where six categories are distinguished:

(1) *dhānya*—of which there are twenty-four kinds;
(2) *ratna*—a comprehensive list again of twenty-four kinds: gold, silver, brass, tin, iron, lead, minted coins, semi-precious stones, diamonds, precious stones, pearls, coral, conches, aloe wood, sandalwood, cotton cloth, woollen cloth, timber, hides, ivory, yaks' tails, perfumes, and resin (*dravyauṣadha*);
(3) *sthāvara*—the three kinds of immovable property are: land (presumably arable land), houses, and orchard land (*taru-gaṇa* explained as 'groves of coconut and similar trees');
(4) *dvipada*—there are two kinds of bipeds: human beings and two-wheeled carts;
(5) *catuṣpada*—ten varieties of livestock are listed as quadrupeds: oxen, buffaloes, camels, goats, sheep, thoroughbred horses (*aśva*, i.e. *jātya*), ordinary horses (*ghoṭaka*, i.e. *ajātya*), mules, asses, and elephants;
(6) *kupya*—implements and utensils of various kinds, no figure being given.

In the traditional Śvetāmbara view the *aticāras* of this *vrata* are:

(i) exceeding the limits set for land and houses by incorporation (*yojanena kṣetra-vāstu-pramāṇātikrama*);

[1] Āv Cū, pt. ii, p. 292. [2] ŚrDK, p. 99. [3] YŚ iii. 95.
[4] CS, p. 7. [5] Ratnaśekhara on *Śraddha-pratikramana-sūtra*, 18.

(ii) exceeding the limits set for gold and silver by donation (*pradānena hiraṇya-suvarṇa pramānātikrama*);

(iii) exceeding the limits set for grain and other foodstuffs by packaging together (*bandhanena dhana-dhānya-pramāṇātikrama*);

(iv) exceeding the limits set for bipeds and quadrupeds by natural reproduction (*kāraṇena dvipada-catuṣpada-pramāṇātikrama*);

(v) exceeding the limits set for household chattels by combination (*bhāvena kupya-pramāṇātikrama*).

All these *aticāras* consist in using various expedients to circumvent the interdictions which devolve from a man's self-imposed restrictions on the extent of his property. Any overt breach of this *vrata* which is a form of *pratyākhyāna* would constitute a *bhaṅga*.

For those Śvetāmbara writers who are influenced by the *Tattvārtha-sūtra*—Siddhasena Gaṇin[1] and Haribhadra—and in general for the Digambara authorities, the *aticāras* imply no more than wilfully exceeding the limits set for the nine categories of possessions ranged under the five heads above. Samantabhadra,[2] though aware of these categories, has established a totally novel series of *aticāras*:

(i) *ati-vāhana*—out of greed of gain driving oxen or other beasts of burden for a greater distance than they can comfortably go;

(ii) *ati-saṃgraha*—hoarding of grain or other commodities in the hope of making a very high profit, so as to obtain a big return on capital;

(iii) *ati-vismaya*—extreme disappointment at having sold something at a price involving a loss;

(iv) *ati-lobha*—excessive greed expressed in wishing for a higher price when a good price has been obtained;

(v) *ati-bhāra-vahana*—overloading of beasts of burden through greed of gain.

More than any other similar provisions of the moral code these *aticāras* are designed exclusively for the trading community; and the fact that the last of them is little more than a repetition of the fifth *aticāra* of the *ahiṃsā-vrata* emphasizes their secondary character. In fact Samantabhadra's innovation in this field was imitated by none of his successors except Sakalakīrti.

[1] T (S) vii. 24. [2] RK iii. 16.

Returning to the original enumeration of the *aticāras* we find the following elucidations in the commentators:[1]

(i) YOJANENA KṢETRA-VĀSTU-PRAMĀṆĀTIKRAMA. The assumption is that a man has taken a vow of *pratyākhyāna* that he will not possess more than a given number of houses or fields. Suppose then, for example, that he acquires an additional field; and to avoid breaking the letter of his undertaking incorporates this with a field already in his ownership by removing a boundary fence. Though he will still have the same number of fields he will have committed an *aticāra* but not a *bhaṅga* of his vow.

(ii) PRADĀNENA HIRAṆYA-SUVARṆA-PRAMĀṆĀTIKRAMA. In this case if a man, perhaps as a gift from a satisfied prince, acquires gold or silver in excess of the limits which he has imposed on himself, for a period of say four months, he may give it to a third party—to his wife, for example—on the understanding that he will get it back when the time limit of his *pratyākhyāna* has passed. Here again he will not have broken the letter of his vow but will, all the same, have committed an *aticāra*.

(iii) BANDHANENA DHANA-DHĀNYA-PRAMĀṆĀTIKRAMA. Suppose that someone has imposed on himself *pratyākhyāna* in respect of the acquisition of grain and other commodities for a period of four months, but is about to receive additional stocks. If he then goes along and has these tied up in bundles with ropes and leaves them where they are until he has sold the stocks already on his premises he will in a similar way have been guilty of an *aticāra*.

(iv) KĀRAṆENA DVIPADA-CATUṢPADA-PRAMĀṆĀTIKRAMA. Here it is assumed that a man has vowed not to increase his live-stock, say, for a year. If they were allowed to breed freely in the meantime he would break the *vrata* completely; accordingly he arranges that a cow, for example, will be in calf when the period of his *pratyākhyāna* expires but will not actually have calved. Though there is thus a potential increase in numbers he will be only guilty of an *aticāra*.

(v) BHĀVENA KUPYA-PRAMĀṆĀTIKRAMA. If a man has undertaken to limit the number of his household utensils and later acquires additional ones he will be guilty of an *aticāra* if, to keep the numbers the same, he has some of them welded together, two

[1] e.g. P (A) 18; NPP 63; YŚ iii. 96.

by two. On the subject of *kupya* an opinion is also recorded by the seventeenth-century writer Yaśovijaya[1] that here the fictitious pretext invoked is donation to a third party.

Certain writers devote themselves to an assessment of the nature of *parigraha*. The Digambaras explain it as *mūrchā*, the 'hallucination' of material possessions; and *mūrchā* in the definition of Amṛtacandra[2] is the development of acquisitive egotism (*mamatva*) arising from the operation of delusion (*moha*). In all forms of *parigraha*, internal and external, *hiṃsā* is implicit. By a graduated progression the internal *parigraha* can be eliminated; whilst the external form, if it cannot be completely extirpated, can at least be rendered as exiguous as possible. For Amitagati[3] every *ārambha* in the world stimulates *parigraha*, and conversely if this is curtailed harmful activity is reduced. Siddhasena Gaṇin[4] expatiates on the evil results to which *mūrchā* can lead. In lust for gain son will murder father, and brother brother. It is for this reason that men bear false witness and rob on the highways.

THE DIG-VRATA

As has already been noted, the original Śvetāmbara grouping of the *guṇa-vratas* covers a certain number of long-term restraints whilst the *śikṣa-vratas* represent recurring exercises in self-discipline, but it is only the *dig-vrata* that is accorded an exact pendant among the latter: the *deśāvakāśika-vrata*, which in the Digambara lists is made to follow directly after it. Except in their temporal and spatial limits these two vows are identical.

The nomenclature of the *aticāras* of the *dig-vrata* is, to all intents and purposes, the same for Śvetāmbaras and Digambaras:

(i) going beyond the limits in an upward direction (*ūrdhva-dik-pramāṇātikrama*);
(ii) going beyond the limits in a downward direction (*adho-dik-pramāṇātikrama*);
(iii) going beyond the limits in a horizontal direction (*tiryag-dik-pramāṇātikrama*);
(iv) expanding the limits of the area of movement (*kṣetra-vṛddhi*);
(v) forgetfulness (*smṛty-antardhāna*).

1 *Dharma-saṃgraha*, 48.
2 PASU iii–28.
3 Śr (A) vi. 75.
4 T (S) vii. 12.

The fundamental idea of the *vrata* is to reduce quantitatively a man's sinful actions by circumscribing the area in which they can be committed. To express this, one simile, incorporated already in the *Āvaśyaka Cūrṇī*, is repeated from author to author among the Śvetāmbaras and is used by some Digambaras, notably Samantabhadra and Āśādhara:

tattāya-gola-kappo pamatta-jīvo 'ṇivāriya-ppasaro
ṣavvattha kiṃ na kujjā pāvaṃ tak-kāraṇāṇugao[1]

Like a heated iron sphere the layman will inevitably, as a result of *pramāda*, bring about the destruction of living creatures everywhere, whether he is walking, or eating, or sleeping, or working. The more his movements are restricted the fewer *trasa-jīvas* and *sthāvara-jivas* will perish.

Although the primary effect of this *vrata* is to curtail travel (Devagupta[2] expressly stipulates that certain roads are to be avoided in order not to destroy frogs) it has also a special association with the preceding *aṇu-vrata*. Thus the *Dvādaśānuprekṣā*[3] emphasizes that the complete restraint thereby imposed makes it possible to extirpate *lobha* which is at the root of *parigraha*. Hemacandra[4] says that the *dig-vrata*, by putting the acquisition of gold and silver and other wealth often out of a man's reach, will free him from the empire of greed, here chosen for an example, as the most tenacious of the *pāpa-sthānas*.

Let us turn back to the individual *aticāras*:

(i) ŪRDHVA-DIK-PRAMĀṆĀTIKRAMA. As it is forbidden to ascend a mountain or to climb to the summit of a tree, a ban on all upward movement outside very narrow limits—perhaps within one's own house—would seem to be intended. Haribhadra[5] and Devagupta preserve a very primitive tradition found in the *Āvaśyaka Cūrṇī*: if a piece of jewellery is carried off by a monkey or a bird it is not permissible to transgress the limits one has imposed for oneself by climbing up to seek it, but if it is dropped one may retrieve it.

(ii) ADHO-DIK-PRAMĀṆĀTIKRAMA. Again the limits appear to be set very narrowly. It is forbidden to descend into a well or the underground store of a village (*grāma-bhūmi-gṛha*) if outside the limits fixed, even if something has been dropped there.

1 Āv Cū, pt. ii, p. 294. 2 NPP 70. 3 KA 341.
4 YŚ iii. 3. 5 Āv (H), p. 827*b*.

(iii) TIRYAG-DIK-PRAMĀṆĀTIKRAMA. This for the Śvetāmbaras applies to normal travelling in all directions, north, south, east, and west; and the boundaries are set fairly wide. (In the explanation of the fifth *aticāra* a figure of a 100 *yojanas* is given by way of example.) Digambara writers[1] refer to the demarcation of limits by the position of well-known seas, rivers, forests, mountains, and states, and to measurement by *yojanas*. At the same time they seem to attempt to maintain a parallelism with the two preceding offences by citing as an instance of this *aticāra* the act of entering a cave in a mountainside which is outside the limits set. In all three cases the transgression is an *aticāra* if committed inadvertently, a *bhaṅga* if done deliberately.

(iv) KṢETRA-VṚDDHI. This is universally explained as an attempt to evade one's obligation by extending the limits in which freedom of movement is allowed.

(v) SMṚTY-ANTARDHĀNA. Suppose that a man has set a limit of 100 *yojanas* for his movements in the eastern direction, but through inattention and carelessness has forgotten the figure he had decided on. Uncertain whether it was 100 or 50, he hesitates. If he then goes outside the radius of 100 *yojanas* he will have committed a *bhaṅga* but owing to the state of mind induced by his uncertainty he will still be guilty of an *aticāra* if he exceeds 50 *yojanas*.[2]

The *aticāras* deal with the spatial but not the temporal limits of the *vrata*, which by contrast with those of the *deśāvakāśika-vrata*—a few hours or at most a day—are considerable: not less than four months (naturally, as later texts show, the four months of the rainy season are intended) or a year or for one's life long.[3] In the *Ratna-karaṇḍa*[4] the *dig-vrata* is defined as the determination, by circumscribing one's range of movement, to desist from minor sin (*aṇu-pāpa*) until death; and the lifelong character of this form of *pratyākhyāna* seems implicit in certain other descriptions. Āśādhara,[5] borrowing a phrase widely current to explain the significance of the *sāmāyika-vrata*, says that in the *dig-vrata* a layman becomes like an ascetic (*jāyate yativad gṛhī*).

In view of the close relationship between the *dig-vrata* and the *deśāvakāśika-vrata* it is perhaps surprising that the *aticāras* of one have not been transposed to the other. Yet the only instance of this

[1] RK iii. 23. [2] P (A) 20. [3] Āv (H), p. 827*a*.
[4] RK iii. 22. [5] SDhA v. 3.

seems to be found in the *Śrāvaka-dharma-pañcāśaka*[1] '*vajjai uddhāikkamam āṇayaṇa-ppesaṇobhaya-visuddham*' where *ānayana* and *preṣaṇa* are introduced from the *deśāvakāśika-vrata*. Abhayadeva's commentary on these words—that they imply the fetching or sending for something—is absorbed into Hemacandra's[2] exhaustive description.

THE BHOGOPABHOGA-PARIMĀṆA-VRATA

For this the older Śvetāmbara writers prefer a designation inherited from the *Upāsaka-daśāḥ*: *upabhoga-paribhoga-parimāṇā-vrata*. Its terms are thus defined:[3]

upabhoga—things used once or used internally such as food, flower garlands, betel, cooling pastes, unguents, incense, or such acts as bathing;

paribhoga—things that can be used repeatedly or used externally such as houses, furniture, women, clothes, jewellery, vehicles.

If a modern term may be allowed to intrude here some items of the second category might roughly be classed as consumer durables. The words *upabhoga* and *paribhoga* are used with these meanings by all the Śvetāmbara authorities except Hemacandra, and also in the *Tattvārtha-sūtra* and the *Cāritra-sāra*. With Hemacandra and the Digambaras the concepts remain the same, but the label *upabhoga* is attached to things used repeatedly whilst things used once are styled *bhoga*. Exceptionally Somadeva and Vasunandin do not adopt the expression *upabhoga* at all but retain *paribhoga* for things used repeatedly and employ *bhoga* for things used once.

Two basic divisions of this *vrata* are recognized by the Śvetāmbaras:[4] it may refer to food eaten or to occupations pursued. The second aspect, expressed in a ban on the pursuit of fifteen cruel trades, is unknown to the Digambaras except Āśādhara,[5] who for this theme is heavily indebted to Hemacandra. Other topics included at least by the Śvetāmbaras under the *bhogopabhoga-vrata* are the *ananta-kāyas*, the *abhakṣyas*, and *rātri-bhojana*.

[1] P (ŚrDh), 20. [2] YŚ iii. 97. [3] P (Y) 21.
[4] e.g. ŚrPr 285. [5] SDhA v. 21–23.

As listed by the Śvetāmbaras the *aticāras* are:

(i) consuming sentient things (*sacittāhāra*);
(ii) consuming what is connected with sentient things (*sacitta-pratibaddhāhāra*);
(iii) consuming uncooked vegetable products (*apakvauṣadhi-bhakṣaṇa*);
(iv) consuming partly cooked vegetable products (*duṣpakvau-ṣadhi-bhakṣaṇa*);
(v) consuming 'empty' vegetable products (*tucchaūṣadhi-bha-kṣaṇa*).

For the third and fifth of these transgressions the Digambaras—and with them Haribhadra[1] (in the *Dharma-bindu*) and Hema-candra—substitute:

(iii) consuming what is mixed with sentient things (*sacitta-sammiśrāhāra*);
(v) consuming what has been conserved by fermentation (*abhiṣava*).

All these offences of course relate very narrowly to what is eaten. Amongst the Digambaras Somadeva[2] has made some modifications in the list: thus the first *aticāra* refers to food that is prohibited (*niṣiddha*) and the fifth to food the preparation of which has not been personally supervised (*avīkṣita*).

Samantabhadra[3] has preferred to establish a completely different list in which the *aticāras* are given a much wider interpretation:

(i) lack of contempt for the poison of sensual pleasure (*viṣaya-viṣato 'nupekṣā*);
(ii) remembrance of it (*anusmṛti*);
(iii) excessive desire for it in the present (*atilaulya*);
(iv) excessive desire for it in the future (*atitṛṣā*);
(v) excessive enjoyment of it (*atyanubhava*).

Sakalakīrti alone follows Samantabhadra in this classification of the *aticāras*.

The conventional list of them shows certain divergencies of treatment:

(i) SACITTĀHĀRA. The Śvetāmbaras[4] define this as the eating

[1] DhB iii. 32. [2] Handiqui, p. 283. [3] RK iii. 44. [4] YŚ iii. 98.

of sentient things, that is, those containing *pṛthvi-kāyas*, *ap-kāyas*, or *vanaspati-jīvas* such as tubers (*kanda*) and roots (*mūla*) or fruits. Siddhasena Gaṇin's[1] commentary on the *Tattvārtha-sūtra* adds to this concept a mention of *ananta-kāyas*. Cāmuṇḍarāya[2] understands by *sacitta* simply a vegetable organism (*harita-kāya*).

(ii) SACITTA-PRATIBADDHĀHĀRA. Haribhadra[3] explains this as the eating of, for example, ripe fruits which are attached to a tree. Abhayadeva[4] offers another interpretation. A person may put a fruit such as a date in his mouth with the intention of eating the flesh which is *acitta* but not the stone which is *sacitta*. Even if he eats only the flesh he will have committed an *aticāra* (not a *bhaṅga*) through this fact of putting it in his mouth. These two explanations are given by succeeding Śvetāmbara authorities and by Āśādhara.[5] Siddhasena Gaṇin[6] chooses a slightly different illustration: he instances the eating of jujubes (*badara*) or *udumbara* fruits which are full of seeds or pips. The Digambara view—that of Pūjyapāda[7] and Cāmuṇḍarāya, for example—is that this *aticāra* implies the consumption of anything that has been in contact with or near to sentient things.

(iii) APAKVAUṢADHI-BHAKṢAṆA. Haribhadra[3] abstains from comment on this as unnecessary but records a variant reading (*pāṭhāntara*): *sacitta-sammiśrāhāra*. Discussing the *Śrāvaka-dharma-pañcāśaka*, Abhayadeva[8] notes that this and the two following *aticāras* refer to grain and pulses whilst the two preceding ones were concerned with fruit and roots. It may be asked why *apakvauṣadhi-bhakṣaṇa* is an *aticāra* for if the substance involved is *acitta* no fault can be found with it and if *sacitta* it will already have been covered by the preceding *aticāras*. This offence has specifically the character of an *aticāra* in relation to the *vrata* if it is done in the belief that even if flour is not cooked the fact that it has been ground will have destroyed its *sacitta* element. The same view is expressed by Yaśodeva and Siddhasena Sūri.

(iv) DUṢPAKVAUṢADHI-BHAKṢAṆA. For Haribhadra[3] and for Siddhasena Gaṇin this means 'half-cooked grains or pulses' in which each individual grain, which may not have been cooked, will be sentient. Hemacandra[9] explains that it is because of the presence

1 T (S) vii. 2 CS, p. 13. 3 Āv (H), p. 828*b*.
4 P (A) 22. 5 SDhA v. 20. 6 T (S) vii. 30.
7 T (P) vii. 35. 8 P (A) 22. 9 YŚ iii. 98.

at the same time of the *acitta* cooked grains and the *sacitta* uncooked grains that the offence is an *aticāra*. On the Digambara side Cāmuṇḍarāya[1] considers *duṣpakvauṣadhi* to mean 'cooked rice spoiled either by excessive moisture or because the grains in the centre are still raw'. Āśādhara[2] explains that whether it is under-cooked or over-cooked some grains will remain raw and therefore sentient.

(v) TUCCHAUṢADHI-BHAKṢAṆA. The traditional definition of this, that of Haribhadra[3] for example, is 'the eating of such grains and pulses as undeveloped *mudga* from which there is little satisfaction of hunger whilst at the same time much harm is done'. In this connexion Devagupta thinks of sugar-cane and other products which are unsatisfying even if eaten in quantity. Abhayadeva,[4] Yaśodeva, and Siddhasena Sūri note that if an 'empty' product were *apakva* or *duṣpakva* there would be an *aticāra* in any case; but, even if it is properly cooked, a person eating it will still have committed an *aticāra* inasmuch as he consumes it out of *gourmandise* after rendering it *acitta* by cooking, even though it does not serve the useful purpose of satisfying hunger. He will have kept the *vrata* in the letter whilst infringing it in the spirit.

(iii) SACITTA-SAMMIŚRĀHĀRA. Siddhasena Gaṇin[5] understands by this either the eating of sweetmeats (*modaka*) mixed with fruits, flowers, or sesamum seeds or the eating of food into which small living creatures such as ants, or *kunthus* have fallen, whilst Haribhadra[3] suggests as an instance the eating of grain mixed with flowers. Hemacandra[6] mentions the consuming of a kind of cake (*pūraṇa*) mixed with ginger, pomegranate seeds, and other fruits or barley meal mixed with sesamum seeds and his examples are copied by Āśādhara.[2] The Digambara[7] writers understand by *sacitta* minute living creatures. For Cāmuṇḍarāya[1] *sammiśra* is what has been mixed in such a way that it cannot be divided whilst *sambaddha* is what has merely been in contact with something else.

(v) ABHIṢAVĀHĀRA. Siddhasena Gaṇin[5] offers two explanations: either wine or spirits produced by the fermentation of various substances or the use of fortifying vegetable substances. Hemacandra[6] has three: alcohol or soul gruel produced by fermentation; or the insertion of pieces of meat; or the use of a

[1] CS, p. 13. [2] SDhA v. 20. [3] Āv (H), p. 828*b*.
[4] P (A) 22. [5] T (S) vii. 30. [6] YŚ iii. 98.
[7] T (P) vii. 35.

fortifiant derived from wine or honey or other vegetable products. Cāmuṇḍarāya[1] interprets as either sour gruel (*sauvīra*) and similar products of fermentation or a stimulant (*vṛṣya*) Āśādhara[2] understands by it the immoderate consumption of liquids such as milk or rice gruel which strengthen the body.

As has been pointed out the orthodox Śvetāmbara[3] view is that the first two offences refer to such things as roots and fruits and the last three to the staple foods: grains and pulses. The Digambaras,[4] who employ a different terminology, do not appear to make this distinction but they recognize in each *aticāra* two elements of fault. Not only are sentient things consumed but the vigour of the sense organs (*indriya-mada*) is thereby stimulated; diseases arising from the wind humour may also be occasioned and there may be an element of sin in the remedies applied to counteract them. In any event the monk must avoid such food when seeking alms.

Cāmuṇḍarāya[1] has a fivefold division, built up from the less explicit model given by Pūjyapāda[5] and Samantabhadra,[6] of *paribhoga* and *upabhoga* to which he gives the common name of *bhoga*: *trasa-ghāta*, *pramāda*, *bahu-vadha*, *aniṣṭa*, *anupasevya*:

(i) always to be avoided are things which involve the killing of living creatures that move (*trasa-ghāta*). Under this head come honey and meat;

(ii) to be avoided in order to eliminate carelessness (*pramāda*) is alcohol which blurs the distinction between what should be done and what should not be done;

(iii) better to be avoided in order to prevent much killing (*bahu-vadha*) are the *ananta-kāyas* such as *arjuna* and *ketakī* flowers, unripe ginger, turmeric, radishes, or margosa flowers for when they are consumed there is great destruction but little profit;

(iv) to be avoided in so far as they are undesirable (*aniṣṭa*)[7] are vehicles, riding animals, ornaments, and similar luxuries. Some are permissible but the rest are not permissible and should be eschewed;

[1] CS, p. 13. [2] SDhA v. 20. [3] YŚ iii. 98.
[4] e.g. CS, p. 13. [5] T (P) vii. 21. [6] RK iii. 38–40.
[7] The late commentator Prabhācandra is probably mistaken in understanding by *aniṣṭa* 'food that is unwholesome because it causes colic or other disorders'.

(v) not to be enjoyed (*anupasevya*)[1] even though not undesirable. Deliberate abstention from such luxuries as gaudy clothes and ornaments is recommended. If they are not abandoned for the duration of one's life their use should be restricted as far as possible for a limited period of time.

Amṛtacandra[2] insists that *bhoga* and *upabhoga* lie at the root of *hiṃsā*. Bearing in mind his own capacity a wise man should eschew even those varieties which are not forbidden and should restrict those which he is unable to abandon altogether. Indeed he should review continually his capacity for self-denial and if possible curtail further each day the limits already set. This of course is in the very spirit of the stories of the *Upāsaka-daśāḥ*.

The *bhogopabhoga-parimāṇa-vrata* is of course, more conspicuously than any other *vrata*, an expression of *pratyākhyāna*. Samantabhadra[3] uses the word to explain the two methods of self-restriction: *niyama* and *yama*. The former is for a limited period of time—a day, a night, a fortnight, a month, two months, six months, and may relate to a wide range of utilitarian or luxury articles.[4] The latter term (apparently used only by the Digambaras) implies renunciation for one's life long.

The *Śrāvaka-dharma-pañcāśaka*[5] enunciates the *bhogopabhoga-parimāṇa-vrata* as covering abstinence from the consumption of the *ananta-kāyas*, the *udumbaras*, and the *atyaṅgas*. The last term (Prakrit *accaṅga*) has presented some difficulty to the commentators. Abhayadeva takes it to mean either honey, alcohol, and meat or the practice of eating by night and use of garlands, sandal-paste, and similar substances, which are all described as occasioning excess of *bhoga*.

RĀTRI-BHOJANA

GREAT importance has always been attached by Jaina writers to the avoidance of taking food by night (*rātri-bhojana*). A passage of the *Daśa-vaikālika-sūtra* gives to this abstention the status of a vow and on this authority Cāmuṇḍarāya[6] in the *Cāritra-sāra* makes

[1] Prabhācandra explains as 'substances which even though *prāsuka* are unfit for consumption by civilized people such as camel's milk, cow's urine, crushed shells, excrement, betel spittle'. [2] PASU 164–6. [3] RK iii. 43.
[4] SDhA v. 14. [5] P (A) 21 (p. 32). [6] CS, p. 7.

it into a sixth *aṇu-vrata* (being imitated in this by Sakalakīrti) whilst Amṛtacandra[1] gives it in his *śrāvakācāra* the position that a sixth vow would have occupied. However, this sixth vow failed to obtain general recognition and no *aticāra* pentad was ever devised for it. For some Digambaras—Kārttikeya[2] and Samantabhadra,[3] for example—and in the *Āvaśyaka Cūrṇī a-rātri-bhojana* is the subject of the fifth *pratimā* and even when this, as in the general Śvetāmbara view, is styled *kāyotsarga-pratimā*, forms still an important element in it. Again in certain enumerations—those of Amitagati and Āśādhara—it figures among the *mūla-guṇas*. In general, however, in the *śrāvakācāras* the topic of *rātri-bhojana* is treated either under the *ahiṃsā-vrata* or, since it is also counted as an *abhakṣya*, under the *paribhogopabhoga-parimāṇa-vrata*.

Samantabhadra[3] defines abstention from *rātri-bhojana* as the abandonment of the fourfold aliments by night out of compassion for living beings. Amṛtacandra,[4] who condemns this practice with especial vehemence, cites as arguments against it that there exist many tiny insects barely discernible by day which are completely invisible by night even when a lamp is lit, and that *rāga* is always more intense in eating by night than in eating by day. Cāmuṇḍarāya repeats Samantabhadra's definition and Vasunandin,[5] like those *ācāryas* who place *a-rātri-bhojana* among the *mūla-guṇas*, regards it as a prerequisite for the observance of the first *pratimā*. At night almost anything—moths, snakes, mice, bits of bones, skin, or hairs—may fall into a bowl of food, and the person who is eating will not be able to see them. And if he kindles a light moths and other tiny *catur-indriya* creatures will be dazzled and drop into the platter. However, as he refers expressly to 'threefold night-eating' Vasunandin[6] would seem to admit that liquids may be consumed; and the *Śrāvaka-dharma-dohaka*[7] expressly permits the taking of betel, medicines, and water during the night.

The Śvetāmbaras seem not to lay quite as much stress as the Digambaras on the avoidance of night eating, which receives only a bare mention under the *paribhogopabhoga-vrata* in the *Śrāvaka-dharma-pañcāśaka* and the *Nava-pada-prakaraṇa*. Hemacandra, however, considers the subject of sufficient importance to devote to it a couple of dozen verses.[8] Four reasons are alleged for exclud-

[1] PASU 129–34. [2] KA 382. [3] RK v. 21.
[4] PASU 132. [5] Śr (V) 314. [6] Ibid. 318.
[7] Doha 37. [8] YŚ iii. 48–70.

ing eating by night: the food may have been contaminated by the touch of *piśācas* or *pretas* or other evil spirits; it may be infested by minute invisible organisms such as *kunthu* and *panaka*;[1] insects may have crawled or fluttered into it; and its contents will in any event be unrecognizable in the dark. To swallow an ant in this way destroys the intelligence, a fly makes one vomit, a louse causes dropsy, and a spider leprosy.[2] Where food has to be cooked and the platters washed up there is even greater *hiṃsā* by night. The ban on eating by night, particularly on the consumption of mangoes and ghee, should also cover the first and last *muhūrtas* of the day when the light is dim'.[3] Addiction to *rātri-bhojana* entails rebirth as an owl or crow, or vulture or cat, or pig or serpent, or lizard or scorpion.[4]

For his condemnation of the practice of eating by night Hemacandra draws support lavishly from Hindu sources; from the Āyurvedic texts[5] for the quasi-medical reasons invoked, and in a more general sense from the mass of Hindu customary law and legends. Night, it is said, is a time of calamity when neither the oblation to fire, nor the offerings to the spirits of the ancestors, nor *dāna*, nor *pūjā* are licit and when bathing is excluded, and it ill behoves a man therefore to eat during the hours of darkness.[6] Again it is traditional that in the morning the *devas* eat, at midday the *ṛṣis*, in the afternoon the *pitṛs*, in the evening the *daityas* and *dainavas*, and in the twilight the *yakṣas* and *rākṣasas*.[7]

Āśādhara[8] takes over all Hemacandra's arguments and at the same time agrees with Amṛtacandra[9] in classing *rātri-bhojana* with the drinking of unfiltered water as a habit in which *rāga* is intense and which provokes great destruction of *jīvas*; both practices are also said to be responsible for disease. The best type of Jaina will eat once a day, the next best, twice, like an animal, whilst the least satisfactory type, comprehending nothing, eats day and night making himself, in Hemacandra's phrase, 'a ruminant though devoid of horns and tail'.[10]

Later Śvetāmbara writers such as Ratnaśekhara and Yaśovijaya quote largely from the *Niśītha-cūrṇī* in discussing *rātri-bhojana* and dwell particularly on the assertion made there that if a *gṛha-godhila* (a kind of house lizard) gets into the food and its excretions

[1] A *kunthu* is described as a very minute *trīndriya* insect and a *panaka* seems to be an organism producing mould.

[2] YŚ iii. 50–52.
[3] Ibid. 57.
[4] Ibid. 67.
[5] Ibid. 60.
[6] Ibid. 56.
[7] Ibid. 58–59.
[8] SDhA iii. 11–15.
[9] PASU 130.
[10] YŚ iii. 62.

or parts of its body are eaten a similar lizard will come into existence by spontaneous generation in the stomach of the eater.[1]

THE ABHAKṢYAS

THE definitions of what is not fit to be eaten are given considerable prominence particularly in the later Jainism. The standard Śvetāmbara list of twenty-two *abhakṣyas* is found as early as the *Pravacana-sāroddhāra*.[2] It has largely ousted the later list of sixteen preferred by Hemacandra.[3] Here are both enumerations:

NEMICANDRA	HEMACANDRA
(1–5) five *udumbaras*	(1–4) four banned *vikṛtis*
(6–9) four banned *vikṛtis*	(5–9) five *udumbaras*
(10) snow (*hima*)	(10) *ananta-kāyas*
(11) poison (*viṣa*)	(11) unknown fruits
(12) ice (*karaka*)	(12) food eaten at night
(13) earth (*mṛd*)	(13) pulses with raw milk products (*āma-go-rasa-sampṛkta-dvidala*)
(14) food eaten at night (*rātri-bhojana*)	(14) rice that has fermented (*puṣpitaudana*)
(15) fruits with many seeds (*bahu-bīja*)	(15) curds kept for more than two days (*dadhy-ahar-dvitīyā-tīta*)
(16) *ananta-kāyas*	(16) tainted food (*kuthitānna*)
(17) pickles (*sandhāna*)	
(18) buttermilk in tiny lumps (*ghola-vaṭaka*)	
(19) aubergines (*vṛntāka*)	
(20) unknown fruits and flowers	
(21) 'empty' fruits (*tuccha-phala*)	
(22) tainted food (*calita-rasa*)	

The basic identity of the two lists is at once apparent. If, as the

[1] *Dharma-saṃgraha*, pt. i, p. 73*b*.

[2] PS, vv. 245–6. These verses are probably older than Nemicandra. They are found again in the *Caitya-vandana-kulaka* of Jinadatta Sūri and are quoted by almost every later writer who refers to the subject.

[3] YŚ iii. 6–7.

commentator says, *ghola-vaṭaka* is an *upalakṣana* for *āma-go-rasa-sampṛkta-dvidala* and *calita-rasa* for *puṣpitaudana* and *dadhy-ahar-dvitīyātīta* Hemacandra has no items that are not found in the longer list. However a list of twenty-five items consisting of Nemicandra's version with these two additions and a mention of *śṛṅgātaka* (*Trapa bispinosa*) is sometimes found.[1]

The relevant verses of the *Pravacana-sāroddhāra* are worth quoting:

> *pañc'-umbari-cau-vigaī hima-visa-karage ya savva-maṭṭī ya*
> *rayaṇī-bhoyaṇagaṃ ciya bahu-bīya-aṇanta-sandhāṇaṃ*
> *ghola-vaḍā vāyaṇgaṇam amuṇiya-nāmāṇi phulla-phalayāṇi*
> *tuccha-phalaṃ caliya-rasaṃ vajjaha vajjāni bāvīsaṃ*

The *udumbaras* and *vikṛtis* (abstinence from which is required for the observance of the *mūla-guṇas*), *rātri-bhojana*, and the *ananta-kāyas* are discussed separately. Of the other elements of the list snow and ice are forbidden because their consumption necessitates the destruction of *ap-kāyas* whilst they are not essential to life like water itself.[2] Poison is not to be taken even if its effect can be counteracted by *mantras* because it will in any event kill innumerable *gaṇḍolaka* organisms in the stomach and because if death ensues it may provoke great delusions in the last hours. Later writers, from the fifteenth century onwards, here mention opium (*ahi-phena*). Earth is prohibited because it contains *pṛthvī-kāyas*, because it may be a source of generation of *trasa-jīvas* with the full five senses like frogs, and because it may cause intestinal maladies. Salt is expressly excluded from the *abhakṣyas* as being essential to life but all other kinds of earth including chalk (*khaṭikā*) are covered by the ban. The *bahu-bīja* class covers fruits like pomegranates in which there is a risk of destroying a *jīva* in each seed. By *sandhāna* are meant pickles or preserves of bael and other fruits. *Ghola-vaṭaka* is said to be used to cover *āma-go-rasa-sampṛkta-dvidala* (*dvidala* being 'pulses which when ground yield no oil'); in it there are organisms so minute that they can be discerned only by a *kevalin*. Aubergines have aphrodisiac properties and provoke a tendency to sleep too much. Unidentified fruits and flowers are to be avoided for if they are forbidden it is wrong to consume them

[1] e.g. in the *Yoga-vidhi* of Candra Sūri.

[2] The explanations in this paragraph are all taken from Siddhasena Sūri's commentary on the above verses.

and if they are poisonous they will occasion loss of life. The expression *tuccha-phala* embraces also flowers, leaves, and roots, 'empty' because they do not satisfy hunger but cause much destruction of *jīvas*. Examples of these are the bael fruits, and rose-apples, and the flowers of mahua, and Indian horse-radish. The term *calita-rasa* (food that has 'gone off') is meant to include by extension boiled rice which has fermented and curds kept for more than forty-eight hours; these are to be rejected because living organisms have started to multiply in them.

Even if the twenty-two *abhakṣyas* are listed for the first time in the *Pravacana-sāroddhāra* their enumeration is adumbrated at a much earlier date. Haribhadra,[1] relying on the *Āvaśyaka Cūrṇī*, situates them under the divisions of the *caturvidhāhāra*. Thus under *aśana* come meat and the *ananta-kāyas*; under *pāna* meat-broth and alcohol; under *khādima* the *udumbaras*; and under *svādima* honey. Devagupta[2] adds to this embryo list butter, *gholavaṭaka*, and *rātri-bhojana*. Yaśodeva,[3] who is posterior to Nemicandra, gives no formal enumeration but mentions the five *udumbaras*, the four *vikṛtis*, ice, earth, *rātri-bhojana*, *bahu-bījas*, *ananta-kāyas*, and pulses mixed with raw milk products (*mugga-gayam āma-goras'-ummīsaṃ*).

The Digambaras have not, at least during the period under review, defined with such precision the *abhakṣyas*. Amitagati[4] enumerates—rather surprisingly under the *anartha-daṇḍa-vrata* *sūrana-kanda* (an *ananta-kāya*)—curds kept for more than two days, boiled rice that has fermented, *droṇa*[5] flowers and *kaliṅga*[6] flowers; and states that in general any *ananta-kāya* and any substance that is tainted and no longer fresh is to be avoided.

Āśādhara[7] gives a more extensive but unnumbered list which he subdivides under the infractions of the *mūla-guṇas*. His *abhakṣyas*, arranged in the order of the Śvetāmbara list are:

(1–4)	four banned *vikṛtis*	
(5–9)	five *udumbaras*	
(10)	water or other liquid in leather containers	(*māṃsa-vrata*)
(11)	honey used as a collyrium	(*madhu-vrata*)

[1] Āv(H), p. 828*b*. [2] NPP 75. [3] P(Y) 21.
[4] Śr(A) vi. 84–85. [5] *Leucas linifolia* Spreng.
[6] *Holarrhena antidysenterica* Wall. [7] SDhA iii. 11–14 and 15–18.

(12) asafoetida (*hiṅgu*) in contact with leather (*māṃsa-vrata*)
(13) any flowers such as those of mahua or marking-nut (*bhallātaka*) (*madhu-vrata*)
(14) food eaten at night
(15) rice gruel that has fermented (*puṣpita-kāñjika*) (*madya-vrata*)
(16) *ananta-kāyas*
(17) pickles (*sandhāna*) (*madya-vrata*)
(18) pods (*simbī*) such as *rāja-māṣa* (*udumbara-vrata*)
(19) aubergines (and jujubes, betel-nuts, &c.) unsplit (*udumbara-vrata*)
(20) unknown fruits (*udumbara-vrata*)
(21) curds kept for more than two days (*madya-vrata*)
(22) tainted food (*vyāpanna-bhojya*) (*māṃsa-vrata*)

There is also an interdiction on eating mangoes, ghee, and a number of other foodstuffs in the last *muhūrta* of the day. Snow and ice, poison and earth are absent from this list; on the other hand Āśādhara includes articles that have been polluted by leather and also flowers (which take the place of empty fruits). Coupled with the *abhakṣyas* is the ban on unfiltered water.

Later Digambara lists closely follow Āśādhara's pattern and make few noticeable additions to the objects forbidden.

There are rudimentary lists too in the *Śrāvaka-dharma-dohaka*[1] and the *Yaśastilaka*.[2] The former understands the *abhakṣyas* to include *nāli*, *sūraṇa*, *mūlaka*, *laśuṇa*, and other *ananta-kāyas*, flowers, curds kept for more than two days, fermented rice, and all tainted food. Somadeva names *ananta-kāyas* and flowers.

THE ANANTA-KĀYAS

AMONGST the substances which a Jaina is forbidden to consume either as food or as medicine are included the *ananta-kāyas* or *sādhāraṇas*, plants which are inhabited, not like the majority of the vegetable kingdom by individual *jīvas*, but by an infinite number of living organisms. Where in the elementary bodies—earth, water, fire, wind—the individual *jīva* wraps itself up only in a tiny part of the material, in the plant bodies additional *jīvas* may attach

[1] Doha 34–36. [2] Handiqui, p. 264.

themselves to the original individual and adhere to it until its development process is complete. Those plants which are classified as *ananta-kāyas* seem to be chosen because of certain morphological peculiarities such as the possession of bulbs or rhizomes or the habit of periodically shedding their leaves; and in general they are characterized by possibilities of vegetative reproduction.[1]

A list of 32 is already conventional by the time of Nemicandra[2] and is repeated by successive writers. It is contained in the following verses:

savvā hu kanda-jāī[3] *sūraṇa-kando ya vajja-kando ya*
adda-haliddā ya tahā addaṃ taha alla-kaccūro
sattāvarī virālī kumāri taha thoharī giloī ya
lhasaṇaṃ vaṃsa-karillā gajjara taha loṇao loḍho
giri-kanni kisala-pattā kaserugā thigga alla-mutthā ya
taha lūṇa-rukkha-challī khelluḍo amaya-vallī ya
mūla tahā bhūmi-rasā viruhā taha ḍhakka-vatthulo paḍhamo
sūyara-vallo ya tahā pallaṅko komal'-ambiliyā
ālū taha piṇḍālū havanti ee ananta-nāmehiṃ
annam aṇantaṃ neyaṃ lakkhaṇa-juttīe samayāo

An attempt is made below to identify the individual plants mentioned:

Prakrit form	Sanskrit form	Botanical name	English name
(1) sūraṇa-kanda	sūraṇa-kanda	*Amorphophallus campanulatus* Br.	
(2) vajja-kanda	vajra-kanda	*Synantherias sylvatica* Schott	
(3) adda-haliddā	moist haridrā	*Curcuma longa* Roxb.	turmeric ginger
(4) adda	ārdraka	*Zingiber officinale* Roscoe	
(5) alla-kaccūra	moist kaccūra	*Curcuma zedoaria* Roscoe	
(6) sattāvarī	śatāvarī	*Asparagus racemosus* Willd.	
(7) virālī	virālika		
(8) kumārī	kumārī	*Elettaria cardamomum* Maton.	cardamom

[1] See J. F. Kohl, 'Pflanzen mit gemeinsamen Körper nach der Lehre der Jainas' in *Zeitschrift für Ethnologie* (1953), Bd. 78, pp. 91 ff.

[2] PS 236–41.

[3] The commentators sometimes consider the first item on the list of thirty-two to be *savvā kanda-jāī* (all sorts of plant growths rooting below the soil, unless in a dried state) in which case *sūraṇa-kanda* and *vajra-kanda* together form the second item.

Prakrit form	Sanskrit form	Botanical name	English name
(9) thoharī[1]	snuhī	*Euphorbia neriifolia* Linn.	
(10) giloī	guḍūcī	*Tinospera cordifolia* Miers.	
(11) lhasaṇa	laśuna	*Allium sativum* Linn.	garlic
(12) vaṃsa-karilla	shoots of vaṃśa		bamboo
(13) gajjara	garjaraka	*Daucus carota* Linn.	carrot
(14) loṇaya[2]	lavaṇaka		
(15) loḍha[3]	loḍhaka		
(16) giri-kanni	giri-karṇikā		
(17) kisala-patta—immature shoots of any kind			
(18) kaseruga	kaśeruka	*Scirpus kysoor* Roxb.	
(19) thigga	thega	*Cyperus bulbosus*	
(20) alla-mutthā	moist mustā	*Cyperus rotundus* Linn.	
(21) lūṇa-rukkha-challi[4]	bark of lavaṇa-vṛksa		
(22) khelluḍa	khelluḍa		
(23) amaya-valli	amṛta-valli		
(24) mūla	mūlaka	*Raphanus sativus* Linn.	radish
(25) bhūmi-rasa—mushrooms or other edible fungi			
(26) viruha (virūḍha)—sprouted pulses or grains			
(27) ḍhakka-vatthula[5]	ṭaṅka-vāstula	*Feronia elephantum* Correa	
(28) sūyara-valli[6]	sūkara-valli		
(29) pallaṅka	palyaṅka	*Beta maritima* Linn.	beetroot
(30) komal'-ambiliyā	immature āmlikā	*Tamarindus indica* Linn.	tamarind
(31) ālu[7]	āluka	*Arum colocasia*	taro
(32) piṇḍālu	piṇḍāluka	*Dioscorea globosa* Roxb.	
ghosāḍaṅkura	ghoṣāṭakī shoots	*Luffa aegyptiaca* Mill.	
karīraṅkura	karīra shoots	*Capparis aphylla* Roth.	caper
komala-tinduga	immature tinduka	*Diospyros embryopteris* Pers.	
varuṇaṅkura	varuṇa shoots	*Crataeva Roxburghii*	
vaḍaṅkura	vaṭa shoots	*Ficus bengalensis*	banyan
nimbaṅkura	nimba shoots	*Melia azadirachta* Linn.	margosa

[1] Sometimes called *vajra-taru*. [2] The ashes are said to yield natron.
[3] This is explained as *padminī-kanda* and is perhaps equivalent to the *nāli* of some Digambara lists. [4] Also called *bhramara-vṛkṣa*.
[5] An *ananta-kāya* in its early stages but not when mature.
[6] Said to be so called because pigs are used to discover it.
[7] Today this word tends to be given the meaning of 'potato'.

The unnumbered *ananta-kāyas* not included in the standard list of thirty-two are mentioned as early as the *Pravacana-sāroddhāra*.

Hemacandra,[1] though he does not adopt the verses quoted above, gives virtually the same enumeration of the *ananta-kāyas*. Of the thirty-two he omits *virālika*, *vaṃśa-karilla*, *garjaraka*, *lavaṇaka*, *khelluḍa*, *bhūmi-rasa*, and *ṭaṅka-vāstula*; however, he mentions also five edible roots: *gṛñjana*, *mudgara*, *palāśa-kanda*, *hasti-kanda*, and *manuṣya-kanda*.

These Śvetambara lists suffered from the disadvantage that they were not exhaustive and named only a few of those *ananta-kāyas* in the vegetable kingdom which might conceivably serve as food. The Digambaras have preferred to abide by a general classification given in a verse of the *Mūlācāra*[2] from which examples can be drawn at will:

> *mūl'agga-pora-bīa sāhā taha khanda-kandha-bīa-ruhā*
> *sammucchimā yā bhaṇiyā patteyāṇanta-kāyā ya*

(1) reproducing from the root (*mūla-bīja*), e.g. *ārdraka*, *haridra*;
(2) ,, ,, ,, tip (*agra-bīja*), e.g. *ketakī* (*Pandanus odoratissimus* Willd.);
(3) ,, ,, ,, nodules (*parva-bīja*), e.g. *ikṣu* (sugar-cane), *vetra*;
(4) ,, ,, ,, branches (*sakha-bīja*),
(5) ,, ,, ,, stem (*skandha-bīja*), e.g. *palāśa*, *sallakī*;
(6) ,, ,, ,, tubers (*kanda-bīja*), e.g. *sūraṇa*, *piṇḍālu*, *palāṇḍu* (onion);
(7) ,, ,, ,, seed (*bīja-ruha*), e.g. *godhūma*, *śāli*;
(8) spontaneously generated (*sammūrchima*).[3]

These plants, which are jointly inhabited by many *jīvas*, have a common source of nourishment and when one perishes the many perish.

The concepts underlying the category of the *ananta-kāyas* have been convincingly explained by J. F. Kohl,[4] who notes that the Jaina concept is based on a thorough insight into plant physiology and morphology as is shown by the recognition of the role of roots and stems in the storage of reserves for future generations.

[1] YŚ iii. 44–46.
[2] *Mūlācāra*, 213.
[3] SDhA v. 174; *Lāṭī-saṃhitā*, ii. 79 ff.
[4] J. F. Kohl, op. cit., and 'Einige Bemerkungen zur Zahlensymbolik und zum Animismus im botanischen System der Jaina-Kanon' in the *Kirfel-Festschrift* (Bonn, 1955), pp. 125–35.

THE PROFESSIONS

As already noted the *bhogopabhoga-vrata* has two aspects: it may refer to food or to occupation. The fifteen trades[1] forbidden under this head are given in the *Upāsaka-daśāḥ*; they form a purely Śvetāmbara category, being unnoticed, for example, in the *Tattvārtha-sūtra*. Āśādhara[2] alone among Digambara writers has included them in his work in an evident borrowing from Hemacandra. The enumeration is as follows:

(1) livelihood from charcoal (*aṅgāra-karman*);
(2) livelihood from destroying plants (*vana-karman*);
(3) livelihood from carts (*śakaṭa-karman*);[3]
(4) livelihood from transport fees (*bhāṭaka-karman*);
(5) livelihood from hewing and digging (*sphoṭa-karman*);
(6) trade in animal by-products (*danta-vāṇijya*);
(7) trade in lac and similar substances (*lākṣā-vāṇijya*);
(8) trade in alcohol and forbidden foodstuffs (*rasa-vāṇijya*);
(9) trade in men and animals (*keśa-vāṇijya*);
(10) trade in destructive articles (*viṣa-vāṇijya*);
(11) work involving milling (*yantra-pīḍana*);
(12) work involving mutilation (*nirlañchana*);
(13) work involving the use of fire (*davāgni-dāna*);
(14) work involving the use of water (*saraḥ-śoṣaṇa*);
(15) work involving breeding and rearing (*asati-poṣaṇa*).

The designations remain virtually the same in all the literature but there are some noticeable divergencies in interpretation.

1. AṄGĀRA-KARMAN. For Haribhadra[4] this is the 'making, buying, and selling of charcoal'. Besides charcoal-burning this includes all occupations involving the use of kilns in which the six forms of living organisms (*ṣaj-jīva-nikāya*) may perish. Under this head come therefore the smelting of iron, the firing of pottery, the refining of gold or silver, the making of bricks and tiles, the

[1] These occupations are noticeably similar to those prohibited for a brahmin who maintains himself as a *śūdra*. See *Yājnavalkya-smṛti*, iii. 36–42.

[2] SDhA v. 21–23.

[3] Hoernle rightly noted that the third forbidden trade is apparently duplicated by the fourth. The *ācāryas* are, however, unanimous in the explanation given and offer no support at all to his suggestion 'livelihood with clothes'. See UD ii. 29.

[4] Āv (H), p. 829*a*.

construction of ovens for roasting chick-peas and other pulses, and in general any working in metals such as tin, copper, brass, bell-metal, or lead.[1]

2. VANA-KARMAN. Haribhadra[2] explains this as 'the purchase of a stand of trees and the felling and sale of the timber'. Hemacandra[3] defines it as the sale of timber, cut or uncut, and of the leaves, shoots and fruits of plants, whether cut or uncut. It also applies to the making of flour from grains and pulses by grinding between two stones (*śilā* and *śilā-putraka*) or by pounding in a mill (*gharaṭṭa*)[4]. It is in the destruction of *vanaspati-kāyas* that the offence lies.

3. ŚAKAṬA-KARMAN. This includes the construction and sale of carts to be drawn by animals and the driving of them, whether done by oneself or at one's instigation. The ban on such occupations would apply equally to the work of a wheelwright. Such trades are sinful because the use of a cart involves the harnessing and beating of the draught beasts and the crushing of living organisms by the animals' hooves and under the wheels as they move.[5]

4. BHĀṬAKA-KARMAN. 'The conveying of merchandise in one's own vehicle or hiring out of draught animals to others for the same purpose' seems to be the original meaning.[6] Hemacandra[7] defines as 'making a livelihood by carting goods in vehicles or on horses, oxen, buffaloes, camels, mules, or asses'. The same destruction of life as in the preceding case would be liable to occur.

5. SPHOṬA-KARMAN. For Haribhadra[8] this is the cultivation of the soil with a plough or digging-stick. By Hemacandra's[9] time the concept has been considerably expanded. He understands it to include the excavating of artificial pools, tanks, and wells, the ploughing of fields, the quarrying of rocks, and shaping of stone. Particularly in the work of cultivation the earth is mercilessly torn up and not only are *pṛthvī-kāyas* destroyed but also *vanaspati-kāyas* and *trasa-jīvas*. Āśādhara[10] adds a further concept: the making and selling of fireworks. Devendra[11] would also include under this head the grinding of grains and pulses into flour (which is more generally held to fall under *yantra-pīḍaṇa*) and the mining of salt.

[1] YŚ iii. 102.
[2] Āv (H), p. 829*b*.
[3] YŚ iii. 103.
[4] Ibid. 104.
[5] SDhA v. 21.
[6] Āv (H), p. 829*b*.
[7] YŚ iii. 105.
[8] Āv (H), p. 829*b*.
[9] YŚ iii. 106.
[10] SDhA v. 21.
[11] ŚrDK, pt. ii, p. 108.

6. DANTA-VĀṆIJYA. Haribhadra,[1] quoting the *Āvaśyaka Cūrṇī*, explains that traders bargain for ivory with the jungle tribes, who then hunt and kill elephants on the understanding that the dealers will come back and purchase it from them. They also make similar arrangements with fishermen for conch-shells. By buying products thus obtained from the slaughter of living beings they are directly provoking that slaughter. While Abhayadeva[2] appears to confine the notion of *danta* to the by-products of the elephant Hemacandra[3] explains that *danta* (ivory) is an *upalakṣaṇa* to indicate any animal by-products such as tail-hairs of yaks, claws of owls, bones i.e. shells of conches, pelts of antelopes or down of geese. Devendra[4] adds to this list the scent glands of musk deer.

7. LĀKṢĀ-VĀṆIJYA. Again here *lākṣā* is an *upalakṣaṇa* designed to include red arsenic (*manaḥ-śilā*), indigo, borax (*ṭaṅkaṇa*), *dhātakī*,[5] and other substances, which have in common the property of serving as dyestuffs or colorants. Devendra[4] mentions too in this connexion yellow orpiment. The objections to the use of and trade in them are based on various grounds. Red arsenic and borax as poisons would properly belong under *viṣa-vāṇijya*; the collection of red lac involves the destruction of endless numbers of tiny insects; *dhātakī* is reprehended because alcohol can be made from its bark and flowers and because its resin is full of insects; and the cultivation of indigo is said to be inseparable from the destruction of living beings.[6]

8. RASA-VĀṆIJYA. From the *Āvaśyaka Cūrṇi*[7] it would seem that originally the reference here was to the manufacture, sale, and consumption of alcohol, which is described as leading to brawling, squabbling, and murder. But for Hemacandra[8] *rasa* in the sense of alcohol becomes an *upalakṣaṇa* to include honey, fat (obtained from meat), and butter, in other words the substances prohibited under the *mūla-guṇa* category. Devendra[4] adds a ban on trade in meat, milk, curds, and ghee.

9. KEŚA-VĀṆIJYA. This is explained as trade in creatures that have hair. Haribhadra[1] understands by this the buying of slave girls in a place where they are cheap and selling them elsewhere to make a profit, which is reprehensible because it implies restricting

[1] Āv (H), p. 829*b*.
[2] P (A) 22 (p. 35).
[3] YŚ iii. 107.
[4] ŚrDK, pt. ii, p. 108.
[5] *Woodfordia floribunda* Salisb.
[6] YŚ iii. 108.
[7] Ibid. 109.
[8] Āv Cū, pt. ii, p. 297.

the liberty of others. Hemacandra[1] distinguishes carefully between this occupation, which affects living beings, human or animal, and *danta-vāṇijya*, which concerns only parts of animals. When bought and sold, animals are bound to suffer from beating and tying up and from hunger and thirst.

10. VIṢA-VĀṆIJYA. This implies a ban on trade in poisons such as aconite, weapons such as swords, mechanical devices such as norias, iron implements such as spades and ploughs, all of which are potentially dangerous to life.[2] Hemacandra includes here yellow orpiment, which Devendra[3] more logically places under *lākṣā-vāṇijya*.

11. YANTRA-PĪḌANA. This is deemed to be the operation of mills and presses for crushing sugar-cane and for expressing oil from sesamum seed, mustard seed, and castor-oil beans as well as the 'crushing' of water in norias. The destruction of life thereby provoked is so great that a popular saying (*laukika*) affirms that an oil-press is as evil as ten slaughterhouses.[4] Devendra[5] includes here all trade in such articles as grindstones, pestles, and mortars.

12. NIRLAÑCHANA. Haribhadra[6] understands by this the gelding of bulls and other animals. Hemacandra[7] extends the meaning to cover the branding, docking, nose-piercing, and cutting off of the ears and dewlaps of livestock.

13. DAVĀGNI-DĀNA. Haribhadra[8] interprets this on the basis of the *Āvaśyaka Cūrṇi* as 'setting fire to the meadows as is the custom in Uttarapatha, so that later on, when the rains come the grass may grow lushly'. Hemacandra[9] 'offers three explanations: either the careless starting of woodland fires by foresters; or the kindling of fires out of piety in the *dīpotsava* festival for a man's future weal at the hour of his death; or the system of predatory cultivation described by Haribhadra. In all cases there is very great loss of life.

14. SARAḤ-ŚOṢAṆA. This is explained as drawing off the water from lakes, tanks, and watercourses so that they dry up and can be sown with crops; thus all forms of aquatic life are destroyed.[9]

15. ASATI-POṢAṆA. For Haribhadra[10] this means the rearing

[1] YŚ iii. 109.
[2] Ibid. 110.
[3] ŚrDK, pt. ii, p. 108.
[4] YŚ iii. 111.
[5] ŚrDK, pt. ii, p. 108.
[6] Āv (H), p. 829*b*.
[7] YŚ iii. 112.
[8] Āv (H), p. 830*a*.
[9] YŚ iii. 114.
[10] Āv (H), p. 830*a*.

of girls for prostitution as is the custom in the Gauḍa country. Hemacandra[1] supplements this to include the breeding and keeping of destructive animals and birds such as parrots, mynahs, peacocks, cocks, cats, dogs, and monkeys. Devendra[2] adds the further idea of rearing eunuchs.

Although the Digambaras have not inherited the tradition of the fifteen forbidden trades they enforce some similar interdictions under other heads. In almost every text, for example, the ban on the keeping of destructive animals and birds is included in the *hiṃsā-pradāna* division of *anartha-daṇḍa* which also embraces everything that is understood by *viṣa-vāṇijya* and *lākṣā-vāṇijya*. Samantabhadra[3] and Cāmuṇḍarāya[4] subdivide the *pāpopadeśa* division of *anartha-daṇḍa* into *kleśa-vāṇijya* (in which it would seem not unreasonable to discern a false sanskritization of a Prakrit *kesa-vāṇijya*) and *tiryag-vāṇijya* which together cover the ground of the ninth forbidden trade.

The eternal dilemma of Jainism in laying down an ethos for the layman has been well put by Āśādhara. The lay estate, he says, cannot exist without activity and there can be no activity without the taking of life; in its grosser form this is to be avoided sedulously but the implicit part of it is hard to avoid. It follows that at least the keeping of animals and contact with any destructive implements are to be eschewed.[5]

At the same time certain Digambara milieux have undoubtedly widened the sphere of occupations open to a believing Jaina and may have consciously rejected some of the interdictions described above. The *Ādi-purāṇa*,[6] for instance, makes provision for a man belonging to a caste which bears arms to retain them if essential to his livelihood.

In general, however, Digambaras and Śvetambaras agree in admitting only a limited number of ways of earning one's living: but *ācāryas* of the school of Jinasena[7] mention various forms of *vārttā* defined as 'the pursuit of a profession in a pure way' which is itself regarded as one of the six daily *karmans*. The later Śvetāmbaras from Ratnaśekhara[8] onwards generally refer to seven licit *upāyas*:

[1] YŚ iii. 113.
[2] ŚrDK, pt. ii, p. 108.
[3] RK iii. 30.
[4] CS, p. 9.
[5] SDhA iv. 12.
[6] MP xxxviii. 125.
[7] e.g. CS, p. 20.
[8] *Śrāddha-vidhi*, p. 90.

ŚVETĀMBARA	DIGAMBARA
(1) *vāṇijya* (trade)	*vāṇijya*
(2) *vidyā* (practice of medicine)	*maṣi* (clerical occupations)
(3) *kṛṣi* (agriculture)	*kṛṣi*
(4) *śilpa* (artisanal crafts)	*śilpa-karman*
(5) *pāśupālya* (animal husbandry)	*asi* (military occupations)
(6) *sevā* (service of a ruler)	
(7) *bhikṣā* (mendicancy)	

The Śvetāmbara list is apparently designed to indicate a sequence of desirability; trade is the best means of getting one's living whilst begging is the worst:[1] it represents a last resort for the blind and the crippled. *Vidyā* covers astrology and divination as well as chemistry and perfumery. For *kṛṣi* the late Digambara work the *Traivarṇikācāra*[2] suggests in preference to tilling the soil a form of *métayage* in which a Jaina business man would provide oxen, seed, and implements for others to use.

Five typical actions symbolizing the round of daily duties in the home are grouped together and styled the 'slaughter-houses' (*sūna*) because they inevitably result in the destruction of living organisms. The following verse detailing them is quoted in Prabhācandra's commentary on the *Ratna-karaṇḍa*:[3]

khaṇḍanī peṣaṇī cullī uda-kumbhaḥ pramārjanī
pañca-sūnā gṛhasthasya tena mokṣaṃ na gacchati.

These *sūnas* which impede the path to *mokṣa* are eliminated, says Āśādhara,[4] by almsgiving to ascetics, and in fact when they are mentioned in the texts it is always under the head of *dāna*. The enumeration is as follows:

(i) pounding (*khaṇḍanī*, *kuṭṭanī*) symbolized by the pestle and mortar;
(ii) grinding (*peṣaṇī*) symbolized by the hand-mill;
(iii) cooking (*cullī*) symbolized by the fire-place;
(iv) cleansing (*uda-kumbha*) symbolized by the water-pot;
(v) sweeping (*pramārjanī*) symbolized by the broom.

The five *sūnas* so styled seem to be peculiar to the Digambaras, being mentioned by Samantabhadra, Āśādhara, and Medhāvin but the enumeration can hardly be strange to the Śvetāmbaras, and

[1] ĀU i. 58. [2] TrA vii. 108. [3] RK iv. 23. [4] SDhA v. 49.

in fact, the *Nava-pada-prakaraṇa* in a quotation[1] mentions five harmful actions from which a layman who keeps the *vratas* must refrain: *kaṇḍaṇa, pīsaṇa, randhaṇa, dalaṇa, payaṇa.* The first three correspond exactly to the first three *sūnas* but then *dalaṇa* appears to duplicate *pīsaṇa* and *payaṇa* to repeat *randhaṇa*; and an embryonic version of the *sūnas* seems here to have been inserted under the *bhogopabhoga-vrata.* In the same connexion Ratnaśekhara[2] in the fifteenth century quotes a verse almost identical with that given in Prabhācandra's commentary, and the *sūnas* are mentioned by Cāritrasundara[3] amongst the forms of *ārambha.*

THE ANARTHA-DAṆḌA-VRATA

THE vow to abstain from harmful activities that serve no useful purpose covers a range of rather disparate topics and overlaps to some extent with the *ahiṃsā-vrata* and the *bhogopabhoga-vrata*, and even with the *mṛṣopadeśa aticāra* of the *satya-vrata* and the *para-vivāha-karaṇa aticāra* of the *brahma-vrata.* Four types of *anartha-daṇḍa* are listed in the canon and maintained by the Śvetāmbaras and to these the Digambaras, perhaps drawing on the definitions of *mithyātva,* have added a fifth. The five are:

(i) evil brooding (*apadhyāna*);
(ii) purposeless mischief (*pramādācarita*);
(iii) facilitation of destruction (*hiṃsā-pradāna*);
(iv) harmful counsel (*pāpopadeśa*);
(v) faulty reading (*duḥ-śruti*).

All the Śvetāmbara authorities, except Siddhasena Gaṇin and Siddhasena Sūri, give the list of four (without *duḥ-śruti*). The *Tattvārtha-sūtra* does not notice any varieties of *anartha-daṇḍa* but the commentator Pūjyapāda[4] mentions the above five and they are found in the *śrāvakācāras* from Samantabhadra[5] onwards.

(i) APADHYĀNA. The older term for this *apadhyānācarita* 'action motivated by evil brooding' is not found outside the canonical texts. Abhayadeva[6] seems to understand in this connexion

[1] NPP 75 (p. 32*b*).
[2] Ratnaśekhara on *Śrāddha-pratikramaṇa-sūtra*, 22.
[3] ĀU iii. 23. [4] T (P) vii. 21. [5] RK iii. 29.
[6] P (A) 23 (p. 36).

'business worries'. ('When should the merchant caravan set out? What goods should it carry? Where should it go? When would be the right time to buy and to sell? &c.') But already in the *Navapada-prakaraṇa* Devagupta[1] has introduced the idea of *ārta-dhyāna* and *raudra-dhyāna* whether expressed in an unwholesome desire ('Would that I might win a kingdom or great wealth, or be exempt from old age and death! Would that my enemy might die!') or the satisfaction felt when that desire is fulfilled ('How glad I am that my enemy is dead!'). This interpretation of *apadhyāna* as *ārta-dhyāna* and *raudra-dhyāna* is established by Hemacandra[2] and maintained by his successors. The generalized Digambara view is virtually the same: it is defined by Pūjyapāda and Cāmuṇḍarāya[3] as 'caressing the ideas of vanquishing, killing, imprisoning, mutilating, and despoiling others'. However, an early text, the *Dvādaśānuprekṣā*,[4] considers it to refer to 'talking of the faults of others, coveting the riches of others, lusting after the wives of others, and watching the disputes of others'. For Amṛtacandra[5] it implies thinking about battles, conquests, hunting, adultery, and theft. Āśādhara,[6] however, adopts Hemacandra's explanation.

(ii) PRAMĀDĀCARITA. Devagupta[7] understands by this the failure to cover with a cloth liquids such as oil, ghee, or molasses, for example, or addiction to vices such as alcoholism and gambling. Yaśodeva[8] and Abhayadeva refer expressly to 'hurt caused through sloth'. To the five *pramādas* normally listed Hemacandra[9] adds a further wide range of purposeless activities to be avoided: watching dancing displays or theatrical representations or listening to concerts out of curiosity (i.e. when these do not treat of a religious theme); study of the *kāma-śāstras*; dicing; games played in pools and watercourses (*jala-krīḍā*); gathering flowers; watching cock-fights or other combats of animals; playing with swings; and the maintaining of inherited enmities. To sleep the whole night is only permissible when one is exhausted by illness or by a journey. These indications of Hemacandra have been largely developed and expanded by Āśādhara,[10] but not under the head of *anartha-daṇḍa*. *Pramādācarita* he defines as the profitless destruction of *pṛthvī-kāyas*, *vāyu-kāyas*, *tejaḥ-kāyas*, and *ap-kāyas* by such actions as

[1] NPP 84. [2] YŚ iii. 75. [3] CS, p. 9.
[4] KA 344. [5] PASU 141. [6] SDhA v. 9.
[7] NPP 84. [8] P (Y) 23 (p. 89). [9] YŚ iii. 78–80.
[10] SDhA v. 10–11.

digging the ground, obstructing the wind, quenching fire with water, irrigating a field, or felling a tree; and under this head he would condemn too all unnecessary travelling. This is in fact the Digambara tradition inherited from Pūjyapāda and Cāmuṇḍarāya, whilst Kārttikeya and Amṛtacandra use very similar terms. It is to be noted that Hemacandra[1] groups under the head of *pramādācarita* those negligent and irreverent actions within a Jaina temple which are later called *āśātanās*.

(iii) HIṂSĀ-PRADĀNA. Haribhadra and succeeding writers[2] explains that it is improper to furnish means of destruction—weapons, fire, or poison to another person whether or not he is under the influence of anger at the time. Hemacandra[3] elaborates this statement by saying that carts, ploughs, swords, bows, pestles, mortars, bellows, or similar objects should not be supplied to another person unless a question of being helpful (*dākṣiṇyāviṣaye*) is involved, since *hiṃsā-pradāna* to a son or other relative is almost unavoidable. Hemacandra's definition has been taken over by Āśādhara; the more general Digambara version is that of Pūjyapāda and Cāmuṇḍarāya:[4] 'the supplying of poison, weapons, fire, rope, whips, staves, and similar objects', whilst Samantabhadra[5] speaks also of chains, swords, axes, and spades. In all these interpretations there are of course no differences except of detail. Kārttikeya,[6] however, includes under this head the keeping of destructive animals such as cats and all trade in such materials as iron or lac.

(iv) PĀPOPADESA. Haribhadra,[7] who etymologizes *pāpa* as that which precipitates (*pātayati*) into hell, regards this as 'instruction in an evil trade', citing such expressions as 'plough the fields' or 'break in the oxen' as unbefitting a Jaina layman. In general *pāpopadeśa*[8] is held to refer to the inevitable but still reprehensible operations of agriculture, but Devagupta[9] includes under it the notion of any advice to marry or procreate. Hemacandra[10] gives a number of additional examples: 'The rains have come, seed time is at hand, so plough the fields', 'geld the stallions', 'set fire to the forest in the hot season'. Like *hiṃsa-pradāna*, *pāpopadeśa* cannot be avoided when a question of being helpful is involved, but it

[1] YŚ iii. 81. [2] Āv (H), p. 830*b*. [3] YŚ iii. 77.
[4] CS, p. 10. [5] RK iii. 31. [6] KA 347.
[7] Āv (H), pt. ii, p. 830*b*: *pātayati narakādāv iti pāpam*. This is more comprehensible if put back into the Prakrit from which it must have been taken: *pāei narayāie tti pāvam*.
[8] Āv (H), p. 830*b*. [9] NPP 84. [10] YŚ iii. 76.

should never be given out of mere garrulity. Samantabhadra,[1] followed by Cāmuṇḍarāya[2] (and by Medhāvin), recognizes four types of it:

(*a*) talk of buying slaves cheap to sell them dear elsewhere (*kleśa-vāṇijya*);
(*b*) talk of buying beasts cheap to sell them dear elsewhere (*tiryag-vāṇijya*);
(*c*) giving word to trappers, hunters, or fowlers of the presence of beasts and birds (*vadhakopadeśa*);
(*d*) giving advice to cultivators which involves destruction of *pṛthvīkāyas*, *tejaḥ-kāyas*, *vāyu-kāyas*, and *ap-kāyas* (*ārambhakopadeśa*).

Pūjyapāda[3] defines it as advice which stimulates others to pursue harmful activities unnecessarily. Āśādhara[4] has widened the field of application of the term considerably to include any advice leading to *hiṃsā*, falsehood, or theft, or concerning methods of livelihood involving wrongdoing. Amṛtacandra[5] insists that *pāpopadeśa* should never be given to men to lead them astray in their professions.

(v) DUḤŚRUTI. The standard definition of this purely Digambara category, that of Pūjyapāda, or Cāmuṇḍarāya, or Amṛtacandra[6] is 'listening to, reciting, or expounding evil stories through which passion and injury are provoked'. Kārttikeya[7] understands by this 'reading *kāmā-śāstras* and listening to the faults of others'. For Samantabhadra[8] it is the study of works which befoul the mind with harmful activities, worldly attachments, violence, false belief, hatred, passion, pride, and lust. The seventeenth-century commentator Prabhācandra[9] offers as examples of texts on false belief those dealing with doctrines such as the Advaita. Āśādhara[10] adopts Samantabhadra's view and stigmatizes as examples of mind-defiling works the *Vātsyāyana-kāma-sūtra* on *kāma*, the *Laṭaka* on *hiṃsā*, the *Vārttā-nīti* on *parigraha*, the *Vīra-kathā* on *sāhasa*, thc *Brahmādvaita* on *mithyātva*, thc *Vaśī-karaṇa-tantra* on *rāga*, and on *mada* such texts as exalt the brahmin's place in the caste system.

The *aticāras* of this *vrata*, according to the Śvetāmbara version,

[1] RK iii. 30. [2] CS, p. 9. [3] T (P) vii. 21.
[4] SDhA v. 8. [5] PASU 142. [6] Ibid. 145.
[7] KA 348. [8] RK iii. 33. [9] Ibid. 30.
[10] SDhA v. 9.

are listed below with an indication of the category of *anartha-daṇḍa* of which they are held to be infractions:

(i)	libidinous speech (*kandarpa*)	*pramādācarita*
(ii)	buffoonery (*kautkucya*)	*pramādācarita*
(iii)	garrulity (*maukharya*)	*pāpopadeśa*
(iv)	bringing together harmful implements (*saṃyuktādhikaraṇa*)	*hiṃsā-pradāna*
(v)	superfluity of luxuries (*upabhoga-paribhogātireka*)	*pramādācarita*

The Digambara lists differ on one important point: the fourth *aticāra* is given as *asamīkṣyādhikaraṇa*, generally interpreted as 'inconsiderate action'. Haribhadra, in the *Dharma-bindu*[1], has preferred this more readily intelligible form, which is none the less an innovation of the *Tattvārtha-sūtra.* Whether this stems from a conscious rationalization or is the fruit of a textual corruption can only be a matter for speculation. Somadeva[2] has a quite personal version of the *aticāras* of this *vrata*: *upadeśād vañcana-pravartana* (practice of deceit on instructions), *ārambha-pravartana* (practice of harmful activity on instructions), *hiṃsā-pravartana* (practice of violence on instructions), *bhārādikya* (overloading of animals), *adhika-kleśa* (inflicting much suffering on them).

(i) KANDARPA. The *Tattvārtha-bhāṣya*[3] defines this as 'indecent language and jesting associated with concupiscence'. Siddhasena Gaṇin[3] develops this: 'language which is provoked by lust or in which the main element is lust; it is accompanied by movements of the mouth, lips, eyes, and eyebrows to arouse laughter.' Haribhadra[4] accepts the first element of this definition and adds that tradition prescribes that it is unbecoming for a Jaina layman to guffaw loudly; if laugh he must, he should confine himself to a slight titter. Abhayadeva, Yaśodeva, Municandra, and Siddhasena Sūri take the same view and Hemacandra[5] adds a further comment that a *śrāvaka* should say nothing to provoke infatuation (*mohodreka*) in himself or others. For Devendra[6] *kandarpa* is no more than roisterous laughter. In the Digambara definition[7] *kandarpa* is coarse (*aśiṣṭa*) language associated with laughter resulting from excessive *rāga* provoked by the rise of *cāritra-moha*.

[1] DhB iii. 33. [2] Handiqui, p. 269. [3] T (S) vii. 27 (p. 112).
[4] Āv (H), p. 830*b*. [5] YŚ iii. 115. [6] ŚrDK, p. 112.
[7] CS, p. 10.

(ii) KAUTKUCYA. The Prakrit *kukkuia* is also sanskritized as *kaukucya*. The commentators prefer to etymologize it as *kut* (in the sense of a pejorative particle)—*kutsitam*—*kucati*; and explain it as 'spasmodic contractions (*saṅkocana*) of the eyebrows, eyes, nose, lips, hands, and feet whilst making various sorts of funny movements'.[1] Haribhadra again cites the traditional statement that a *śrāvaka* ought not to speak in such a way as to make other people laugh, and he is followed by all the Śvetāmbara *ācāryas*. The Digambaras consider this *aticāra* to be 'vulgar speech accompanied by laughter and by undesirable gesticulation'.[2]

(iii) MAUKHARYA. Siddhasena Gaṇin[3] holds this to be speech that is vulgar, prolix, nonsensical (*asambaddha*), and impertinent (*mukhara* being an epithet applicable to anyone who speaks without due consideration). That is the general Śvetāmbara view. The Digambaras define it as 'constant purposeless talking through self-conceit'.[4]

(iv) SAṂYUKTĀDHIKARAṆA. The traditional Śvetāmbara interpretation is unvarying: the keeping together of any two objects (*adhikaraṇa*—etymologized as 'that by which one's *ātman* is guided to an evil fate'), generally implements or parts of implements, used for any of the activities (*ārambha*) of daily life which inevitably involve destruction of *jīvas*.[5] If they are kept apart there may be some reduction quantitatively in *ārambha* as the person wishing to use them may be dissuaded from doing so if they are not immediately available. Typical examples of such linked *adhikaraṇas* are pestle and mortar, plough and coulter, cart and yoke, bow and arrows. Siddhasena Gaṇin[6] gives a rather similar interpretation to the *asamīkṣyādhikaraṇa* of the *Tattvārtha-sūtra*, mentioning the supplying of grindstones (*śilā-putraka*), mill-stones (*godhūma-yantraka-śilā*), or sickles (*datra*), but noting the Digambara definition 'excessive and improper use of an object without consideration for the aim in view'. For the same term in the *Dharma-bindu*[7] Municandra offers a purely Śvetāmbara explanation. Pūjyapāda's[8] definition is practically identical with that of Siddhasena but there is no identification of the harmful objects. With Cāmuṇḍarāya[9] the concept is more complicated: *asamīkṣyādhikaraṇa* may be of three kinds: mental, vocal, or physical. Thinking of unprofitable

[1] Āv (H), p. 830*b*.
[2] CS, p. 10.
[3] T (S) vii. 27 (p. 113).
[4] CS, p. 10.
[5] Āv (H), p. 831*a*.
[6] T (S) vii. 27.
[7] DhB iii. 33.
[8] T (P) vii. 32.
[9] CS, p. 10.

literary productions would be an example of the first type; the second would cover the recounting of purposeless stories or indeed any form of the spoken word through which pain was caused to others; whilst the third would include the cutting, breaking, bruising, or throwing away purposelessly of any sentient or non-sentient leaves, flowers, or fruit. Āśādhara[1] sees in this offence 'the taking more of anything than is needed for use'.

In the *pratikramaṇa* texts there is a special avowal of offences under this head: weapons, fire, pestles, mechanical devices (*yantra*), grass, wood, *mantras*, roots (*mūla*), drugs (*bhaiṣajya*) given or caused to be given to any person. Devendra[2] explains *yantra* to mean such things as carts; grass may be used to clean maggots from wounds or for besoms, and wood for staves or for norias; whilst *mūla* means roots such as *nāga-damani*[3] used, for example, to assuage fever or to procure abortion.

(v) UPABHOGA-PARIBHOGĀTIRIKTITA. Haribhadra[4] records a traditional teaching on moderation in the use of *upabhogas*: if one man takes an excessive amount of oil and myrobalan for his toilet then other people attracted by this luxury go to the bathing tank and many bathe who would not otherwise have done so; and as a result many *ap-kāyas* and small aquatic creatures perish unnecessarily. Excessive indulgence in betel and flower garlands brings about similar profitless destruction. Accordingly a man who desires to bathe should either do so at home or, failing that, rub oil and myrobalan on to his head at home and, when they are completely dissolved should go to the tank and wash by taking up water in his hands. Abhayadeva, Yaśodeva, Municandra, and Hemacandra repeat the same view. Siddhasena,[5] in his commentary on the *Tattvārtha-sūtra*, explains that bathing and the use of ornaments as well as the consumption of food and drink and unguents must be on a moderate scale and adapted to one's needs. The Digambaras[6] regard this *aticāra* merely as the accumulation of *upabhogas* and *paribhogas* beyond the limit of one's needs. Āśādhara,[7] who calls this transgression *sevārthādhikatā*, prefers Hemacandra's explanation.

Here again the *pratikramaṇa*[8] texts enjoin the confession of faults committed in connexion with bathing, unguents (*udvartana*),

[1] SDhA v. 12. [2] Devendra on *Śrāddha-pratikramaṇa-sūtra*, 24.
[3] *Artemisia vulgaris* Linn. [4] Āv (H), p. 831*a*. [5] T (S) vii. 27.
[6] CS, p. 11. [7] SDhA v. 12. [8] *Śrāddha-pratikramaṇa-sūtra*, 25.

cosmetics (*varṇaka*), cooling pastes (*vilepana*), sounds, shapes, tastes, smells, clothes, couches, and ornaments. The washing of the body after anointing should not be done at a spot where there are *trasa-jīvas*, nor at a time when there are many *sampātima* creatures abroad, nor with unfiltered water. Unguents should not be dropped in the dust where they may become infested with maggots only to be eaten later by dogs or trodden under foot. *Varṇakas* such as musk and in *vilepanas* such as sandal-paste or saffron may also give rise to *sampātima* creatures. Under the head of *śabda* the following are reprehended: the sounds of musical instruments when listened to out of mere curiosity, and the noise made to arouse house lizards at night so that they come out to eat flies. Similarly undesirable are the shapes of women viewed at theatrical performances or described to others, and the savour of tasty dishes described to others to increase their *gourmandise*.

One point emerges clearly from all the texts: it is because unnecessary evil actions (*nirarthaka-pāpa*) bind on additional karma that *anartha-daṇḍa* is to be at all costs avoided. But here a careful distinction has to be made between what is *artha* and what is *anartha*. By *artha*, for example, Haribhadra[1] understands 'the practical interests of the family'. Devagupta's[2] definition is more explicit: whatever harmful action is done for the sake of religion (such as building a temple), or for the bodily organs (*indriya*) (such as eating nourishment or taking betel), or in order to produce food (such as farming) is *artha*; any similar action for other ends—such as the cutting down of creepers or the killing of lizards is *anartha*.

Certain writers tend to stigmatize as a grave form of *pramādācarita* some of the offences commonly called the *vyasanas*, particularly gambling and the frequentation of prostitutes. This point is made particularly by Devagupta. For Amṛtacandra,[3] too, gambling takes precedence over all other forms of *anartha* and leads to lying and stealing.

Somadeva[4] attempts a general definition of the various elements comprised under the term *anartha-daṇḍa*. It would include all acts done to spite, sadden, or denigrate others, or through which others are hurt or deprived of liberty. More specifically it refers to the keeping of harmful animals and the provision of harmful objects.

[1] ŚrPr 290. [2] NPP 83. [3] NPP 84.
[4] PASU 146. [5] Handiqui, p. 269.

A narrower view is that of Vasunandin:[1] the observance of the *anartha-daṇḍa-vrata* implies a ban on the selling of iron rods or snares, the keeping of destructive animals, and measuring with false balances.

As has already been noted the main differences in the scope of this vow, as understood by Śvetāmbaras and Digambaras, are to be found in the addition by the Digambaras of *duḥ-śruti* to the four categories listed in the *Upāsaka-daśāḥ* and in the replacement of *saṃyuktādhikaraṇa* by *asamīkṣyādhikaraṇa*. The ban on the keeping of such creatures as destroy other lives—cats, dogs, mongooses, cocks, vow only by the parrots, peacocks, and mynahs—seems to be introduced by the Digambaras, almost all of whom insist on this.

Amitagati[2] appears to have included under the *anartha-daṇḍa-vrata* certain elements which elsewhere are covered by the *bhogopabhoga-vrata*. Thus he stipulates that iron, lac, indigo, saffron, bees-wax (*madana*), hemp, weapons, pickles (*sandhānaka*), *sūraṇa-kanda*, flowers, curds that have been left for two days, rice that has sprouted or fermented, water-melons, and *droṇa* flowers are to be eschewed.

THE SĀMĀYIKA-VRATA

FOR all the *ācāryas* the *sāmāyika* is at the same time the first *śikṣā-vrata* (except for Āśādhara and Samantabhadra, who make it the second, and for Vasunandin, who omits it altogether) and the third *pratimā*. At the same time it is one of the six *āvaśyakas* and, to mention a category which is outside the sphere of this survey, one of the five *cāritras*. As an *āvaśyaka* it belongs to the life of the layman when it is temporary (*itvarika*) and to that of the monk when it is lifelong (*yāvat-kathita*).

Two explanations of the term are usually current. For Siddhasena Gaṇin[3] it is an exercise in *samāya* etymologized as the attainment (*aya*) of equanimity or tranquillity of mind (*sama*). Pūjyapāda[4] holds *samaya* to be 'the process of becoming one (*ekatva-gamana*), of fusion of the activities of body, mind, and speech with the *ātman*', and the practice designed to achieve this

[1] Śr (V) 215. [2] Śr (A) vi. 81–85.
[3] T (S) vii. 16 (p. 91). [4] T (P) vii. 21.

end is the *sāmāyika*. In any event the *sāmāyika* in Haribhadra's[1] definition implies at the same time the cessation of all blameable activity and the concentration on blameless activity.

The Śvetāmbara texts give a ritual for the *sāmāyika* based on the *Āvaśyaka Cūrṇī*, a distinction being made between the ordinary and the affluent layman. For a man of great wealth or invested with the authority of a ruler special rules are laid down in order to increase the prestige of the Jaina community by emphasizing the fact that he has adhered to the sacred doctrine. In the former case the following procedure is prescribed[2]:

The *sāmāyika* may be performed in one's own house or in a temple, or in a specially designed fasting-hall (*poṣadha-śālā*), or in the presence of a *sādhu*, or in a place where one is resting or not engaged in any activity. The individual intending to perform the rite must not be in fear of anyone or in dispute with anyone or indebted to anyone, nor should there be other cause for anxiety to sway his mind in any direction. He must, like a *sādhu*, observe the five *samitis* and the three *guptis* and avoid all harmful (*sāvadya*) speech, and before picking up or setting down any object he must not neglect *pratilekhana* and *pramārjana*.[3] He should try to avoid spitting or blowing his nose, but if he cannot help doing so, should first find a bare patch of ground and carry out *pratilekhana* and *pramārjana*. Then, making obeisance to the *sādhus*, he is to repeat the following formula:

karemi bhante sāmāiyaṃ sāvajjaṃ jogam paccakkhāmi jāva sahu pajjuvāsāmi duvihaṃ tivihenaṃ maṇeṇaṃ vāyāe kāyeṇaṃ na karemi karāvemi tassa bhante paḍikkamāmi nindāmi garihāmi appāṇaṃ vosirāmi.

I engage, lord, in the *sāmāyika*, making *pratyākhyāna*, for as long as I worship the *sādhus* of harmful activities whether I have done them or caused them to be done by others; neither with mind, speech nor body will I do them or cause them to be done by others; I confess them, lord, and reprehend and repent of[4] them, and I cast aside my past self.

Each word of this formula—usually styled the *sāmāyika-sūtra*—is analysed in detail by the commentators. Thus the Prakrit vocative *bhante* is interpreted as an invocation of him 'who makes an end to existence, to reincarnation' (*bhavānta*). *Nindāmi* and *garihāmi* are

[1] Āv (H), p. 831*b*. [2] Āv (H), p. 832*a*

[3] *pratilekhana* is the scanning of the ground or of any object for the presence of living creatures and *pramārjana* the removing of such living creatures by means of a monk's broom (*rajo-haraṇa*).

[4] It will be recalled that *garhā* is one of the *guṇas* of *samyaktva*.

said to have the same meaning; but the former expresses reprobation made in one's own mind and the latter reprobation voiced in the presence of a guru. *Pratyākhyāna* of course refers to harmful activities in the future, *pratikramaṇa* to those already past; and it is the self which is the author of past harmful activity (*sāvadya-yoga*) which is cast aside.[1]

After reciting this formula the layman must make *airyāpathikī-pratikramaṇa* and then *ālocanā*. After *vandana* to the *ācāryas* in order of seniority and to his preceptor he is to make *pratilekhana* and sit down to engage in *svādhyāya*. If (as happens when any of the impediments mentioned at the beginning exist) the *sāmāyika* is performed in one's own home or in the *poṣadha-śālā* the question of the arrival formalities does not arise.

A king or very rich man will come with *cāmaras* and *chattras* and regal ornaments, there will be horses and elephants and foot-soldiers and chariots in his retinue, and as he goes to the presence of the *sādhu* or to the temple, the common people will bow down and praise him crying, 'Blessed is the sacred law.' When he arrives he will lay aside the insignia of royalty and take off shoes, and sword, and diadem; and then only is he to make *Jina-pūjā* and *guru-vandana*. If, when he has performed the *sāmāyika*, he were to go away as he came with much pomp and a great retinue it would be from the religious angle undesirable, so he departs on foot. As the *sādhus* cannot fittingly stand up when he arrives, since he is only a *śrāvaka*, a seat is disposed beforehand so that he may be given the honours fitting to his rank while the *ācāryas* await him standing up. Thus the delicate question of whether or not they should rise does not present itself; and on arrival he makes the *sāmāyika* and then *pratikramaṇa* and then pays reverence to the *sādhus*. During this time he lays aside his ear-rings, signet-ring, flower garlands, betel, and outer garment, but opinions differ as to whether he should or should not take off his diadem.[2]

It is reiterated in many places that in the *sāmāyika* the layman becomes like an ascetic and for that reason it should be performed often. The assertion seems to stem originally from the *Āvaśyaka-niryukti*:[3]

> *sāmāiyammi u kae samaṇo iva sāvao havai jamhā*
> *eeṇa kāraṇeṇaṃ bahuso sāmāiyaṃ kujjā*

[1] YŚ iii. 82 (p. 505).
[2] Āv (H), p. 832*a–b*; YŚ iii. 82 (pp. 508–9).
[3] Āv (H), p. 832*a*.

A similar verse is to be found in the *Śrāvaka-prajñapti*,[1] whilst in the *Pratimā-pañcāśaka*[2] the *sāmāyika* is described as the layman's highest temporary *guṇa-sthāna*; it may exert such an effect on him that he is led to renounce the world altogether. However, this assimilation of the *śrāvaka* to the *yati* is to a greater or less extent a feature of all the necessary rites, and even in the *sāmāyika* where the identity of layman and ascetic is most nearly achieved too much stress can be laid on the comparison. Haribhadra[3] warns that the likeness will never be more than partial just as when reference is made to a *candra-mukhī strī*: her face resembles the moon only in its roundness (*pārimāṇḍalya*), affability (*saumyatā*), and grace (*kānti*) but differs from it in many other ways. Since the householder when he 'empties his senses' with mind concentrated on the Jina attains in effect to the *māha-vratas* at a particular point in time and space it might be supposed that he would achieve perfect restraint and self-control (*saṃyama*). However, as Pūjyapāda[4] points out, the *karmans* and *kaṣāyas* are still present so that the term *mahā-vrata* can only be held to be used figuratively, just as *caitra* is said to be present everywhere in a royal household.

Samantabhadra[5] envisages the layman who is performing the *sāmāyika* as a monk on whom clothes have been draped, and this phrase becomes a cliché with succeeding Digambaras. Cāmuṇḍarāya[6] takes the view that by overcoming the *pariṣahas* and *upasargas*, by maintaining silence, and by refraining from all manifestation of *hiṃsā* he does in fact achieve the *mahā-vratas*. Elsewhere, however, it is emphasized that there is no real cessation of attachment to material things or disapproval for those activities of daily life which constitute *ārambha*. Where the *sādhu* has recourse to the *mahā-vratas* the *śrāvaka* relies on the *aṇu-vratas*; nor does the latter necessarily maintain the full ritual prescriptions, for example, those governing the use of the *mukha-vastrikā* and *rajo-haraṇa*, even during the *sāmāyika*.[7]

The older Śvetāmbara texts generally lay down that the *sāmāyika* should be carried out as often as possible.[8] Amongst the Digambaras Amṛtacandra[9] recommends morning and evening and whenever possible outside those times, and Āśādhara[10] the night-

[1] ŚrPr 293. [2] P (ŚrUP) 11. [3] Āv (H), p. 833*b*.
[4] T (P) vii. 21. [5] RK iv. 12. [6] CS, p. 11.
[7] ŚrPr 310. [8] Āv (H), p. 832*b*. [9] PASU 149.
[10] SDhA v. 29.

time and the end of day; but usually the three *sandhyās* or links of time—dawn, noon, and sunset—are indicated as proper for the practice of the rite, which should last for a minimum of one *muhūrta*.

As has already been noted, the choice of a place for its performance is, for the Śvetāmbaras, the same as that offered for the other *āvaśyakas*, and the *Pratimā-pañcāśaka*[1] even refers expressly to a communal *sāmāyika* observance in the *poṣadha-śālā*. The Digambaras lay more stress on silence and solitude: Kārttikeya[2] insists on a place where there are no gnats or other disturbing insects, no babble of sounds (*kalayala*), and no tumult of many people; Samantabhadra[3] suggests a solitary forest clearing, a sanctuary, or one's own home; Vasunandin[4] a temple, one's own home, or any undefiled spot facing north or facing south; and Āśādhara[5] is content merely with solitude.

Śvetāmbaras and Digambaras give the *aticāras* of this *vrata* alike:

(i) misdirection of mind (*mano-duṣpraṇidhāna*);
(ii) misdirection of speech (*vāg-duṣpraṇidhāna*);
(iii) misdirection of body (*kāya-duṣpraṇidhāna*);
(iv) forgetfulness of the *sāmāyika* (*smṛty-akaraṇa*);
(v) instability in the *sāmāyika* (*anavasthita-karaṇa*).

(i) *Mano-duṣpraṇidhāna*. For Haribhadra[6] this means 'wondering whether household tasks have been rightly performed'. He quotes from the *Śrāvaka-prajñapti*[7] a verse to the effect that the *sāmāyika*, when performed by a *śrāvaka* who under the influence of *ārta-dhyāna* becomes a prey to mundane anxieties, is ineffective. Siddhasena Gaṇin[8] explains that *duṣpraṇidhāna* arises when the mind is swayed by eddies of anger, avarice, deceit, pride, and envy: and this interpretation is followed by later Śvetāmbaras. Pūjyapāda and Cāmuṇḍarāya[9] hold that this *aticāra* implies a failure to surrender the mind to meditation.

(ii) *Vāg-duṣpraṇidhāna*. Haribhadra[10] defines this as the use of indecent, harsh, or hurtful language. The *Śrāvaka-prajñapti*,[11] again repeatedly quoted on this point, lays down that is essential to speak with discretion and avoid any words that can have a harmful effect; otherwise the *sāmāyika* becomes impossible. For Siddhasena Gaṇin[12] this *aticāra* amounts to confused and hesitant

[1] P (ŚrUP) 12. [2] KA 353. [3] RK iv. 9.
[4] Śr (V) 274. [5] SDhA v. 28. [6] Āv (H), p. 834*a*.
[7] ŚrPr 313. [8] T (S) vii. 28. [9] CS, p. 11.
[10] Āv (H), p. 834*b*. [11] ŚrPr 314. [12] T (S) vii. 28.

enunciation of the syllables and inability to comprehend the meaning of the text. The same view is taken by Hemacandra and by Pūjyapāda, Cāmuṇḍarāya, and Āśādhara.

(iii) *Kāya-duṣpraṇidhāna*. Haribhadra[1] understands by this the failure to make *pratilekhana* and *pramārjana* of the ground and of all material objects, and to keep the hands and feet and other limbs of the body from moving, amounting to *pramāda* in the performance of the *sāmāyika*. In this connexion he speaks of making *pramārjana* with the soft flap of a garment. On the nature of this *aticāra* there is general agreement among Śvetāmbaras and Digambaras.

(iv) *Smṛty-akaraṇa*. This is generally held to be an inability through extreme carelessness to remember when the *sāmāyika* is to be performed or whether or not it has been performed. Thus since the whole of the religious life depends on mindfulness the *sāmāyika* is nullified.[2] Unlike *mano-duṣpranidhāna* which implies a temporary deviation of the mental processes this *aticāra* can vitiate the practice of the *sāmāyika* over long periods.[3] Lack of concentration is the simple Digambara definition.[4]

(v) *Anavasthita-karaṇa*. This is explained as a failure to observe the proper formalities in carrying out the *sāmāyika*, or a readiness to give it up after a very short time, or the taking of food immediately after it is finished.[5] The Digambaras apply the designation *anādara* to this *aticāra*, explaining it as a lack of zeal in the performance of the *sāmāyika*.[6]

The nature of the *sāmāyika*, as it is presented in the early Śvetāmbara texts, is obscured or altered at an early date among the Digambaras, at least as an element of the lay life. The concept of a brief period of detachment from the world and its cares, of a respite from the tyranny of love and hate, is still to the fore in Pūjyapāda, Samantabhadra, Cāmuṇḍarāya, and above all Amṛtacandra[7] but with this are gradually being associated, as aids to the attainment of this state of mind, elements of ritual from the other *āvaśyakas*. Thus Samantabhadra[8] prescribes for the *sāmāyika* the ritual movements and other requirements (*āvarta*, *praṇāma*, *yatha-jāta*,

[1] Āv (H), p. 834*b*. [2] T (S) vii. 28. [3] YŚ iii. 116 (p. 577).
[4] T (P) vii. 33. [5] YŚ iii. 116. [6] CS, p. 11.
[7] PASU 148; RK iv. 10. The general picture is that of the *sainte indifférence* of St. François de Sales.
[8] RK v. 18.

niṣadya, *tri-yoga-śuddhi*) that form part of the *vandanaka* in the Śvetāmbara canonical writings; whilst *āvartas* and *praṇāmas* are mentioned by Kārttikeya.[1]

Posture and symbol assume an increasing importance. The *saṅketa* types of *pratyākhyāna* offer a model for Samantabhadra[2] when he proposes that the *sāmāyika* should be maintained for as long as the hair is tied up, or the fist clenched, or the garment knotted. These symbolic limits for its duration—*keśa-bandha*, *muṣṭi-bandha*, and *vastra-bandha*—are noted again by Cāmuṇḍarāya[3] and by Āśādhara.[4] Various *mudrās* find a place in Amitagati's[5] description of the rite: they include the three—*Jina-mudrā*, *yoga-mudrā*, and *muktā-śukti-mudrā*—that have been incorporated in the standard Śvetāmbara *caitya-vandana* ritual, as well as a *vandana-mudrā* in which the devotee stands with his hands clasped in the form of a half-open lotus on his stomach. Five forms of obeisance (*praṇāma*) are noted by Amitagati:[6] with one limb (the head), with two limbs (the hands), with three limbs (the head and hands), with four limbs (the hands and knees), and with five limbs (the head, hands, and knees). These types are fairly generally accepted and are noted by Hemacandra.[7] The third *praṇāma* is the *ardhāvanata* and the fifth the *pañcāṅga* of the *caitya-vandana* ritual. There are more considerable divergencies in the recommendations for the postures to be adopted in the *sāmāyika*: Kārttikeya[8] mentions the *paryaṅkāsana* and the seated *kāyotsarga* to which Samantabhadra[9] and Āśādhara[10] add the upright *kāyotsarga*; Amitagati[11] envisages the *padmāsana*, *paryaṅkāsana*, *vīrāsana*, and *gav-āsana*; Cāmuṇḍarāya[12] speaks of the *paryaṅkāsana* and *makara-mukhāsana*; and Somadeva[13] notes the *padmāsana*, *vīrāsana*, and *sukhāsana*. Kārttikeya[14] lists seven requisites for the *sāmāyika*: fitting time (*kāla*) and place (*kṣetra*), posture (*āsana*) and mood (*vilaya*), purity of mind (*manaḥ-śuddhi*), of speech (*vacana-śuddhi*), and of body (*kāya-śuddhi*).

But the most significant extraneous element which is absorbed into the *sāmāyika* is the custom of making offerings. Samantabhadra[15] envisaged the *pūjā* as an aspect of *dāna*, but the more general trend is to associate it with the *sāmāyika*, and from this stems the

[1] KA 371. [2] RK iv. 8. [3] CS, p. 11.
[4] SDhA v. 28. [5] Śr (A) viii. 51–56. [6] Ibid. 63–64.
[7] YŚ, p. 612. [8] KA 355. [9] RK iv. 8.
[10] SDhA v. 28. [11] Śr (A) viii. 45–48. [12] CS, p. 11.
[13] Handiqui, p. 281. [14] KA 352. [15] RK iv. 30.

injunction that it is to be performed at the three *sandhyās*. Even Amṛtacandra[1] regards *pūjā* with *prāsuka* substances as part of the *sāmāyika* ritual whilst Vasunandin[2] comprises under this the adoration of the sacred doctrine, the images, and the *parameṣṭhins*. The logical development is already clearly apparent in the *Yaśastilaka*[3] where the discussion of the *sāmāyika-vrata* covers *dhyāna* as well as every form of *dravya-pūjā* and *bhāva-pūjā*.

With the Śvetāmbaras a more rigid tradition maintains the separate identity of the *sāmāyika-vrata* but at the same time, as will be seen, many elements from it are incorporated into the *caitya-vandana*. Thus the five *abhigamas* of that ritual are drawn from the description of the arrival of the ruler or rich disciple desirous of performing the *sāmāyika*. In fact, as with the Digambaras, this slanting of the concept had begun at an early date. Abhayadeva,[4] in his commentary on the *Pañcāśakas*, expressly admits the possibility of performing, for example, *Jina-snapana-pūjā* during the *sāmāyika* inasmuch as *pūjā* does not fall within the definition of *sāvadya-yoga*.

However, *sāmāyika* and *caitya-vandana* are still felt to be sufficiently distinct to receive separate treatment in the *Śrāddha-dina-kṛtya*. In the section devoted to the *sāmāyika* Devendra notes the traditional distinction of the rich and poor disciples and the description of the ritual given in the *Āvaśyaka Cūrṇī*, adding one significant detail that is of later origin. If the vocative *bhante* is used in the recitation of the *sāmāyika-sūtra* it is obligatory on the devotee, if no monk is present, to set up a *sthāpanācārya*—a symbolic representation of the guru—to which adoration is offered just as the Jina image is worshipped in place of the Jina, who is for ever absent from the world. For this *sthāpanācārya* Devendra uses the term *sūri*.[5] The *sāmāyika* is also mentioned in another passage of the *Śrāddha-dina-kṛtya* where it appears to designate any worship offered in the home when, because of some impediment, a man is unable to go to the temple.[6]

The diminishing importance of the *sāmāyika* in the lay life is manifest in the fifteenth-century *Śrāddha-vidhi*[7] where it figures among the practices which are possible only during the leisure of the rainy season. In that connexion Ratnaśekhara comments signi-

[1] PASU 155.
[2] Śr (V) 275.
[3] Handiqui, pp. 269–82.
[4] P (A) 25 (p. 38).
[5] ŚrDK 230.
[6] Ibid. 77.
[7] *Śrāddha-vidhi*, p. 158*a*.

ficantly that the acceptance of the *sāmāyika* is difficult for a rich man whilst the *pūjā* is easy.

A brief allusion deserves to be made to the resemblance between the *deśāvakāśika-vrata* and *sāmāyika-vrata* noted by some Digambara *ācāryas*. Samantabhadra[1] defines the latter as the complete avoidance of those five sins which are the subject of the *aṇu-vratas*. Āśādhara insists[2] that a distinction must be made between them, explaining that in the *deśāvakāśika-vrata* all *pāpa* outside a tiny radius ceases whilst in the *sāmāyika-vrata* for a brief moment all *pāpa* everywhere is eliminated.

THE DEŚĀVAKĀŚIKA-VRATA

IN character closely related to the *dig-vrata*, of which it is a reduced version in time and space, this vow is considered by the Śvetāmbaras to be the second of the *śikṣā-vratas*; but the Digambaras in the main prefer to place it among the *guṇa-vratas* immediately after the *dig-vrata*. However, Samantabhadra (with Sakalakīrti) and Āśādhara (with Medhāvin) hold it to be the first, and Kārttikeya the last, of the *śikṣā-vratas*. Perhaps because considered to be basically identical with the *dig-vrata* the *deśāvakāśika-vrata* is omitted by those *ācāryas* who make *sallekhanā* the subject of the last *śikṣā-vrata*.

Abhayadeva[3] describes this *vrata* as an assumption for a limited time (*avakāśa*) of the restrictions of place (*deśa*) set forth in the *dig-vrata* since freedom of movement is restricted to a tiny part of the area previously measured out. Where previously the boundaries were measured in hundreds of *yojanas* and the restrictions were to operate for a lifetime or a year or, at the very least, for four months, it is the surroundings of one's home and the limits of a day that are now prescribed. It is in fact a symbolic epitome of all the *vratas*. Its intensity, says the *Śrāvaka-prajñapti*,[4] should be contained within a small compass like the poison of the serpent's eye. Haribhadra explains this illustration thus: at one time the serpent's poison eye could kill at a radius of twelve *yojanas* but later a magician drove it away and limited its range to one *yojana*. In the same way a layman

[1] RK iv. 7. [2] SDhA v. 28. [3] P (A) 27. [4] ŚrPr 319.

is to contract his harmful activities and reduce the danger caused by them by imposing narrower limits on his own 'poison eye'—those movements which kill living beings.

For the spatial dimensions of the *deśāvakāśika-vrata* Siddhasena Gaṇin[1] prescribes a room of a house, a whole house, a village, or a township, and, as an example of its duration, the period from dusk to dawn. Other time limits suggested are a night, a day, five days, a fortnight, or for even shorter periods such as a *prahara* or a *muhūrta*.[2]

Spatial limitations with the Digambaras are similar. Samantabhadra[3] suggests as suitable boundaries a house, a merchant caravan, a village, a wood, or, in terms of measurements, one *yojana*. Cāmuṇḍarāya[4] proposes the suppression of all journeying except for the walk from one's home to the bathing tank and back. Amṛtacandra[5] would confine movement to a village, a street, a market, or a house. There is a tendency among later Digambaras to read into this *vrata* a ban on certain types of travel irrespective of limits set. Thus Medhāvin[6] condemns under this head all journeying to countries where the Jaina teaching is unknown and its prescriptions not observed. In regard to time the Digambaras would seem to admit much longer periods for the observance of the *deśāvakāśika-vrata* than do the Śvetāmbaras. Samantabhadra[7] speaks of a fortnight, a month, two months, four months, six months, a year, and Kārttikeya[8] mentions a year 'or other period'.

The basic idea underlying both the *dig-vrata* and the *deśāvakāśika-vrata* is that if a man reduces his freedom of movement to a restricted area, small or large, his absence from all the area not comprised within the self-imposed limits will mean that he can be said to be keeping the *mahā-vratas*, the rigid vows of an ascetic, in that wider area; whilst at the same time constant awareness of these spatial limits will result in added vigilance in the observation of the *aṇu-vratas* within them.

All the *śrāvakācāra* texts record the *aticāras* of this vow in the same form:

(i) having something brought from outside (*ānayana-prayoga*)
(ii) sending a servant for something from outside (*preṣya-prayoga*);
(iii) communicating by making sounds (*śabdānupata*);

[1] T (S) vii. 16 (p. 90). [2] YŚ iii. 117. [3] RK iv. 3.
[4] CS, p. 9. [5] PASU 139. [6] Śr (M) vii. 40.
[7] RK iv. 4. [8] KA 367.

(iv) communicating by making signs (*rūpānupata*);

(v) communicating by throwing objects (*bahya-pudgala-prakṣepa*).

(i) Ānayana-prayoga. This would seem from the evidence of the texts to mean 'getting somebody to take a message in order to obtain something from outside one's self-imposed limits'.[1] Hemacandra[2] explains that the essence of the *vrata*—the avoidance of harm to living organisms through moving to and fro outside the designated area—is violated even by causing someone else to make such movements on one's behalf. The Digambaras style this *aticāra* simply *ānayana* and render as 'giving orders to have something brought from outside the limits'.[3]

(ii) Preṣya-prayoga. The older Śvetāmbara texts distinguish this offence from the preceding one by implying an element of compulsion: 'giving orders to a servant to have something brought from outside'.[1] The Digambaras interpret it as 'causing work to be done by a servant outside one's self-imposed limits:'[4] in both this and in the previous *aticāra* orders are given to an employee.

(iii) Śabdānupata. The picture of this *aticāra* given by the Śvetāmbaras is more or less as follows: a man stands just inside the wall or enclosure of his house (which he has chosen as the boundary of his activity) and by making noises such as sneezing or coughing attracts the attention of people who are near at hand, and then employs them on various errands.[5] The Digambaras consider that the offence consists in attracting the attention of men working outside in the hope that they will understand and do what is required of them without delay.[6]

(iv) Rūpānupata. This is exactly parallel to the preceding *aticāra* except that signs and gestures are used to attract attention.

(v) Pudgala-prakṣepa. Again there is an exact parallelism (both for Digambaras and Śvetāmbaras). Here clods of earth, sticks, stones, or bricks are thrown to attract attention.

[1] Āv (H), p. 835*a*. [2] YŚ iii. 117. [3] T (P) vii. 31.
[4] CS, p. 9. [5] Āv (H), p. 835*b*. [6] CS, p. 9.

THE POṢADHOPAVĀSA-VRATA

FOR the Prakrit *posaha* (corresponding to *upavasatha*) there have come into existence a number of false sanskritizations *pauṣadha*, *proṣadha*, *poṣadha*—of which the last seems to have attained the most general currency. It is commonly held to mean the *parvan*, the day of the moon's periodic change and the etymologically tautological *poṣadhopavāsa* is accordingly interpreted as 'the fast on the *parvan* day'. Whilst this is the only explanation admitted by some texts, by the *Tattvārtha-bhāṣya*,[1] for example, elsewhere the fantasy is given free play and the *poṣadha* becomes 'that which strengthens or fattens the religious life'. (*poṣam puṣṭim prakramād dharmasya dhatte poṣadha*).[2] For Cāritrasundara it is a contraction of *paramauṣadha* 'the supreme medicament'. In ordinary usage of course *poṣadha* is synonymous with *poṣadhopavāsa*.

There are some major divergencies between Digambaras and Śvetāmbaras in *poṣadha* observance. The Digambara texts explicitly or implicitly indicate that the fast should continue from noon on the day preceding the *poṣadha* (the *dhāraṇaka*) till noon on the following day (the *pāraṇaka*) that is, for a total of forty-eight hours. The Śvetāmbara writers, however, mention a period of twenty-four hours (*aho-rātra*)[3] and some of the later authorities admit even a shorter term.[4] There are four *poṣadha* days—the *catuṣparvī* made up of *aṣṭamī*, *caturdaśī*, *purṇimā*, and *amāvāsī*—in a month but some Śvetāmbaras admit the possibility of additional days. Thus the most widespread view is that of the *Tattvārtha-bhāṣya*,[5] which names specifically the *aṣṭamī*, *caturdaśī*, and *pañcadaśī* of each half-month with the possibility of other optional *poṣadha* days (for which Siddhasena Gaṇin suggests the *pratipadā*), and the late *Ācāropadeśa*[6] would regard the 2nd, 5th, 8th, 11th, and 14th of each *parvan* as *poṣadha* days. In the main, however, the texts are silent on this point.

In the classifications of the doctrine the *poṣadha* has two niches: it is the third (or for some Digambaras the second) *śikṣa-vrata* and,

1 T (S) vii. 16 (p. 92).

2 YŚ iii. 85.

3 However, it would seem that this might in practice be longer as the layman should not break his fast till he has fed the ascetics, that is, not until after the first *pauruṣī* of the day.

4 e.g. Ratnaśekhara in the *Śrāddha-vidhi*, p. 153*b*.

5 T (S) vii. 16 (p. 92).

6 ĀU v. 4–12.

at the same time, it is the fourth *pratimā*. It is also sometimes regarded as a form of *tapas*. It will be convenient to treat together any references to the *poṣadha*, irrespective of the category to which they are assigned, and to commence by a description of the ritual as the later Śvetāmbaras have codified it.

From the canonical texts onwards the Śvetāmbaras list four spheres of application for the *poṣadha*, which may in each case be either partial (*deśatas*) or entire (*sarvatas*):

(i) In respect of food (*āhāra*):

- (*a*) partial—eating once or twice only during the period, or eating tasteless food (*nirvikṛtya*) only, or taking only rice and water (*ācāmāmla*), or taking only water;
- (*b*) entire—complete abstinence from the fourfold aliments.

(ii) In respect of bodily care (*deha-satkāra*):

- (*a*) partial—omitting some aspect of the toilet such as bathing;
- (*b*) entire—complete abstinence from bathing, massaging, cooling pastes, perfumes, and all other forms of care for the person.

(iii) In respect of sexual intercourse (*maithuna*):

- (*a*) partial—continence during the day only, or for a period of one or more *praharas*, or limitation to one or two acts of intercourse during the full period;
- (*b*) entire—complete abstinence from sexual relations.

(iv) In respect of worldly occupations (*vyāpāra*):

- (*a*) partial—refraining from certain of the harmful activities of a householder;
- (*b*) entire—complete abandonment of all activities.

It would appear that it is only in regard to food that the Digambara *ācāryas* admit the possibility of partial restraints: they insist on total abstinence in all other respects. Thus Amitagati[1] stipulates for the performance of the *poṣadha* the relinquishment of all bodily adornment (*saṃskāra*) including garlands, perfumes, unguents, and even betel (which is generally considered as *āhāra*), and of worldly duties, as well as a state of *brahma-carya*. Similarly Kārttikeya's[2] ruling is clear: that without complete cessation of *ārambha* no *poṣadhopavāsa* is effective.

[1] Śr (A) vi. 89. [2] KA 374.

With regard to food there are then three possibilities:[1]

(i) the best (*uttama*)—*upavāsa* (a complete fast);
(ii) the next best (*madhyama*)—*anupavāsa* (a fast in which the taking of water is permitted);
(iii) the least satisfactory (*jaghanya*)—*eka-sthāna* or *sakṛd-bhojana* (the taking of one meal a day).

All these food restrictions are of course forms of *pratyākhyāna*. There is fairly general agreement on the nature of the *uttama* and *madhyama* types but for the *jaghanya* type Āśādhara[2] prefers *ācāmāmla* (taking only rice and water) or *nirvikṛtya* (taking only food without *vikṛtis*) whilst Vasunandin[3] offers a choice of *eka-sthāna*, or *eka-bhakta*, or *ācāmāmla*, or *nirvikṛtya*, and Vāmadeva[4] mentions only *kañjikāhāra* (which is equivalent to *ācāmāmla*).[5]

Pūjyapāda[6] and Cāmuṇḍarāya regard the *poṣadhopavāsa* as a relinquishment of the pleasures of the five senses even of such as are afforded to the ear by sounds. Cāmuṇḍarāya[7] indeed etymologizes the word *upavāsa* as 'the state in which the sense organs abide (*vasanti*) after reaching (*upetya*) quiescence'. In general it is held that the primary aim of the *poṣadhopavāsa* is to enable the *sāmāyika* to be properly performed: wherever it is entire there of necessity the *sāmāyika* exists, where it is partial the *sāmāyika* may or may not be attained. Āśādhara[8] takes up from Samantabhadra the cliché that a man performing the *poṣadha* appears to onlookers as a *muni* on whom clothes have been draped.

According to the Śvetāmbaras the fast, like the *āvaśyakas* in general, may be carried out in a temple, in a *poṣadha-śālā*, in the presence of a *sādhu*, or in one's own home. The Digambaras are generally content to say that any secluded spot is suitable but Pūjyapāda and Cāmuṇḍarāya[9] recommend a temple, or the abode of a *sādhu*, or one's own fasting-room (*sva-poṣadhopavāsa-gṛha*). Somadeva[10] mentions a temple, one's home, a hill-top, or a forest glade. The whole time should be spent in meditation (*dhyāna*) or scriptural study (*svādhyāya*).

The *poṣadha* ritual is given in considerable detail in the later

[1] RK iv. 19. [2] SDhA v. 35. [3] Śr (V) 292.
[4] BhS (V) 508.
[5] For an explanation of these terms see p. 209.
[6] T (P) vii. 21. [7] CS, p. 12. [8] SDhA vii. 5.
[9] CS, p. 12. [10] Handiqui, p. 282.

Śvetāmbara writings. The following description is taken from Yaśovijaya[1], who has used a number of older texts:[2]

On the *poṣadha* day the layman is to lay aside ornaments of gold and jewels and to remove garlands, *vilepanas* and *varṇakas* and to break off all his worldly occupations. Then taking all he requires for the *poṣadha* he should go to the *poṣadha-śālā* or to the presence of a *sādhu*, choosing a suitable piece of bare ground for defecation and micturition. If no *sādhu* is present he sets up a *sthāpanācārya* after reciting the *namaskāra*, then makes *airyā-pathikī-pratikramaṇa* and recites a *kṣamā-śramaṇa*.[3] After examining his *mukha-vastrikā* for living organisms he again recites a *kṣamā-śramaṇa* followed by a declaration of his intention to carry out the *poṣadhopavāsa* either partially or entirely in the four kinds. After further repetitions of the *kṣamā-śramana* he performs *sāmāyika* and *svādhyāya*. Then he again examines his *mukha-vastrikā* and also his clothes, and *rajoharaṇa*, and the *sthāpanācārya*. Then he makes *pratilekhana* of his bedding and brushes the *poṣadha-śālā*, and after *airyā-pathikī-pratikramaṇa* again, engages in *svādhyāya* like a *sādhu*. He may then, if it is the proper occasion, make *pūjā* in the temple. If his *poṣadhopavāsa* is not to be a complete fast (that is, if it is to be *ekāśana*, or *ācāmāmla*, or *nirvikṛtya*, or *anupavāsa*) he may go home to eat or drink or else have food or drink brought to him in the *poṣadha-śālā* by his servants but should not obtain his meal by begging as a *sādhu* would. Returning to the *poṣadha-śālā* he follows the same routine as before. If he has to satisfy a bodily need he must observe the same precautions as a *sādhu*. If required he should perform *viśrāmaṇā* for the *sādhus*. At the end of the appointed time he declares that the *poṣadha* is completed, stands up, and recites the *namaskāra* and then, kneeling with his head touching the ground, recites verses in praise of disciples of Mahāvīra, who performed the *poṣadha*.

Āśādhara[4] gives the following directions for the performance of the *poṣadhopavāsa*. After eating and feeding the *sādhus* at noon the layman should go to a secluded spot and fast. He should spend the rest of that day meditating on religion and, after performing the evening *pūjā* and other necessary duties, should pass the night on a

[1] *Dharma-Saṃgraha*, pp. 90 ff.

[2] As, for example, Haribhadra's commentary on the *Āvaśyaka Sūtra*.

[3] For an explanation of this and other terms used see pp. 199 ff.

[4] SDhA v. 36–38.

bed which is devoid of living organisms, devoting himself to *svādhyāya*, and letting his mind dwell on the *anuprekṣās*. After the six *praharas* of the night are over he is to get up and carry out the dawn *pūjā* and necessary duties, to pass the remaining ten *praharas* in similar fashion, and at noon on the morrow of the *parvan* day to take a moderate repast, at the same time feeding the *sādhus*. During the fast *pūjā* should be made either mentally or with *acitta* materials such as *akṣata* to Jinas, *śāstra* and gurus, and all such diversions as music and dancing which lead the mind astray should be avoided.

More extensive information is given by Vasunandin.[1] On the *saptamī* and *trayodaśī* days of each half-month the layman, after eating and feeding the *munis*, is to wash his face and hands and feet, and clean out his mouth, and go to the temple for worship. After paying obeisance to the guru and carrying out the necessary duties in his presence he is to fast from the fourfold aliments also in his presence. The rest of that day he will spend reciting the scriptures, listening to *dharma-kathās*, and thinking on the *anuprekṣās*. He performs the evening *pūjā* and passes as much of the night as he can in the *kāyotsarga* posture. Having made *pratilekhana* of the ground and prepared a bed in a small compass he is to sleep in the temple or in his own house; or else he may pass the whole night in the *kāyotsarga*. Rising at dawn he will carry out the morning worship of Jina, *śāstra* and gurus with *dravya-pūjā* and *bhāva-pūjā*. According to the same pattern he will pass the actual *poṣadha* day and the morning of the *pāraṇaka* day which follows, and will then return home to eat and to feed the *sādhus*.

There is little factual difference in the *aticāras* recognized by Śvetāmbaras and Digambaras but there are two ways of arrangement of them: one traditionally Śvetāmbara, and the other adopted by the Digambaras and also by Haribhadra in the *Dharma-bindu*[2] and by Hemacandra in the *Yoga-śāstra*.[3] The former scheme is:

(i) failure to examine the sleeping-place (*apratilekhita-śayyā*);
(ii) failure to examine the place of excretion (*apratilekhita-sthaṇḍila*);
(iii) failure to sweep the sleeping-place (*apramārjita-śayyā*);
(iv) failure to sweep the place of excretion (*apramārjita-sthaṇḍila*);
(v) improper general performance of the fast (*samyag ananupālana*).

[1] Śr (V) 280–9. [2] DhB iii. 36. [3] YŚ iii. 118.

The second schema is more convenient as a basis for the present study:

(i) excreting without examining and sweeping the spot (*apratyupekṣitāpramārjitotsarga*);
(ii) picking up or laying down an object without examining and sweeping the spot (*apratyupekṣitāpramārjitādāna-nikṣepa*);
(iii) making one's bed without examining and sweeping the spot (*apratyupekṣitāpramārjita-saṃstāra*);
(iv) lack of zeal in performance (*anādara*);
(v) forgetfulness (*smṛty-anupasthāpana*).

The *aticāras* as here presented are clearly modelled on those given for the *sāmāyika-vrata* with which the *poṣadhopavāsa* is closely associated. It is of course the *Tattvārtha-sūtra*[1] that is responsible for the innovation and it is from this work that Haribhadra and, in his wake, Hemacandra have borrowed it.

(i) APRATYUPEKṢITĀPRAMĀRJITOTSARGA. A suitable spot of ground must be chosen, examined, and swept either with a monk's broom (*rajo-haraṇa*) or with the flap of one's garment before voiding faeces, urine, spittle, or any bodily discharge. The Śvetāmbara writers specify that neither must there be a failure to do this nor must it be done distractedly (*udbhrānta-cetasā*), if the destruction of living organisms by the dropped excreta is to be avoided.

(ii) APRATYUPEKṢITĀPRAMĀRJITĀDĀNA-NIKṢEPA. Siddhasena Gaṇin[1] understands by this the picking and laying down of sticks, boards, stools, and similar objects without the due precautions already mentioned. Pūjyapāda and Cāmuṇḍarāya[2] explain this *aticāra* as the handling of objects used in the *Jina-pūjā* or in the obeisance to the guru such as perfumes, garlands, sandalwood paste, and incense or of articles of personal use such as pots and pans and clothing. The word *nikṣepa* does not always figure in the nomenclature of the *aticāra* but according to Hemacandra[3] is always implied. Although this *aticāra* is missing from the traditional Śvetāmbara list the *ācāryas*, taking *śayyā* and *sthaṇḍila* as *upalakṣanas*, regard it as included.

(iii) APRATYUPEKṢITĀPRAMĀRJITA-SAṂSTĀRA. Haribhadra,[4] defining the *śayyā* or *saṃstāra* as 'consisting of *darbha* grass,

[1] T (S) vii. 29. [2] CS, p. 12. [3] YŚ iii. 118.
[4] Āv (H), p. 836*b*.

kuśa grass, blankets, or clothes', says that *pratilekhana* is obligatory before going to bed, before lying down again after easing nature, before strewing grass on the ground, and indeed before entering the *poṣadha-śālā*. As in the case of the two preceding *aticāras* inspection and cleaning are everywhere held to be essential before mats and garments are spread on the ground. Hemacandra[1] points out that in the designations of these three *aticāras* the negatives are used in a pejorative sense just as the term *abrāhmaṇa* is applied contemptuously to an unworthy brahmin.

(iv) ANĀDARA. For Siddhasena Gaṇin[2] this means a lack of zeal, and for Pūjyapāda and Cāmuṇḍarāya[3] more expressly a lack of zeal expressed in failure to perform the necessary duties (*āvaśyaka*) owing to the travail of hunger. To this *aticāra* corresponds the *samyag ananupālana* of the traditional Śvetāmbara list defined by Haribhadra[4] as a 'failure to carry out the fast according to the ritual with unflinching mind'. In this connexion Abhayadeva[5] and Siddhasena Sūri give the following elucidation. Vexed by hunger and thirst whilst performing the *poṣadhopavāsa* the layman thinks: 'Tomorrow I shall have an excellent meal cooked, with *ghṛta-pūrṇa* cakes and other delicacies and shall drink grape-juice and other refreshing drinks, I shall bathe and anoint myself and make my toilet with saffron paste and comb my hair elegantly, if it is hot I shall sprinkle myself with water.' Thus he continues to desire the pleasures of the senses and to recall with lascivious words and gestures the joys of venery and to ponder on the problems of worldly business which will confront him, so that there is no virtue in his fast. Devendra,[6] in the *Śrāddha-dina-kṛtya*, records a divergent designation for this *aticāra*: *bhojanābhoga* ('the enjoyment of food'), which, by taking *bhojana* as an *upalakṣaṇa*, he interprets in the same way.

(v) SMṚTY-ANUPASTHĀPANA. Siddhasena Gaṇin[7] explains this as 'inability to remember whether one has or has not performed the *poṣadhopavāsa* or whether one is or is not to perform it'. This is a fatal defect as the attainment of *mokṣa* is rooted in mindfulness. For the Digambaras this *aticāra* is no more than lack of concentration and Āśādhara[8] in fact applies to it the name *anaikāgrya* 'an unsteadiness of the mind in fulfilling the necessary duties'.

[1] YŚ iii. 118. [2] T (S) vii. 29. [3] CS, p. 12.
[4] Āv (H), p. 836*b*. [5] P (A) 30. [6] ŚrDK, pt. ii, p. 126.
[7] T (S) vii. 29. [8] SDhA v. 40.

As in other cases Somadeva[1] has a very personal interpretation of this *vrata*. He holds the five *aticāras* to be: failure to examine the ground (*anavekṣā*), failure to sweep the ground (*apratilekhana*), wrong physical activity (*duṣkarmārambha*), wrong mental activity (*durmanaskāra*), and failure to carry out the necessary duties (*āvaśyaka-virati*).

The commentators show considerable interest in whether a layman is to use the monk's broom (*rajo-haraṇa*) for the operation of sweeping the ground, which is an essential part of the *poṣadhopavāsa*. Haribhadra, Siddhasena Gaṇin, Hemacandra, and the Digambaras do not refer to the question but the other Śvetāmbaras all mention its use. Abhayadeva[2] and Yaśodeva discuss the point at some length quoting the *Āvaśyaka Cūrṇī* and other texts. If the layman who is making the *poṣadhopavāsa* is with a *sādhu* he is to ask him for his *rajo-haraṇa*, if he is at home he will use a *rajo-haraṇa* if one is available, if not, the end of his garment.

THE DĀNA-VRATA (VAIYĀVṚTTYA-VRATA, ATITHI-SAMVIBHĀGA-VRATA)

THIS *vrata* covers the most important single element in the practice of the religion for, without almsgiving by the laity, there could be no ascetics and therefore no transmission of the sacred doctrine. But *dāna* in its largest sense may include the giving of one's daughters to wife and the transmission of property to one's heirs (in other words questions of marriage and succession), the exercise of charity to relieve want even outside one's own community (a form of *ahiṃsā*), the construction of temples and communal institutions such as *poṣadha-śālās*, and even the performance of *pūjā* (viewed as the giving of flowers, incense, flagstaffs, and similar offerings to the Jina). In the categories used to elaborate the doctrine *dāna* also figures as one of the six *karmans* to be carried out continually by the layman and as one of the constituents of the fourfold *dharma*.

The designation usually applied to this *vrata* is *atithi-saṃvibhāga*

[1] Handiqui, p. 283. [2] P (A) 29.

('sharing with the guest'). The word *atithi* has in fact been specialized by the Jainas to signify a *sādhu* on his almsround and is explained to mean 'one who has no *tithi*', i.e. who is unfettered by the fixed dates—the *parvan* days or the festivals (*utsava*)—which are important in the secular life. Samantabhadra replaces the term *atithi-saṃvibhāga* by *vaiyāvṛttya* which is more generally used to indicate the physical services rendered by laymen or monks to other monks in need. Kundakunda and Kārttikeya prefer the form *atithi-pūjā* and Amṛtacandra *atithi-dāna*; whilst Somadeva is alone in employing the simple expression *dāna*.

Though agreeing on essentials Śvetāmbaras and Digambaras differ considerably in their formulation of the subject. It is generally recognized that five factors have to be considered:[1]

(i) the recipient (*pātra*);
(ii) the giver (*dātṛ*);
(iii) the thing given (*dātavya*, *dravya*);
(iv) the manner of giving (*dāna-vidhi*);
(v) the result of giving (*dāna-phala*).

The first four of these are set out in a separate *sūtra* at the end of the seventh *adhyāya* of the *Tattvārtha-sūtra*.[2] Pūjyapāda, commenting on this, states that the recipient is of superlative quality if possessed of attributes which lead to *mokṣa*, the giver if devoid of envy and dejection, the thing given if it conduces to study and religious austerities, the manner of giving if the *atithi* is welcomed with fitting reverence. He adds that the excellence of the reward is proportionate to these qualities just as a rich harvest depends on the fertility of the soil, the grade of the seed, and similar factors.

The Śvetāmbaras regard *dāna* as conditioned by five factors to which it must be appropriate (the enumeration is canonical and is found in all their *śrāvakācāra* texts from the *Śrāvaka-prajñapti* onwards):

(i) place (*deśa*), i.e. whether the area produces rice or wheat or other cereals or pulses;
(ii) time (*kāla*), i.e. whether there is famine or abundance;
(iii) faith (*śraddhā*), i.e. whether the giver is in a state of purity of mind;

[1] Śr (V) 220. [2] T (P) vii. 39.

(iv) respect (*satkāra*), i.e. whether due attention is shown to the *atithi*;

(v) due order (*krama*), e.g. whether the boiled rice (*odana*) or the rice gruel (*peya*) is offered first.

The *Tattvārtha-bhāṣya* refers to these factors as the *vidhi* and Siddhasena Gaṇin[1] interprets them rather differently from the other *ācāryas*. For him the mention of *deśa* means that the spot must be free of *sthāvara-jīvas* and *trasa-jīvas*, *kāla* implies a meal-time by day and not by night or a suitable occasion for offering clothes and begging bowl, *śraddhā* signifies a desire to give alms, whilst by *krama* are intended the traditional usages of a country in such matters as apparel or else the classification of *pātras* into *uttama*, *madhyama*, and *jaghanya*. Like the other Śvetāmbaras he understands by *satkāra* what the Digambaras call the *puṇyas*.

With this goes a conventional description[2] enjoining that the alms offered must be *nyayāgata* ('righteously acquired' by oneself or by one's forebears and not the product of reprehended occupations) and *kalpanīya* ('suitable', i.e. in the case of food, in conformity with the canonical prescriptions as to what may be eaten); and that they must be given with deep devotion, in the consciousness that it is the *atithi* who confers rather than receives a favour. In fact, as the *Tattvārtha-sūtra*[3] says, *dāna* is an outpouring of one's substance to benefit both the recipient who takes food and drink and the giver who finds the recompense of his action in another life.

To return to the five topics enumerated by Vasunandin both Śvetāmbaras and Digambaras recognize a classification set out in full by Amṛtacandra,[4] Amitagati,[5] Vasunandin,[6] and Āśādhara into three or, if the undesirable types are included, five *pātras*:

(i) the best recipient (*uttama-pātra*)—a Jaina ascetic (*sakala-virata*);

(ii) the next best recipient (*madhyama-pātra*)—a Jaina layman who is mounting the ladder of the *pratimās* (*viratāvirata*);

(iii) the least satisfactory recipient (*jaghanya-pātra*)—a non-practising layman who has the right belief (*avirata-samyag-dṛṣṭi*);

[1] T (S) vii. 34 (p. 119).
[2] Āv (H), p. 837*b*.
[3] T (S) vii. 33.
[4] PASU 171.
[5] Śr (A) x. 1–38.
[6] Śr (V) 221–3.

(iv) a poor recipient (*ku-pātra*)—a person of righteous life but without right belief (*samyaktva-vivarjita*);

(v) a wrong recipient (*a-pātra*)—a person devoid of right belief and of all good qualities, delighting in meat, alcohol, and honey (*samyaktva-śīla-vrata-varjita*).

Somadeva[1] seems to be the originator of another classification of the *pātras* designed to put a premium on erudition:

(i) ascetics and laymen who are the support of the faith (*samayin*);

(ii) astrologers and specialists in other sciences of practical utility (*sādhaka*);[2]

(iii) orators, debaters, and littérateurs (*samaya-dīpaka* or *samaya-dyotaka*);

(iv) ascetics and laymen who have accomplished austerities and observe the *mūla-guṇas* and *uttara-guṇas* (*naiṣṭhika*, *sādhu*);

(v) leaders of the community in the field of religion (*gaṇādhipa*, *sūri*).[3]

Āśādhara[4] has incorporated this classification into his own work, slanting it slightly by substituting *naiṣṭhika* for *sādhu* and *gaṇādhipa* for *sūri*, since both these terms may be understood to cover laymen as well as ascetics.

Somadeva[5] seems also to be responsible for a general classification of *dāna* not found elsewhere except as a quotation in the commentary to the *Sāgāra-dharmāmṛta*.[6]

(i) *sāttvika*—alms offered to a worthy recipient by a giver possessed of the seven *dātṛ-guṇas*;

(ii) *rājasa*—alms offered in self-advertisement for momentary display and in deference to the opinion of others;

(iii) *tāmasa*—alms offered through the agency of slaves or servants without considering whether the recipient is good or worthy or unworthy and without showing marks of respect.

Of these the first is the best and the last the worst. Here as elsewhere Somadeva shows his indebtedness to vedāntist influences.

[1] Handiqui, p. 284.

[2] The meaningless *śrāvaka* of the printed text should certainly be emended to *sādhaka*.

[3] These *pātras* cover the same categories of individuals as those listed by Hemacandra as *prabhāvakas* (p. 45).

[4] SDhA ii. 51. [5] Handiqui, p. 285. [6] SDhA v. 47.

He goes on to explain[1] that a meritorious ascetic is the most deserving of all *pātras* but where no *sādhu* is available charity may be given to any co-religionist. To test the worthiness of the recipient is unnecessary since the mere act of giving purifies the layman; he will in any event have to disburse money, and *dāna* is the best way of employing his wealth. Almsgiving to adherents of other faiths can do little good, and they should never be entertained in one's own house as their presence there might vitiate the ritual of the nine *puṇyas*. In particular a rigorous ban is placed on all contact with Buddhists, Cārvākas, Śaivas, and Ajīvakas.

The Digambaras have established a list of qualities which should be manifested in a giver. These seven *dātṛ-guṇas* are:

(i) faith (*śraddhā*)—confidence in the result attained by the alms given;
(ii) devotion (*bhakti*)—love for the virtues embodied in the recipient;
(iii) contentment (*tuṣṭi*)—joy in giving;
(iv) zeal (*sattva*)—even when one is not rich, that energy in practising *dāna* which excites the admiration of the very rich;
(v) discrimination (*vijñāna*)—awareness of what is fit or unfit to be given;
(vi) disinterestedness (*lobha-parityāga*, *alubdhatā*, *alaulya*)—lack of desire for worldly reward;
(vii) forbearance (*kṣamā*)—absence of anger even when there are grounds for it.

Such is the list given by Devasena,[2] Amitagati,[3] and Cāmuṇḍarāya.[4] A less developed Śvetāmbara version of this is found in Siddhasena Gaṇin's commentary on the *Tattvārtha-sūtra*:[5] *śraddhā*, *sattva*, *vitṛṣnatā*, *kṣamā*, *vinaya*, *śakti*.

Another Śvetāmbara version is given in the *Tattvārtha-bhāṣya*:[6]

(i)	absence of ill will towards the recipient (*anasuyā*)	(*anasuyatva*)
(ii)	absence of dejection in giving (*aviṣāda*)	(*aviṣāditva*)
(iii)	absence of condescension towards the recipient (*aparibhāvitā*)	(*nirahaṅkāritva*)

[1] Handiqui, pp. 284–5. [2] BhS (D) 496. [3] Śr (A) ix. 3–10.
[4] CS, p. 14. [5] T (S) vii. 33 (p. 117). [6] Ibid. 34 (p. 120).

(iv)	joy in giving (*prīti-yoga*)	(*muditva*)
(v)	auspicious frame of mind (*kuśalābhisandhitā*)	(*kṣamā*)
(vi)	lack of desire for worldly result (*dṛṣta-phalānapekṣitā*)	(*aihika-phalānapekṣā*)
(vii)	straightforwardness (*nirupadhatva*)	(*niṣkapaṭatā*)
(viii)	freedom from hankering for another rebirth (*anidānatva*).	

The forms given in brackets on the right belong to the list of seven *dātr-guṇas* of the Digambara Amṛtacandra.[1] It is apparent, therefore, that the *dātṛ-guṇas* vary between six and eight in number, with the figure of seven stabilized in the standard list of the later Digambara texts.

Amitagati[2] considers that the best giver is a man who practises *dāna* merely from hearing about it, the next best he who practises it because he has seen it carried out, and the least satisfactory he who fails to practise it even though he has both seen and heard of it. Almsgiving is totally ineffective if performed by one who beats or hurts or intimidates others or commits such offences as theft. It must always be accompanied by fair words for, offered ungraciously, it provokes enmities. If a giver still regards what he has given as his own property all his possessions will be stolen from him by his sons or wives or by thieves.

The Digambaras give a fourfold classification of the *dātavya*:[3]

(i) shelter to living beings in fear of death (*abhaya*);
(ii) food (*āhāra, anna*);
(iii) medicaments (*auṣadha*);
(iv) knowledge (*jñāna*).

Naturally this *caturvidha-dāna* represents a purely conventional division and applies only in part to the *atithi-saṃvibhāga-vrata*.

A variant classification of the *caturvidha-dāna* is given by Pūjyapāda and Cāmuṇḍarāya:[4]

(i) food (*bhīkṣā*);
(ii) religious accessories (*dharmopakaraṇa*) which fortify the *ratna-traya*;

[1] PASU 169. [2] Śr (A) ix. 40–43.
[3] e.g. Śr (V) 233–8. [4] CS, p. 14.

(iii) medicaments (*auṣadha*);
(iv) shelter (*pratiśraya*).

This schematization of course restricts the concept to almsgiving.

The concept of what may licitly be given varies. As suitable for almsgiving Haribhadra[1] recommends food and drink, clothes, almsbowls, and medicaments (*auṣadha*, *bheṣaja*), and expressly excludes money (*hiraṇya*). Siddhasena Gaṇin[2] enumerates food, clothes, almsbowls, and staves (*daṇḍaka*). The food should be rice, wheat, or other cereals, excellent of its kind, well-cooked, and well-flavoured. Devagupta[3] lists food such as sweetmeats, drink such as milk or grape-juice, clothes, almsbowls, medicaments, blankets, and lodging (*śayyā* explained as *vasati*). Abhayadeva[4] and Yaśodeva repeat Haribhadra's list of *dātavya* again insisting that no money may be given.

Hemacandra[5] remarks that it is sometimes suggested that there is no canonical authority for *dāna* in any form other than food and drink and goes on to quote texts permitting the offering of clothes, blankets, bedding, *rajo-haraṇas*, and other necessary accessories, to ascetics. Such gifts are justified because the monk is thereby enabled through care for his body to pursue the religious life. Clothes obviate the need to seek the warmth of a fire which would destroy brushwood and they help him to concentrate his mind on *śukla-dhyāna* and avoid the disturbance of sickness. The use of an almsbowl makes it easier for him to avoid swallowing food which is impure or water in which there are minute forms of aquatic life. It is irrelevant to say that there is no record of the *tīrthaṅkaras* possessing clothes or almsbowls and that accordingly their disciples do not need them, since by their supernatural knowledge the Jinas can distinguish between tainted and untainted food and between sterile water and water containing living creatures, and so do not need almsbowls. Again when *sādhus* are obliged to go outside during the rainy season the blanket helps to avoid the destruction of *ap-kāyas* whilst the merciful purpose of the *rajo-haraṇa* is too well known to need description. Similarly the *mukha-vastrikā* serves to preserve *sampātima-jīvas*, saves *vāyu-kāyas* from perishing in the stream of hot air emanating from the mouth, and

[1] Āv (H), p. 837*b*.
[2] T (S) vii. 34 (p. 119).
[3] NPP 121.
[4] P (A) 31.
[5] YŚ iii. 87 (pp. 521–6).

prevents *pṛthvī-kāyas* entering in the form of dust. In the rainy season, too, the use of planks (*phalaka*) and stools (*pīṭha*) to lie and sit on is essential, since it is forbidden to lie on ground which is covered with mould (*panaka*) and tiny living creatures (*kunthu*), whilst bedding is required in the hot and cold seasons. Most beneficial to the life of the ascetics is the provision of lodging, for an *upāśraya* furnishes them with food and drink and clothing and beds at the same time, and protects them from cold and heat, and thieves, and stinging insects. In fact it can be said that there is no objection to any article required for the religious life and the giving of such articles is therefore meritorious.

Hemacandra[1] is equally explicit in his definition of undesirable gifts (*ku-dāna*). Gold and silver inflame the passions of anger, greed, and lust, iron provokes the death of living beings, sesamum seeds afford a breeding ground for the spontaneous generation of living organisms. Nor can there be any merit in the gift of a cow which destroys living creatures with its hooves, eats unclean things (even though its dung is esteemed holy), and is the cause of suffering to its calf each time it is milked; *go-dāna* is therefore a form of *mūḍhatā*, of foolish superstition. Similarly *kanyā-dāna* the gift of a daughter in marriage cannot be regarded as meritorious: whatever fools may think, even the dowry given at a wedding is no more than an oblation that falls in the dust, for a woman is the key to the door that leads to an evil destiny and bars the way of salvation, it is she who steals away the treasure of the religious life. Offerings to the spirits of the ancestors are equally vain: those who seek to nourish the dead are in effect watering a wooden club in the belief that it will sprout into growth. It is absurd to imagine that the ancestors will derive sustenance from food given to brahmins. Offerings made or ascetic practices pursued by a son cannot absolve a parent from sin. Special condemnation is reserved for the offering of meat to recipients of alms.

Devendra[2] recommends as licit alms for a *sādhu*, in addition to the fourfold aliments, medicaments, clothes, woollen or cotton, almsbowls, books, staves of wood or bamboo, blankets, and *rajo-haraṇas*. But the best of all forms of *dāna* is the gift of a dwelling-place (*vasati*) for in addition to food and shelter this gives the possibility for study and meditation and development of the righteous life.

[1] YŚ iii. 87 (the *antara-ślokāḥ* on pp. 527–32). [2] ŚrDK 176–8.

Among Digambara *ācāryas* Amitagati[1] furnishes the fullest information about what may or may not be given. Forbidden objects include anything by which a living being may be killed, by which harmful activities may be provoked, through which misfortune is occasioned or disease spread, or as a result of which fear is inspired or the recipient ruined. There is an express ban on the gift of land —the earth is compared to a pregnant woman whose foetus, represented by the *jīvas* living within it, is destroyed by ploughing—and houses, as in them harmful activities which prolong the cycle of transmigration are carried on. The other items on his list are virtually the same as those enumerated by Hemacandra: iron, gold, money, sesamum seed, meat, *kanyā-dāna* (marriage is the concentration of all harmful activities) offerings to the *pitṛ*, and *go-dāna* (the cow is the object of false beliefs and is given by people who follow a false path). Licit *dāna*[2] on the other hand includes anything which destroys disease, has a beneficial effect for another person or strengthens devotion to religion; and in addition to the *caturvidha-dāna*, clothes, almsbowls, and shelter (*āśraya*) as distinct from landed property.

Somadeva,[3] after listing the *caturvidha-dāna*, remarks, in connexion with *āhāra-dāna*, that food offered as alms should not have been touched by evil persons or consecrated to *devas* or Yakṣas; nor should it have been bought in the market or be prepared with unseasonable commodities. Food, shelter, and books are to be supplied to the monks so that they can devote themselves to study and meditation which are impossible without comforts. Physical toil and the career of arms demand less effort from a man than intellectual concentration.

In contrast to Somadeva, who mentions only the *caturvidha-dāna* to ascetics, Vasunandin[4] enjoins the giving of food not only to the monk on his almsround, but to the very young and the very old, the blind, the dumb, and the deaf, strangers from another land, and sick people; this is the practice of *karuṇa-dāna*. To all who are weakened by disease, fasting, fatigue, or anxiety, salutary medicines are to be given. *Jñāna-dāna* implies arranging for the study and recitation of the scriptures as well as the distribution of texts that have been copied out.

In the treatment of *ku-dāna* Āśādhara propounds certain

[1] Śr (A) ix. 44–69.
[2] Śr (A) ix. 81–107.
[3] Handiqui, p. 284.
[4] Śr (V) 235–7.

distinctions. In agreement with Amitagati he lays down that a *naiṣṭhika* layman may give nothing that is prejudicial to right conduct and right belief. Offerings to the spirits of the ancestors, donations of lands to brahmins for the performance of special ceremonies, gifts made to ward off untoward consequences at eclipses of the sun or moon, and astrological conjunctions all come under this ban. It applies also to gifts of land and gold on the occasion of the marriage of a daughter where the recipients may make evil use of them so that in general the *ku-dāna* for a *naiṣṭhika* includes land, houses, iron, cattle, and horses.[1] However, a *pākṣika* layman is not only not forbidden but is enjoined to give his daughter and with her lands, house, gold, jewels, horses, elephants, and carriages to suitable co-religionists. Such *kanyā-dāna* is a form of *sama-datti*.[2] As an expression of *karuṇa-dāna*[3] one should support those who are in need because they have no livelihood, whether or not they are one's dependants, by giving them food by day, and water, betel, cardamums, and medicines even by night.

The primary form of *dāna* is of course food and as an ascetic must live by begged food it must always be the most important. The *Dvādaśānuprekṣā*[4] affirms that the giving of food embodies all gifts since the diseases of hunger and thirst occur every day. It preserves life and through the strength given by it *sādhus* study the scriptures night and day.

The *abhaya-dāna*, extolled as the noblest of all gifts and repeatedly illustrated by the famous apologue[5] of the four queens and the robber, is only in name a form of *dāna* and belongs properly to the sphere of *ahiṃsā*.

Successive Śvetāmbara writers[6] give a ritual for *dāna* quoted from the *Āvaśyaka Cūrṇī*. When a layman has completed the *poṣadhopavāsa* he is under an obligation to feed monks before he breaks his fast but at other times he may eat either before or after the almsgiving. When the mealtime approaches he puts on his best clothes and ornaments and goes to the *sādhus'* lodging to invite them to come and accept alms. If able to, they accept and two of them—one should not go alone—return with him, walking in front with the layman behind them. Directing them to his house he in-

[1] SDhA vi. 53. [2] SDhA ii. 56–57. [3] SDhA 75–76.
[4] KA 363–4.
[5] A summary of this tale in English is to be found in Jacobi's introduction to his edition of the *Samarāditya-kathā*. The Prakrit text appears on pp. 785–7.
[6] e.g. YŚ iii. 87 (pp. 526–7).

vites them to sit down. Either he himself gives them food and drink or else he holds the platter whilst his wife offers the alms. Then he makes obeisance to them and accompanies them for a few steps as they leave, after which he may take food himself. If there are no *sādhus* in the village where he lives he should go to the door when it is time to eat and look carefully in all directions giving expression to the pious wish: 'If only there were *sādhus* then I should find the way to salvation (*nistarito 'bhaviṣyam*).' The layman should in any event only consume the same food as has been offered to the monks, but the food should not have been specially prepared for them, though what is given must be of the best quality.

Devendra[1] describes the layman as making *pūjā* to the household images when the time to eat comes. Having prepared the best gruel he invites the *sādhus*, and as soon as he espies them coming towards his house he goes to meet them. Surrounded by his household he makes obeisance to them. Then like a physician to a sick man he should apply the treatment of *dāna*, taking into consideration time and place and circumstances (*avasthā*—explained as 'whether there is famine or abundance'), and the individual (*puruṣa*—explained as signifying whether he is *ācārya*, *upādhyāya*, young, old, in good or in ill health). These elements recall the five factors listed earlier as conditioning the giving of alms.

The Digambaras treat the ritual (*dāna-vidhi*) as made up of nine elements termed *puṇyas*: these are mentioned by Kārttikeya and Samantabhadra and enumerated by Vasunandin, Āśādhara, and Vāmadeva as follows:

(i) reception (*pratigraha*, *sthāpana*)—seeing the monk at the door of his house or inviting him from a distance the layman should welcome him with the words: *Namo 'stu tiṣṭha*;

(ii) giving a seat of honour (*ucca-sthāna*, *yogyāsana*)—if he accepts the proffered alms he is to be brought into the house and led to the best seat;

(iii) washing the feet (*andhri-kṣālana*, *caraṇa-kṣālana*, *pādodaka*)—his feet are then reverently washed;

(iv) worship (*arcana*)—the layman then pours the *pādodaka* (water in which the feet have been washed) on his own head and makes *pūjā* to the *sādhu* with perfumes, flowers, *akṣata*, *naivedya*, incense, fruits, and lamps;

[1] ŚrDK 171–5.

(v) obeisance (*ānati*, *praṇāma*)—next after putting on him a garland of flowers and reciting the *pañca-namaskāra* he bows down to him;

For the act of *dāna* purity under four aspects is necessary, the first three referring to the donor:

(vi) purity of mind (*manaḥ-śuddhi*)—freedom from *ārta-dhyāna* and *raudra-dhyāna*;
(vii) purity of speech (*vacana-śuddhi*)—the avoidance of harsh words;
(viii) purity of body (*kāya-śuddhi*)—firm control of the senses;
(ix) purity of food (*anna-śuddhi*).

The sixth, seventh, and eighth items of this list represent another manifestation of the familiar category of the *tri-yoga*—mind, speech, and body.

The impurities of food (*piṇḍa-doṣa*) in other words the defects that preclude its acceptance as alms by monks form a canonical category familiar both to Śvetāmbaras and Digambaras. They belong rightly to the field of *yaty-ācāra* but are enumerated by some writers on the lay life. A figure of fourteen is usually set for them though a late Digambara writer, Vāmedeva[1] notes sixteen. Here is the list as given in a verse quoted by Vasunandin from the *Mūlācāra*:[2] nails, living organisms, bones, excrement, hair, specks of dirt, meat, blood, skin, tubers, roots, fruits, seeds, and particles of grain.

In their developed form as a category of nine the *puṇyas* are peculiar to the Digambaras; however, the Śvetāmbaras include the same elements under what they term *satkāra*. Thus Haribhadra[3] mentions standing up (*abhyutthāna*), offering a seat (*āsana-pradāna*), worship (*vandana*), and following the departing guest (*anuvrajana*). To these Siddhasena Gaṇin[4] adds massaging the feet (*caraṇa-pramārjana*) the final *ādi* indicating that the enumeration is not complete. Siddhasena Gaṇin[5] notes that any gift may be either

(i) solicited (*prerita*) like the food begged by a *sādhu*; or
(ii) accepted (*anumata*) like the clothes given to an *ācārya* who, desirous to show favour to the giver, approves the offering made; or

[1] Bh (V) 530. [2] *Mūlācara*, 484. [3] Āv (H), p. 837*b*.
[4] T (S) vii. 16 (p. 94). [5] Ibid. 34 (p. 118).

(iii) not rejected (*anirākṛta*) like the offerings of flowers or incense made to the Jina.

As a postcript to the discussion of the *dātavya* it is worth noting that a fifteenth-century writer Ratnaśekhara[1] distinguishes three types of licit *dāna*: first, the fourfold aliments; secondly, clothes, almsbowl, blanket, and *rajo-haraṇa*; and thirdly such articles as needles (*sūci*), sewing-thread (*pippalaka*), nail-cutters, and ear-cleaners. In his view[1] there should be annually a presentation of certain articles including clothes, blankets, *rajo-haraṇas*, thread, wool, almsbowls, jugs (*udaṅkaka*), water jars (*tumbaka*), staves, needles, and pins (*kaṇṭaka*).

The insistence on the results of *dāna* is proportionate to its pre-eminence among religious duties. Like other meritorious acts it can contribute to the extinction of karma or to the amassing of a favourable karma or may find requital in the present life. Even though the scriptures teach that all almsgiving is vitiated if done for worldly fame it is still true, as Vasunandin[2] says, that the ignorant are loath to perform any action from which they can expect no material result. Samantabhadra[3] has written that the feeding of ascetics wipes away the karma heaped up by the activities of the household life just as water washes away blood.

Though the older texts mention various auspicious results from almsgiving the Digambaras[4] come more and more to associate *dāna* with rebirth in the fairy-tale world of the *bhoga-bhūmis*. In fact a regular equation is established: gifts to an *uttama-pātra* bring rebirth in an *uttama-bhoga-bhūmi*, to a *ku-pātra* in a *ku-bhoga-bhūmi*, and so on, whilst gifts to an *apātra* lead to no result whatever; Amitagati, Vasunandin, Āśādhara, Devasena all dwell on this theme. The Śvetāmbaras do not seem to regard this kind of reincarnation as having any special connexion with *dāna*.

Amṛtacandra,[5] concerned as always to stress the unique importance of *ahiṃsā* and its permeation of every *vrata*, affirms that, since acquisitiveness (*lābha*) which is a manifestation of *hiṃsā* is overcome by *dāna*, almsgiving brings about a cessation of *hiṃsā*. That man is full of *lobha* who fails to feed the monk who comes to his house like a bee in flight without causing injury in his path.

[1] *Śrāddha-vidhi*, p. 161*a*. [2] Śr (V) 239. [3] RK iv. 24.
[4] Śr (A) xi. 62–88; Śr (V) 239–70; BhS 497–533. [5] PASU 172–4.

The *aticāras* of the *atithi-saṃvibhāga-vrata* are enumerated similarly by all writers, Śvetāmbara and Digambara, except Samantabhadra:

(i) depositing alms on sentient things (*sacitta-nikṣepa*);
(ii) covering alms with sentient things (*sacitta-pidhāna*);
(iii) transgressing the appointed time (*kālātikrama*);
(iv) pretending that the alms belongs to others (*para-vyapadeśa*);
(v) jealousy in almsgiving (*matsaritā*).

Samantabhadra[1] replaces the third *aticāra* by *anādara* (lack of respect) a vague term taken from the *sāmāyika-* and *poṣadhopavāsa-vratas*.

(i) SACITTA-NIKṢEPA. Siddhasena Gaṇin[2] explains this as the depositing of the licit fourfold aliments on sentient uncooked grains of rice, wheat, or barley with the intention of avoiding almsgiving since such *dāna*, though offered, cannot be accepted by the *sādhu*; thus the fame of an almsgiver will be obtained at no cost. Haribhadra[3] takes the same view. Abhayadeva[4] and Yaśodeva interpret as 'depositing on the earth' (which is full of *pṛthvī-kāyas*). Hemacandra[5] offers the choice of both explanations. Pūjyapāda[6] and Cāmuṇḍarāya consider that the *aticāra* refers to the placing of food on a lotus leaf or other leaf; this would be a mistake on the giver's part but not necessarily evidence of a niggardly intention. Āśādhara[7] suggests that it may mean 'depositing on the ground, on water or on plant leaves'.

(ii) SACITTA-PIDHĀNA. The Śvetāmbaras all interpret this in the same way: covering the alms offered with fruit, leaves, flowers, or roots with the same intention as in the previous *aticāra*. The Digambaras Pūjyapāda and Cāmuṇḍarāya[8] speak only of lotus leaves.

(iii) KĀLĀTIKRAMA. The Śvetāmbaras understand by this the offering of *dāna* either when the time has passed for the monks to eat or when the time has not yet come, so that in either case they are obliged to refuse. As before, the covert intention is to avoid almsgiving. Haribhadra,[3] in fact, quotes a verse to the effect that the real value of giving lies in giving at the right time. The Digambaras describe this *aticāra* as 'offering alms at an unfitting time'.[8]

[1] RK iv. 31. [2] T (S) vii. 31. [3] Āv (H), p. 838*b*.
[4] P (A) 32. [5] YŚ iii. 119. [6] T (P) vii. 36.
[7] SDhA v. 54. [8] CS, p. 14.

(iv) PARA-VYAPADEŚA. For Haribhadra[1] and Siddhasena Gaṇin[2] this implies an artifice of the following kind: if a monk arrives in quest of alms at the time that a layman is breaking his fast after the *posadhopavāsa* he is merely told 'this does not belong to us but to someone else' or 'this belongs to so-and-so, go and ask him'. This interpretation is followed by the later Śvetāmbaras and by Āśādhara. Pūjyapāda[3] and Cāmuṇḍarāya suggest that the *aticāra* consists in offering some other person's alms as if it were one's own.

(v) MATSARITĀ. Two possibilities of interpretation are uniformly admitted by the Śvetāmbara authorities.[2] Either *matsaritā* means a state of resentment or anger aroused by the monk's solicitation even though alms are actually given; or a feeling of envy (defined as 'dejection at the excellence of an another person') provoked by the sight of a well-to-do neighbour giving generously. This again will stimulate egoistic emulation. Pūjyapāda and Cāmuṇḍarāya[4] understand by *matsaritā* a lack of respect in almsgiving even though an offering is made. Āśādhara[5] combines the Śvetāmbara and Digambara versions.

All these offences are *aticāras* because whatever the artifices adopted the rightness of *dāna* is never called in question and the external marks of respect for the mendicant which constitute the *satkāra* are observed; actual impediments to the giving of alms or dejection of mind for that cause would, as Devagupta[6] points out, constitute a *bhaṅga*.

There is another general classification, again Digambara, of the act of giving, in this case more usually termed *datti*:

(i) almsgiving (*pātra-datti*);
(ii) giving shelter (*dayā-datti*) equivalent to *abhaya-dāna* or *karuṇa-dāna*;
(iii) transfer of one's entire property to a son or kinsman before abandoning the lay life (*sakala-datti* or *anvaya-datti*);
(iv) gifts to equals (*sama-datti*) covering such subjects as transfers of property during one's lifetime or the marriage of a daughter.

The distinction of the first and fourth types is inevitably blurred at many points.

[1] Āv (H), p. 838*b*. [2] T (S) vii. 31 (p. 115).
[3] T (P) vii. 36. [4] CS, p. 14. [5] SDhA v. 54.
[6] NPP 127.

This fourfold *datti* is perhaps best defined as the treatment given to *dāna* when regarded as one of the six daily duties. The classification introduced, it would seem, by Jinasena[1] is taken up by Cāmuṇḍarāya,[2] who is indebted on more than one score to the *Mahāpurāṇa*, and later by Āśādhara, and finds a last distant echo in Medhāvin. Of its four elements *pātra-datii* has already been discussed, *dayā-datti* belongs really to *ahiṃsā*, and *sakala-datti* will be dealt with later under the *kriyās*. *Sama-datti* is defined by Jinasena[3] as the giving to an excellent recipient—similar to oneself in respect of *kriyā*, *mantra*, and *vrata*—of land, and gold, and horses, and elephants, and chariots, and daughters; such an *uttama-pātra* is styled *nistāraka* (one who assists or rescues). If no person equal to oneself in these respects is to be found such *dāna* may be made to a *madhyama-pātra*. Āśādhara[4] understands by *kriyā* such ceremonies as the *garbhādhāna* described in the *Mahāpurāṇa*, by *mantra* the *pañca-namaskāra* and other ritual formulae, and by *vrata* the *pūjā* and the *mūla-guṇas*. The distinction between *pātra-datti* and *sama-datti* is pointed again by Āśādhara[5] in a verse which proclaims that a *dharma-pātra* is to be entertained for the sake of one's well-being in a future life and a *kārya-pātra* for the sake of one's repute in this world. *Kanyā-dāna*, so strongly condemned by Hemacandra or by Amitagati,[6] is extolled on the other hand from the angle of *sama-datti* as the path to happiness in this world, since a wife, says Āśādhara,[7] punning in a way that reflects a turn of phrase of the neo-Indian languages, is called a house (*gṛha*), but a mere mass of walls and matting cannot be called a house.

The question how much of one's property is to be devoted to *dāna* is raised with increasing frequency in the later texts. The earliest writer to give a clear-cut answer to this question seems to have been Devasena,[8] who takes the view that a wise man should divide his property into six parts. The first is for the *dharma*, the second for the upkeep of his family, the third for luxuries (*bhoga*), the fourth for maintaining his servants, and the fifth and sixth shares together are to be used for performing *pūjā*.

It would appear that Hemacandra[9] is the author of a more

[1] MP xxxviii. 35. [2] CS, p. 20. [3] MP xxxviii. 38–39.
[4] SDhA ii. 57. [5] Ibid. 50. [6] Śr (A) ix. 57–58.
[7] SDhA ii. 59. The phrase is borrowed from Somadeva.
[8] BhS (D) 578–80. Other views on the proper distribution of one's material wealth are given by Jinamaṇḍana (ŚrGuV, p. 34*b*).
[9] YŚ iii. 120 (pp. 583–95).

schematic presentation of *dāna* in the form of the seven fields (*kṣetra*), though the term *kṣetra* at least is older for Haribhadra uses it twice in the *Dharma-bindu*: *vibhavocitam vidhinā kṣetra-dānam*[1] 'give alms in proportion to one's substance, and in accordance with the ritual, to the *kṣetras*' and *vītarāga-sādhavaḥ kṣetram*[2] 'the *kṣetra* is made up of those who excel in the law of the Jina'. The commentator here explains *kṣetra* as 'a recipient worthy to be given alms'. Hemacandra describes as an illustrious disciple (*mahā-śrāvaka*) the man who abides by the *vratas* and sows his wealth on the seven fields with compassion for those in great misery.[3] The seven *kṣetras* are:

(i) Jaina images (*Jina-bimba*)—wealth is sown on them by setting them up, by performing the eightfold *pūjā*, by taking them in procession through the city, by adorning them with jewels, and by dressing them with fine clothes.
(ii) Jaina temples (*Jina-bhavana*)—new ones are to be built and old ones restored.
(iii) Jaina scriptures (*Jināgama*)—the copying of the sacred texts and the giving of them to learned monks to commentate.
(iv) Monks (*sādhu*)—ordinary almsgiving.
(v) Nuns (*sādhvī*)—ordinary almsgiving.
(iv) Laymen (*śrāvaka*)—the inviting of co-religionists to birth and marriage festivals, distributing food, betel, clothes, and ornaments to them, constructing public *poṣadha-sālās* and other buildings for them, and encouraging them in religious duties. Charity is to be extended to all those who have fallen into evil circumstances.
(vii) Laywomen (*śrāvikā*)—all the duties under the last head apply equally in respect of women, who are not naturally more perverse than men.

The last four *kṣetras* are the familiar four limbs (*catur-aṅga* or *catur-varṇa*) of the Jaina community.

Hemacandra[4] goes on to say that a *mahā-śrāvaka* should use his wealth indiscriminately to assist all who are in misery or poverty, or who are blind, deaf, crippled, or sick, irrespective of whether recipients or not. Such sowing of one's substance is to be made

[1] DhB iii. 71. [2] Ibid. 73. [3] YŚ iii. 120 (verse).
[4] Ibid. (p. 595).

with limitless compassion but not with devotion (*bhakti*) as in *pātra-dāna*.

Subsequent Śvetāmbara writers take over from Hemacandra the seven *kṣetras* as a convenient method of treating the subject of *dāna* and Āśādhara[1] refers to them when discussing the appropriateness of giving alms to laywomen and nuns.

A later development is apparent in the *saṅgha-pūjā* or distribution of blankets, cloth, needles, thread, staves, almsbowls, *rajoharaṇas*, and other objects useful to an ascetic. Ratnaśekhara[2] and Cāritrasundara[3] recommend that this should be carried out annually.

THE SALLEKHANĀ-VRATA

Sallekhanā,[4] generally interpreted as ritual suicide by fasting, the scraping or emaciating of the *kaṣāyas* forms the subject of a *vrata* which, since it cannot by its nature be included among the formal religious obligations, is treated as supplementary to the twelve *vratas*; however, in a few cases—by Kundakunda, Devasena, Padmanandin, and Vasunandin—it has been incorporated, rather anomalously, into the twelve as the last *śikṣā-vrata*. Early in the Śvetāmbara tradition the *Śrāvaka-prajñapti*[5] expressly states that *sallekhanā* is not restricted to ascetics; but already in the *Śrāvaka-dharma-pañcāśaka*[6] it is given only a perfunctory mention; it is absent completely from those chapters of the *Dharma-bindu* which deal with the lay life; even Hemacandra,[7] despite the amplitude of his coverage of *śrāvakācāra*, devotes only a very short space to the subject, and after his day the *śrāvakācāra* texts are in general silent.

The *Nava-pada-prakaraṇa*[8] seems to be the only Śvetāmbara *śrāvakācāra* to treat *sallekhanā* in detail. It lists the seventeen possible forms of voluntarily chosen death of which three only are permissible for a Jaina.[9] In fact these three are fused together but the name of only one—*prāyopagamana* (by the later Śvetāmbaras often falsely sanskritized from Prakrit *pāovagamana* as *pādapagamana* and by the Digambaras sometimes abbreviated to *prāya*)—

[1] SDhA ii. 73. [2] *Śraddha-vidhi*, p. 161*a*. [3] ĀU vi. 19.
[4] CS, p. 23. [5] ŚrPr 382. [6] P (ŚrDh) 40.
[7] YŚ iii. 149–53. [8] NPP 129–35.
[9] For a consideration of these see von Kamptz, *Über die vom Sterbefasten handelnden älteren Paiṇṇa des Jaina-Kanons*, Hamburg, 1929.

is retained to become synonymous with *sallekhanā* itself, which is also often called *samādhi-maraṇa*.

Various reasons may decide a man to perform *sallekhanā*. The Śvetāmbara *Tattvārtha-bhāṣya*[1] mentions time (explained as time of famine), physical weakness (*saṃhanana-daurbalya*), calamity (*upasarga*), and the approach of death which renders the performance of the *āvaśyakas* impossible. Hemacandra insists on this last motivation. Devagupta[2] suggests that the rite should take place in a Jaina temple or at a *kalyāṇa-sthāna* (place of birth, ordination, enlightenment, or *nirvāṇa* of a *tīrthaṅkara*), or if this is impracticable, in one's own house (*gṛha*) or in the wilderness (*araṇya*). In default of a *kalyāṇa-sthāna* Hemacandra[3] advocates *gṛha* or *araṇya*; but by the former he understands a monks' lodging and by the latter a place of pilgrimage such as *Śatruñjaya*. Whatever the place chosen, the piece of ground on which the prospective suicide is to lie down must be devoid of living organisms and *pratilekhana* and *pramārjana* must have been performed.

For the Śvetāmbaras the actual practice of *sallekhanā* seems, as in the canonical sources, to begin with a progressive withdrawal of food. The *Tattvārtha-bhāṣya*[1] speaks of a gradually increasing severity of fasting of the *avamaudarya* type (in which one meal is missed and then another taken) culminating in complete abstinence from food and drink. The *Nava-pada-prakaraṇa*[4] prefers the canonically approved method of first abandoning all solid food and then making the fast complete by extending it to include liquids. The confession of one's faults (*ālocanā*) and forgiveness of all offences committed against oneself (*kṣāmaṇā*) make a man fit for the so-called *saṃstāra-dīkṣā* or death-bed consecration expressed in a special form of confession (*vikaṭanā*) and reinforcement (*uccāraṇa*) of the vows (not, however, the administration of the *mahā-vratas*). His last moments on earth will then be spent in concentration on the *pañca-namaskāra* and on the *catuḥ-śaraṇa* and in meditation on the *anuprekṣās* and on all that is covered by the term *ārādhanā*.[5] And even in these last moments he will need to be steadfast to withstand the assaults of *parīṣahas* and *upasargas*.[6]

There are some variations in the presentation of *sallekhanā* by

[1] T (S) vii. 17 (p. 95). [2] NPP 129. [3] YŚ iii. 150.
[4] NPP 131. [5] YŚ iii. 151 (p. 757).
[6] For these see Glasenapp, *Der Jainismus* p. 207. Hemacandra lists and describes them: YŚ iii. 153 (pp. 758–61).

the Digambaras, the generally current views being exemplified by Samantabhadra[1] and Cāmuṇḍarāya,[2] who would seem to enjoin the same ritual for layman and ascetic. In a rather brief reference Vasunandin[3] describes a rite appropriate to *śrāvakas* only; and a distinction between *śrāvaka* and *yati* is maintained in Āśādhara's long and detailed treatment of the theme.

Samantabhadra[4] prescribes *sallekhanā* when the individual is overcome by calamity (*upasarga*), famine, old age, or incurable disease. In this last rite (*anta-kriyā*) he is to put aside affection and enmity, and all attachment and acquisitiveness, and then to seek forgiveness of his kin and his household and his friends, at the same time expressing his forgiveness to them in gentle words. Only when he has confessed without any concealment all his transgressions, *kṛta*, *kārita*, or *anumata*, is he fit to assume the *mahā-vratas* in their entirety for as long as his life lasts. Abandoning dissatisfaction, sorrow, fear, dejection, and turpitude, and stimulating courage and steadfastness he is to soothe his mind with the nectar of the scriptures. Once he has taken the *mahā-vratas* he begins the fasting ritual which is in three stages, involving a gradual reduction in the intake, first of solid food, then of fatty liquids (*snigdha-pāna*), then of acid liquids (*khara-pāna*), until finally all nourishment is abandoned. As he repeats the *pañca-namaskāra* he is to keep his mind fixed on the five *parameṣṭhins* until at last he abandons his body.

Sallekhanā in Vasunandin's[3] conception differs little from the Śvetāmbara model and does not imply for a layman the assumption of the *mahā-vratas*. He is to abandon all *parigraha* except for clothing and after making *ālocanā* in the presence of a guru is to perform the rite in his own home or in a temple, abstaining first from solid food and then fasting completely.

Āśādhara[4] devotes a whole *adhyāya* to the consideration of *sallekhanā* and the accompanying *ārādhanā* meditations and, it would seem, regards it as the normal conclusion of human life except where sudden death makes this impossible. Preparation for it is to be made when the individual is afflicted by old age or calamity and the actual fast will begin when the physical deterioration of the body or omens, obtained from astrological data or from ornithomancy, indicate that the moment has come. He is, if pos-

[1] RK v. 1–7. [2] CS, pp. 22–24. [3] Śr (V) 271–2.
[4] SDhA viii.

sible, to repair to a place of great sanctity such as a *kalyāṇa-sthāna* or else to a Jaina temple, in which case, even if he dies on the way, the intention in his mind will have a very favourable effect on his next reincarnation. Then he is to make *ālocanā* to a guru (remaining exempt thereafter from the three *śalyas*) and to forgive all offences against himself. He is now fit to receive the *mahā-vratas* but if he feels a sense of shame either because he has been very rich or because his family are unbelievers or because nudity offends his sense of propriety he may avoid a frequented place and choose a solitary spot for this *saṃstāra-dīkṣā* which entails nakedness.[1] In this last hour it is proper even for a woman to divest herself of all clothes.[2] For the performance of the death fast external and internal expressions of purity, in each case fivefold, are required; these refer to the following points:[3]

EXTERNAL (*bāhiraṅga*)	INTERNAL (*antaraṅga*)
(1) the bed (*saṃstāra*)	right belief (*samyag-darśana*)
(2) the monkish insignia (*upadhi*)	right knowledge (*samyag-jñāna*)
(3) the confession (*ālocanā*)	right conduct (*samyak-cāritra*)
(4) food (*anna*)	*vinaya*
(5) *vaiyāvṛttya*	the six *āvaśyakas*

Whether the aspirant has taken the *mahā-vratas* or whether, unable to give up attachment to clothes, he has retained his lay status he is now ready to undertake the fast which is carried out in stages as described by Samantabhadra. In very hot weather or in a desert climate or in the case of certain diseases the dying man may be permitted to go on drinking water almost until the last and only *in extremis* will he relinquish completely the four aliments.[4] Then all those present wili stand in the *kāyotsarga* to promote the successful outcome of this holy death and the guru will whisper in the dying man's ear a few last words of exhortation: 'Vomit forth unbelief and imbibe pure religion, make firm your faith in the Jinas, have joy in the *namaskāra*, guard the *mahā-vratas*, overcome the *kaṣāyas*, tame the sense organs and by yourself see yourself within yourself (*ātmānam ātmanātmani paśya*).'[5]

[1] SDhA viii. 37. [2] Ibid. 38. [3] Ibid. 42–43.
[4] Ibid. 63–64. [5] Ibid. 68–69.

Five *aticāras* are recorded for the *sallekhanā-* as for other *vratas*:

(i) desire for a fortunate rebirth as a man (*iha-lokāśaṃsā*);
(ii) desire for a fortunate rebirth as a divinity (*para-lokāśaṃsā*);
(iii) desire for continuing life (*jīvitāśaṃsā*);
(iv) desire for death (*maraṇāśaṃsā*);
(v) desire for sensual pleasures (*kāma-bhogāśamsā*).

For the last *aticāra* of the Śvetāmbaras the Digambaras use the term *nidāna*, already familiar as one of the *śalyas*, which is practically identical with one interpretation of *kāma-bhogāśaṃsā*. The first and second infractions are given by the Digambaras as:

(i) attachment to comfort (*sukhānubandha*);
(ii) affection for friends (*mitrānurāga*).

Samantabhadra[1] is alone in regarding *bhaya* (fear) as the first *aticāra*. The *Nava-pada-prakaraṇa*[2] would consider as a *bhaṅga* of *sallekhanā* any request for food or proposal to eat again, once the fast has been begun.

(i) IHA-LOKĀŚAṂSĀ. This is the desire to be reborn in a human incarnation in which one may enjoy the good things of the world—as a guildsman or a king's minister, says Haribhadra,[3] as a universal monarch, suggests Devagupta,[2] or in Hemacandra's[4] phrase, in any position of wealth and fame.

(ii) PARA-LOKĀŚAṂSĀ. This is the desire to be reborn in the *deva-loka* and more particularly in a high position among the *devas*.

(iii) JĪVITĀŚAṂSĀ. The Śvetāmbaras[3] and Āśādhara[5] explain this as meaning either a general desire for continuing life or as a wish to go on enjoying the high consideration accorded to a person engaged in the rite of *sallekhanā*, with many people about him engaged in reciting the scriptures and performing *vaiyāvṛttya* for him and extolling his great qualities. Pūjyapāda and Cāmuṇḍarāya[6] regard this *aticāra* as 'reluctance to abandon this body which is as ephemeral as a bubble of water'.

(iv) MARAṆĀŚAṂSĀ. This is, for the Śvetāmbaras, the direct antithesis of the preceding *aticāra*.[3] It means that a man conceives the desire to die as quickly as possible because he is disappointed that no one comes to wait on him and pay him respect on his

[1] RK v. 8. [2] NPP 135. [3] Āv (H), p. 840*a*.
[4] YŚ iii. 152. [5] SDhA viii. 45. [6] CS, p. 23.

deathbed. Pūjyapāda and Cāmuṇḍarāya understand by it the hope of speedy death in order to put an end to the miseries of disease or calamity.[1]

(v) KĀMA-BHOGĀŚAṂSĀ or NIDĀNA. The same interpretation[2] may be given to *kāma* and *bhoga* as in the fifth *aticāra* of the *brahma-vrata*, but the Śvetāmbaras in general[3] specify here a desire for rebirth as a Vāsudeva, or as a very handsome or very rich man. The Digambaras[4] understand by this *aticāra* a desire that the performance of the grim rite of *sallekhanā* may result in unbounded satisfaction of sensual desires in another incarnation.

(i) SUKHĀNUBANDHA. This is to be understood as the recollection of the comforts and the pleasures one has enjoyed in former days.[4]

(ii) MITRĀNURĀGA. This is the recollection of the friends one has loved, of the games of childhood, of merry festivities, and of shared pleasures of all kinds.[4]

It is not surprising that the duty, or at least the recommended practice, of ritual suicide is an aspect of Jainism that has been remarked and reprobated by non-Jainas. Some *ācāryas*—Amṛtacandra[5] and Pūjyapāda, for example—have therefore felt it necessary to defend *sallekhanā*. Pūjyapāda[6] maintains that it cannot be called suicide because of the complete absence of *rāga* which is always present when a person under the sway of passion or hate or delusion poisons or otherwise destroys himself. He compares the layman undertaking *sallekhanā* to a householder who has stored goods in a warehouse. If danger threatens he tries to save the whole building but if that proves impossible he does his best to preserve at least the goods. The householder's warehouse is the body and his goods the *vratas*. He does not seek the destruction of his body but if he cannot maintain it he tries at least to safeguard the vows he has taken. Āśādhara[7] employs a rather similar turn of phrase: it is the *dharma*, he says, which fulfils the desires of the necessarily perishing body; the body itself is recuperable in another incarnation but the *dharma* is very hard to recover. *Sallekhanā* alone, according to Amṛtacandra,[8] will enable a man in dying to take away with him all his stock of *dharma*.

[1] T (P) viii. 37. [2] UD 57. [3] YŚ iii. 152.
[4] CS, p. 24. [5] PASU 177–80. [6] T (P) viii. 22.
[7] SDhA viii. 7. [8] PASU 175.

The underlying motive for *sallekhanā* is perhaps best put by Āśādhara:[1] if at the hour of death there is an offence against the *dharma* a lifetime of religious observance and meditation will be vain, but if the final meditation is pure even deeply encrusted sin will be eradicated.[2] It is the physical weakness and the mental delusion that are often associated with old age or grave infirmity that provoke the evil forms of *dhyāna* and make it difficult or impossible to keep up the daily *āvaśyakas* that help to make firm the mind. A healthy body is to be guarded from disease but one that fails to respond to treatment is to be rejected just as an evil man is shunned by the good.[3] In such circumstances it is easier to let the body waste away than to attempt to maintain the religious life; and *sallekhanā* will be, in Hemacandra's[4] vivid phrase, in some sort an *udyāpana*[5] for the whole *śrāvaka-dharma*.

And when this body, which is like a withering leaf or like a lamp in which the oil is running low,[6] is at last abandoned, there is hope that the *jīva* may burst asunder the cage of existence or at least abridge by many hundreds of incarnations his wanderings in the *saṃsāra*.[7] In default of *mokṣa*, it is abundantly stressed, the correct practice of *sallekhanā* will certainly lead to rebirth in the *deva-loka*.

THE PRATIMĀS

THE eleven stages of spiritual progress—the word *pratimā* means a statue and is used in another specifically Jaina sense to designate the *kāyotsarga*—have been described by Schubring[8] as, so to speak, a vertical projection of the horizontally conceived *vratas*; their enumeration would represent partly a theoretical graduation and partly the possibility of choice. The medieval *ācāryas*, however, quite plainly conceive of the *pratimās* as forming a regular progressing series in Amitagati's words, a *sopāna-mārga*, a ladder on each rung of which the aspirant layman is to rest for a number of months proportionate to its place on the list before he is fit to

[1] SDhA viii. 16.

[2] For some literary parallels illustrating the significance of the hour of death, see K. Bruhn, *Śīlāṅkas Cauppaṇṇamahāpurisacariya*, pp. 107–8.

[3] SDhA viii. 4.

[4] YŚ iii. 149 (p. 755).

[5] For the meaning of this word see p. 231.

[6] Handiqui, p. 287.

[7] SDhA viii. 28.

[8] Schubring, *Die Lehre der Jainas*, pp. 180–1.

supplement and reinforce his achievement by the practice of the succeeding stage.

The *pratimās* are listed below in the Śvetāmbara (including the *Āvaśyaka Cūrṇī*) and the Digambara enumerations, which diverge slightly:

	Śvetāmbara	Digambara	Āvaśyaka-Cūrni
(1)	darśana	darśana	darśana
(2)	vrata	vrata	vrata
(3)	sāmāyika	sāmāyika	sāmāyika
(4)	poṣadha	poṣadha	poṣadha
(5)	kāyotsarga	sacitta-tyāga	rātri-bhojana-parijñā
(6)	abrahma-varjana	rātri-bhakta	sacitta-tyāga
(7)	sacitta-tyāga	abrahma-varjana	diva-brahmacarya
(8)	ārambha-tyāga	ārambha-tyāga	divo-rātri-brahmacarya
(9)	preṣya-tyāga	parigraha-tyāga	ārambha-tyāga
(10)	uddiṣṭa-tyāga	anumati-tyāga	preṣya-tyāga
(11)	śramaṇa-bhūta	uddiṣṭa-tyāga	uddiṣṭa-tyāga-śramana-bhūta

The differences in these lists are more apparent than real and in fact concern two points: the position of *sacitta-tyāga* in the series and the insertion of *parigraha-tyāga* by the Digambaras. What is called the *kāyotsarga-pratimā* or *pratimā-pratimā* embraces a provision for continence by day and moderate sexual congress by night; in other words it is equivalent to the *rātri-bhakta-pratimā* as understood by the majority of Digambaras. The point at issue therefore is simply whether the cessation of sexual relations is to precede or to follow the abandonment of *sacitta* foodstuffs. Not even all the Digambaras are in agreement here for Somadeva reverses the positions of *sacitta-tyāga* and *ārambha-tyāga* in the table. In regard to the second point the Digambaras would seem, even if they have deliberately inserted the *parigraha-tyāga*, to have eliminated the *śramaṇa-bhūta* only in name, for from the time, at least, of Vasunandin onwards, the eleventh *pratimā* is divided into two grades to which in modern times the terms *ailaka* and *kṣullaka* are attached and the second of which seems to correspond to the canonical descriptions of the *śramaṇa-bhūta*.

In reality the most important divergence on the list is that which the nomenclature conceals: whether the *rātri-bhakta-pratimā* is to be interpreted as the restriction of sexual relations to the night time or as the abandonment of eating by night. In view of the commentators' descriptions of the *kāyotsarga-pratimā* there is little reason to question the former explanation and it would seem probable that Kārttikeya and Samantabhadra[1] (in this as in so many other matters an innovator) were led to their view by the ambiguity of the term *bhakta* and by the importance ascribed to the avoidance of night eating.

The *Dvādaśānuprekṣā*[2] is exceptional in referring to twelve stages of the lay life, the first *pratimā* implying the possession of *samyaktva* and the second the avoidance of the grosser faults (*sthūla-doṣas*) such as drinking alcohol (in effect the practice of the *mūla-guṇas*). Generally the Digambaras regard both of these qualifications as implicit in the *darśana-pratimā*. Kārttikeya lists the remaining *pratimās* in their normal Digambara order.

In the following discussion of the individual *pratimās* the Śvetāmbara view will be represented by the *Pratimā-pañcāśaka* and by Abhayadeva's commentaries on this and on the *Upāsaka-daśāḥ*, since later Śvetāmbaras appear to attach little importance to this formulation of the layman's duty. Even Hemacandra seems to have omitted it from the section of the *Yoga-śāstra* devoted to the *śrāvakācāra*, and the belated description of the *pratimās* furnished apparently for the sake of completeness by Yaśovijaya in the seventeenth century is no more than perfunctory.

1. The stage of right views (*darśana-pratimā*)

The *Pratimā-pañcāśaka*[3] begins by explaining the word *pratimā* as meaning 'body' (Prakrit *bondi*), that body which is the vehicle of the human incarnation and which in the *darśana-pratimā* is purified from misconceptions (*ku-graha*) through the elimination of *mithyātva* which is compared to a poison infecting the system. The characteristic of this stage is the avoidance of the *aticāras* of *samyaktva*.

The Digambaras from Samantabhadra[4] onwards add to this a second requirement: the observance of the *mūla-guṇas*. (Kārttikeya, of course, as was noted above, makes these into two separate *pratimās*.) Samantabhadra[4] further stipulates for this stage a lack of attachment to creature comforts and worldly life, and devotion to Jina and gurus. Amitagati[5] speaks of fostering the *guṇas* of *samyaktva*, Vasunandin[6] stresses particularly the eschewing of the seven *vyasanas*, and Āśādhara[7] insists in more general terms on

[1] RK v. 21. [2] KA 305. [3] P (ŚrUP) 4–6. [4] RK v. 16.
[5] Śr (A) vii. 67. [6] Śr (V) 57. [7] SDhA iii. 7–8.

purity of moral conduct; whilst the *Śrāvaka-dharma-dohaka*[1] characterizes the first *pratimā* very simply as 'refraining from eating the *udumbara* fruits'.

2. THE STAGE OF TAKING THE VOWS (*vrata-pratimā*)

This in the *Pañcāśaka*[2] is described as the assumption and observance of the *vratas* and the avoidance of their *aticāras* and the comprehension that the essence of the law is compassion. Abhayadeva makes it plain that here the *aṇu-vratas* are intended.

Samantabhadra,[3] however, states unambiguously that this *pratimā* implies also the observance of the *guṇa-vratas* and *śikṣā-vratas*, and from the statements of other *ācāryas* this may be taken as the generally accepted Digambara view. Freedom from the three *śalyas* is, of course, a prerequisite for the taking of the vows.

3. THE STAGE OF PRACTISING THE SĀMĀYIKA (*sāmāyika-pratimā*)

When his observance of the *aṇu-vratas* is satisfactory the aspirant to spiritual progress is fit to perform the *sāmāyika*, which, as the commentators never tire of repeating, temporarily assimilates him to the status of an ascetic. The frequency with which this is to be carried out is not clearly defined. Abhayadeva[4] considers the morning and evening twilight periods as the proper times.

Where the Śvetāmbaras see in the *sāmāyika* a purification of the soul by meditation some Digambaras like Samantabhadra[5] regard it as an act of worship of the Jina comprising the gestures of reverence associated with the *vandanaka*, and performed thrice daily. Others such as Somadeva seem to extend the concept to cover the full ritual of the *caitya-vandana*.

4. THE STAGE OF FASTING (*poṣadha-pratimā*)

This involves the keeping of four fasts in each month.[6] The differences in observance are noted under the head of the *poṣadhopavāsa-vrata*.

5. THE STAGE OF CONTINENCE BY DAY (*kāyotsarga-pratimā*, *rātri-bhakta-pratimā*)

According to Abhayadeva[7] the requirements of this *pratimā* are that on the *parvan* days when fasting a man should spend the whole night in the *kāyotsarga* posture, steadfast in heart and conscious

[1] Doha 10. [2] P(ŚrUP) 10. [3] RK v. 17. [4] P (ŚrUP) 11–12.
[5] RK v. 18. [6] RK v. 19. [7] P (ŚrUP) 18.

of his aim, and that at other times he should avoid sexual congress by day and 'make only moderate use' of his wife by night. He should also, in the words of the *Pañcāśaka*, be *vikaṭa-bhojin* (explained as 'refraining from night eating').

Amongst the Digambaras Kārttikeya[1] and Samantabhadra[2] (followed by Rājamalla) interpret this *pratimā* to mean the refusal to take food by night. The existence of this view is noted by Āśādhara[3] but he, with Cāmuṇḍarāya,[4] Somadeva, Amitagati, and Vasunandin (and also Medhāvin and Vāmadeva), prefers to understand by it the abstinence from sexual relations during the day. Āśādhara[5] indeed would seem to extend this interdiction at this stage to cover all intercourse unless during the *ṛtu* and expressly for the procreation of children.

6. The stage of absolute continence (*abrahma-varjana-pratimā*)

In this *pratimā* according to the *Pañcāśaka*[6] the layman is to avoid not only all physical contact with a woman, but he is never to allow himself to be alone with a woman, nor to engage in conversation about women; and he must also avoid any care for his personal appearance or for the clothes and ornaments he wears.

The Digambaras[7] take the opportunity here to stress the value of meditation on the impurity of the human body (the literature is very rich in verses on this theme) and the inborn wickedness of women, as an aid to carrying out this *pratimā*, in which of course are also comprised the cessation of all sexual activity and the extinction of all desire.

7. The stage of purity of nourishment (*sacitta-tyāga-pratimā*)

The *Pañcāśaka*[8] explains that from among the fourfold aliments the layman must now avoid in the *aśana* category, *inter alia*, *taṇḍula*, *umbikā*,[9] chick-peas (*caṇaka*), and sesamum (*tila*); in the *pāna* category all unboiled water as well as liquids that contain salt; in the *khādima* category the five *udumbara* fruits and *cirbhaṭika*;[10] and in the *svādima* category myrobalans (*harītakī*), betel, and the use of a

[1] KA 382–3.
[2] RK v. 21.
[3] SDhA vii. 13.
[4] CS, p. 19.
[5] SDhA vii. 14.
[6] P (ŚrUP) 20–21.
[7] e.g. RK v. 22.
[8] P (ŚrUP) 23–25.
[9] The lexicographers explain this to mean 'fried stalks of wheat or barley'.
[10] *Cucumis utilissimus*.

toothpick. As Abhayadeva points out he would also have to refrain from eating any grains or pulses, uncooked or insufficiently cooked, and any of the foodstuffs that are styled *tucchauṣadhis*.

The Digambaras[1], who nearly all make this *pratimā* the fifth on the list, exclude here the consumption of all roots and tubers, green leaves and shoots, and seeds and fruits in an uncooked state. Āśādhara[2] comments that the man who would hesitate to crush a growing plant with his foot should not be ready to pick and eat that same plant. By this *pratimā* the layman in fact engages himself to observe the same food restrictions as are incumbent on a monk.

8. THE STAGE OF ABANDONMENT OF ACTIVITY (*ārambha-tyāga-pratimā*)

In this stage the layman must relinquish all harmful activity done by himself, but is not yet strongwilled enough to abandon all activity exercised indirectly through agents or servants for the sake of a livelihood.[3]

The Digambaras state that in order to avoid *hiṃsā* all activity exercised for a livelihood—commerce equally with agriculture—is to be abandoned, but from this prohibition the *ārambha* inherent in such religious practices as *pūjā* is expressly excluded.[4]

9. THE STAGE OF BREAKING THE TIES WITH THE HOUSEHOLD LIFE (Śvetāmbara *preṣya-tyāga-pratimā*, Digambara *parigraha-tyāga-pratimā* and *anumati-tyāga-pratimā*)

The description of the ninth stage in the *Pañcāśaka*[5] is fair warrant for asserting that it corresponds both to the 'abandonment of acquisitiveness' and the 'abandonment of approval for the household life' which figure in the Digambara enumeration. In this *pratimā* when he ceases to have work done by servants the layman is to lay down the burden of worldly cares on his sons or brothers or on other members of his household (this would in effect correspond to what the Digambaras call *sakala-datti*), to reduce to the minimum his acquisitive hankerings (*mamatva*) and to foster the longing for final release (*saṃvega*).

For the Digambaras *parigraha-tyāga* is the abandonment of the ten external attachments since in Cāmuṇḍarāya's[6] words *parigraha* is the begetter of the four *kaṣāyas*, of *ārta-* and *raudra-dhyāna*, and

[1] e.g. RK v. 20.
[2] SDhA vii. 9.
[3] P (ŚrUP) 26.
[4] SDhA vii. 21.
[5] P (ŚrUP) 29–31.
[6] CS, p. 19.

of fear. Āśādhara[1] takes up the question of *sakala-datti* and prescribes the formalities for its accomplishment: they are, he says, required to prevent the resurrection of the tiger of delusion. Samantabhadra[2] notes that *anumati-tyāga* is expressed in three ways: the refusal to approve attachment to possessions (*parigraha*), harmful activities (*ārambha*), or the affairs of this world (*aihika-karman*). At this stage says Āśādhara[3] the layman should spend his time in the temple carrying out *svādhyāya* and after the midday *vandana* should take his meal, when summoned, in his own or in somebody else's house, reflecting that soon he will no longer be eating specially prepared food but only what is given as alms. This stage is essentially one of preparation for the eleventh *pratimā* when the world is renounced. Vasunandin[4] comments that the only *parigraha* permissible from the ninth stage onwards is attachment to clothes, this being gradually reduced in the succeeding *pratimās*. In this stage the layman is to refuse to express any opinion on household affairs even when it is sought by those dearest to him.

10 and 11. The stage of renunciation of the world (*uddiṣṭa-tyāga-pratimā* and *śramaṇa-bhūta-pratimā*)

In the *uddiṣṭa-tyāga-pratimā*[5] the layman, according to the *Pañcāśaka*, avoids all food specially prepared for him and goes about with shaven pate or wearing a top-knot, indifferent to mundane business. In the *śramaṇa-bhūta*[6] stage he is either to keep his head shaven or to perform the *loca*—the tearing out of the hair, traditionally in five handfuls, supposedly obligatory on every monk on ordination—and to carry the monastic requisites—the broom (*rajo-haraṇa*) and the begging-bowl (*avagraha*). He is then said to be touching or supporting the *dharma* with his body. Even if on his almsround he goes to his own kith and kin he may only beg his food and eat only what is licit for a *sādhu*.

The earlier Digambaras know only one form of the eleventh *pratimā*. Kundakunda[7] lays down that the layman is to make the begging round practising *īryā-samiti*. Samantabhadra[8] says that he is to repair to a sylvan retreat of ascetics (*muni-vana*) and to assume the *vratas*; he will then live by alms begged, wearing but one piece of cloth and pursuing asceticism. Cāmuṇḍarāya[9] agrees that he is

[1] SDhA vii. 27–28. [2] RK v. 25. [3] SDhA vii. 31–33.
[4] Śr(V) 299. [5] P (ŚrUP) 32–33. [6] P (ŚrUP) 35–37.
[7] *Sūtra-prābhṛta*, 21. [8] RK v. 26. [9] CS, p. 19.

to live by alms and to wear only one piece of cloth and adds that he is to eat from the hollow of his hand and to reject food or any other form of *dāna* that has been specially reserved for him.

The first text to mention two divisions of the eleventh *pratimā* seems to be the *Śrāvaka-dharma-dohaka*:[1] in the former, one piece of cloth is worn, in the second, only a loincloth (*kaupīna*), the hair of the head being removed either by tonsure or by the *loca*. It is not, however, until the sixteenth century that the names by which these two types of laymen are still known are applied to them for the first time: Rājamalla, in the *Lāṭī-saṃhitā*,[2] calls the former *kṣullaka* and the latter *ailaka*. The word *kṣullaka* is used as a Jaina technical term from an early date and undoubtedly the sense to be ascribed to it is that later attested in the *Ācāra-dinakara*[3] where the *kṣullakatva-vidhi*—of which ample details are given—appears as a sort of provisional ordination which does not bind the ordinand to the monastic life if he has not the vocation (*tatah saṃyamasya yathokta-pālane pravrajyā, vrata-bhaṅge punar gārhasthyam*). The meaning is not peculiar to the Śvetāmbaras for it is clearly thus that Cāmuṇḍarāya[4] uses the term *kṣullaka-rūpena* in describing the *avalamba-brahmacārin*; whilst he applies to what is today called the *kṣullaka* the designation *naiṣṭhika-brahmacārin*, a layman pledged to chastity, shaven save for a top-knot, and wearing only a loincloth; in the provision that it is to be either white or red lies perhaps a hint of the subsequent distinction of *kṣullaka* and *ailaka*,[5] for according to Medhāvin[6] the former wears white and the latter is clad in red. Medhāvin though he distinguishes two types of the eleventh *pratimā* still uses the word *kṣullaka* in the older sense.[7]

[1] Doha 17. [2] *Lāṭi-saṃhita*, vii. 55–56.

[3] *Ācāra-dinakara*, pp. 726–36. [4] CS, p. 20.

[5] Hiralal Jain, in his introduction to the *Vasunandi-śrāvakācāra*, has discussed at length the meaning and origin of the terms *kṣullaka* and *ailaka*. Basing himself on the views expressed in the *Ādi-purāṇa* and on the use of the word *kṣullaka* in a work the *Prāyaścitta-cūlika* to which he perhaps ascribes too early a date, he would consider *kṣullaka* or *kṣudraka* to designate a person unworthy and ineligible to become a monk owing to lowly birth. This argument can with difficulty be sustained, for in the tenth century *Kathā-kośa* of Hariṣena, in the tale of Yaśodhara, the young prince and princess who are Jaina devotees appear as *kṣullakas* in the train of an *ācārya*. In regard to the suggested derivation of *ailaka* from *acelaka* it can only be pointed out that—leaving aside the philological difficulty—the *ailaka* is in fact expressly described as *cela-khaṇda-dhara*. See Śr (V): *Bhūmikā*, pp. 60–64.

[6] *Dharmā-saṃgraha-śrāvakācāra*, viii. [7] Ibid. ix. 21.

From Vasunandin[1] and Āśādhara[2] onwards the Digambara authorities all describe the two varieties of the *uddiṣṭa-tyāga-pratimā* and the general delineation remains the same. The *kṣullaka* is to wear one piece of cloth (Āśādhara speaks of a white loincloth), to cut off his hair and beard either with scissors or with a razor, to take food seated, either from a bowl or from the hollow of his hand, and to perform *pratilekhana* with a soft piece of tissue. The *ailaka* may wear no more than a loincloth, must make the *loca* and eat from the palm of his hand, and will carry a peacock's feather *rajo-haraṇa* to make *pratilekhana*.

Both *kṣullaka* and *ailaka* are enjoined to observe rigidly the complete *poṣadhopavāsa* on the *parvan* days, and both must beg their food according to the following routine. The quasi-ascetic when he goes, begging-bowl in hand, to a layman's house is either to show himself and wait silently or to pronounce the *dharma-lābha* (the benediction used by a monk in greeting to a layman); and if he receives no alms he must not be dispirited but is to repeat the request elsewhere. When he has obtained enough food to satisfy the craving of hunger he should eat no more. He may drink only water that has been rendered sterile by boiling (*prāsuka*). Then having washed his almsbowl he should go back to his guru to make *pratyākhyāna* followed by *ālocanā* or confession of his faults.[3] But the *kṣullaka* or *ailaka* may, if he chooses, make a vow or *niyama* to beg only from one house (*eka-bhikṣā-niyama*); in that event he is to follow a monk on his begging round and if he meets with a refusal must of necessity fast.[4] Again he may prefer to stay all the time in a *muni-vana* engaging in *tapas* and performing the ten kinds of *vaiyāvṛttya* for the ascetics.[5]

Certain features of the monk's life remain forbidden to the layman even in the eleventh *pratimā*. He is not allowed to study the mysteries of the sacred texts. He may not engage in the *kāyotsarga* for a whole day (*dina-pratimā*), nor pursue the almsround (*vīra-caryā*) as does a monk, nor practise the *tri-kāla-yoga*, the form of asceticism which consists in meditating on a hill-top in the hot season, under a tree during the rains, and by a river's bank in winter. Pride in one's own knowledge or asceticism is severely

[1] Śr (V) 301–13. [2] SDhA vii. 34–50.

[3] Śr (V) 303–10. It is curious to find the term *dharma-lābha* used in a Digambara text.

[4] SDhA vii. 46. [5] Ibid. 47.

to be condemned and the form of greeting used by the laity *icchākāra* remains the only one which *kṣullaka* and *ailaka* may properly use.[1]

The conception of the *pratimās* seems to have suffered certain modifications in the history of Jainism. As delineated in the *Upāsaka-daśāḥ* they are a means to achieve a spiritual development which will in the end lead the devotee to take his own life by *sallekhanā*. It is therefore natural to expect that in course of time if fewer Śvetāmbara laymen tend to have recourse to ritual suicide the *pratimās* lose their significance. Where among the Digambaras *sallekhanā* remains at least in an attenuated form ('in the event of mortal illness or famine or calamity')[2] part of the pattern of life, for the ordinary layman great importance continues to attach to the *pratimās*. By placing them in the *sallekhanādhikara* of his *śrāvakācāra* Samantabhadra clearly emphasizes the connexion whilst Āśādhara expressly states that the *kṣullaka* and *ailaka* should always keep in mind the possibility of recourse to *sallekhanā*, or put in other terms, the *naiṣṭhika-śrāvaka* has still to become a *sādhaka-śrāvaka*.[3] In fact, for various reasons in the Digambara community—some have suggested that the conquest of large areas of India by Moslems who disapproved of nudity was responsible—laymen in the eleventh *pratimā* came, to a large extent, to take the place of monks. Perhaps because of the importance of these quasi-monks the sequence that led, through the *pratimās*, automatically to *sallekhanā* was broken.

There is, as certain Digambara *ācāryas*[4] imply, a special connexion between the *pratimās* and the *śikṣā-vratas*: the third and fourth *pratimās* are at the same time *śikṣā-vratas* and the fifth, sixth, and seventh all relate to the *paribhogopabhoga-vrata*, food being the main *paribhoga* and women the principal *upabhoga*; and even the last three *pratimās* are concerned, *inter alia*, with the progressive diminution of attachment to another *upabhoga*—clothing. Classifications of *śrāvakas* according to their progress through the *pratimās* are offered by some Digambaras such as Somadeva and Āśādhara.

[1] SDhA vii. 49–50. [2] RK v. 1. [3] SDhA vii. 61.

[4] SDhA iii. 1–8. For an elaboration of this subject see Śr (V): *Bhūmikā*, pp. 54–58.

THE DINA-CARYĀ

After outlining the traditional pattern of the layman's duties as expressed in the *vratas*, Hemacandra lays down that if he fulfils these and also practises charity reverently to the seven *kṣetras* and compassionately to the needy he is to be designated a *mahā-śrāvaka*,[1] a term, not it would seem, previously employed but adopted later by Āśādhara and by some Śvetāmbaras. This ideal layman is expected to carry out the obligations of his religion in a uniform round which Hemacandra calls the *dina-caryā*[2] and which serves as a framework for a description of the *pūjā* and *caitya-vandana* and the various *āvaśyakas*.

If the expression is Hemacandra's the idea is very much older. As early as the *Śrāvaka-prajñapti* the exposition of the *vratas* is followed by a rather rough-and-ready description of the *abhigrahas*.[3] This word, which in normal usage is the equivalent of *niyama* (a vow), appears already in this text, specialized in the meaning of any duty incumbent on a layman: it may include even such obligations as the provision of ghee for monks who have just performed the *loca*. It reappears in this sense in such later works as the *Śrāddha-dina-kṛtya*.[4]

In the *Śrāvaka-dharma-pañcāśaka*[5] the picture of the *dina-caryā* is already taking shape. The pious Jaina is to recite the *pañca-namaskāra* on waking and to say to himself: 'I am a *śrāvaka* and have taken the vows.' Before starting his work he goes to the temple and performs the *pūjā* and *caitya-vandana*. When he returns home he eats at the fitting time and again repairs to the temple to listen to the scriptures, perform *pūjā*, and wait on the ascetics. At night he will go to sleep, as he woke, with the *namaskāra*.

The *sūtras* of the *Dharma-bindu*[6] offer a concise notation of all the daily duties; and on this description Hemacandra[7] has drawn largely. The *śrāvaka* is to get up at the *brahma-muhūrta* (the fourteenth of the night) with the *namaskāra* on his lips and recalling his vows. A long description of the *caitya-vandana* follows and then of the *pratikramaṇa* and *pratyākhyāna*. After the morning's work the layman is to make the midday *pūjā* before taking his meal.

[1] YŚ iii. 120.
[2] YŚ iii. 122 (p. 597).
[3] ŚrPr 376.
[4] ŚrDK 269.
[5] P (ŚrDh) 42–46.
[6] DhB iii. 46 ff.
[7] YŚ iii. 122–32.

The afternoon he spends in questioning the monks about the scriptures after which he performs the evening *pūjā* and the *āvaśyakas*. He will now, if he is in the habit of eating twice a day, take his second meal. When he lies down to sleep he is to pursue his meditations on the scriptures, avoiding if he can all sexual relations and indeed all erotic ideas.

In the sixth *adhyāya* of the *Sāgāra-dharmāmṛta* Āśādhara[1] took over Hemacandra's picture of the *dina-caryā* beginning with the moment of waking when the *śrāvaka* asks himself: 'Who am I? What are my vows? What is my *dharma*?' but he did not find imitators among the later Digambaras, and there is only a faint echo of Hemacandra in Medhāvin's[2] use of the expression *mahā-śrāvaka*.

The real importance of the *dina-caryā* lies in its adoption as the preferred model for the later *śrāvakācāras*. The most important, and one of the first works constructed on these lines, is the *Śrāddha-dina-kṛtya* of Devendra. In general terms the *abhigrahas* which he prescribes for laymen may be set out as follows.[3]

The *śrāvaka* awakens with the *namaskāra* and as the torpor of sleep falls away calls to mind the religion to which he belongs, the family into which he has been born and the vows which he has assumed. When after defecation, tooth-cleaning, tongue-scraping, mouth-rinsing, and bathing he is in a state of cleanliness, of ritual purity, he is to make *dravya-pūjā* and *bhāva-pūjā* to the Jina image in the chapel of his own home and to undertake the form of *pratyākhyāna* appropriate to the time of day. Before engaging in this act of worship he should if possible perform the six *āvaśyakas*. The adoration of the Jina is then repeated in the form of *pūjā* and *caitya-vandana* in the temple. The devotee then seeks out the religious teachers and, repeating the *pratyākhyāna* before them, listens to their exposition of the scriptures. He is enjoined to inquire formally after their well-being and to perform for them various personal services, including the provision of medicaments for the sick. His work must then claim his undivided attention.

When he returns from his place of business he is to carry out the noon *pūjā* and, after providing alms for any monks who may require to be fed, he is to take his midday meal, eating in moderation. He will then reaffirm the *pratyākhyāna* and meditate on the meaning of the scriptures. At the close of the afternoon he performs the

1 SDhA vi. 1–9.

2 Śr (M) vii. 136.

3 ŚrDK 2–7: these opening verses summarize the *dina-caryā*.

evening *pūjā* and the six *āvaśyakas*. He is then to engage in *svādhyāya* and if necessary to minister to the bodily needs of the ascetics (*yati-viśrāmaṇā*) by massaging their limbs and in other ways.

Finally he will go home and, after giving religious instruction to his household, lie down to sleep: sleep, like food, is to be indulged in with moderation. If possible he should abstain from sexual intercourse and to this end he should, during the intervals of sleep, direct his mind to meditation on the impurity of the human body and the innate wickedness of women and to emulation of those who have renounced the world.

THE NECESSARY DUTIES

THE six daily *āvaśyakas*[1] or necessary duties are traditionally:

(1) *sāmāyika*—this is the subject also of a *vrata* and of a *pratimā*;
(2) *caturviṃśati-stava*—praise of the twenty-four Jinas (this is comprised in the *caitya-vandana*);
(3) *vandanaka*—worship (generally restricted to the ritual expression of respect to a monk or to the community of monks);
(4) *pratikramaṇa*—the recitation of the formulae of confession of past faults;
(5) *pratyākhyāna*—the recitation of formulae for the forfending of future faults generally expressed in the form of abstinence from food and drink and comforts;
(6) *kāyotsarga*—'the abandonment of the body' for a limited time.

The numbering of the *āvaśyakas* is that of the Śvetāmbaras; the Digambaras reverse the positions of *kāyotsarga* and *pratyākhyāna*.

This list was perhaps never wholly satisfactory. In particular the *kāyotsarga* is different in its nature from the other *āvaśyakas* to which it is properly an adjunct; keeping the body motionless for a limited period of time serves as an aid to concentration of mind but is not an end in itself. To judge from the details of the mediaeval texts the Śvetāmbaras would probably have regarded the most important *āvaśyakas* as *pūjā*, *caitya-vandana*, and *guru-vandana* and even the notion of 'daily' duties must have tended to be lost, if the

[1] See Schubring, *Die Lehre der Jainas*, p. 170.

fifteenth-century Ratnaśekhara,[1] who includes the *sāmāyika* and the *caitya-vandana* among the religious practices recommended specifically for the enforced leisure of the rainy season, is to be regarded as reflecting the practice of his age.

The Digambaras seem tacitly to accept that the *āvaśyakas* are rather a matter for the ascetic than for the layman and writers like Cāmuṇḍarāya[2] and Āśādhara, who treat both of *śrāvākācāra* and *yaty-ācāra* refer, their readers to the latter for information about these rites. Those *ācāryas* who follow the tradition of Jinasena have virtually replaced the *āvaśyakas* by a list of six daily *karmans* to be performed by the layman:[3]

(1) *pūjā*—which in fact covers the *sāmāyika*, *caturviṃśati-stava*, and *vandanaka*;
(2) *vārttā*—the exercise of an honest livelihood;
(3) *dāna*—almsgiving; this is the subject also of a *vrata*;
(4) *svādhyāya*—study of the scriptures;
(5) *saṃyama*—the carrying out of the five *aṇuvratas* with complete self-discipline;
(6) *tapas*—which includes *pratikramaṇa*, *pratyākhyāna*, and *kāyotsarga*.

THE NAMASKĀRA

THE basic ritual formula of Jainism is the *pañca-namaskāra* or *pañca-parameṣṭhi-stuti*,[4] the invocation which runs:

namo arihantāṇaṃ namo siddhāṇam namo āyāriyāṇaṃ namo uvajjhāyāṇaṃ namo loe savva-sāhūṇaṃ

to which is sometimes added the complementary verse:

eso pañca-namokkāro savva-pāva-ppanāsaṇo
maṅgalāṇaṃ ca savvesiṃ paḍhamaṃ havai maṅgalaṃ

Hail to the Jinas, to those who have attained *mokṣa*, to religious leaders, to religious teachers and to all monks in the world. This fivefold salutation which destroys all sin is pre-eminent as the most auspicious of all auspicious things.

[1] *Śrāddha-vidhi*, p. 158*a*.

[2] Thus CS, p. 26: *vandanā . . . tat-prapañcas tūttaratra vakṣyate.* This reference is taken up on p. 69 of the section *anagāra-dharme tapo-varṇanam* where details of the *vandanā* are given.

[3] MP xxxviii. 24; CS, p. 21.

[4] See Glasenapp, op. cit., p. 367.

'This supreme prayer, this best object of meditation'[1] serves as a quarry for magic formulae of varying lengths and different potency: thirty-five syllables—or sixty-eight if the complementary verse is added—are counted in the full *namaskāra* (*sarvākṣara-mantra*) but various abbreviations, of which the most popular is the use of the initial *akṣaras* of the five *parameṣṭhins* (*mukhyākṣara-mantra*), are employed to give totals of sixteen, six, five, and two *akṣaras*.[2] The whole *namaskāra* can also be concentrated in the single syllable *oṃ* which is held to be a contraction of the *mukhyākṣara-mantra*, *siddha* being replaced by *aśarīra* and *sadhu* by *muni* to give *a*, *a*, *ā*, *u*, *m*. Audibly muttered in an unending repetition, these formulae play an important part in the *pada-stha-dhyāna*. This practice of *japa* (as it is called) is accompanied by the telling of the beads, which may be of gold or gems or merely of lotus seeds.[3]

The recitation of the *pañca-namaskāra*, the *aparājita-mantra* as it is styled, comes to be synonymous with acceptance of the Jaina creed and it is with this prayer on his lips that the pious layman should wake each morning.[4] Twice a day at the morning and evening twilights he is to meditate on the excellent protection derived from it.[5] Its magic powers grow in the popular imagination as witness the late *Ratna-mālā* which says that whoso remembers this imperishable *mantra* will never be seized by *rākṣasas* or bitten by cobras.[6]

With the *namaskāra* is associated the *catuḥ-śaraṇa*, the recourse to the four refuges of the *arhats*, the *siddhas*, the *ācāryas*, and the community, and both are mentioned particularly as a source of support in the final trial of the *sallekhanā*,[7] when they form the symbolic quintessence of the scriptures, which are too long to be borne in mind in that hour. The *catuḥ-saraṇa* runs as follows:

arahante saraṇaṃ pavvajjāmi, siddhe saraṇaṃ pavvajjāmi, sāhū saraṇaṃ pavvajjāmi, kevali-pannattaṃ dhammaṃ pavvajjāmi

The use of *mantras* as a feature of worship develops more and more, under the influence of Hinduism. The biggest impetus to this trend seems to have come from Jinasena, who prescribed their use with all *kriyās*.[8]

[1] ŚrDK 10. [2] Śr (V), p. 466. [3] Handiqui, p. 272.
[4] ŚrDK 2. [5] *Dharma-rasāyana*, 152. [6] *Ratna-mālā*, 43.
[7] YŚ iii. 151 (p. 758). [8] MP xxxviii. 75.

THE CAITYA-VANDANA

THE *caitya-vandana*, which comprises elements of the *sāmāyika*, *caturvimśati-stava*, and *vandanaka*, the first three necessary duties, is given an extensive treatment in the *Āvaśyaka* literature. Understood as the 'veneration of the Jina's image', it is closely associated with the *pūjā* 'the making of offerings to the Jina', and Devendra defines it as the combination of the *dravya-pūjā* (actual offerings) and *bhāva-pūjā* (hymns of praise and mental concentration). Hemacandra, it must be admitted, describes the *pūjā* only as an element of the *caitya-vandana*, but in the much earlier Prakrit *Pañcāśakas* the two topics are kept separate in different sections. It would seem more appropriate to follow the *Pañcāśakas* in restricting the term *caitya-vandana* to the *bhāva-pūjā* and to what in effect constitutes the Jaina liturgy, and to apply the designation *pūjā* to the bathing and adorning of the images and the making of offerings to them, both in the temple and in the home. The following consideration of the *caitya-vandana* is virtually limited to Śvetāmbara sources, since, at least during the medieval period, the Digambara treatises on the lay life barely touch on the subject.

From the *Āvaśyaka* texts onwards the *ācāryas* divide the *caitya-vandana* into twelve sections devoted to specific objects of worship (*adhikāra*) and five chants (*daṇḍaka*):

Adhikāra	Daṇḍaka	Appropriate passage of liturgy
(1) Bhāva-jina	Praṇipāta	*Śakra-stava* without final verse
(2) Dravya-jina	,,	final verse of *Śakra-stava*
(3) Eka-caitya-sthāpanā-jina	Arhac-caitya-stava	*caitya-stava*
(4) Nāma-jina	Nama-jina-stava	*nāma-stava*[1]
(5) Tri-bhuvana-sthāpanā-jina	,,	*caitya-stava* preluded by the words *savva-loe*
(6) Virahamāna-jina	Śruta-stava	first verse of *śruta-stava*
(7) Śruta-jñāna	,,	rest of *śruta-stava*
(8) Sarva-siddha-stuti	Siddha-stava	first verse of *siddha-stava*
(9) Tīrthādhipa-vīra-stuti	,,	second and third verses of *siddha-stava*
(10) Ujjayanta-stuti	,,	fourth verse of *siddha-stava*
(11) Aṣṭāpada-stuti	,,	fifth verse of *siddha-stava*
(12) Sudṛṣṭi-smaraṇa	,,	*sura-smṛti-sūtra*

[1] This is the *caturviṃśati-stava*. For a translation and discussion see Leumann, *Übersicht über die Āvaśyaka-Literatur*, pp. 6–7.

Each *adhikāra* concerns a special object of worship:

1. *Bhāva-jina*—this implies the visualization of the Jinas endowed with *kevala-jñāna* as they are present in the *samavasaraṇa*.
2. *Dravya-jina*—this is the worship of the *arhatva-dravya*, the raw material of the quality of Jina, i.e. the *jina-jīvas* who will one day in this or in another life attain to final release.
3. *Eka-caitya-sthāpanā-jina*—the worship of Jina images in temples everywhere.
4. *Nāma-jina*—worship of the names of the twenty-four Jinas who have appeared in the present era in Bharata-kṣetra. This corresponds to the second *āvaśyaka*, the *caturvimśati-stava*, in its narrower sense.
5. *Tri-bhuvana-sthāpanā-jina*—the worship of Jina images in *śāśvata* and *aśāśvata* temples in the three worlds.
6. *Virahamāna-jina*—worship of the infinite number of absent Jinas, past and future, in the universe.
7. *Śruta-jñāna*—worship of the holy writ.
8. *Sarva-siddha-stuti*—worship of all those beings who have attained to *mokṣa*.
9. *Tīrthādhipa-Vīra-stuti*—worship of Mahāvīra the last Jina.
10. *Ujjayanta-stuti*—worship of the twenty-second Jina Ariṣṭanemi, who entered into *nirvāṇa* on Mount Ujjayanta.
11. *Aṣṭāpada-stuti*—worship of the other twenty-two Jinas, who entered into *nirvāṇa* on Mount Aṣṭāpada.
12. *Sudṛṣṭa-smaraṇa*—worship of those *devas* who like the Gomukha Yakṣas attained to *samyaktva* and performed *vaiyāvṛttya* to Mahāvīra.

Haribhadra recognizes only nine *adhikāras*, the second, tenth, and eleventh being omitted, but the *daṇḍakas* and the pattern of the ritual of course remain the same. In fact the ritual as set forth in the *Vandana-vidhāna-pañcāśaka*, in such *Āvaśyaka* commentaries as the *Lalita-vistarā* of Haribhadra and the *Caitya-vandana-bhāṣya* of Devendra, and in Hemacandra's *Yoga-śāstra*[1] shows almost no variation. It is given a numerical framework by division into five preparatory features (*abhigama*) and ten triads (*trika*) or groups of three related actions, or of actions requiring to be performed three times:

[1] YŚ iii. 124 (pp. 599–644).

THE FIVE ABHIGAMAS[1] (which are extracted from the conventional descriptions of the ruler or rich man arriving to perform the *sāmāyika*) are:

1. Discarding of all sentient (*sacitta*) objects such as flowers, betel, *siddhārthaka*, *durva* grass, that may be on one's person.
2. Retaining of certain non-sentient (*acitta*) objects. There is some uncertainty on this point but in any event vehicles, footwear, swords, knives, *cāmaras*, and *chattras* are to be left behind on entering the temple, whilst it would appear that all ornaments except diadems are to be retained.
3. Donning of an outer garment in the form of a wide piece of cloth.[2]
4. Making the *añjali* at sight of the Jina image with the words 'Hail to the friend of the world' (*namo bhuvana-bandhave*).
5. Concentrating one's mind on worship.

THE TEN TRIADS (*trika*):[3]

1. Three *naiṣedhikīs*:
   - (i) The first *naiṣedhiki*[4] signifies the relinquishment or prohibition (*niṣedha*) of the mundane activities (*gṛha-vyāpāra*). It is to be pronounced on entering the main gate of the temple.
   - (ii) The second *naiṣedhikī* implies the abandonment of all activities connected with the temple (*Jina-gṛha-vyāpāra*) and is spoken when one enters the inner sanctuary (*garbha-gṛha*).
   - (iii) The third *naiṣedhikī* expresses the end of activities (*Jina-pūjā-vyāpāra*) connected with the *pūjā* ceremony (which must of necessity involve some harmful *ārambha*). It is pronounced before carrying out the actual *caitya-vandana*.

[1] CVBh 19–20.

[2] The commentaries make it clear that a man is therefore expected to wear two pieces of cloth and a woman three, of which one will be the *kañcuka* or bodice.

[3] The clearest description of these is to be found in the *Saṅghācāra* commentary of Dharmaghoṣa: CVBh 6–19.

[4] The symbolism of the *naiṣedhikī*, as interpreted in the *Volksetymologie*, is lost if the correct sanskritization of *nisīhiya* is restored. For a discussion of the subject see Leumann, op. cit., pp. 9–10 (who explains): '*Man hat unter die Āvassiyā eine leise Verabschiedung und unter die Nisīhiyā eine leise Begrüssung zu verstehen. Ebenso soll man bei jeder Ankunft mit dem Wort nisīhiyā eine gewisse Weihe verbreiten.*'

2. Three circumambulations (*pradakṣiṇā*).

3. Three reverences (*praṇāma*):[1]

   (i) The *añjali*.
   (ii) The *pañcāṅga*, i.e. a reverence in which the five limbs —head, two hands, and two knees—all touch the ground.
   (iii) The *ardhāvanata*, i.e. a reverence in which the body is 'half-bent', the head and hands touching the ground.

   These are each to be made three times and to be accompanied by the words 'Hail to the Jinas' (*Jinebhyo namaḥ*).

4. Three forms of *pūjā*:

   (i) *aṅga-pūjā*;
   (ii) *agra-pūjā*;
   (iii) *bhāva-pūjā*.

These are discussed at length in the section on *pūjā*: it is only the third—the immaterial acts of worship in the form of *stuti*—that belongs to the *caitya-vandana* in its narrower sense, embracing the twelve *adhikāras* and five *daṇḍakas* listed above.

5. Meditation (*dhyāna*) on the three states (*avasthā*) of the Jina:

   (i) on the *chadma-stha* state in which he is still travestied as an ordinary mortal. To this the *piṇḍa-stha-dhyāna* applies. It is again divided into three phases:
      (*a*) birth—the meditation is stimulated by the images of the *snāpakas*, the gods mounted on elephants, who pour water from ewers (*kalaśa*);
      (*b*) kingship—the meditation is stimulated by the images of the *arcakas*, the votaries who bring garlands;
      (*c*) the monkish condition—the meditation is provoked by the sight of the Jina's hairless head;

   (ii) on the *kaivalya* state in which he has attained infinite knowledge. To this belongs the *pada-stha-dhyāna*, which arises from the vision of the eight *prātihāryas*,[2] the miraculous manifestations which took place when the Jina attained to *kevala-jñāna*;

[1] The Digambara Amitagati lists five kinds of *praṇāma* (Śr (A) viii. 62–64).
[2] For the *prātihāryas* see Glasenapp, op. cit., p. 253.

(iii) on the *siddhatva* state in which he has reached *nirvāṇa*. Here the meditation, the *rūpātīta-dhyāna*, is to be achieved by performing the *kāyotsarga* in the *paryaṅkāsana* posture.

(The *rūpa-stha-dhyāna*,[1] which arises from the mere sight of the image, is expressly excluded from this *trika*.)

6. Abstention from looking in the three directions (*tri-diṅ-nirīkṣaṇa-virati*). The worshipper is not to look to the right or to the left or behind him (in another interpretation neither upwards nor downwards nor transversally) but is to keep his gaze fixed on the image.

7. Making *pramārjana* three times of the ground under foot (*pada-bhūmi-pramārjana*).

8. Fulfilling the three requirements of the liturgy (*varṇādi-trika*):
   (i) reciting distinctly and without omissions or additions the words of the *stutis*;
   (ii) reflecting on their meaning;
   (iii) representing to oneself mentally the objects of adoration.

9. The three *mudrās*:[2]
   (i) *Jina-mudrā*—the two hands hang down loosely and the feet do not touch. The purpose of this *mudrā* is to remove obstacles.
   (ii) *yoga-mudrā*—the two hands are joined with the fingers interlocking and the elbows resting on the abdomen. The *mudrā* is calculated to achieve all desires.
   (iii) *muktā-śukti-mudrā*—the two hands are clasped evenly together and raised so as to touch the middle of the forehead. (A divergent view holds that they should be close to the eyes without actually touching the forehead.)

10. The threefold final prayer (*praṇidhāna*),[3] the concentration of mind, body, and speech in the form of *caitya-vandana*, *guru-vandana*, and *prārthanā* (invocation).

[1] The four types of *dhyāna* are described by Amitagati (Śr (A) xv. 30–56).

[2] Amitagati describes in addition to these three a *vandana-mudrā* (Śr (A) viii. 52–56) and many other *mudrās* are found in the ritual literature.

[3] The term *praṇidhāna* seems to be used approximately in this sense in the *Śrāvaka-prajnapti* (368–73).

(i) the first *praṇidhāna*, called from its opening words the *jāvanti-ceiyāiṃ*

jāvanti ceiyāiṃ uddhe ya ahe ya tiriya-loe ya
savvāiṃ tāiṃ vande iha santo tattha santāiṃ

From here I adore all such images as exist there in the upper world and the middle world and the nether world;

(ii) the second *praṇidhāna*, called the *jāvanta-kei-sāhū*

jāvanta kei sāhū Bharah'-Eravaya-Mahāvidehe ya
savvesiṃ tesiṃ paṇao tivihena ti-daṇḍa-virayāṇaṃ

I bow down to all those *sādhus* averse from evil in word, in thought, or in act who are to be found in Bharata, Airāvata, and Mahāvideha;

(iii) the third *praṇidhāna*, called the *jāya-vīyarāya* or *praṇidhāṇa-sūtra*.

The text of this is given below in its place at the end of the liturgy.

The numerical plan of the *caitya-vandana* includes in addition to the five *abhigamas* and ten *trikas* a mention of three *avagrahas* (*utkṛṣṭa*, *madhyama*, and *jaghanya*), the distance from the image at which the votary is to stand—the best *avagraha* is six *hastas* away—and of the *vāma-dik* and *dakṣiṇa-dik*. Men, it is said, are to stand on the right of the image when worshipping, because of their pre-eminence in the *dharma*, and women on the left.

From the elaborate details the sequence of the elements of the *vandana* would seem, at least in Devendra's picture, to be as follows:

On arriving at the temple and catching sight of the image above the door, the worshipper makes the *añjali*. As he enters, and leaves behind the cares of the world, he utters the first *naiṣedhikī*. He goes into the sanctuary and, as he circumambulates the images, he pronounces the second *naiṣedhikī*. He then carries out the *pūjā* for which he has brought with him the necessary materials, first bathing and dressing the image, and then setting the offerings before it, and burning incense and waving lamps. When this is done he utters the third *naiṣedhikī*, makes the *pañcāṅga-praṇāma*, and, adopting the *yoga-mudrā*, commences the recitation of the *Śakra-stava*, replacing it by the *Jina-mudrā* for the *caitya-stava*. When the five *daṇḍakas* are completed he recites the three *praṇidhānas* accompanying them by the *muktā-śukti-mudrā*. The *caitya-vandana* is then at an end.

The *caitya-vandana* liturgy in its narrower sense may be outlined as follows:

The worshipper recites the *pañca-namaskāra*, performs *pratikramaṇa* and *ālocanā* using the *airyāpathikī-sūtra*,[1] and then engages in the *kāyotsarga* reciting the *uttari-karaṇa-sūtra*[2] and *kāyotsarga-sūtra*.[3] He concentrates his mind and his gaze on the Jina, and 'his body horripilating from the force of *saṃvega* and *vairāgya* and his eyes moist with tears'[4] he makes the *pañcāṅga-praṇāma* and using the *yoga-mudrā* starts to recite the *praṇipāta-daṇḍaka*.

1. Praṇipāta-daṇḍaka.[5]

The *Śakra-stava*, so-called because in the legends it is usually spoken by Indra,[6] runs as follows:

namo 'tthu arihantāṇaṃ bhagavantāṇaṃ, āigarāṇaṃ titthayarāṇaṃ sayaṃsambuddhāṇaṃ, puris'-uttamāṇaṃ purisa-sīhānam purisa-vara-puṇḍarīyāṇaṃ purisa-vara-gandha-hatthīṇaṃ, log'-uttamāṇaṃ loga-nāhāṇaṃ loga-hiyāṇaṃ loga-paīvāṇaṃ loga-pajjoya-garāṇaṃ, abhaya-dayāṇaṃ cakkhu-dayāṇaṃ magga-dayāṇaṃ saraṇa-dayāṇaṃ bohi-dayāṇaṃ, dhamma-dayāṇaṃ dhamma-desayāṇaṃ dhamma-nāyagāṇaṃ dhamma-sārahīṇaṃ dhamma-vara-cāuranta-cakkavaṭṭīṇaṃ, appaḍihaya-vara-nāṇa-daṃsaṇa-dharāṇaṃ viyaṭṭa-chaumāṇaṃ, jiṇāṇaṃ jāvayāṇaṃ tiṇṇāṇaṃ tārayāṇaṃ buddhāṇaṃ bohayāṇaṃ muttāṇaṃ moyagāṇaṃ, savvannūṇaṃ savva-darisīṇaṃ sivam ayalam aruyam aṇantam akkhayam avvābāham apunarāvitti-siddhi-gai-nāmadheyaṃ thāṇaṃ sampattāṇaṃ namo jiṇāṇaṃ jiya-bhayāṇaṃ

je ya aīyā siddhā je ya bhavissanti 'ṇāgae kāle
sampai ya vaṭṭamāṇā savve tivihena vandāmi

Praise to the *arhats*, the blessed ones, who are the cause of the beginnings, who provide the path across, who have of themselves attained enlightenment, the best among men, the lions among men, the lotuses among men, the *gandha-hastins*[7] among men, the best of those in the world, the lords of the world, the benefactors of the world, the lights of the world, the irradiators of the world, those who give freedom from fear, who give insight, who give the right direction, who give refuge, who give enlightenment, who give the sacred doctrine, who expound the sacred doctrine, who are the authorities on the sacred doctrine, the guides to the sacred doctrine, the oecumenical monarchs of the sacred doctrine, those who maintain the irrefutable knowledge and insight,

[1] See p. 163. [2] See p. 173. [3] See p. 173. [4] YŚ, p. 612.
[5] YŚ, pp. 612–29; LV, pp. 7a–76b. [6] YŚ, p. 629.
[7] The *gandha-hastin* or 'perfume-elephant', a familiar creature of legend, is regarded as the noblest of beasts.

who have thrown off all travesties, the Jinas, who drive away evil, who have crossed over, who aid others across, the enlightened and the enlighteners, the liberated and the liberators, the omniscient, the all-seeing, those who have reached that place that is called *siddhi-gati* from which there is no return, and which is bliss immutable, inviolable, endless, imperishable, and undisturbed; praise to the Jinas who have overcome fear.

In the threefold way I worship all the *siddhas*, those who have been, and those who are, and those who in future time will be.

Haribhadra and Hemacandra have felt it necessary to give a very detailed interpretation of this and the following *stavas*, and it is possible here to mention only a few of the points made. Special interest attaches to the popular etymologies, almost invariably false, by which the associations of a word are evoked.

Thus the *arhat* is explained either as the one who is worthy (*arha*) of *vandana* and *pūjā*; or (in the form of Prakrit *arihanta*) as the destroyer of the enemies (*ari*),[1] these being the evil qualities such as *moha* which are responsible for the growth of karma, or karma itself in its various forms; or again (in the Prakrit variant *aruhanta*) those in whom the seed of karma can no longer grow (*ruhati*). The *bhagavat* is the possessor of *bhaga* defined lexically by fourteen terms which (after subtraction of the inappropriate meanings *arka* and *yoni*) become the twelve *ālāpakas* to be recorded in the praise of the Jina: knowledge (*jñāna*), glory (*māhātmya*), fame (*yaśas*), asceticism (*vairāgya*), final release (*mukti*), beauty (*rūpa*), courage (*vīrya*), energy (*prayatna*), longing (*icchā*), religion (*dharma*), abundance (*śrī*), wealth (*aiśvarya*). The *tīrthaṅkaras* are lions because of their courage in combatting the enemy that is karma, they are lotuses because they have made to blossom in the mire of the *saṃsāra* the flower of the *dharma*, whilst all calamities are driven away by the presence of the *tīrthaṅkara* just as lesser elephants are driven away by the *gandha-hastin*.

2. Arhac-caitya-stava-daṇḍaka[2]

The worshipper, making the *Jina-mudrā*, recites the *caitya-stava*:

arihanta-ceiyāṇaṃ karemi kāyussaggam vandana-vattiyāe pūyaṇa-vattiyāe sakkāra-vattiyāe sammāṇa-vattiyāe bohi-lāha-vattiyāe niruva-sagga-vattiyāe saddhāe mehāe dhiīe dhāraṇāe aṇuppehāe vaddhamāṇīe ṭhāmi kāussaggaṃ

[1] For these see p. 229. [2] YŚ, pp. 629–32; LV, pp. 76*b*–89*b*.

For the sake of the images of the *arhats* I make the *kāyotsarga*, for the sake of worship, for the sake of making offerings, for the sake of making gifts, for the sake of making praise, for the sake of obtaining enlightenment, for the sake of final release, I stand in the *kāyotsarga* with faith, with intelligence, with steadfastness, with mindfulness, with reflection, with intensity.

Hemacandra understands here by *pūjana* the offering of flowers and garlands, by *satkāra* the giving of ornaments and clothes, and by *sammāna* hymns of praise (in other words the three forms of *pūjā*). These are legitimate for a layman; and an ascetic, though he may not make *dravya-pūjā* himself, may yet approve it or get others to perform it.

When several worshippers are engaged in the *caitya-stava* together, one only will recite the words whilst the others stand silent in the *kāyotsarga*. On completion of the *kāyotsarga* the *pañca-namaskāra* is to be repeated. The next phase is the praise of the twenty-four *tīrthaṅkaras* of the present era.

3. Nāma-Jina-stava-daṇḍaka[1]

1. *logassa ujjoya-gare dhamma-titthayare jiṇe*
   arihante kittaissaṃ cauvīsaṃ pi kevali
2. *Usabham Ajiyaṃ ca vande Sambhavaṃ Abhinandanaṃ ca Sumaiṃ ca*
   Paumappahaṃ Supāsaṃ jinaṃ ca Candappahaṃ vande
3. *Suvihiṃ ca Pupphadantaṃ Siyala-Sejjaṃsa-Vāsupujjaṃ ca*
   Vimalam Anantaṃ ca jinaṃ Dhammaṃ Santiṃ ca vandāmi
4. *Kunthum Aram ca Malliṃ vande Muṇisuvvayaṃ Nami-jinaṃ ca*
   vandāmi Riṭṭhanemiṃ Pāsaṃ taha Vaddhamāṇam ca
5. *evaṃ mae abhithuā vihūya-raja-māla pahīna-jara-maraṇā*
   cauvīsaṃ pi jiṇa-varā titthayarā me pasīyantu
6. *kittiya-vandiya-mahiyā jee logassa uttamā siddhā*
   ārogga-bohi-lāham samāhi-varam uttamaṃ dentu
7. *candesu nimmalayarā āiccesu ahiyaṃ payāsayarā*
   sāgara-vara-gambhīrā siddhā siddhiṃ mama disantu

I shall praise the twenty-four Jinas, the *arhats* of perfect knowledge, who have illuminated the world and created the sacred doctrine as a way across . . . [*The names are listed*]. . . . Thus I have extolled the twenty-four Jinas who have shaken off impurities and defilements and rejected old age and death; may they, the *tīrthaṅkaras*, be gracious to me; may

[1] YŚ, pp. 632–42; LV, pp. 89*b*–96*b*.

they, the *siddhas*, the best of beings give me enlightenment and tranquillity and final release, they who have been praised and worshipped and adored. May the *siddhas*, purer than the moons, more radiant than the suns, and profound as the oceans, give me bliss.

After this *nāma-stava* the *caitya-stava* is repeated, the words *savva-loe* being prefixed to it.

4. Śruta-stava-daṇḍaka[1]

1. *Pukkhara-vara-dīv'aḍḍhe Dhāyaīkhaṇḍe ya Jambudīve ya*
   Bharah'-Eravaya-Videhe dhamm'-āigare namaṃsāmi
2. *tama-timira-paḍala-viddhaṃsaṇassa sura-gaṇa-narinda-mahiyassa*
   sīmā-dharassa vande papphoḍiya-moha-jālassa
3. *jāi-jara-maraṇa-soga-paṇāsaṇassa kallāṇa-pukkhala-visāla-suhāva-hassa*
   ko deva-dāṇava-narinda-gan'-acciyassa dhammassa sāram uvalabbha kare pamāyaṃ
4. *siddhe bho payao jiṇa-mae nandi sayā saṃjame devaṃ-nāga-suvaṇṇa-kinnara-gaṇa-sab-bhūya-bhāv'-accie*
   logo jattha paiṭṭhio jagam iṇaṃ telokka-macc'-asuram dhammo vaddhau sāsao vijayao dhamm'-uttaram vaddhau
   suyassa bhagavao karemi kāussaggam

I bow down to those who have established the sacred doctrine in Puṣkaradvīpa, in Dhātakīkhaṇḍa and in Jambudvīpa, in Bharata, Airavata, and Mahāvideha.

I worship the *śruta-dharma*, which contains the rules of conduct, which dispels the veil of the darkness of ignorance, which is adored by gods and kings, which rends asunder the net of delusion, which ends the sorrows of birth, old age, and death, which brings the full and ample bliss of final release. Who, if he understands its essence, can be neglectful of the sacred doctrine worshipped by gods and demi-gods and kings? O *siddhas*, I am devoutly attached to the Jaina creed; well-being always lies in the religious life extolled with veritable devotion by *devas*, *nāgas*, *jyotiṣkas*, and *kinnaras*. May the eternal sacred doctrine prosper this world of *devas*, mortals, and *asuras* where the people are firmly established in it, may it be victorious and may it prosper the primacy of the *dharma*.

The first verse is devoted to the infinite number of absent Jinas in other continents of which there is no knowledge; the rest is in praise of the holy writ.

[1] YŚ, pp. 642–6; LV, pp. 96*b*–106*a*.

5. Siddha-stava-daṇḍaka[1]

1. *siddhāṇaṃ buddhāṇaṃ pāra-gayāṇaṃ paramparā-gayāṇaṃ*
loy'-aggam uvagayāṇaṃ namo sayā savva-siddhāṇaṃ
2. *jo devāṇa vi devo jaṃ devo pañjali namaṃsanti*
taṃ deva-deva-mahiyaṃ sirasā vande Mahāvīraṃ
3. *ekko vi namokkāro jiṇa-vara-vasahassa Vaddhamāṇassa*
saṃsāra-sāgarao tārei naraṃ va nāriṃ va
4. *Ujjenta-sela-sihare dikkhā nāṇam nisīhiya jassa*
taṃ dhamma-cakkavattim Ariṭṭhanemim namaṃsāmi
5. *cattāri aṭṭha dasa do ya vandiyā jiṇa-varā cauvīsaṃ*
paramaṭṭha-niṭṭhiy'-aṭṭhā siddhā siddhiṃ mama disantu

Praise to the *siddhas*, the enlightened ones who have gone to the further shore, who have gone there by stages, who have reached the summit of the worlds, praise always to all *siddhas*.

I bow down my head to Mahāvīra, who is the god of gods, who is adored by lords of gods, and whom gods worship joining their hands. Even one *namaskāra* offered to the excellent Jina Vardhamāna will carry a man or a woman across the ocean of the cycle of transmigration.

I worship Ariṣṭanemi that oecumenical monarch of the sacred doctrine who on the summit of the Ujjayanta mountain received the initiation and attained to *kevala-jñāna* and to *mokṣa*.

May the twenty-four *siddhas*—the twenty-two Jinas and the two others who have been celebrated—whose significance is firmly established in reality, show me final release.

These verses make up the *siddhi-stava*; and the *daṇḍaka* is completed by an invocation of the *vaiyāvṛttya-karas* which is sometimes styled the *sura-smṛti-sūtra*.

veyāvacca-garāṇaṃ santi-garāṇaṃ sammad-diṭṭhi-samāhi-garāṇaṃ karemi kāussaggaṃ

I make the *kāyotsarga* for those who render service, who create tranquillity, who create absorption in right belief.

Hemacandra explains that the *paramparā-gatānām* of verse 1 refers to the progression through the *guṇasthāna*, the Jina is called *devānām deva* because he is worshipped by *devas* such as the Bhavana-vāsis and he is also worshipped by the *deva-devas* such as Śakra. He is called Mahāvīra because he directs (*īrayati*) to *mokṣa*. To the words *nāriṃ va* there attaches a special importance. In this connexion both Haribhadra and Hemacandra quote a passage from the lost *Yāpanīya-tantra* stressing that women equally with men

[1] YŚ, pp. 646–53; LV, pp. 106*b*–118*b*.

can reach the summit of the religious life. Hemacandra says that the last two verses of the *siddha-stava* are not, in the opinion of some authorities, an essential part of the ritual but may be omitted.

When the *siddha-stava-daṇḍaka* and the accompanying *kāyotsarga* are completed the worshipper is again to recite the *Śakra-stava* and then, making the *muktā-śukti-mudrā*, to pronounce the *praṇidhāna-sūtra*:

1. *jaya vīya-rāya jaga-guru hou mama tuha ppahāvao bhayavaṃ bhava-nivveo maggāṇusāriyā iṭṭha-phala-siddhī*
2. *loga-viruddha-ccão guru-jana-pūā par'-attha-karaṇaṃ ca suha-guru-jogo tav-vayaṇa-sevaṇā ā-bhavam akhaṇḍā*

Hail, Jina, preceptor of the world, through your grace, blessed lord, may I achieve these things: disgust for the world, regular pursuit of the right path, attainment of desired results, abandonment of whatever is ill-famed in the world, respect for preceptors and parents, practice of help to others, attachment to a good guru, and full obedience to his words for all existence.

It is evident from this description of the ritual that a considerable amount of time is required to carry out the *caitya-vandana*. In theory the layman should imitate the monk in performing it seven times a day, or if that is not possible five times, or if that too is beyond his powers, at least three times—at dawn, noon, and dusk. Not surprisingly therefore from an early date an abbreviated ritual is admitted. Three possibilities are in fact envisaged:[1]

(i) the best (*uttama*)—the complete ritual of the five *daṇḍakas* preceded by the *airyāpathikī-pratikramaṇa*;

(ii) the next best (*madhyama*)—this is considered to be either one chant (*daṇḍaka*) (the *arhac-caitya-stava*), and one verse (*stuti*); or two *daṇḍakas* (*arhac-caitya-stava* and *Śakra-stava*), and two *stutis*;

(iii) the least satisfactory (*jaghanya*)—the *namaskāra* alone, or the *Śakra-stava* alone.

[1] CVBh 23; Ratnaśekhara, *Śraddha-vidhi*, p. 56*b*; *Vandhana-vidhāna-pañcāśaka*, 2.

THE VANDANAKA

BY its basic meaning of reverent salutation (*vandana* or *vandanaka*), the third *āvaśyaka* would apply equally to the worship paid to the Jina, to the guru, or to the sacred scriptures; but though the *Vandana-vidhāna-pañcāśaka*, for example, is actually devoted to the *caitya-vandana*, this term is usually specialized in the sense of *guru-vandana*. In his explanation of the subject Hemacandra[1] notes that, although in the texts quoted by him the person performing the *vandanaka* is always referred to as a monk, the ritual can equally well be carried out by a layman; yet it has to be admitted that of all the elements transferred from the monastic ritual this has been the least successfully accommodated to the *śrāvakācāra*.

In the form in which it appears in the works of Hemacandra[2] and Devendra[3] the ritual has been subdivided into twenty-five essential constituents or *āvaśyakas* (not of course to be confused with the six daily necessary duties). The Digambaras, though not adhering to this figure, give a very similar classification:

ŚVETĀMBARA	DIGAMBARA
2 avanamana	2 niṣadya or āsana
1 yathā-jāta	1 yathā-jāta
12 āvartana or āvarta	12 āvarta
4 śiras, or śiro-'vanati	4 namaskāra or praṇāma
3 gupta	3 śuddhi
2 praveśa	
1 niṣkramaṇa	

Hemacandras's list is in fact, save for the last three items which are not counted by the Digambaras, identical with those given by Samantabhadra[4] and Cāmuṇḍarāya.[5]

The ritual passage to be recited by Śvetāmbaras during the *vandanaka* is known as the *dvādaśāvarta-vandanaka-sūtra* or (from the phrase of address which recurs in it) *kṣamā-śramaṇa*. It runs as follows:[6]

icchāmi khamā-samaṇo vandiuṃ jāvaṇijjāe nisīhiyāe (the guru: *chandeṇa*) *aṇujāṇaha me miy'-oggahaṃ* (the guru: *aṇujāṇāmi*) *nisīhi aho kāyaṃ*

[1] YŚ iii. 130 (p. 679). [2] YŚ iii. 130 (pp. 659–86).
[3] *Guru-vandana-bhāṣya.* [4] RK v. 18. [5] CS, p. 69.
[6] Both text and translation of this ritual passage are given with extensive explanatory details in Leumann, op. cit., pp. 7–10.

kāya-samphāsaṃ khamaṇijjo bhe kilāmo appa-kilantāṇam bahu-subheṇa bhe divaso vaikkanto (the guru: *taha tti*) *jattā bhe* (the guru: *tubbham pi vaṭṭai*) *javaṇijjaṃ ca bhe* (the guru: *evaṃ*) *khāmemi khamā-samaṇo devasiyaṃ vaikkamaṃ* (the guru: *aham avi khāmemi*) *āvassiyāe paḍikkamāmi khamā-samaṇāṇaṃ devasiyāe āsāyaṇāe tettīs' annayarāe jaṃ kiṃci micchāe maṇa-dukkaḍāe vaya-dukkaḍāe kāya-dukkaḍāe kohāe māṇāe māyāe lobhāe savva-kāliyāe savva-micchovayārāe savva-dhammāikkamaṇāe jo me aiyāro kao tassa khamā-samaṇo paḍikkamāmi nindāmi garihāmi appāṇaṃ vosirāmi.*

I desire to worship you, forbearing monk,[1] with very intense concentration. (*The guru*: Willingly.) Allow me to enter the measured space. (*The guru*: I allow you.) Allow my bodily contact on the lower part of your body. Please suffer this annoyance. You will have spent the whole day fortunately little disturbed. (*The guru*: Yes.) You are making spiritual progress. (*The guru*: Yes and so are you.) You are unperturbed by your sense organs? (*The guru*: Yes.) I ask pardon, forbearing monk, for my daily transgressions. (*The guru*: I too ask pardon.) Necessarily I make *pratikramaṇa* to you, forbearing monk, for any day-by-day lack of respect, for any of the thirty-three *āśātanās*, anything done amiss through mind, speech, or body, through anger, pride, deceit, or greed, through false behaviour and neglect of the sacred doctrine at any time; whatever offence may have been committed by me, forbearing monk, I confess and reprehend and repent of it and cast aside my past self.

The stages or *sthānas* of the *vandanaka* are marked by the responses (*abhilāpa*) of the guru, which have been given the following labels, taken from the expressions used in the text:

(1) icchā;
(2) anujñāpanā;
(3) avyābādha;
(4) yātrā;
(5) yāpanā;
(6) aparādha-kṣāmaṇā.

The following description of the ritual is furnished by Hemacandra: as he intends it to apply to the lay life the word *śiṣya* (neophyte) is here throughout replaced by 'layman':

The layman who wishes to perform the *vandanaka* waits some distance away from the monk, holding a *rajo-haraṇa* in his hand and wearing a *mukha-vastrikā*, which he has subjected to *pratilekhana*. He begins to recite the formula and when the guru says '*chandeṇa*' he makes the first *avanamana* or reverence and comes up to him making *pratilekhana* and *pramārjana*. Putting his *rajo-haraṇa* on the ground close to the monk and taking off his *mukha-vastrikā*, he leaves it on his left knee. He then touches the

[1] This rendering is chosen to harmonize with Hemacandra's interpretation.

rajo-haraṇa with his hands and then his own forehead. Six *āvartas* —this is the name given to a gesture in which the joined palms of the hands are moved from right to left—are made whilst he slowly repeats the third *sthāna*. Then keeping his gaze fixed on the guru and making the *añjali* he continues to recite. The movement of hands between *rajo-haraṇa* and forehead is resumed as the recitation continues until he has completed the sixth *sthāna*. At the words *khāmemi khamā-samaṇo* he applies both his hands and his forehead to the *rajo-haraṇa* and when reaches the phrase *tassa khamā-samaṇo paḍikkamāmi* he gets up and moves out of the proximity of the monk. After this exit and a second entry he repeats the same ritual.

Hemacandra's description apparently refers to the third variety of *vandanaka* mentioned at the commencement of Devendra's *Guru-vandana-bhāṣya*,[1] where the following types are listed:

(i) *spheṭa* (Prakrit *phiṭṭa*)—consisting of inclinations of the head (addressed to the congregation of monks);
(ii) *chobha*—a double recitation of the *kṣamā-śramaṇa* (addressed to ordinary individual monks);
(iii) *dvādaśāvarta*—the full ritual, this too being repeated (destined for ascetics of higher standing).

Certain elucidations of the ritual are available from the texts particularly from Hemacandra[2] and from Siddhasena Sūri's commentary on the *Pravacana-sāroddhāra*.[3] Thus the expression *kṣamā-śramaṇa* is understood by the former as implying that an ascetic is possessed of the ten elements making up the *dharma* the first of which is *kṣamā* 'forbearance'. One *avanamana* or obeisance is made at the end of the first *sthāna* in each recitation of the *kṣamā-śramaṇa*. By *yathā-jata* is meant the full accoutrement of the monk: *rajo-haraṇa* (the little broom that is used to carry out *pramārjana*), *mukha-vastrikā* (the strip of cloth worn in front of the mouth), and the pieces of material allowed —at least by the Śvetāmbaras—for clothing. The monastic initiation is conceived of as a second birth, the hands clasped in the *añjali* being held to symbolize the folded hands of the child issuing from the womb. Whether the layman should make use of the *rajo-haraṇa* and *mukha-vastrikā*, the special symbols of the ascetic condition, is sometimes questioned but the Śvetāmbara texts used in

[1] *Guru-vandana-bhāṣya*, 1. [2] YŚ iii. 130 (pp. 665–76). [3] PS 93–174.

this study depict them as essential in a number of rites. The six *āvartas* of each repetition are to accompany the following words or phrases of the ritual: *aho, kāyaṃ, kāya-samphāsaṃ, jattā bhe, javaṇijjaṃ bhe*, two being assigned to the last. Two *śiras* (inclination of the head) are to be made in each repetition of the ritual: one by the layman when he recites *khāmemi khamā-samaṇo devasiyaṃ vaikkamaṃ* and one by the monk when he replies *aham avi khāmemi tume*. At the first *sthāna* of the *kṣamā-śramaṇa* the monk may, if he is not in a position at the moment to accept the *vandanaka*, reply *tiviheṇa* ('Make your reverence in mind, speech, and body') thereby cutting short the ritual. The repetition which is characteristic of the full ritual is explained on the analogy of an envoy bringing a message to a king and making obeisance both before and after speaking.

Other elements of the *vandanaka* are given the form of numerical apothegms, in particular the thirty-two faults (*doṣas*)[1] and the thirty-three failures to express respect (*āśātanās*)[2] but, devoted as these are to the minutiae of monkish life, they cannot be said to have any real existence in the lay ritual though enumerated by Hemacandra and Devendra. It will be enough to mention here the division of the *gurv-āśātanās* into three types:[3]

(i) most conspicuous (*utkṛṣṭa*)—those concerned with actions contrary to the guru's command;
(ii) next most conspicuous (*madhyama*)—those referring to contact with impurities;
(iii) least conspicuous (*jaghanya*)—those concerned with touching the feet or other limbs of the guru.

The *vandanaka* is associated with a number of other rites such as the *pratikramaṇa*, in fact it might be said to be implicit in any rite which involves the concourse of the guru. If no monk is present a convenient device for which canonical authority is claimed[4] exists to ensure the satisfactory completion of the rite: this is the fiction of the *sthāpanācārya*.

Just as the Jina can be conceived in terms of *nāma, sthāpanā, dravya*, and *bhāva* so can these categories be applied to the *ācārya*, and the *sthāpanācārya* will then signify the guru represented by a statue or by some symbolic object. To this the worshipper performs

[1] YŚ iii. 130 (pp. 661–4).
[2] Ibid. (pp. 676–8).
[3] *Śrāddha-vidhi*, p. 71*a*.
[4] ŚrDK 230.

the *vandanaka*, keeping the guru present in his mind. Special *āśātanās* are devised to cover actions implying lack of respect to the *sthāpanācārya*.[1] The practice is clearly set out in Devendra's *Śrāddha-dina-kṛtya*[2] and Hemacandra[3] had earlier laid down that one should imagine in one's mind an embodiment of the guru if he is not himself present (*guru-virahe guru-sthāpanāṃ manasikṛtvā*).

THE PRATIKRAMAṆA AND ĀLOCANĀ

THE *pratikramaṇa*, the fourth of the *āvaśvakas*, generally linked with an avowal of past transgressions (*ālocanā*) is a manifestation of contrition and desire for amendment expressed by the recitation of certain confession formulae.[4] Various types of *pratikramaṇa*, mainly based on the period of time to which the confession refers, are recognized:[5]

(1) performed at nightfall and referring to the past day (*daivasika*);
(2) performed at dawn and referring to the past night (*prābhātika* or *rātrika*);
(3) covering the past *pakṣa* or half-month (*pākṣika*);
(4) covering the past four months (*cāturmāsika*);
(5) covering the past year (*vārṣika*);
(6) referring to the unwitting harm caused by all movement (*airyāpathikī*).

The acceptance of *pratikramaṇa* only as an annual duty or as a duty to be carried out only during the additional leisure of the *caturmāsa* or rainy season is a characteristic of later texts.[6]

It will be convenient to deal first with the *airyāpathikī-pratikramaṇa*,[7] which has a special importance notably as forming the prelude to the *caitya-vandana*. The *airyāpathikī-sūtra* runs as follows:

icchāmi paḍikkamiuṃ iriyā-vahiyāe virāhaṇāe gamaṇ'-āgamaṇe pāṇ'-akkamaṇe bīy'-akkamaṇe hariy'-akkamaṇe osāy'-uttiṅga-paṇaga-daga-maṭṭi-makkaḍa-santāṇa-saṃkamaṇe je me jīvā virāhiyā eg'-indiyā

[1] *Śrāddha-vidhi*, p. 73*b*.
[2] ŚrDK 230, where the term *sūri*, explained as *sthāpanācārya*, is used.
[3] YŚ iii. 124 (p. 611).
[4] See Schubring, *Die Lehre der Jainas*, p. 177.
[5] YŚ iii. 130 (p. 687).
[6] *Śrāddha-vidhi*, p. 158*b*.
[7] YŚ iii. 124 (pp. 605–7).

be-indiyā te-indiyā caur-indiyā pañc'-indiyā abhihayā vattiyā lesiyā saṅghāiyā saṅghaṭṭiyā pariyāviyā kilāmiyā uddaviyā ṭhāṇāo ṭhāṇaṃ saṃkāmiyā jīviyāo vavaroviyā tassa micchāmi dukkaḍaṃ

I want to make *pratikramaṇa* for injury on the path of my movement, in coming and in going, in treading on living things, in treading on seeds, in treading on green plants, in treading on dew, on beetles, on mould, on moist earth, and on cobwebs; whatever living organisms with one or two or three or four or five senses have been injured by me or knocked over or crushed or squashed or touched or mangled or hurt or affrighted or removed from one place to another or deprived of life—may all that evil have been done in vain.

Hemacandra says that *īryā-patha* may be taken in the literal sense as 'the path of one's going' or it may be understood to mean 'the line of conduct of an ascetic' the primary infraction of which would be the destruction of any form of life: the import of the *sūtra* remains in either case the same. The *avaśyāya* (Prakrit *osāya*) is explained as a *jala-viśeṣa*; the *uttiṅga* is an insect of the form of a dung-beetle which makes holes in the ground; *panaka* is explained as *pañca-varṇolli*; the moist earth will contain *ap-kāyas* and *pṛthvī-kāyas*. The phrase which recurs in all the *pratikramaṇa* formulae *micchāmi dukkaḍaṃ* is given its proper sanskritization *mithyā me duṣkṛtam* ('may the evil of it be in vain') but at the same time the individual *akṣaras* are said to have the following symbolic meaning:[1]

mi—miu-maddava	'gentleness'
chā—dosāṇaṃ chāyaṇa	'the veiling of faults'
mi, me—a-merāe thiya	'abiding in the limitless'
du—dugañchāmi appāṇaṃ	'I loath myself'
ka—kaḍaṃ me pāvaṃ	'I have committed sin'
ḍa—ḍevemi taṃ uvasameṇaṃ	'I go beyond it through attaining to calm'

In general, apart from the recitation of the *airyāpathikī* formula, the performance of *pratikramaṇa* requires the presence of a guru. The ritual passages used for this and for the *ālocanā* are given below in the sequence in which they normally follow the *vandanaka* formula, beginning with the *aticārālocanā*:[2]

icchā-kāreṇa saṃdisaha bhagavaṃ devasiyaṃ āloiuṃ (the guru: *āloaha*) *icchaṃ āloemi jo me devasio aiyāro kao kāio vāio māṇasio ussutto ummaggo akappo akaraṇijjo dujjhāyo duvvicintio aṇāyāro aṇicchiyavvo asāvaga-*

[1] YŚ iii. 124 (p. 607). [2] YŚ iii. 130 (pp. 679–82).

pāoggo nāṇe daṃsaṇe cārittācaritte sue sāmāiye tiṇhaṃ guttīnaṃ cauṇhaṃ kasāyāṇaṃ pañcaṇhaṃ aṇu-vvayāṇaṃ tiṇhaṃ guṇa-vvayāṇaṃ cauṇhaṃ sikkhā-vayāṇam bārasavihassa sāvaga-dhammassa jaṃ khaṇḍiyaṃ jaṃ virāhiyaṃ tassa micchāmi dukkaḍaṃ.

Instruct me, lord, at my own desire to make *ālocanā* for the day. (*The guru*: Do so.) I wish to make *ālocanā*: whatever fault has been committed by me during the day in body, speech, or mind, in contravention of the scriptures and of right conduct, unfitting and improper to be done, ill meditated and ill conceived, immoral and undesirable, unbecoming for a layman, in regard to knowledge and philosophy and the lay life and the holy writ and the *sāmāyika*, and whatever transgression or infraction I may have committed in respect of the three *guptis* and four *kaṣāyas*, and the five *aṇu-vratas*, three *guṇa-vratas*, and four *śikṣā-vratas*, that is to say, the layman's twelvefold rule of conduct—may that evil have been done in vain.

Hemacandra explains that *cāritrācāritra* is equivalent to *deśa-virati*. *Khaṇḍita* implies a partial violation of the religious duties and *virādhita* a more serious violation but neither of them amounts to a complete *bhaṅga*.

After this *ālocanā* formula the worshipper is to recite the *pratikramaṇa-bīja-sūtra*:[1]

savvassa vi devasiya duccintiya dubbhāsiya duccetthiya icchā-kāreṇa sandisaha bhagavaṃ (the guru: *paḍikkamaha*) *tassa micchāmi dukkaḍam*

Instruct me at my own desire to make *pratikramaṇa* for all that I have done amiss this day in thought, in speech, and in act (*The guru*: Do so) —may that evil have been done in vain.

Then comes the request for forgiveness, the *kṣāmaṇā-sūtra*:[2]

icchā-kāreṇa sandisaha bhagavaṃ abbhuṭṭhio 'mhi abbhintara-devasiyaṃ khāmeuṃ icchaṃ khāmemi devasiyaṃ jaṃ kiṃci apattiyaṃ para-pattiyaṃ bhatte pāṇe viṇaye veyāvacce ālāve saṃlāve ucc'-āsane sam'-āsaṇe antara-bhāsāe uvari-bhāsāe jaṃ kiṃci majjha viṇaya-parihīṇaṃ suhumaṃ vā bāyaraṃ vā tubbhe jāṇaha ahaṃ na jāṇāmi tassa micchāmi dukkaḍaṃ

Instruct me, lord, at my own desire; I am come forward to seek forgiveness for what is within the day: I want to seek forgiveness for whatever unfriendly or excessively unfriendly thing I have done this day in regard to eating and drinking, in regard to *vinaya* and *vaiyāvṛttya*, in regard to speech and conversation, in regard to seating oneself at a higher or at the same level as the guru, or in interrupting him when he

[1] Ibid. (pp. 682–3). [2] Ibid. (pp. 683–5).

is speaking, or in speaking louder than he, may whatever offence against *vinaya*, great or small, which you know and I do not know, have been done in vain.

In all these formulae the word *daivasika* will be replaced by the appropriate variant if the *pratikramaṇa* refers to the night or to some other period.

The great importance of the *pratikramaṇa* in Jainism is evident from the way in which the meaning of the term is extended to cover all edifying religious practices, the scope of the numerous *pratikramaṇa-sūtras* being very wide indeed.[1] Amongst the faults to be avowed are all forbidden things done and all duties left undone, all infringements of the twelve *vratas*, all offences against the *ratna-traya*, all the evil results of *parigraha* and *ārambha*, all actions motivated by passion and hate, all partiality for false creeds and dissemination of false dogmas, and all wrong done in the course of one's daily business or one's household duties.

The best-known *pratikramaṇa* commentary is the *Vandāru-vṛtti* of Devendra. Here as elsewhere *pratikramaṇa* for the eighteen sources of sin (*pāpa-sthānas*) is recommended. It may therefore be not inappropriate to list these here:[2]

(1) killing (*prāṇi-vadha, hiṃsā*) (2) lying (*asatya*) (3) thieving (*adattādana*) (4) unchastity (*abrahma, maithuna*) (5) acquisitiveness (*parigraha*)	the themes of the five *aṇu-vratas*
(6) anger (*krodha*) (7) pride (*māna*) (8) deceit (*māyā*) (9) greed (*lobha*)	the four *kaṣāyas*
(10) attachment (*rāga, preman*)	
(11) hatred (*dveṣa*)	
(12) disputation (*kalaha*)	
(13) false accusation (*abhyākhyāna*)	
(14) backbiting (*paiśunya*)	
(15) denigration (*parivāda, nindā*)	

[1] The *pratikramaṇa* is sometimes given a more ornate literary form as in the elegant *Pañcaviṃśatika* of Ratnākara Sūri. In this poem the Jina is invoked almost as a personal god.

[2] See PS 1351–3 and ŚrDK 300–3.

(16) depression and elation (*arati-rati*)
(17) deceitful speech (*māyā-mṛṣā*)
(18) false belief (*mithyātva*).

In another version[1] of the eighteen *pāpa-sthānas* eating by night (*rātri-bhojana*) is inserted in the list after *parigraha* and *arati-rati* omitted.

The keynote of the *pratikramaṇa* is best expressed in the well-known verse from the *sūtra*:

khāmemi savva-jīve savve jīve khamantu me
metti me savva-bhūesu veraṃ majjha na keṇavi[2]

I ask pardon of all living creatures, may all of them pardon me, may I have friendship with all beings and enmity with none.

It is probably because in this way the *pratikramaṇa* represents the pervasion of the mind by the feeling of *ahiṃsā* that it comes to be regarded as the central feature of the *āvaśyakas*. Like the other *āvaśyakas* it may be performed either in the temple or in a *poṣadha-śālā*, or in the presence of a monk or at home, and like them it requires the elimination of all *ārta-dhyāna*. It is sometimes said that like *pratyākhyāna* it is best expressed three times, first mentally when alone, then before the image of the Jina, and finally aloud before the guru. It is not always necessarily confined to past time and may therefore overlap with *pratyākhyāna*.

Together with *ālocanā* it is often given the designation of *prāyaścitta* but the *kāyotsarga* too is a form of *prāyaścitta*.

THE PRATYĀKHYĀNA

THIS, the fifth, or, according to the Digambaras, the sixth, *āvaśyaka* has been defined by Amitagati[3] as the avoidance of what is unfitting in order to prevent the commission of sin in the future. In a sense it is the equivalent of *pratikramaṇa* translated into future time. Ideally it should be performed three times[4] in solitude, before the Jina image and in the presence of a guru when it is linked with the *vandanaka*.

[1] Siddhasena Sūri on PS 1351–3.
[2] *Pratikramaṇa-sūtra*, 49.
[3] Śr (A) viii. 35.
[4] *Śraddha-vidhi*, p. 73*b*.

Pratyākhyāna[1] is said to be of two kinds according to whether it relates to the *mūla-gunas* (i.e. in the case of laymen the *aṇu-vratas*) or to the *uttara-guṇas* (i.e. the *guṇa-* and *śikṣā-vratas*), many of which may in fact be regarded as expressions of *pratyākhyāna*; that is particularly true of the *dig-*, *deśāvakāśika-*, *bhogopabhoga-*, and *poṣadhopavāsa-vratas*. Renunciation of any form of enjoyment is implicit in the concept but in practice it most often implies abstention from food, or from a particular kind of food, for a certain period of time.

There are traditionally ten categories of *pratyākhyāna*; but Hemacandra,[1] recognizing that these are without relevance for the lay doctrine, has preferred to discuss only the ninth and tenth: *saṅketa-pratyākhyāna* and *addha-pratyākhyāna*, which, he says, are in daily use. The former, as its name indicates, is symbolic; the devotee refrains from taking food for as long, for example, as he keeps his hand clenched, and by this renunciation he recalls his mind to his religious duties. Eight types of *saṅketa-pratyākhyāna* are listed:[1]

(1) *aṅguṣṭha*—'as long as I do not unclasp my thumb';
(2) *muṣṭi*—'as along as I do not unclench my hand';
(3) *granthi*—'as long as I do not loosen this knot';
(4) *gṛha*—'as long as I do not enter my house';
(5) *sveda*—'as long as these sweat drops do not dry';
(6) *ucchvāsa*—'as long as these respirations continue' (i.e. for a given number of them);
(7) *stibuka*—'as long as the drops of moisture do not dry on this bed';
(8) *jyotiṣka*—'as long as this lamp is not extinguished.'

Much more important is the *addhā-pratyākhyāna* for which a full ritual appropriate rather to the monastic, than to the lay, life, exists. This is classified into ten categories:[1]

(1) *namaskāra-sahita*—abstention from food for the duration of a *muhūrta*;
(2) *pauruṣī*—abstention from food for the duration of a *pauruṣī*;
(3) *dina-pūrvārddha*—abstention from food for the first half of the day;
(4) *ekāśana*—eating only one meal during the day;

[1] YŚ iii. 130 (p. 697).

(5) *eka-sthāna*[1]—taking food only in one position, i.e. without moving any limbs except the hands and mouth;
(6) *ācāmāmla*—eating only *ācāmāmla*;
(7) *abhaktārtha* (*upavāsa*)—fasting from the fourfold aliments or from three of them;
(8) *carama*—abstention from food until the end of the twenty-four-hour period, or from certain things until the end of one's life;
(9) *abhigraha*—a special vow of some kind; it may cover various types of *kāla-niyama* or any of the forms of *saṅketa-pratyākhyāna* previously listed;
(10) *vikṛti-niṣedha*—abstention from consuming any of the *vikṛtis*.

The formulae used in each case are as follows:[2]

1. *uggae sūre namokkāra-sahiyaṃ paccakkhāmi cauvvihaṃ pi āhāraṃ asaṇaṃ pāṇaṃ khāimaṃ sāimaṃ annatth' aṇābhogeṇaṃ sahasāgāreṇaṃ vosirāmi*

When the sun is risen I renounce for as long as the *namaskāra* lasts the fourfold aliments and except for cases of unawareness or of *force majeure* abandon them.

Hemacandra here refutes the argument that as no period of time is mentioned this should be properly called a form of *saṅketa-pratyākhyāna*. There are two licit grounds for breaking this *pratyākhyāna* termed *ākāras*.[3]

2. *porisīyaṃ paccakkhāmi uggae sūre cauvvihaṃ pi āhāraṃ asanaṃ pāṇaṃ khāimaṃ sāimaṃ annatth' aṇābhogeṇaṃ sahasāgāreṇaṃ pacchanna-kāleṇaṃ disā-moheṇaṃ sāhu-vayaṇeṇaṃ savva-samāhi-vattiy'-āgāreṇaṃ vosirāmi*

When the sun is risen I renounce for the duration of a *pauruṣī* the fourfold aliments and except for cases of unawareness or of *force majeure* or of overcast skies or of confusion of north and south or of instructions from a monk or except in order to attain full tranquillity of mind I abandon them.

The possibilities of legitimately breaking this *pratyākhyāna* are

[1] In the Digambara tradition this is held to mean 'taking only once from a platter'.

[2] YŚ iii. 130 (pp. 698–710) and ŚrDK 79 (pt. i, pp. 228–35).

[3] This word seems to have acquired the sense here of 'contingency' because of its repeated occurrence in the compounds which express the possibilities of exception to the vow.

six in number. The third and fourth are admitted because the passage of time has to be calculated from the varying length of one's shadow. The last is designed to provide for the contingency that a person may be suddenly afflicted by an acute pain provoking *ārta-dhyāna* or *raudra-dhyāna*; his tranquillity of mind is lost until he takes medicine to alleviate it.

3. *sūre uggae purim'-aḍḍham paccakkhāmi cauvvihaṃ pi āhāraṃ asaṇaṃ pāṇaṃ khāimaṃ sāimaṃ annatth' aṇābhogeṇaṃ sahasāgāreṇaṃ pacchanna-kāleṇaṃ disā-moheṇaṃ sāhu-vayaṇeṇaṃ mahattar'-āgāreṇaṃ savva-samāhi-vattiy'-āgāreṇaṃ vosirāmi*

An additional contingency (*ākāra*) is inserted: 'or except for more important business', this being understood to mean something done on behalf of the community that a third party could not perform and of equal spiritual merit with the *pratyākhyāna.*

4. *egāsaṇaṃ paccakkhāmi cauvvihaṃ pi āhāraṃ asaṇaṃ pāṇaṃ khāimaṃ sāimaṃ annatth' aṇābhogeṇaṃ sahasāgāreṇaṃ sāgāriy'-āgāreṇaṃ āuṇṭaṇa-pasāreṇaṃ guru-abbhutthāṇeṇaṃ pāriṭṭhāvaṇiy'-āgāreṇaṃ mahattar'āgāreṇaṃ savva-samāhi-vattiy'-āgāreṇaṃ vosirāmi*

I take only the *ekāśana* otherwise renouncing the fourfold aliments and except for cases of unawareness or of *force majeure* or of householder's business or except when the food offered has to be rejected or except for more important business or except in order to attain full tranquillity of mind I abandon them, not moving except for contortions and stretchings of the body or in rising to salute the guru.

There are now eight *ākāras* in this form of *pratyākhyāna.* It is noted that the Prakrit *egāsaṇa* may be interpreted either as 'eating one meal' or 'eating in one posture'. Certain of the *ākāras* refer to posture and not to actual fasting.

5. *ega-thāṇaṃ paccakkhāmi cauvvihaṃ pi āhāraṃ asaṇaṃ pāṇaṃ khāimaṃ sāimaṃ annatth' aṇābhogeṇaṃ sahasāgāreṇaṃ sāgāriy'-āgāreṇaṃ guru-abbhutthāṇeṇaṃ pāriṭṭhāvaṇiy'-āgāreṇaṃ mahattar'-āgāreṇaṃ savva-samāhi-vattiy'-āgāreṇaṃ vosirāmi*

This is identical with the preceding formula except for the omission of *āuṇṭaṇa-pasāreṇaṃ.*

6. *āyambilaṃ paccakkhāmi annatth' aṇābhogeṇaṃ sahasāgāreṇaṃ levāleveṇaṃ gihattha-saṃsaṭṭheṇaṃ ukkhitta-vivegeṇaṃ pāriṭṭhāvaṇiy'-āgāreṇaṃ mahattar'-āgāreṇaṃ savva-samāhi-vattiy'-āgāreṇaṃ vosirāmi*

For the *ācāmāmla-pratyākhyāna* I renounce and abandon everything and except for cases of unawareness or of *force majeure* or where other food has stuck to or been scraped off the platter or where other food has not been separated or where the householder's pot contains other substances or when the food offered has to be rejected or for more important business or in order to attain to full tranquillity of mind I abandon them.

7. *sūre uggae abhatt'-aṭṭham paccakkhāmi cauvviham pi āhāraṃ asaṇaṃ pāṇaṃ khāimaṃ sāimaṃ annatth' aṇābhogeṇaṃ sahasāgāreṇaṃ pāriṭṭhāvaṇiy'-āgāreṇaṃ mahattar'-āgāreṇaṃ savva-samāhi-vattiy'-āgāreṇaṃ vosirāmi*

When the sun is risen I renounce for this fasting the fourfold aliments and except for cases of unawareness or of *force majeure* or when the food offered has to be rejected or except for more important business or except in order to attain full tranquillity of mind I abandon them.

Here the *pāriṣṭhāpanika* contingency is not in fact applicable if the fourfold aliments are renounced.

pāṇassa levāḍeṇa vā alevāḍeṇa vā accheṇa vā bahuleṇa vā sasittheṇa vā asittheṇa vā vosirāmi

I abandon the fourfold aliments except for liquids viscous or non-viscous or transparent or turbid or mixed with rice grains or not mixed with rice grains.

These six *ākāras* are formulated to cover the case of the modified form of fasting in which liquids may still be taken.

8. *divasa-carimaṃ bhava-carimaṃ vā paccakkhāmi cauvvihaṃ pi āhāraṃ asaṇaṃ pāṇaṃ khāimaṃ sāimaṃ annatth' aṇābhogeṇaṃ sahasāgāreṇaṃ mahattar'-āgāreṇaṃ savva-samāhi-vattiy'-āgāreṇaṃ vosirāmi*

Whether this is to last till the end of the day or to the end of one's life four *ākāras* apply, and for this reason it is in the former meaning distinct from *ekāśana-pratyākhyāna*. On the other hand abstention from *rātri-bhojana* is an expression of *bhava-carima-pratyākhyāna*.

9. For the various types of *kāla-niyama* and *saṅketa-pratyākhyāna* four *ākāras* prevail: *annatth' aṇābhogeṇaṃ sahasāgāreṇaṃ mahattar' āgāreṇaṃ savva-samāhi-vattiy'-āgāreṇaṃ*. However, in the case of a vow to renounce clothing (*aprāvaraṇābhigraha*) a fifth *ākāra* '*cola-paṭṭag'-āgāreṇaṃ*' is also operative.

10. *vigaīo paccakkhāmi annatth' aṇābhogeṇaṃ sahasāgāreṇaṃ levāle-veṇaṃ gihattha-saṃsaṭṭheṇaṃ ukkhitta-vivegeṇaṃ paḍucca-makkhieṇaṃ pariṭṭhāvaṇiy'-āgāreṇaṃ mahattar'-āgāreṇaṃ savva-samāhi-vattiy'-āgāre-ṇaṃ vosirāmi*

I renounce the *vikṛtis* and except for cases of unawareness or of *force majeure* or where other food has stuck to and been scraped off the platter or where the householder's pot contains other substances or where other food has not been separated or because the butter has been kept beyond its due time or when the food offered has to be rejected or except for more important business or except in order to attain to full tranquillity of mind I abandon them.

A rough-and-ready test is applied in the case of the sixth of these *ākāras*.

As has already been noted, the *bhogopabhoga-vrata* is one of the *vratas* expressing forms of *pratyākhyāna*. The *yamas* mentioned by Samantabhadra[1] would belong under *bhava-carima-pratyākhyāna* and the *niyamas* under *abhigraha-pratyākhyāna*. Corresponding to the latter the Śvetāmbaras have a traditional list of fourteen *niyamas* expressed in the following verse:

saccitta-davva-vigai-vāṇaha-tambola-vattha-kusumesu
vāhaṇa-sayaṇa-vilevaṇa-bambha-disi-nhāṇa-bhattesu[2]

The two lists are closely related, both of course depending ultimately on the twenty-one *abhigrahas* or undertakings to observe restraint, which are accorded an important place in the *Upāsaka-daśāḥ*:

Śvetāmbara	Samantabhadra
(1) *sacitta* (green leaves and shoots)	*sangīta* (instrumental music)
(2) *dravya* (food other than *sacitta* and *vikṛti*)	*gīta* (singing)
(3) *vikṛti* (the licit six)	
(4) *upānah* (sandals)	
(5) *tambola* (betel)	*tambola*
(6) *vastra* (clothes)	*vasana*
(7) *kusuma* (flowers)	*kusuma*
(8) *vāhana* (vehicles, riding animals)	*vāhana*

[1] RK iii. 42.

[2] Quoted by Ratnaśekhara (*Śrāddha-vidhi*, p. 73*a*) and Yaśovijaya (*Dharma-saṃgraha*, i. 73).

(9)	*śayana* (beds)	*śayana*
(10)	*abrahma* (sexual intercourse)	*manmatha*
(11)	*vilepana* (cooling pastes and unguents)	*aṅga-rāga*
(12)	*dik*[1] (restriction of movement to fixed limits)	
(13)	*snāna* (bathing)	*snāna*
(14)	*bhakta* (restriction of food to fixed quantities).	*bhojana*.

THE KĀYOTSARGA

THE *kāyotsarga*, the fifth, or for the Digambaras the sixth, *āvaśyaka* is also for the Śvetāmbaras the fifth *pratimā*. Despite its status in the literature as a separate *āvaśyaka* it is, in reality, an adjunct to other rites, in Amitagati's[2] words 'the undisturbed abandonment of the body in all *āvaśyakas*'.

The so-called *kāyotsarga-sūtra* runs as follows:[3]

tassa uttarī-karaṇeṇaṃ pāyacchitta-karaṇenaṃ visohī-karaṇeṇaṃ visallī-karaṇeṇaṃ pāvāṇaṃ kammāṇaṃ nigghāyaṇ'-aṭṭhāe ṭhāmi kāussaggaṃ annattha ūsasieṇaṃ nīsasieṇaṃ khāsieṇaṃ chīeṇaṃ jambhāieṇaṃ uḍḍueṇaṃ vāya-nisaggeṇaṃ bhamalīe pitta-mucchāe suhumehiṃ aṅga-sañcālehiṃ suhumehiṃ khela-sañcalehiṃ suhumehiṃ diṭṭhi-sañcālehiṃ evam-āiehiṃ āgārehiṃ abhaggo avirāhio hujja me kāussaggo jāva arihantāṇaṃ bhagavantāṇaṃ namokkāreṇaṃ na pāremi tāva kāyam thāṇeṇaṃ māṇeṇaṃ jhāṇeṇaṃ appāṇaṃ vosirāmi

Making an additional effort, making penance, making purification, extracting evil from myself, I stand in the *kāyotsarga* in order to make an end to sinful acts. With the exception of inhaling and exhaling, coughing and sneezing, yawning and hiccoughing, breaking wind, giddiness, and swooning, very slight movements of the limbs, the eyes, and the saliva, and similar involuntary acts may my *kāyotsarga* be unbroken and unimpaired; until I have completed the recitation of the *namaskāra* to the blessed *arhats* I shall cast aside my body in the standing position, in silence and in meditation.

Hemacandra etymologizes *prāyaścitta* as 'that which in general (*prāyas*) purifies the mind (*citta*)'. By the final phrase he understands

[1] This of course is, in effect, the *dig-vrata*.
[2] Śr(A) viii. 36. [3] YŚ iii. 130 (pp. 607–11).

that the termination of any *kāyotsarga* is to be marked by the recitation of the *pañca-namaskāra*. He further notes that the word *appānam* is omitted in some texts: if it is to be retained it must mean 'body'.

In another passage Hemacandra defines the *kāyotsarga*[1] as 'standing silent in meditation without other movement than the involuntary movements of the body such as breathing, for a definite time until the *pañca-namaskāra* is recited'. It may be performed either:

(i) because of activities (*ceṣṭā*), for example, in connexion with the *airyāpathikī-pratikramaṇa*; or
(ii) for the sake of self-mastery (*abhibhava*), i.e. to win victory over *upasargas*.[2]

The former type is always brief, varying from eight to a thousand *ucchvāsas*. The latter will not be less than a *muhūrta* and may, as in the case of Bāhubali,[3] last for as long as a year.[4]

Numerous forms of the *kāyotsarga*, characterized by slight differences of posture, are noted in the monastic discipline. For the layman Hemacandra[4] recognizes three main types: upright, (*ucchrita*), seated (*upaviṣṭa*), and recumbent (*śayita*). Each of these again can be subdivided into four categories which for the upright position would be:

(i) upright physically and upright spiritually (the mind being in *dharmya-* or *śukla-dhyāna*);
(ii) upright physically but not spiritually;
(iii) upright spiritually but not physically;
(iv) upright neither spiritually nor physically.

This classification, for which there are many parallels in other spheres of Jainism, lies at the basis of that used by Amitagati:[5]

(i) *upaviṣṭopaviṣṭa*—a seated posture with *ārta-* or *raudra-dhyāna*;
(ii) *upaviṣṭotthita*—a seated posture with *dharmya-* or *śukla-dhyāna*;

[1] YŚ iii. 130 (p. 693).
[2] For a description of the *upasargas* see YŚ iii. 153.
[3] The figure whose *kāyotsarga* is represented in the famous statue of Śrāvana Belgola.
[4] YŚ iii. 130 (p. 694).
[5] Śr (A) viii. 57–61.

(iii) *utthitopaviṣṭa*—an upright posture with *ārta-* or *raudra-dhyāna*;

(iv) *utthitotthita*—an upright posture with *dharmya-* or *śukla-dhyāna*.

But such classifications represent little more than the subtleties of the schoolmen; the essential, it is stressed, is that without pure meditation the *kāyotsarga* can serve no purpose.

As has already been noted the *kāyotsarga* is, properly, an accessory to the performance of the *āvaśyakas* and of such rites as the *poṣadhopavāsa*. Amitagati[1] and Āśādhara,[2] for example, prescribe a total of twenty-eight *kāyotsargas* for the necessary duties: six for the *vandanaka*, eight for the *pratikramaṇa*, two for the *yoga-bhakti*, and twelve for the *svādhyāya*; and the precise duration of each of them in *ucchvāsas* is also fixed. The same minutiae of detail are found in the descriptions of the blemishes (*doṣas*) of the *kāyotsarga*: Hemacandra[3] notes twenty-one such faults, the *Mūlācāra* gives twenty-three, and Amitagati[4] raises the figure to thirty-two. All these lists relate in fact to the monastic life and have no real relevance to the *śrāvakācāra*.

When the layman engages in the *kāyotsarga* particularly, as Abhayadeva[5] notes, by night at a crossroads he will need to be of stout heart for he will be assailed by *upasargas* and *parīṣahas*.[6] These he must withstand but there are some legitimate reasons for interrupting the exercise: he is to be excused if he utters a cry because he himself or another person has been bitten by a snake or because bandits make an incursion or again if he interposes himself to save a living creature, as, for example, a mouse from the claws of a cat.[7] But the ideal picture of the *kāyotsarga* remains that of Hemacandra's verse: 'At dead of night he stands in the *kāyotsarga* outside the city wall and the bullocks taking him for a post rub their flanks against his body.'[8]

[1] Śr(A) viii. 66–67.
[2] SDhA vi. 27.
[3] YŚ iii. 130 (pp. 694–6).
[4] Śr (A) viii. 88–98.
[5] P (ŚrUP) 17.
[6] For the *parīṣahas* see YŚ iii. 153.
[7] YŚ iii. 124 (p. 610).
[8] YŚ iii. 144.

THE PŪJĀ

Pūjā, often called *ijyā* or *yajña*, the one form of 'sacrifice' possible to a Jaina, is the only major element of the layman's religion which is not discussed in the canonical works and the only one which may be said to belong exclusively to the lay life. Closely associated with the *āvaśyakas*,[1] it is often by the Śvetāmbaras voluntarily confounded with the *caitya-vandana*, which is sometimes held to be equivalent to *dravya-pūjā* and *bhāva-pūjā* together, sometimes to *bhāva-pūjā* alone. It will be convenient to make a distinction by treating under the head of *pūjā* those matters which form part of the *Pūjā-vidhāna-pañcāśaka* and under *caitya-vandana* those which make up the subject-matter of the *Vandana-vidhāna-pañcāśaka*.

Pūjā is not of course restricted to the adoration of the Jina's image, the *caitya*, either in the temple or in one's home; it may be offered to all those who, like the Jinas, have attained to final release, to monks whether *sādhus* or *ācāryas*, to the holy writ, and even to parents and elders.[2] Sometimes the meaning of the word is arbitrarily expanded to include the construction of temples and images, the carrying out of pilgrimages, the copying of the scriptures, the foundation of almshouses, the recitation of *mantras*, even the giving of alms (regarded as the *pūjā* of the *atithi*).[3] On the other hand it may be presented as a mere aspect of *dāna*—in Hemacandra's terms, the sowing of wealth on the *Jina-bimba-kṣetra*.[4]

The custom of *pūjā* is manifestly one of Jainism's earliest conscious imitations of the Hindu world around, a transference which was all the easier because the ceremony can be conceived as a simulacrum of the *samavasaraṇa*, that gathering where the Tīrthaṅkara preached to men and gods who rendered *pūjā* to him with all that was most priceless. On entering the temple, advises Āśādhara,[5] one should say to oneself, 'This is the *samavasaraṇa*, this is the Jina, and these are they who sit in the assembly'. Medhāvin even devotes the first three or four *adhikāras* of his *śrāva-*

[1] It has already been mentioned that the *sāmāyika*, originally conceived of as a period of meditation, gradually took on the character of a formal act of worship, in which praise was offered to the Jina. It was then but a step to the offering of material objects—the *pūjā*.

[2] YŚ iii. 124 (p. 655).

[3] SDhA ii. 25.

[4] YŚ iii. 120 (p. 584).

[5] SDhA vi. 10.

kācāra to a description of a *samavasaraṇa.* But this worship of the Jina, even if it responds to a basic human need, can yield only a subjective satisfaction. The *Tīrthaṅkaras*, immersed in their timeless beatitude, are inaccessible to human entreaties, derive no satisfaction from the offerings of their votaries.[1] And, since neither the lifeless image nor the being it represents are benefited by the *pūjā*, how can this be commendable since it inevitably involves destruction of life? To this objection the reply is that the individual who offers the *pūjā* achieves through viewing the image a tranquillity that is a source of *puṇya.* For those therefore whose livelihood necessarily provokes the destruction of living creatures it is hypocrisy to shy at the *Jina-pūjā* on the ground that it involves *hiṃsā.*[2]

Certain Digambaras—Jinasena,[3] Cāmuṇḍarāya,[4] and Āśādhara[5] (as well as Medhāvin and Vāmadeva)—give a rather unreal division of *pūjā* into five types:

(i) the daily worship (*nitya-maha*)—the ordinary *pūjā* in one's home or in the temple. This term is also used to cover the construction of temples;

(ii) *pūjā* made by diademed kings (*caturmukha* or *sarvatobhadra* or *mahā-maha*);

(iii) *pūjā* made by *cakravartins* to fulfil all desires (*kalpa-druma*);

(iv) *pūjā* lasting for eight days (*aṣṭāhnikī*) offered by the rulers of the *devas* in *Nandīśvara-dvīpa* or by mortals during the *Nandīśvara-parvan*;

(v) *pūjā* offered by the *devas* at the five *kalyāṇas* and in uncreate temples (*aindra-dhvaja*).

Of these the first type alone is germane to the discussion; the fourth is best considered under the head of *yātrā* with other festivals; and the other three have but a theoretical significance, the third and fifth belonging really to the realm of mythology.

The daily *pūjā*, like the *āvaśyakas*, may, as in Vasunandin's work, be classified on rather artificial lines according to the categories of *nāma*, *sthāpanā*, *dravya*, *kṣetra*, *kāla*, and *bhāva*:

(i) reciting the names of the Jinas (*nāma-pūjā*);[6]

[1] Haribhadra's commentary on ŚrPr 345.

[2] P (Pūjā) 41–45 and ŚrPr 344–50.

[3] MP xxxviii. 26–32.

[4] CS, p. 21.

[5] SDhA ii. 24–28.

[6] Śr (V) 382.

(ii) representing the Jina in an image (*sthāpanā-pūjā*).[1] This may be either:

(*a*) *sad-bhāva*—the attribution of the Jina's qualities to an object having form; or

(*b*) *asad-bhāva*—the imagining mentally of a divine presence in the *akṣata* or other objects offered in the *pūjā*;

(iii) offering in an act of worship substances such as perfumes (*dravya-pūjā*);[2]

(*a*) *sacitta*—to the Jina or to the gurus;

(*b*) *acitta*—to the holy writ;

(iv) worshipping places associated with the Jinas, their *kalyāṇa-sthānas* (*kṣetra-pūjā*);[3]

(v) making *pūjā* on the anniversaries of the *kalyāṇas* or on such occasions as the *Nandīśvara-parvan* (*kāla-pūjā*);[4]

(vi) worshipping mentally or by muttering formulae (*japa*) or by *dhyāna* (*bhāva-pūjā*).[5]

More significant in fact, however, is the simpler division, as given, for example, by Amitagati,[6] into worship with offerings (*dravya-pūjā*) and worship by mental concentration (*bhāva-pūjā*).

Various lists of the offerings which should constitute the *pūjā* are given by different writers often with indications of their symbolism; but before comparing them it is well to note the constituents of the act of worship at least as understood by the Digambaras:[7]

(i) bathing the image (*snapana, abhiṣeka*);

(ii) making the offerings (*bali, arca, pūjā*);

(iii) chanting the praise of the Jina (*stava, stuti*);

(iv) muttering the sacred formulae (*japa*).

The Śvetāmbaras have a rather similar basic threefold division of *pūjā* which figures in all the descriptions of the *caitya-vandana*.[8]

(i) *aṅga-pūjā* symbolized by *puṣpa*—flowers, clothes, ornaments, unguents;

(ii) *agra-pūjā* symbolized by *āhāra*—water, fruit, rice, lamps;

(iii) *bhāva-pūjā* symbolized by *stuti*—hymns of praise.

[1] Śr (V) 383–4. [2] Śr (V) 448–51. [3] Śr (V) 452.
[4] Śr (V) 453–5. [5] Śr (V) 456–8. [6] Śr (A) xii. 12.
[7] SDhA v. 31. [8] CVBh 10.

At the same time there exist the distinctions of *snapana* (bathing) and *sthāpana* (making offerings) and of *dravya-pūjā* and *bhāva-pūjā*.

Here for purposes of comparison are the Śvetāmbara lists of 8, 17, and 21 forms of *pūjā*, the unnumbered list of the *Pañcāsaka*,[1] and the Digambara list of 11 given by Vāmadeva, as well as some items mentioned by Vasunandin[2] and in the *Śrāvaka-dharma-dohaka* (see p. 220).[3]

The eightfold worship (*aṣṭopahāra*) is the commonest numerical form given to the elements of the *pūjā*: it has superseded an earlier fivefold classification identical with the first five items on the list of eight, and has obtained general acceptance among Digambaras as well as Śvetāmbaras, being noted at a rather earlier date by the former. Devasena,[4] Hemacandra,[5] Devendra,[6] and Āśādhara[7] are amongst the writers who give the list. The figure is expanded in subsequent times; thus Vāmadeva among the Digambaras prefers a figure of eleven whilst among the Śvetāmbaras the *Pūjā-prakaraṇa*, which has been fathered on Umāsvāti but can scarcely be older than the fourteenth century, catalogues twenty-one elements of *pūjā* which are almost identical with those noted by Cāritrasundara in the *Ācāropadeśa*.[8] The other list with seventeen items which appears to be anterior to the list of twenty-one is quoted by Yaśovijaya.[9]

The earliest work devoted exclusively to the *pūjā* would seem to be the *Pūjā-pañcāśaka*. The author introduces the subject with some prudence: just as the labours of agriculture yield a good return if performed in due season so all religious duties should be carried out at the right times, these being in the case of the *pūjā* the three *sandhyās*.[10] If done in such a way that the householder's livelihood is interrupted they will in the end lead to no good, for the full religious life is possible only for the ascetic.[11] But when the householder makes *pūjā* even the servants assisting him have a share in its good results whilst those who continue their normal duties have only toil.[12]

The first requisite for the votary is purity of body and mind.

[1] P (Pūjā) 14–15.
[2] Śr (V) 483–92.
[3] Doha 181–204.
[4] BhS(D) 461–87. However, in this list for *naivedya* is substituted the triad of milk products: milk, curds, ghee.
[5] YŚ iii. 124 (p. 601).
[6] ŚrDK 26.
[7] SDhA ii. 30.
[8] ĀU ii. 35–36.
[9] *Dharma-saṃgraha*, p. 134*b*.
[10] P (Pūjā) 4–5.
[11] P (Pūjā) 7.
[12] P (Pūjā) 21.

	Standard list of eight	List of twenty-one	List of seventeen	Pañcāśaka	Vāmadeva	Other Digambaras (Vasunandin, etc.)
1.	gandha	vāsa	vāsa	gandha, gorocana	gandha	candana
2.	puṣpa-mālā, puṣpa	puṣpa	puṣpāruhana	sarvauṣadhi	puṣpa-mālā	puṣpa
3.	akṣata	taṇḍula	—	akṣata	akṣata	akṣata
4.	dhūpa	dhūpa	dhūpotkṣepa	dhūpa	dhūpa	dhūpa
5.	dīpa	dipa	dīpa	dīpa	dīpa	dīpa
6.	naivedya, caru	naivedya	naivedya	bali	caru	naivedya
7.	phala	phala	sukha-phala-ḍhaukana	—	phala	phala
8.	jala	jala	—	jala	jala	jala
9.	—	dāman	mālāruhana	kusuma-dāman	puṣpāñjali	puṣpāñjali
10.	—	pattra	puṣpa-prakara	dadhi	śānti-dhārā-traya	ghṛtā-payas
11.	—	pūga	puṣpa-gṛha	siddhārthaka	ghaṇṭā	ghaṇṭā
12.	—	bhūṣana	ābharaṇa	kañcana-ratna-mauktika	—	—
13.	—	snātra	snapana-vilepana	surabhi-vilepana	—	abhiṣeka
14.	—	vilepana	ārātrika	—	—	ārātrika
15.	—	cāmara	cūrṇa	—	—	cāmara
16.	—	chattra	varṇaka	—	—	chattra
17.	—	vāditra	vāditra	—	—	—
18.	—	nṛtya	nṛtya	—	—	—
19.	—	gīta	gīta	—	—	—
20.	—	stuti	—	—	—	—
21.	—	kośa-vṛddhi	—	—	—	—

His normal livelihood must be unobjectionable, he must put away all evil and improper thoughts, concentrating his mind on religion, and he must avoid all actions within the temple that can be considered as *āśātanās*. Whilst taking precautions to minimize the *hiṃsā* inherent in bathing he must wash himself before making the *pūjā* since physical cleanliness for the layman both fosters and symbolizes spiritual purity through the destruction of *pāpa*.[1] Āśādhara[2] mentions five forms of bathing (*snāna*): as far as the feet, the knees, the loins, the neck, or the head; ranging in other words from the mere washing of the feet to the full cleansing. As a preliminary to the *pūjā* one must bathe as far as the head or at least as far as the neck; or else its performance will have to be delegated to another person. Cāritrasundara[3] recommends bathing as far as the neck: only in cases where this is ritual pollution in the home is bathing as far as the head desirable. For going to the temple clean clothes are always to be worn and muddy paths avoided.

A special ritual[4] is laid down for the setting up (*pratiṣṭhā*) of a Jina image, which is accounted a form of *pūjā* in its larger significance, and here again the concept of a representation of the *samavasaraṇa* dominates.

The ritual for the occasion, as described by Vasunandin,[4] is of a rather special kind but its elements are those which recur in all descriptions of *pūjā*,[5] Digambara and Śvetāmbara.

Hemacandra[5] sites the *pūjā* within the *caitya-vandana* ceremony after the triple circumambulation of the Jina image. It commences with the bathing ceremony followed by the designing of the *tilaka* with *śrī-khaṇḍa* sandalwood paste and by the burning of incense. The image is then placed in a *kalaśa* full of water to which various herbs have been added, garlands of flowers are set before it, it is bathed with milk and ghee together with water perfumed with camphor, saffron, *śrī-khaṇḍa*, agallochum, and other scents, and anointed with the finest sandal paste. Then garlands of *jātī*, *campaka*, *śatapattra*, *vicakila*, and *kamala* flowers are placed before the Jina; it is dressed with clothes and with ornaments of gems, gold, pearls; the eight *maṅgalas* are designed with *siddhārthaka*, *śāli*, and *taṇḍula* seeds; lamps, and offerings of ghee and curds and sweet

[1] P (Pūjā) 9–13. [2] SDhA ii. 34. [3] ĀU ii. 3–8.

[4] Vasunandin says that what he describes here is a form of *sad-bhāva-sthāpanā-pūjā* as the *asad-bhāva* form is dangerous in a world deluded by false beliefs.

[5] YŚ 124 (pp. 600–1).

cakes are placed before it; a *tilaka* is made with sandal paste on the forehead, and lamps are waved before it in the *ārātrika* ceremony.

The eight *maṅgalas*[1] are:

(1) svastika;	(5) bhadrāsana (throne);
(2) śrī-vatsa;	(6) kalaśa;
(3) nandyāvarta;	(7) matsya (two fishes);
(4) vardhamānaka;	(8) darpaṇa (mirror).

A description and explanation of these is given by Kirfel.[2]

Devendra, in the *Śrāddha-dina-kṛtya*, notes that for *pūjā* in the home the worshipper is to be clad in white and to wear a *mukha-vastrikā*. Bathing of the image in water perfumed with sandal and camphor and inunction with *go-śīrṣa* sandal are enjoined. Clothes and ornaments are to be put on it and flowers and fruit offered.[3] A similar but more elaborate procedure is to be followed for *pūjā* in the temple. The limbs of the image are to be rubbed with a delicate cloth well perfumed and smeared with a paste of sandal, camphor, and saffron. The eight *maṅgalas* are to be designed with *akṣata* and *pūjā* then made to them with five-coloured flowers. Incense is to be burned, and the devotee, if he has the necessary talent, will himself dance before the Jina.[4] After the recitation of the *pranidhāṇa-sūtra* he is to make a *puṣpa-gṛha* (flower-house) with fragrant blossoms of many colours, this once again being a symbol of the *samavasaraṇa*.[5] And finally the worshipper plays or gets others to play various musical instruments.[6]

Probably because of the absence of a rigidly fixed canonical tradition the *pūjā* has continued to develop with increasing complexity since the medieval period. Thus the *Pūjā-prakaraṇa* assigns different types of offerings to different hours of the day: perfumes at dawn, flowers at noon, incense and lamps at eventide, and requires the marking of the image with no less than nine *tilakas*.[7] *Pūjā* is to be made in the *padmāsana* posture with downcast eyes and in silence; the worshipper should face the west and if he fails to observe this rule various ills such as poverty will befall him.[8]

The *Ācāropadeśa* gives details of the *pūjā* very similar to those of the *Pūjā-prakaraṇa*. *Tilakas* are to be made on the forehead,

[1] ŚrDK 66. [2] Kirfel, op. cit., pp. 153–5. [3] ŚrDK 23–26.
[4] ŚrDK 57–70. [5] ŚrDK 71–73. [6] ŚrDK 74–75.
[7] *Pūjā-prakaraṇa*, 8–10; ĀU ii. 29–30. [8] *Pūjā-prakaraṇa*, 4–6.

chest, neck, and abdomen of the image. Flowers are never to be cut in two as *pāpa* would be provoked by the severing of leaves or flowers, there being a special objection to splitting the buds of *campaka* flowers.[1] A sevenfold purity—of mind, body, speech, dress, ground, utensils, and ritual—is to be observed before the *pūjā* can be made.[2]

Whilst the Śvetāmbaras tend to augment continually the lists of possible forms of *pūjā* the later Digambaras develop the *pūjā* in other directions. Vāmadeva,[3] for example, mentions as a requisite a triple ablution: *vrata-snāna* (purification by observance of the vows) and *mantra-snāna* (purification by recitation of *mantras*) as well as the ritual bathing of the body (*kāya-snāna*). Again, after asperging the image the votary is to pour the remains of the scented *abhiṣeka* water on his own head.

Dharmakīrti, in his *Saṅghācāra* commentary on the *Caitya-vandana-bhāṣya*,[4] explains the *aṅga-pūjā* as comprising the picking up and sweeping away of the remains of the offerings and the faded garlands, the washing of the body of the image, the garlanding, bathing, and inunction, the marking of the *tilaka*, the adorning with jewels, the burning of incense, and the placing in the hand of the image of a coconut, betel nut, *nāgavallī* leaf, or similar offering.

The *agra-pūjā*, the putting before the image of *amiṣa*—literally 'meat' but defined in the dictionaries as 'anything comestible'—includes *naivedya*, betel, fruits, leaves, sugar-cane, and lamps.

Another late writer, Ratnaśekhara, is interesting for his development of the details of the *pūjā*. He too insists that the worshipper should, in the inner sanctuary, meditate on the Jina seated in the *samavasaraṇa* and should also visualize the whole temple as the *samavasaraṇa*.[5] He is particularly concerned with the disposal of the *nirmālya* by which is meant anything put on or before a Jina image—*akṣata*, fruits, sweet cakes, flowers, clothes—that has become devoid of lustre, perfume, or freshness. As in the rainy season the *nirmālya* will contain insects it is to be discarded, together with the water that has been used for bathing the image, in a spot where people do not tread.

As already explained the *aṅga-pūjā* commences by the removal of the *nirmālya*, the wiping and washing of the limbs, and the brushing of the hair. After the offering of flowers the image is

[1] ĀU ii. 29–31. [2] ĀU ii. 12. [3] BhS (V) 470.
[4] CVBh 10. [5] *Śrāddha-vidhi*, p. 53*a*.

bathed with the *pañcāmṛta*[1]—ghee, curds, milk, water, and sugar-cane juice—and then with sterile (*prāsuka*) water. The limbs are next to be rubbed with a scented cloth which must be soft in texture and red in colour and then anointed with *go-śīrṣa* sandal. In using sandal paste flowers or other forms of *aṅga-pūjā*, care is to be taken that the eyes and mouth of the Jina are not covered. The image is now clothed and adorned with ornaments of gold, pearls, and gems and with gold and silver flower designs. Garlands, crowns, and flower-houses are fashioned with flowers of *campaka*, *ketaka*, *śatapattra*, *sahasrapattra*, and *jāti* and in the Jina's hand is placed a citron, coconut, betel nut, *nāgavalli* leaf, sweetmeat, or coin (*nāṇaka*).[2]

The *agra-pūjā* includes the designing of the eight *maṅgalas* with grains of rice or mustard seed or, better still, with grains of gold or silver, the disposing of little heaps of food (the *caturvidhāhāra*) in groups of three, the waving of lamps before the image, the offering of nosegays of flowers (*puṣpa-prakara*). The *ārātrika* lamps may be alimented with ghee, sugar, camphor, and other perfumed substances.[3]

It is stressed that *pūjā* must first be made to the *mūla-bimba* (principal image) within the inner sanctuary just as when making *guru-vandana* the first salutation is for the *ācārya* and not for those *munis* who may happen to be nearest. It would be very undesirable, for example, if *pujā* were first made to the image at the door (*dvāra-bimba*) only to find that there were not sufficient flowers to make *pūjā* to the principal image. But within the limits of one's means the same ritual is to be followed for all images including those in one's private chapel (*gṛha-caitya*). The image is to be well rubbed dry each day to prevent the formation of mould (*śyāmikā*).

In all the texts there is a clear insistence that the variety and richness of the *pūjā* depend on one's financial means. A poor man will content himself with the simple meditation of the *bhāva-pūjā* though he may assist others in making offerings by threading garlands of flowers.

[1] Compare with this the *pañca-ratna* (gold, silver, copper, coral, and pearls) and the *pañca-gavya*, both of which enter into the later ritual.

[2] *Śraddha-vidhi*, pp. 53 ff.

[3] Ibid., pp. 56 ff.

THE ĀŚĀTANĀS

THE term as employed in the canonical texts covers any act on the part of a younger monk implying a lack of respect to an older monk. Thirty-three such *āśātanās* of the *vandanaka* ritual, listed in the *Āvaśyaka* texts, are described by Hemacandra[1] and Devendra[2] but are with difficulty applicable[3] to the layman performing this rite. Others are devised to cater for the replacement of the guru by the *sthāpanācārya*; and at some stage the concept of *āśātanā* is transferred to the *caitya-vandana* ritual and developed to a point where the word comes virtually to signify a sacrilege or profanation of the temple. Though the designation seems never to be used by them some Digambara writers[4] note a number of acts which should be avoided in the presence of an ascetic (no special category is devised for the temple). These, though more general and less ritualistic in character, are in effect identical with the *gurv-āśātanās*.

They are given below, together with the ten *devāśātanās* of Nemicandra,[5] which becomes the standard later list, and the ten mentioned by Hemacandra[6] and repeated by Āśādhara.[7]

	DIGAMBARA	NEMICANDRA	HEMACANDRA
(1)	yawning (*jṛmbhana*)	sleeping (*svapna*)	sleeping (*nidrā*)
(2)	laughter (*hāsya*)	laughter (*hāsa*)	laughter (*hāsa*)
(3)	jesting (*narma*)	wearing sandals (*upānah*)	sporting (*vilāsa*)
(4)	gesticulation (*vikāra*)	micturating (*mūtra*)	quarrelling (*kalaha*)
(5)	spitting (*niṣṭhīvana*)	defecating (*uccāra*)	spitting (*niṣṭhyūta*)
(6)	making one's toilet (*aṅga-saṃskāra*)	copulation (*strī-bhoga*)	evil gossip (*duṣkathā*)
(7)	lying (*asatya*)	eating (*bhojana*)	consuming the fourfold aliments (*bhojana*)
(8)	calumniating (*abhyākhyāna*)	drinking (*pāna*)	(*pāna*)
(9)	leaning (*avaṣṭambha*)	betel (*tambola*)	(*svādima*)
(10)	clapping the hands (*kara-tāḍana*)	dicing (*dyūta*)	(*khādima*)
(11)	stretching the hands (*kara-sphoṭa*)		
(12)	stretching the feet (*pāda-prasāraṇa*)		
(13)	stretching the body (*gātra-bhañjana*)		

Reference is made to profanations of the temple (*vajjeyavvam tu taya dehammi vi kaṇḍuyana-m-āi*) as early as the *Pūjā-vidhāna-pañcāśaka*[8] though the term *āśātanā* is not there used. Abhayadeva

[1] YŚ iii. 130 (pp. 676–7).
[2] ŚrDK 79 (pp. 224–5).
[3] Hemacandra's remark that 'in the descriptions of the *vandanaka* the celebrant is a monk not a layman' (p. 679) suggests that he was aware of this.
[4] Śr (A) xiii. 40–41.
[5] PS 432.
[6] YŚ iii. 81.
[7] SDhA vi. 14.
[8] P (Pūjā).

explains the phrase quoted as referring not only to scratching an itching sore, but to spitting, stretching the limbs, and talking idly. Nemicandra, who gives the ten *devāśātanās* enumerated above, also sets out a longer list of eighty-four.[1] This embraces some very disparate elements of which one or two may perhaps be the result of textual corruptions for the Prakrit text is, as so often in such enumerations, very unsatisfactory; in any event it includes the ten mentioned above together with a number which are based on infringements of the five *abhigamas* of the *caitya-vandana* ritual. As a curiosity rather than for its practical importance it is given below:

(1) *khela*—spitting
(2) *keli*—pastimes
(3) *kali*—wrangling
(4) *kalā*—practising arts such as bowmanship
(5) *kulalaya*—rinsing the mouth (comm. *gaṇḍūṣa*)
(6) *tambola*—chewing betel
(7) *udgālana*—spitting out betel
(8) *gālī*—vulgar abuse
(9) *kaṅgulikā*—micturation and defecation
(10) *śarīra-dhāvana*—cleansing the body
(11) *keśa*—arranging the hair
(12) *nakha*—paring the nails
(13) *lohita*—letting blood drip from cuts or sores
(14) *bhaktoṣa*—eating at one's ease
(15) *tvac*—picking off the scab from a sore
(16) *pitta*—vomiting bile
(17) *vānta*—vomiting
(18) *daśana*—cleaning the teeth
(19) *viśrāmaṇā*—massaging the body
(20) *dāmana*—tethering of animals (another explanation is 'breaking in of horses')

<table>
<tr><td>(21) danta—</td><td rowspan="8">letting discharges or secretions of these organs or excrescences fall on the floor of the temple</td><td>teeth</td></tr>
<tr><td>(22) akṣi—</td><td>eye</td></tr>
<tr><td>(23) nakha—</td><td>nails</td></tr>
<tr><td>(24) gaṇḍa—</td><td>boil</td></tr>
<tr><td>(25) nāsikā—</td><td>nose</td></tr>
<tr><td>(26) śiras—</td><td>head</td></tr>
<tr><td>(27) śrotra—</td><td>ear</td></tr>
<tr><td>(28) chavi—</td><td>skin</td></tr>
</table>

[1] PS 433–6.

(29) *mantra*—use of *mantras*
(30) *mīlana*—meeting old men to discuss marriage contracts
(31) *lekhyaka*—business transactions
(32) *vibhajana*—settlement of inheritances
(33) *bhaṇḍāra*—storing of property
(34) *duṣṭāsana*—sitting with one leg crossed over the other
(35) *chāṇī*—making pats of cowdung

(36) *karpaṭa*—	concealing these and other commodities in the temple to escape taxation	cloth
(37) *dāli*—		pulses
(38) *parpaṭa*—		cakes of rice
(39) *vaṭikā*—		cakes of pulses

(40) *nāśana*—taking refuge in the temple to evade justice
(41) *ākranda*—wailing, lamentation
(42) *vi-kathā*—idlc gossip (or perhaps more specifically the *vi-kathās*)
(43) *śara-ghaṭana*—fabrication of bows and arrows
(44) *tiryak-saṃsthāpana*—stabling of animals
(45) *agni-sevana*—kindling fires
(46) *randhana*—cooking
(47) *parīkṣana*—testing of coins
(48) *naiṣedhikī-bhañjana*—failure to observe the *naiṣedhikī*

(49) *chattra*—	failure to leave such objects outside the temple	parasol
(50) *upānah*—		footwear
(51) *śastra*—		weapons
(52) *cāmara*—		yak's tail fly-whisk

(53) *mano-'nekatva*—failure to concentrate one's mind
(54) *abhyaṅgana*—inunction of the body with oil
(55) *sacittānām atyāga*—failure to remove sentient objects such as flowers
(56) *ajīve tyāga*—removal of non-sentient objects such as necklaces
(57) *dṛṣṭau no-añjali*—failure to make the *añjali* on sight of the Jina image
(58) *eka-sāṭottarāsaṅga-bhaṅga*—failure to put on an outer garment
(59) *mukuṭa*—wearing a diadem on one's head
(60) *mauli*—wearing a tiara on one's head
(61) *siraḥ-śekhara*—wearing a wreath of flowers on one's head
(62) *huḍḍa*—making wagers

(63) *kaṇḍuka-geḍḍikādi-ramaṇa*—playing with a ball and stick
(64) *jyotkāra*—burning lamps for the spirits of the ancestors
(65) *bhaṇḍa-kriyā*—making indecent remarks
(66) *re-kāra*—making contemptuous remarks
(67) *dharaṇa*—restraining wrongdoers
(68) *raṇa*—fighting
(69) *vālānām vivaraṇa*—combing one's hair
(70) *paryastikā*—spreading one's bed
(71) *pādukā*—keeping on one's sandals
(72) *pāda-prasāraṇa*—stretching out one's feet
(73) *puṭa-puṭi*—whistling
(74) *paṅka*—making the floor muddy by washing one's body
(75) *rajas*—making the floor dusty by shaking one's feet
(76) *maithuna*—copulation
(77) *yūka*—removing lice from the head
(78) *jemana*—eating
(79) *guhya*—not covering the sexual organs (there is a v.l. *yuddha* —wrestling)
(80) *vaidya*—practising medicine
(81) *vāṇijya*—buying and selling
(82) *śayyā*—sleeping on a bed
(83) *jala*—drinking water or letting it drop
(84) *majjana*—bathing

The sanskritizations given above are those of Siddhasena Sūri and represent in themselves an interpretation of the original Prakrit. There are slight divergencies in the list given by Devendra[1] but that of the fifteenth-century Ratnaśekhara[2] tallies completely with the *Pravacana-sāroddhāra*.

It is to Ratnaśekhara[3] that we must turn for the full picture of the *āśātanās* as a category of Jainism. They are classified as follows:

1. In respect of *jñāna*:
 (i) *jaghanya*, e.g. letting a drop of spittle fall on a manuscript or rosary; pronouncing a syllable too little or too much;
 (ii) *madhyama*, e.g. reciting at the wrong time; touching a book with one's foot out of *pramāda*; dropping a book on the ground; eating when the *jñānopakaraṇa* is close at hand;

[1] ŚrDK 123 (p. 270).
[2] *Śrāddha-vidhi*, p. 73*b*.
[3] Ibid., pp. 71*a* ff.

(iii) *utkṛṣṭa*, e.g. wiping the characters on manuscripts with spittle; sitting or lying on a manuscript; defecating when the *jñānopakaraṇa* is close at hand; expressing reprobation of the sacred knowledge and its repositories.

2. In respect of *deva*:

(i) *jaghanya*—the list of ten already given;
(ii) *madhyama*—a list of forty, which is clearly less original than either the ten or the eighty-four *āśātanās* and seems to have been constructed from them: in any event it contains no new elements;
(iii) *utkṛṣṭa*—the list of eighty-four given above.

3. In respect of the guru:

(i) *jaghanya*—concerned with touching the guru's feet;
(ii) *madhyama*—concerned with contact with mucus, spittle, or other impurities;
(iii) *utkṛṣṭa*—concerned with acting contrary to the guru's command.

All these are taken from the conventional enumeration of thirty-three *āśātanās* of the *vandanaka*.

4. In respect of the *sthāpanācārya*:

(i) *jaghanya*, e.g. moving it about, touching it with the feet;
(ii) *madhyama*, e.g. letting it fall on the ground, dropping it in contempt;
(iii) *utkṛṣṭa*, e.g. destroying it, smashing it to pieces.

The destruction of temple property is said to be also a very serious *āśātanā*.

PRAMĀDA

PRAMADA (carelessness) or *pramatta-yoga* (careless activity) is a primary cause of *hiṃsā*. Amṛtacandra dwells on this fundamental concept laid down in the *Tattvārtha-sūtra*[1] and finds *pramatta-yoga*, and therefore *hiṃsā*, in *asatya* and all other transgressions of the moral law.[2] The *anartha-daṇḍa-vrata*, which is largely a reinforcement of the *ahiṃsā-vrata*, contains a special section devoted to

[1] T (P) vii. 13. [2] e.g. PASU 99–100.

abstinence from activities resulting from *pramādācarita*. In that connexion *pramāda* is fivefold:

(i) drinking alcohol (*madya*), which is also condemned as an infringement of the *mūla-guṇas*;
(ii) sensual pleasures (*viṣaya*);
(iii) the passions (*kaṣāya*);
(iv) sleep (*nidrā*);

Sleep as a form of *pramāda* is often mentioned. Like food it should always be enjoyed only in moderation, and according to many texts from the *Pañcāśaka*[1] onwards one should always in any interval of sleep meditate on the foulness of the human body, for if one realizes that the bodies of women are only outwardly attractive, Kāma's arrows will be but empty feathers. In any event sleep during daytime is to be rigorously eschewed, and at night it is to be restricted to the minimum.

(v) unprofitable conversation (*vi-kathā*).

Four (or sometimes seven) types of *vi-kathā* or *aśubha-kathā* are generally listed:

(i) Talk of women (*strī-kathā*)—this is understood to mean talking about women's dresses, ornaments, looks, or gait, as, for example, saying that a woman is slender or full-breasted or skilled in love-making or else that she squawks like a crow and waddles like a buffalo. It may also cover comparisons between women of different countries.

(ii) Talk of food (*bhakta-kathā*)—this applies to descriptions of various kinds of dishes or of what one plans to eat at one's next meal such as saying how delicious are cakes made with ghee and honey.

(iii) Talk of places (*deśa-kathā*)—as examples of this are cited the statements that in the south there is abundant food and desirable women, or in the east wine and sugar and rice and cloth, or that in the north there are brave men, swift horses, abundant saffron, and sweet grapes and pomegranates, wheat being the main crop, whilst in the west there are sugar-cane and cool waters and cloth of fine texture. Śānti Sūri suggests rather similar examples: that Gurjara is a land difficult of access, the people of Lāṭa are great warriors, or that it is pleasant to live in Kashmir.

[1] P (ŚrDh) 46.

(iv) Talk of kings (*rāṭ-kathā*)—this would refer to statements such as these: our ruler is very heroic or the king of Gauḍa has many elephants; or again, that there was a terrible battle between two neighbouring kings.

(v) Sentimental talk (*mṛdu-kāruṇikī kathā*)—this is defined as tales calculated to soften the hearts of the auditors such as descriptions of persons in misfortune separated from their loved ones.

(vi) Irreligious talk (*darśana-bhedinī kathā*)—this term would apply to discourses destructive of right belief such as praise of, for example, Buddhist doctrines by people who imagine themselves to be very knowledgeable. It is practically equivalent to the *para-pāṣaṇḍi-praśaṃsā aticāra* of *samyaktva*.

(vii) Unethical talk (*cāritra-bhedinī kathā*)—by this is meant stories in which the repeated transgressions of moral precepts can offer a bad example to those who listen to them.

These seven *vi-kathās* are listed by Śānti Sūri[1] in the *Dharma-ratna-prakaraṇa* but in general, as, for example, by Hemacandra[2] only the first four are taken into account.

Just as *pramāda* finds expression in idle speech so can it be avoided by silence. Amitagati[3] recommends the undertaking of a vow of silence (*mauna-vrata*) which may be either for a limited period or for one's life long. In the former case its completion will be marked by a festival in the temple with the dedication of a bell (*ghaṇṭikā*), any such offering made in celebration of a successfully accomplished vow, being styled an *uddyotana* or, more commonly, an *udyāpana*.

The maintenance of silence is regarded as essential for auspicious meditation (*śukla-dhyāna*) and for the *āvaśyakas* as the list of the *maunas* or occasions for silence shows. Amitagati notes four of these: eating, excretion, *pāpa-kārya*, and *āvaśyaka*, but at least from Āśādhara onwards a figure of seven is fixed, the actual enumeration varying slightly from author to author. Here are some examples:

ĀŚĀDHARA[4]	MEDHĀVIN[5]	CĀRITRASUNDARA[6]
(1) bhojana	bhojana	bhojana
(2) maithuna	maithuna	maithuna
(3) snāna	snāna	snāna

[1] DhRP 20. [2] YŚ iii. 79 (p. 500).

[3] Śr (A) xii. 108–10. Āśādhara here clearly borrowed from Amitagati (SDhA iv. 36–37). [4] SDhA iv. 38. [5] Śr (M) vi. 44. [6] ĀU ii. 51.

	Āśādhara	Medhāvin	Cāritrasundara
(4)	mala-kṣepa	hadana	viḍ-utsarga
(5)	vamana	mūtraṇa	vamana
(6)	pāpa-kārya[1]	pūjā	danta-dhāvana
(7)	āvaśyaka	āvaśyaka	nirodha

The term *nirodha* is a little unclear: if it means the 'stoppage of breath' in yogic exercises conducing to meditation the Śvetāmbara list of Cāritrasundara will be parallel with the Digambara lists: in both cases the Jaina notion of religious rites will have been appended to an enumeration of physical activities—eating, copulation, bathing, vomiting, excretion, tooth-cleaning—regarded by the primitive mind as exposing the individual to danger from the unseen.

THE YĀTRĀ

Devendra, in the *Śrāddha-dina-kṛtya*,[2] classifies the *yātrā* into three types representing in fact different concepts, the last of which has little in common with the others but the name:

(1) *aṣṭāhnika-yātrā*—the festival of the *Nandīśvara-parvan*;
(2) *ratha-yātrā*—the processions in which the sacred images are carried through the streets;
(3) *tīrtha-yātrā*—pilgrimages to holy places.

This threefold division is not, it would seem, found earlier—Hemacandra, for example, does not deal with the subject in the *Yoga-śāstra*, though he describes a *ratha-yātrā* in detail in the *Pariśiṣṭa-parvan*—but it is repeated by Ratnaśekhara in the *Śrāddha-vidhi*.[3]

1. The *aṣṭāhnika-yātrā* takes place in *Nandīśvara-parvan* from *aṣṭamī* to *paurṇimā* in the bright fortnights of the months of Kārttika, Phālguna, and Āṣāḍha. This act of worship—one of the forms of *pūjā* listed by Jinasena[4]—is a surrogate for the adoration of the Jina images by the gods in the temples of the *Nandīśvara-dvīpa*, which is inaccessible to mortals. It would appear to be the only festival of the Jaina calendar to which the older *śrāvakācāras* devote any attention.

[1] *Pāpa-kārya* is explained by Āśādhara himself as actions involving *ārambha*.
[2] ŚrDK 292 (pt. ii, pp. 206–8).
[3] *Śrāddha-vidhi*, p. 163*b*.
[4] MP xxxviii. 26.

2. The *ratha-yātrā*, in Devendra's[1] brief description, is essentially a chariot festival: the Jina images are paraded through the streets on a flower-decorated chariot with white *chattras*, *cāmaras*, and pennants to the accompaniment of musical instruments and the dancing of men and women. It is not clear from the texts whether there is any essential difference between this and the preceding *yātrā*. Both probably combine the same elements and the *Yātrā-pañcāśaka*[2] in fact speaks only of a *Jina-yātrā*—Jaina, that is, and not Hindu—though Abhayadeva, commenting the *Stava-vidhi-pañcāśaka*,[3] defines the word *yātrā* as *aṣṭāhnika-mahimā pūjā ca.* Probably the *aṣṭāhnika* festival offered a model for other popular celebrations in which profane spectacles like dancing and drama could, like folk-tales, be given a *nihil obstat* when adapted to religious ends. It is the *kalyāṇas* of the Jinas, particularly of the last Jina, Mahāvīra, that are held to be the most suitable times for the carrying out of *yātrās*.

These *kalyāṇas*,[4] so-called, according to the *Pañcāśaka*,[5] because they bring benefit (*kalyāṇa*) to living beings, are generally four or five in number, though there are some divergencies in the listing of them:

PAÑCĀŚAKA[6] AND DIGAMBARAS	VASUNANDIN	HEMACANDRA, DEVENDRA	JINAPRABHA[7]
(1) garbhādhāna	janma	janma	cyavana
(2) janma	niṣkramaṇa	dīkṣā	garbhāpahāra
(3) niṣkramaṇa	jñāna	jñāna	janma
(4) jñāna	tīrtha-cihna	nirvāṇa	dīkṣā
(5) nirvāṇa	nirvāṇa		jñāna

About birth, renunciation of the world, attainment of illumination, and final release there is little dispute; but the notation of the *garbhāpahāra* (removal from the womb), which mirrors faithfully the *Kalpa-sūtra* story, seems to be rather unusual; of course *cyavana* corresponds to *garbhādhāna* (conception).

The early date of the *Pañcāśaka* makes its description of a *yātrā*[8] of great value and worth quoting *in extenso*.

[1] ŚrDK, pt. ii, p. 206.
[2] P (Yātrā) 3.
[3] *Stava-vidhi-pañcāśaka*, 3.
[4] Āśādhara wrote a short work, the *Kalyāṇā-mala*, in which the calendar of these festivals for the twenty-four *tīrthaṇkaras* is versified. Hemacandra lists the *kalyāṇā-sthānas*: YŚ iii. 150 (pp. 758–9).
[5] P (Yātrā) 30.
[6] P (Yātrā) 31.
[7] Śr (V) 452.
[8] P (Yātrā) 6–11.

The *yātrā*, as an external manifestation of the importance and material prosperity of those who profess the Jaina religion, is a form of *prabhāvanā* which again is one of the constituent elements or *aṅgas* of *samyaktva* or right belief. Its proper accomplishment is achieved by the combination of the following factors:

(i) *dāna*—the distribution of largesse. This includes not only almsgiving to monks but charity to the needy without distinction of creed or calling—even 'killers' such as fishermen are to share in it. It should mark the commencement of the *yātrā*.

(ii) *tapas*—austerities which in practice mean food restrictions (*ekāśana-pratyākhyāna* is cited as an example). The purpose is to emphasize the solemnity of the occasion and to induce a proper frame of mind in the participants.

(iii) *śarīra-satkāra*—bodily adornment. People are to wear their best clothes and to use the best unguents and garlands.

(iv) *gīta-vāditra*—music and song. These should be pleasing, fitting for the occasion, and calculated to inspire a religious frame of mind.

(v) *stuti-stotra*—hymns of praise. These should not be merely sonorous but of deep significance and should tend to generate a desire to seek release from the world. They are also to be *sama* (the commentator explains either this as 'not harsh in sound' or as 'easily understandable').

(vi) *prekṣaṇaka*—spectacles. These are to be understood as religious dramas (*dharma-nāṭaka*) dealing with such themes as the Jina's birth, life, and renunciation of the world and accompanied by displays of dancing. They are to be performed preferably at the beginning of the *yātrā*.

The culmination of the festival occurs when the Jina image is taken out of the temple and borne in procession on a chariot through the city together with religious pictures; this is the *ratha-yātrā* properly so-called.[1] All expenditure and efforts for this end are praiseworthy because the moral effect of the *yātrā* contributes to the avoidance of *hiṃsā* and enables some people to attain to enlightenment.[2]

3. The *tīrtha-yātrā* seems to be a later development.[3] There is

[1] P (Yātrā) 26–28. [2] Ibid. 18.

[3] For a study of Digambara and Śvetāmbara places of pilgrimage see Premī, op. cit., pp. 185–250.

no indication of its being known to the author of the *Pañcāśaka* but the custom must have existed in Abhayadeva's time for in his commentary[1] he is careful to explain that the treatise deals with a festival and not with journeying to another country.

For a description of the *tīrtha-yātrā* as a well-established custom it is necessary to turn to a writer who is later than the limits set for the study. Ratnaśekhara[2] defines the expression as meaning the visiting of such places as Satruñjaya and Raivata where the atmosphere is hallowed by association with the birth, initiation, enlightenment, or *nirvāṇa* of *tīrthaṅkaras*.

The would-be pilgrim to these holy places must observe certain interdictions: he must not take more than one meal a day, he must not wear garlands or other *sacitta* objects, he must abstain from sexual relations, he must sleep on the ground, and he should travel on foot even if he possesses horses and carriages or other means of transport. The pilgrimage is naturally envisaged as a communal effort. A man of substance will first seek the authorization of the local ruler, get together a party from among his own household and kinsfolk and co-religionists rather as if he were organizing a merchant caravan, and invite suitable religious preceptors. Then, assembling provisions and baggage animals as well as vehicles for those unable to travel afoot and hiring armed guards for the expedition, he will set out at an auspicious astrological conjuncture after festal *pūjās* in the temples. On the journey he will look after the welfare of the members of the convoy, providing food, betel, and clothes and encouraging the faint-hearted. *En route* he will hold *pūjā* services and provide for the restoration of ruined temples in towns and villages. When the place of pilgrimages comes into sight he will distribute alms to his co-religionists. The actual celebrations at the *tīrtha* will include the full eightfold *pūjā*, a major *pūjā* with a *puṣpa-gṛha* and *kadali-gṛha*, a night wake, a festival of music and dance, and a period of fasting. The party will then return home.

Ratnaśekhara's description, by its very completeness, attests a long tradition for the *tīrtha-yātrā* by his day; and in fact Āśādhara advises rich men to organize them in order to spread right beliefs in the world,[3] and refers to their beneficial effect in counteracting the spurious attractions of the Kali age.[4]

[1] P (Yātrā) 4. [2] *Śrāddha-vidhi*, pp. 164*b* ff.
[3] SDhA ii. 84. [4] SDhA ii. 37.

THE CAITYA

THE term is used to designate both the image and, equivalent to *caityālaya*, the temple. In the former sense there is an old classification into five types noted by Nemicandra:[1]

(i) *bhakti-caitya*—an image set up in the home for devotional purposes and used at the three *sandhyās*;
(ii) *maṅgala-caitya*—an image set in the middle of the door lintel as an auspicious symbol;
(iii) *niśrā-kṛta-caitya*—an image used by a particular *gaccha*;
(iv) *aniśrā-kṛta-caitya*—an image common to all *gacchas*;
(v) *śāśvata-caitya*—an uncreate image existing since all eternity in some temple in the three worlds.

Hemacandra[2] notes the first, second, and fifth types of these. He also advocates the construction of temples, the restoration of derelict ones, and the rebuilding of ruined ones. As in similar activities of a pious nature any injury to living beings caused by the work of excavation and construction is outweighed by the good done in promoting the cause of religion.

Devendra[3] has a slightly different classification:

(i) *bhakti-caitya*—an image or temple for devotional purposes;
 (*a*) *aniśrā-kṛta*—without lodging for monks as at Aṣṭāpada;
 (*b*) *niśrā-kṛta*—with lodging for monks;
(ii) *maṅgala-caitya*—as at Mathurā;
(iii) *śāśvata-caitya*—as in *Nandīśvara-dvīpa*;
(iv) *sādharmika-caitya*—an image for the use of co-religionists.

The temple, says Āśādhara, destroys the spurious attraction of the present age and provides an *āśrama* for ascetics where the laity can rid themselves of the worldly life through contact with religious ceremonies.[4] Attached to the temple there should be a garden with a water-supply and a lotus pool to provide offerings for the *pūjā*. Food-distribution centres (*sattra*) and medical-treatment centres (*cikitsā-śālā*) should also be set up.[5]

Devendra has a series of verses in praise of those who rebuild or restore ruined Jaina temples: they will enjoy the esteem of their fellow men and will be reborn, if not as *devas* at least in an exalted family on earth. Knowledge and artistic skill and intelligence, if

[1] PS 659. [2] YŚ iii. 120 (p. 585).
[3] ŚrDK 151. [4] SDhA ii. 37. [5] Ibid. 40.

they are to be worth while, must be used in the service of the Jina.[1] If, on the other hand, any man appropriates or allows others to appropriate religious property (*Jina-dravya*) he will experience misfortunes of every kind in the cycle of transmigration, so he should take a vow never to touch it. Temple property comprises valuables such as gold and silver and also the actual construction material—bricks, stone, and timber.[2] Grouped together within the same aura of untouchability are the monastic property, i.e. the clothes, begging bowls, and other objects used by monks (*guru-dravya*); the learned property or books (*jñāna-dravya*); and all that has been bequeathed to the community 'to sow on the seven fields or *kṣetras*' (*sādhāraṇa-dravya* or *prabhāsva*).

SVĀDHYĀYA

SVĀDHYĀYA (study), regarded as one of the six forms of internal *tapas* and by the Digambaras as one of the six daily *karmans*[3] of the householder, is a feature of the lay life that has been transferred directly from the textbooks of monastic discipline. It is traditionally divided into five elements:[4]

(i) *vācanā*—reciting of the sacred texts;
(ii) *praśna*—asking the guru questions about them;
(iii) *parivartanā*—repetition of the texts in order not to forget those previously learned;
(iv) *anuprekṣā*[5]—imbuing oneself with the meaning;
(v) *dharma-kathā*—listening to the exposition of religious parables.

Without the light that comes from study it is impossible, says Amitagati,[6] to rid oneself of the darkness of ignorance. For Vāmadeva[7] *svādhyāya* is one of the four *anuyogas* propounded by the Jina. Āśādhara[8] recommends the construction of *svādhyāya-śālās* since 'where there is no opportunity of study the minds of monks, tossed about by an inconstant wind, walk not in primacy in the doctrines of religion'.

[1] ŚrDK 99–110. [2] ŚrDK 126–39. [3] CS, p. 21.
[4] Śr (A) xiii. 81; T (P) ix. 25. See Schubring, *Die Lehre der Jainas*, p. 169.
[5] Here the word *anuprekṣā* has a rather special meaning. See A. N. Upadhye, *Introduction to KA*, pp. 7–8. The other four elements of *svādhyāya* are sometimes considered as supports (*ālambana*) of *dharmya-dhyāna* to which four *anuprekṣās* are then assigned. [6] Śr (A) xiii. 83. [7] BhS (V) 599.
[8] SDhA ii. 39.

TAPAS

THIS term would seem to embrace any form of self-discipline or training for the spiritual life. By the Digambaras it is accounted the sixth of the daily *karmans* and by both Digambaras and Śvetāmbaras is held to be either external (*bāhya*) or internal (*abhyantara*). The six varieties of the latter are:[1]

(1) Confession to a guru (*prāyaścitta*); this includes *pratikramaṇa* and *ālocanā*.
(2) Expression of respect to ascetics (*vinaya*).
(3) Rendering of personal services to ascetic (*vaiyāvṛttya*).
(4) Studying, memorizing and expounding, the sacred lore (*svādhyāya*).
(5) Abandonment of the body (*utsarga, vyavasarga*).
(6) Meditation (*dhyāna*), i.e. concentration on one thought for up to a maximum time of one *muhūrta*.

There is some confusion in this list. *Svādhyāya* is also of its own right the fourth of the six daily *karmans*; and *vinaya* and *vaiyāvṛttya* together make up *bhakti*, which is one of the five *bhūṣaṇas* of *samyaktva*.[2] The term *vaiyāvṛttya-vrata* is also used by some writers as a synonym of *dāna-vrata*.

The six varieties of *bāhya-tapas* are:[3]

(1) Fasting (*anaśana*).
(2) Taking only part of a full meal (*ūnaudarya, avamaudarya*).
(3) Limiting of food according to the range of choice or according to the time, place, and posture in which it is offered (*vṛtti-saṃkṣepa, vṛtteḥ saṅkhya*).
(4) Abstention from luxury foods (*rasa-parityāga*).
(5) Avoidance of all that can lead to temptation (*saṃlīnatā, vivikta-śayyāsana*).

(6) Mortification of the flesh (*kāya-kleśa*), e.g. by heat, cold, insect bites. The first four of these are variants of fasting and go together with others mentioned in the sections on *pratyākhyāna* and *posadhopavāsa-vrata*. *Bāhya-tapas* is virtually synonymous with fasting, even the expression *kāya-kleśa* being used in that

[1] PASU 199; ŚrDK, pt. ii, p. 76. See Schubring, op. cit., pp. 196–7.
[2] YŚ ii. 16.
[3] PASU 198; ŚrDK, pt. ii, p. 76. See Schubring, op. cit., p. 196.

sense by Vasunandin.[1] In fact asceticism for the Jaina lies first and foremost in depriving oneself of food, its extreme expression being found in *sallekhanā*.

DHYĀNA

DHYĀNA, one of the forms of *abhyantara-tapas* is defined in the *Tattvārtha-sūtra*[2] as 'the concentration of thought on a single object for up to one *muhūrta*'. It may be of four types, the first and second being inauspicious (*apraśasta*) and the third and fourth auspicious (*praśasta*)[3] and each type is again subdivided to cover four possible themes:[4]

1. Painful (*ārta*):

(*a*) contact with what is unpleasant (*amanojña-samprayoga*) and desire for its removal. 'What is unpleasant' would cover hostile persons, material discomforts, hurtful words, and disagreeable emotions;

(b) separation from what is pleasant (*manojña-viyoga*), for example, through losing one's loved ones or one's wealth, and desire to get them back again;

(*c*) the sensation of suffering (*vedanā*) as from an illness and the desire to rid oneself of it;

(*d*) hankering for sensual pleasures (*nidāna*). The same term of course recurs as one of the three *śalyas* and as an *aticāra* of the *sallekhanā-vrata*.

2. Harmful (*raudra*):

(*a*) the infliction of hurt (*hiṃsā*);

(*b*) falsehood (*anṛta*);

(*c*) theft (*steya*);

(*d*) the hoarding of wealth (*dhana-saṃrakṣaṇa*).[5]

1. Moral (*dharmya*):

(*a*) discerning the command of the Jina (*ājñā-vicaya*);

(*b*) discerning the nature of what is calamitous (*apāya-vicaya*);

[1] Śr (V) 351. [2] T (P) ix. 27. [3] CS, p. 74.

[4] Śr (A) xv. 9–15; T (P) ix. 28–39.

[5] Hemacandra (YŚ iii. 73) covers *ārta-* and *raudra-dhyāna* only, in discussing the *śrāvakācāra*.

(*c*) discerning the consequences of karma (*vipāka-vicaya*);
(*d*) discerning the structure of the universe (*saṃsthāna-vicaya*).[1]

4. Refulgent (*śukla*):

(*a*) consideration of diversity (*pṛthaktva-vitarka*);
(*b*) consideration of unity (*ekatva-vitarka*);
(*c*) maintenance of subtle activity (*sūkṣma-kriyā-pratipāti*);
(*d*) complete destruction of activity (*vyuparata-kriyā-nivartini*).

Together *ārta-dhyāna* and *raudra-dhyāna* constitute *apadhyāna*, which is one of the manifestations of *anartha-daṇḍa*. Strictly they should apply only to the lay life since a monk who gives way, for example, to *raudra-dhyāna* has already lapsed from his vocation.[2] The other forms of *dhyāna* are proper for an ascetic and *śukla-dhyāna* is in fact only possible for one who has reached a very high stage of spiritual development. For this reason doubtless some writers such as Cāmuṇḍarāya[3] and Āśādhara treat the whole subject as belonging to the *yaty-ācāra*.

Amitagati[4] gives to the topic of *dhyāna* a theoretical treatment parallel to that of *dāna*. Four aspects are considered:

(i) the meditator (*dhyātṛ*), who must be pure in heart;
(ii) the object of meditation (*dhyeya*);
(iii) the technique (*vidhi*);
(iv) the result obtained (*phala*), which is *svarga* or *mokṣa*.

Cāmuṇḍarāya[5] has a rather similar classification.

It is only the second of these aspects that is of any practical significance, four objects of *dhyāna* being distinguished under this head:[6]

(i) meditation on the syllables of the sacred *mantras* (*pada-stha*);
(ii) meditation on the group of magic powers possessed by the Jina (*piṇḍa-stha*);
(iii) meditation on the form of the Jina materialized in the statue (*rūpa-stha*);
(iv) meditation on the Jina as a disembodied *ārhat* (*rūpātīta*).

[1] There is a special association of *svādhyāya* with the *dharmya-dhyānā*. See p. 237.
[2] T (P) ix. 35.
[3] CS, pp. 74–95.
[4] Śr (A) xv. 23.
[5] CS, p. 74.
[6] Śr (A) xv. 30–56.

Reduced to a triad by the omission of the third type of meditation, this enumeration finds a place in the conventional *caitya-vandana* ritual of the Śvetāmbaras under the designation of the *avasthā-trika* and again in the Digambara ritual with Somadeva[1] and Vasunandin.[2]

VINAYA AND VAIYĀVṚTTYA

BOTH of these are classed as forms of *abhyantara-tapas*, and both relate initially to the monastic life. They may also be viewed as the twin manifestations of that devotion (*bhakti*) to the sacred doctrine which is listed by Hemacandra as one of the *bhūṣaṇas* of *samyaktva*.[3]

Vinaya, originally the outward expression of respect for a hierarchical superior, is divided by Vasunandin[4]—and, in his section on *yaty-ācāra*, by Cāmuṇḍarāya[5]—into five categories following the *Tattvārtha-sūtra*[6] (which has four):

(i) respect for right belief (*darśana-vinaya*) expressed by fulfilling the *guṇas* of *samyaktva*;
(ii) respect for right knowledge (*jñāna-vinaya*) and for those who are its repositories;
(iii) respect for right conduct (*cāritra-vinaya*);
(iv) respect for ascetic practices (*tapo-vinaya*);
(v) respect expressed, for example, to a guru by considerate attentions (*upacāra-vinaya*), which may take the form of a favourable mental attitude, of courteous words, or of appropriate actions. This last aspect—the *kāya-vinaya*—includes a number of features which have been given a numerical classification by Hemacandra[7] as the eightfold *upacāra-vidhi*; for the most part these are also mentioned by Vasunandin and Cāmuṇḍarāya:
   (*a*) rising from one's place (*abhyutthāna*);
   (*b*) going towards him (*abhiyāna*);
   (*c*) making the *añjali* (*añjali-karaṇa*);
   (*d*) oneself offering him a seat (*svayam āsana-ḍhaukana*);
   (*e*) acceptance by him of the seat (*āsanābhigraha*);

1 Handiqui, pp. 272–82.
2 Śr (V), 458–76.
3 YŚ ii. 16.
4 Śr (V) 320.
5 CS, pp. 65–66.
6 T (P) ix. 23.
7 YŚ ii. 16 (p. 185).

(*f*) reverent salutation (*vandanā*);
(*g*) waiting upon him (*paryupāsana*);
(*h*) accompanying him as he leaves (*anugamana*).

Vasunandin[1] also here includes some actions which might more properly be described as forms of *vaiyāvṛttya*, such as massaging the limbs and preparing a bed. The *upacāra-vinaya* just described (another form of which is to be found in the nine *puṇyas*[2] prescribed for welcoming an *atithi* to whom *dāna* is given) is applicable when a guru is present, but similar respect may be shown when he is absent by mental reverence and words of praise.

Like the *vandanaka* ritual (itself an expression of *vinaya*) *vinaya* is envisaged as rendered by monk to monk or by layman to monk. Vasunandin,[3] however, goes a step further by laying down that laymen may fittingly make *kāya-vinaya* both to ascetics and to laymen.

A similar development, far more important in its implications, has also occurred with the practice of *vaiyāvṛttya*, which is the term used in the canonical texts for bodily services rendered to monks, in particular attendance on the sick. The traditional enumeration[4] of the objects of *vaiyāvṛttya* is worth noting:

(1) *ācārya*—the head of a community;
(2) *upādhyāya*—a preceptor;
(3) *tapasvin*—monk engaged in fasting or other austerities;
(4) *śaikṣa*, *śikṣaka*—neophyte;
(5) *glāna*—a sick monk;
(6) *gaṇa*—a group of monks senior not in age but in religious knowledge;
(7) *kula*—a group of monks with the same *ācārya;*
(8) *saṅgha*—the community of monks;
(9) *sādhu*—a monk of long standing;
(10) *samanojña*—a distinguished or highly respected monk.

Amitagati[5] has introduced certain variations into this list: the *sādhu* figures as a *vṛddha* (aged monk) and *kula* and *samanojña* disappear to make way for *pravartaka* and *gaṇa-rakṣa*, which appear to indicate special types of *ācārya*. He particularly enjoins the practice of *vaiyāvṛttya* in times of famine or epidemic disease or when the monks are harassed by *pariṣahas* or by thieves or rulers.

[1] Śr (V) 328. [2] Śr (V) 225. [3] Śr (V) 330.
[4] T (P) ix. 24. [5] Śr (A) xiii. 62–64.

From this list it is clear that the scope of *vaiyāvṛttya* covers all reciprocal assistance within the community of monks and is not confined to services rendered by an inferior to a superior. It also includes services rendered by laymen (for whom this represents a privilege) to individual ascetics or to the community of monks: the concept is that expressed by the word *yati-viśrāmaṇā*.[1] It is probably the term *saṅgha* interpreted already by Siddhasena Gaṇin[2] as the *catur-varṇa-saṅgha* (the fourfold community of monks, nuns, laymen, and laywomen) that is at the origin of a further extension of the meaning which is fully manifest in Vasunandin's description.

For all those, he says,[3] within the fourfold community who are very young or very old or afflicted by disease or physically exhausted *vaiyāvṛttya* is to be performed: this will include the massaging of arms, legs, back, and head, asperging, anointing with oil, and application of cooling pastes; if they are dirty the filth will be removed and whilst their bodies are washed their beds will be cleaned and made ready; and food and drink and medicines will be provided for them. Such actions bring their own reward both in this life and in succeeding lives.

The mention of providing food recalls another aspect of *vaiyāvṛttya* that comes to the fore in the *Cāritra-sāra*.[4] When monks are assailed by diseases, *pariṣahas*, or false beliefs (*mithyātva*) *prāsuka* medicaments and food and drink, shelter and bedding, blankets and religious accessories (*dharmopakaraṇa*) are to be given them to help to strengthen them in the faith; these amount in fact to almsgiving. With this in mind it is not difficult to understand that in the *Ratna-karaṇḍa*[5] *vaiyāvṛttya* is used as a synonym of *dāna*.

The idea of community self-help, implicit in Vasunandin's concept of *vaiyāvṛttya*, more often finds expression with the Śvetāmbaras in the discussion of *vātsalya*, one of the *guṇas* or *aṅgas* of *samyaktva*. All co-religionists, says Devendra,[6] are to be regarded as dear friends with whom disputes and quarrels are unthinkable. He who strikes a fellow Jaina in anger is guilty of an *āśātanā*—a sacrilege. Money or effort expended in the interests of one's co-religionists is always well spent whether they belong to one's own country and caste or whether they have come from afar.

At the same time the individual has a duty to look to the moral

[1] ŚrDK 243. [2] T (S) ix. 24 (p. 257). [3] Śr (V) 337–40.
[4] CS, p. 67. [5] RK iv. 21. [6] ŚrDK 198–206.

welfare of his fellows. Those who are lukewarm in their zeal for the performance of religious duties should be stimulated in every possible way, even if encouragements or admonitions meet with a testy answer from the person to whom they are addressed. They are to be prodded with questions such as: 'Why, my friend, did I not see you yesterday in the temple or in the *poṣadha-śālā* or at the feet of the *sādhu*?' in order to save them from the grip of *pramāda*.[1]

THE ANUPREKṢĀS

THE subject of the twelve *anuprekṣās*[2] or themes of meditation has already been treated in many works on Jainism and it would be otiose to discuss it here,[3] though certain writers on *śrāvakācāra* cover the topic. These are mainly Digambaras—Kundakunda, Kārttikeya, Somadeva, Amitagati,[4] Āśādhara,[5] Cāmuṇḍarāya[5]—but Śvetāmbara works dealing with the subject as an aspect of monastic discipline include the *Yoga-śāstra*.[6] These apply to the *anuprekṣās* the designation *bhāvanā* (not to be confused with the twenty-five *bhāvanās* of the *mahā-vratas* nor with the sixteen Digambara *bhāvanās*). Here, for the purpose of comparison, are the twelve *anuprekṣās*:

(1) on impermanence (*anitya*);
(2) on helplessness (*aśaraṇa*);
(3) on the cycle of transmigration (*saṃsāra*);
(4) on solitariness (*ekatva*);
(5) on the separateness of the self and the body (*anyatva*);
(6) on the foulness of the body (*aśucya*);
(7) on the influx of karma (*āsrava*);
(8) on the checking of karma (*saṃvara*);
(9) on the elimination of karma (*nirjara*);
(10) on the universe (*loka*);
(11) on the difficulty of enlightenment (*bodhi-durlabha*);
(12) on the preaching of the sacred law (*dharma-svākhyatatva*).

[1] ŚrDK 207–19.

[2] For the canonical origins of the *anuprekṣās* see Schubring, op. cit.

[3] For a comprehensive treatment of the meditations see K. K. Handiqui, *Yaśastilaka and Indian Culture* (chap. xi: 'The *anupreksās* and Jaina religious poetry'), and A. N. Upadhye, *Introduction to KA*, pp. 6–42.

[4] Śr (A) xiv.

[5] The *anuprekṣās* are treated both by Cāmuṇḍarāya (CS, pp. 78–92) and Āśādhara (*Anagāra-dharmāmṛta*, vi. 57–82) as a feature of *yaty-ācāra*.

[6] YŚ iv. 55–110.

THE BHĀVANĀS

BHĀVANĀ—'meditation' or 'contemplation'—is the designation more commonly used by the Śvetāmbaras for the *anuprekṣās*. Some Digambaras, however, apply this name to another series of mental attitudes, sixteen, not twelve, in number. Here is the list of their themes as given by Cāmuṇḍarāya:[1]

(1) purity of belief (*darśana-śuddhi*);
(2) perfection of *vinaya* (*vinaya-sampannatā*);
(3) faultless observance of the *vratas* and the *śīlas*[2] (*śīla-vrateṣv anaticara*). *Śīla* here signifies the avoidance of anger and similar virtues;
(4) continuous cultivation of knowledge (*abhīkṣṇa-jñānopa-yoga*);
(5) fear of the cycle of reincarnation and its vicissitudes (*saṃvega*);
(6) the practice of the fourfold *dāna* within the limits of one's power (*śaktitas tyāga*);
(7) the practice of austerities within the limit of one's power (*śaktitas tapas*). The body is vile but may yet be used as a vehicle for spiritual progress;
(8) removing impediments to the practice of austerities by monks (*sādhu-samādhi*). This is compared to the extinguishing of a fire that threatens a storehouse;
(9) the tending of ascetics in misfortune (*vaiyāvṛttya-karaṇa*);
(10) devotion to the Jinas (*arhad-bhakti*);
(11) devotion to the gurus (*guru-bhakti*);
(12) devotion to those learned in holy writ (*bahu-śruta-bhakti*);
(13) devotion to the sacred doctrine (*pravacana-bhakti*);
(14) zealous performance of the six necessary duties (*āvaśyakā-parihāṇi*);
(15) glorification of the sacred doctrine (*mārga-prabhāvanā*) by *tapas*, *jñāna*, and *pūjā*;
(16) affection towards the expounders, i.e. exemplary ascetics

[1] CS, pp. 24–27.

[2] One would expect the word *śīla* here to mean the *guṇa-vratas* and *śikṣa-vratas* but Cāmuṇḍarāya himself explains it as 'the avoidance of anger, &c. in order to keep the *vratas*' (CS, p. 25).

and laymen[1] (*pravacana-vātsalya*). (The alternative explanation of this *bhāvanā*: 'affection for the sacred doctrine' seems too nearly a repetition of *pravacana-bhakti* to be tenable.)

These *bhāvanās* though they are mentioned both by Āśādhara[2] and by Medhāvin[3] as types of meditation are in fact totally distinct from the *anuprekṣās*.[4] They have rather the nature of those *bhāvanās* which are designed to fortify the *mahā-vratas*, that is they are observances to be followed in order to achieve progress in the spiritual life.

They represent in fact a transcription of the passage of the *Tattvārtha-sūtra*[5] which lists the *āsravas* which bring about the auspicious *tīrthaṅkara-nāma-karman*, and which Pūjyapāda, in his commentary, terms the sixteen *bhāvanās*.

THE KALĀS

THE seventy-two arts or accomplishments of men belong to the canonical literature and scarcely survive, save as an archaism, in the medieval *śrāvakācāras*. Devendra[6] seems to be alone in listing them in full, though Vasunandin[7] ascribes to the inhabitants of the *bhoga-bhūmis* the knowledge of the seventy-two *kalās* and to their womenfolk the acquaintance with the sixty-four *guṇas*.

In view of the abundant literature on the subject it is pointless to detail them here.[8]

[1] Pūjyapāda explains as 'co-religionists'.
[2] SDhA vii. 55.
[3] Śr (M) x. 100.
[4] The *anuprekṣās* are treated by Cāmuṇḍarāya under the head of *yaty-ācāra* (CS, pp. 78–92) and considered to be an aspect of *dharmya-dhyāna*.
[5] T (P) vi. 24.
[6] ŚrDK 106 (pt. i, pp. 265–6).
[7] Śr (V) 263.
[8] For a full description of the seventy-two *kalās* and a comparison with the list of sixty-four in the *Kāma-sūtra*, see, for example, the article by Amulyachandra Sen in the *Calcutta Review*, March 1933, pp. 364 ff.

THE SEVEN VYASANAS

THESE are listed as:

(1) dicing, gambling (*dyūta*);
(2) boozing, drinking alcohol (*madya*, *surā*);
(3) meat-eating (*māṃsa*);
(4) whoring (*veśyā*);
(5) hunting (*kheṭa*, *pāparddhi*, *mṛgayā*);
(6) thieving (*caurya*, *stena*);
(7) adultery (*para-dāra*).

By definition these vices are specific forms of *pāpa* which entail an evil reincarnation (*durgati*), generally in hell.[1] In fact some later writers assign each *vyasana* to a special *naraka*.[2] Amitagati[3] opposes the seven vices to an integral concept of *śīla*[4] (the maintenance of all vows assumed) to which they form an impediment.

As a category the *vyasanas* are treated only in the Digambara *śrāvakācāras*, being expressly mentioned by Vasunandin,[5] Āśādhara,[6] and Padmanandin (and by Medhāvin, Sakalakīrti, and Śivakoṭi). Without employing this designation, Amitagati[7] covers the same subject in detail. The oldest discussion, of the topic is therefore not earlier than the eleventh century though reference is made to the *vyasanas* in *kathās*, both Śvetāmbara and Digambara, before that date. There is considerable irregularity of treatment in the literature because thieving is already condemned by the third *aṇuvrata* and adultery by the fourth, while eating meat, drinking alcohol, and hunting can all be regarded as violations of *ahiṃsā*. Furthermore the Digambara category of the *mūla-guṇas* covers the abstention from eating and drinking alcohol and, according to some writers, from gambling.[8]

It is on the theme of the *vyasanas* that the moral teaching of Jainism is most clearly sited in a social context; and this morality

[1] Śr (V) 59.
[2] *Praśnottara-śrāvakācāra*, xii; *Padmanandi-śrāvakācāra*, 12.
[3] Śr (A) xii. 41–53.
[4] In Digambara texts the word is of course used as a collective name for the *guṇa-vratas* and *śikṣā-vratas* but it can also be synonymous with *brahmacaryā* chastity.
[5] Śr (V) 60–124.
[6] SDhA iii. 16–23.
[7] Śr (A) xii. 54–100 and v. 1–26.
[8] Hiralal Jain would like to regard the mention by Jinasena of *dyūta* in his list of the *mūla-guṇas* as an *upalakṣaṇa* for the *vyasanas*, but this view seems hardly tenable.

is that of the common man who adheres to the conventions of the world, avoiding anything that can evoke obloquy or derision from his neighbours. Even *ahiṃsā* is relegated to the background, as, for example, when alcohol is condemned not, as in the earlier texts, because its preparation involves the destruction of life but because intoxication causes a man to act in an indecorous and ridiculous fashion. In some spheres this newer, worldly, morality can lead to contradictions with the older doctrines. Admitting, however reluctantly, a dispensation from perfect chastity for the lay adherent, primitive Jainism forbade him intercourse with all women who where the property of others but allowed him to frequent the woman who was common property—the village prostitute. The inclusion of *veśyā* under the seven *vyasanas* represents in effect, therefore, the revocation of an older dispensation.

The conventional description of the seven vices is given by Amitagati, Vasunandin, Āśādhara, Gunabhūṣaṇa, Śivakoṭi, and Medhāvin in terms so nearly identical that they must be taken from a common source. Dicing, for example, is said to engender anger, delusion, pride, and greed in their most intense forms. Blinded by his infatuation the gambler loses all sense of shame, takes false oaths, and lies so inveterately that even his own mother will not believe him. In a fit of anger he is ready to kill even those nearest to him. So absorbed is he by his vice that he will not heed parents or teachers and will even neglect food and sleep.[1]

Meat and alcohol are *vikṛtis* and are given a more extensive treatment from another angle under the heading of the *mūla-guṇas*. As a *vyasana* meat-eating is condemned mainly because it is a concomitant to other vices: in particular it is said to produce an addiction to alcohol, which in itself makes the pursuit of the religious life impossible.[2]

The consequences of drunkenness are realistically portrayed. Under the influence of *madya* a drinker's intelligence runs away like the wife of a man who has fallen into misfortune. His alcoholic state is manifested in giddiness, lassitude, nausea, trembling fits, red eyes, and unsteadiness of gait. He tries to commit incest with mother or sister or daughter, and treats his servant as if he were a ruler and his ruler as if he were a servant. He falls down in a drunken stupor in the highroad or in his courtyard and when the dogs lick his face and urinate in his mouth he imagines in his

[1] Śr (V) 60–69; Śr (A) xi. 54–62.

[2] Śr (V) 86.

delusion that he is drinking sweet wine. Thieves remove his clothes as he lies there and when he recovers consciousness he stumbles around drunkenly threatening to kill the man who has robbed him. Then, going home in a daze, he takes his own kin for enemies and smashes his own chattels with a stick. By turns he sings, screams, talks slurringly, vomits, tries to dance, gesticulates, uses obscene language, is hilarious, or is plunged in gloom.[1]

The vices of meat-eating and drinking are said to be always found in a harlot whilst her body is polluted by the embraces of the base-born. A man who spends even one night with a prostitute eats the leavings of ordinary workpeople and of outcastes and aliens. And if he becomes infatuated with her she will wheedle everything out of him and leave him but skin and bones. To every lover she tells the same story—that he is the only man for her. The love of a harlot means only humiliation for a man however high his birth and talents.[2]

When the vice of hunting is considered, the accent shifts back to *ahiṃsā*, for this *vyasana* is said to destroy all compassion. Since a righteous man will not even kill an evildoer if he comes seeking asylum with *tṛṇa* grass between his teeth why should he kill an innocent deer that pastures on grass? If there is sin in the killing of cows and brahmins, there is sin, too, in the killing of other living beings, and as much of it incurred in one day from hunting as in a long period of time from eating meat and drinking alcohol.[3]

The last two *vyasanas* differ from the other five in being punishable in a non-Jaina society as crimes, so that they not infrequently bring retribution in the present life. Thus the thief who has taken another man's property is presented as apprehensively quitting his home, trembling in every limb, and pursuing a circuitous path, always anxious lest he has been seen. His heart patters and his feet stumble. He is obsessed by fear to the point of being unable to sleep because he has taken away either by force or by deceit the property of others, perhaps even of parents, teachers, and friends, unheedful of his good repute in this world or of what awaits him in the next life. If he is caught by the constables he is at once bound with ropes by a low-caste jailer and promenaded around the streets on the back of an ass with the placard: 'This is a thief, and any other caught like him will receive the same retribution.' Then

[1] Śr (V) 70–79; Śr (A) v. 1–12.
[2] Śr (V) 88–93; Śr (A) xi. 63–76.
[3] Śr (V) 94–100; Śr (A) xi. 92–100.

he is quickly carried outside the city where the executioners tear out his eyes or amputate his limbs or impale him alive.[1]

Adultery leads to a similar fate. A man who lusts after another's wife and cannot resist his own desires will sigh, weep, sing, beat his head, fall on the ground, and utter incoherent speech.[2] Tormented by uncertainty whether the woman will accept his advances he cannot sleep or eat and abandoning family traditions gives way to drink. Sometimes he makes advances and is rebuffed and put out of countenance. If he succeeds in waylaying the woman of his choice and taking her by force against her will what pleasure can he derive? Or if again the woman herself is so lost to shame that she gives herself to him under the impulse of lust what enjoyment will there be in a hurried, furtive union in an empty house or ruined temple? At the slightest sound he will run away and crouch down, looking in all directions, terrified. And if he is discovered and brought before the royal tribunal he will be castrated and then, like a thief, mounted on an ass and paraded through the city before being executed. He can have no reliance even on the woman with whom he is infatuated, for she who betrays her husband will also betray her lover just as a cat that eats its kittens will certainly eat mice.[3]

The cautionary tales related in connexion with the seven *vyasanas* are as stereotyped as the descriptions and for that reason are worth a mention. They are amongst the best known in Indian literature. For *dyūta* the example is Yudhiṣṭhira; for *madya* the Yādavas; for *māṃsa* Bakarakṣa; for *veśyā* Cārudatta; for *pāparddhi* Brahmadatta; for *caurya* Śrībhūti; and for *para-dāra* Rāvaṇa; while addiction to all seven vices at the same time is personified by Rudradatta.

Āśādhara[4] (and following him Medhāvin)[5] has conceived of a sub-category of ancillary (*sodara*) vices, adumbrated rather than systematically set forth under each *vyasana*:

(1) *dyūta*[6]—gambling for the sake of amusement (presumably for purely nominal stakes) because this can still provoke *rāga* and *dveṣa*;

[1] Śr (V) 101–11.

[2] This concurs with the description of love unfulfilled, ranged into a numerical category as quoted by Yaśodeva (P (Y)).

[3] Śr (V) 112–24; Śr (A) xi. 77–91.

[4] Śr (V) 125–33. [5] Śr (M) v. 164–8. [6] SDhA iii. 19.

(2) *madya*[1]—eating or drinking anything at all which is the product of fermentation, selling alcohol, sleeping with women who drink alcohol;

(3) *māṃsa*[2]—consuming anything which has been kept in leather containers;

(4) *veśyā*[3]—enjoyment of the *taurya-trika* (vocal and instrumental music and dancing), idle strolling around, associating with pimps and other disreputable company;

(5) *pāparddhi*[4]—making representations of hunting scenes whether on coins or in books or on cloth;

(6) *caurya*[5]—exploiting the favour of a ruler to take property from a rightful heir, concealing anything which forms part of a joint family property;

(7) *para-dāra*[6]—seducing an unmarried girl: this specifically includes a condemnation of the *gandharva-vivāha*.

As has been noted the Śvetāmbara *śrāvakācāras* do not treat of the *vyasanas* as a category though these are mentioned casually at times as in the commentary of the *Dharma-ratna-prakaraṇa*.[7] However, the same condemnations are of course implicit in their teaching and sometimes Hemacandra's[8] verses, for example, parallel very closely those of Amitagati or Vasunandin.

THE GATIS

If the ultimate aim of escape from the *saṃsāra*—*mokṣa* is sometimes called the fifth *gati*—is not attained when this life is extinguished there are four possibilities of reincarnation: as a human being again (*mānuṣya-gati*), as an animal (*tiryag-gati*), as a celestial being (*deva-gati*), or as a denizen of hell (*naraka-gati*). There is also what might be called a sub-category of the *mānuṣya-gati*: reincarnation in a *bhoga-bhūmi*, 'a land of ease', as distinguished from normal human life, which is passed in a *karma-bhūmi*, 'a land of toil'[9]; but in most respects such a fairy-tale world is nearer to life in the *deva-loka*. The *tiryag-gati* also includes the possibility of reincarnation in the vegetable kingdom as a *vanaspati-kāya*. This

1 SDhA iii. 9–11. 2 Ibid. 12. 3 Ibid. 20.
4 Ibid. 22. 5 Ibid. 21. 6 Ibid. 23.
7 DhRP 7. 8 e.g. on *madya* YŚ iii. 8–12. 9 T (P) iii. 37.

complicated edifice of continuing existence can, it is obvious, respond to the most subtle gradations of merit and demerit, but no lasting bliss is possible except through release from it since life, even in the most exalted realms of the *deva-loka*, will still be tinged with some sadness.

All Jaina writers of course stress the retribution that evil acts bring upon themselves either in this life—sometimes directly through the action of the law when they are of a criminal character, sometimes through supernatural intervention, and sometimes through visitation by disease and other calamities—or through the automatic operation of karma in another incarnation. The Śvetāmbaras have never apparently felt that the discussion of a future life belonged to the sphere of a *śrāvakācāra*, but the Digambaras, particularly the popular writers, deal at considerable length with the subject, giving a standardized, but still vivid, picture of hell and of the *bhoga-bhūmis*. While Amṛtacandra finds in the ideal of *mokṣa* the only incentive to a righteous life Vasunandin[1] expressly states that the masses must be coerced by the fear of punishment and the hope of material reward.

Hell[2] is conceived of as a region immeasurably spacious, divided into seven mansions, each of which, it is sometimes said,[3] provides the fitting retribution for one of the seven *vyasanas*. Mention again is sometimes made of four entries into hell (*naraka-dvāra*) each wide open to receive the perpetrators of specified evil actions. It is a place of mental as well as physical suffering the capacity for which is never exhausted until the appointed incarnation reaches its close for the body of a hell-dweller even when cut to pieces by tortures will always be re-created to suffer anew and the mind will always be open to fear.[4]

In hell a *jīva* becomes spontaneously existent on a surface of ground so rough that he at once gets up only to fall again.[5] Then the demons, whose enmity towards their victims is like that of snake and mongoose, attack him with spears, clubs, tridents, arrows, and swords. The *Dharma-rasāyana*[6] mentions—but the concept is rather an aberrant one—that those who first strike the *jīva* are the beasts that were aforetime slain by him in offerings to the ancestors

[1] Śr (V) 239.

[2] The Jaina picture of hell is of course very close to the descriptions given in Buddhist and Hindu texts. See Kane, *History of Dharma-śāstra*, iv. 167.

[3] *Padmanandi-śrāvakācāra*, 12.

[4] Śr (V) 176; *Dharma-rasāyana*, 71.

[5] Śr (V) 137.

[6] *Dharma-rasāyana*, 25.

and to bloodthirsty divinities. He is put in a flaming pot and as he emerges he is prodded with pikes so that he gnaws his own fingers with the pain; nor do appeals for mercy bring any response from his tormentors.[1] This, according to Vasunandin, is the reward that awaits the gambler.[2]

Escaping from this torture he rushes into a mountain ravine imagining that he will find a refuge there but now rocks begin to fall on him, smashing his body into tiny fragments. Yet the severed parts at once reunite like drops of quicksilver. If he has consumed honey and alcohol in a former life he is made to drink molten iron[3] and if has eaten *udumbara* fruits he must swallow live coals.

Next he rushes terrified into a forest only to find that the leaves which fall on him are sharp as swords[4]. With blood streaming from the gashes he seeks to escape but is seized again by the demons, who hold him down and, cutting off lumps of his flesh, force him to swallow them, jeering as they tell him that this meat will be as sweet as that which he ate in his human life.[5]

A red-hot ploughshare is forced into his mouth, and to seek relief from the pain he crawls into a river flowing near by, but its waters are corrosive and at the same time full of putrefaction and blood.[6] When he emerges from it he is pounded like sugar-cane in a press and acid is then applied to his wounds and needles forced under his finger-nails.[7] Then the demons constrain him, if he has committed adultery or fornication, to embrace a statue of red-hot iron;[8] if he has been guilty of acquisitiveness he must bear a heavy stone on his back, if he has lied his tongue is torn out.[9] Whatever karma a *jīva* has bound on himself laughing, that he will not escape by weeping.[10]

Next the demons take the forms of vultures or cocks or crows and tear at his flesh with their beaks, whilst others gouge out his eyes or smash in his teeth.[11] Monstrous beasts such as eight-footed jackals come to devour him and he is stung by insects and serpents.[12] Nor is this all: the demons stir up in the minds of the hell-dwellers the memory of former enmities and they fight, tearing each other to pieces.[13]

[1] Śr (V) 141–50.
[2] Śr (V) 143.
[3] Śr (V) 151–5.
[4] *Dharma-rasāyana*, 57.
[5] Śr (V) 156–9.
[6] Śr (V) 160–2.
[7] *Dharma-rasāyana*, 47–49.
[8] Śr (V) 164–5.
[9] *Dharma-rasāyana*, 51–56.
[10] Śr (V) 165.
[11] Śr (V) 166–9.
[12] *Dharma-rasāyana*, 61–62.
[13] Śr (V) 170.

Evil-doing may also be expiated in the *tiryag-gati*. A *jīva* may wander through countless incarnations in the most primitive forms of life before attaining to rebirth as a *pañcendriya* animal which will suffer from mutilations, heavy burdens, lack of food and drink, and separation from its offspring, and which may be killed and eaten.[1]

In the *mānuṣya-gati* it may happen that a child is abandoned at birth only to die from exposure or starvation, or if it is abandoned later during childhood it will live miserably as a servant in another's household. Again a man who has given generously to others when he was rich may fall on evil days and not obtain even a plate of gruel when he begs for it. Another may be smitten by a loathsome disease (*pāpa-roga*) such as leprosy and obliged to live outside the city cut off from friends and kin.[2]

But the *mānuṣya-gati* includes also rebirth in the *bhoga-bhūmis*. The descriptions of these fairy-tale worlds are doubtless an inheritance from popular folk-lore but they have been incorporated into the Jaina cosmography and find mention even in the necessarily brief epitome of the *Tattvārtha-sūtra*.[3] The Digambara *śrāvakācāra* texts are notable for the way in which they link rebirth in the *bhoga-bhūmis* with the performance of *dāna*. No interest is shown in the geographical location of these regions but their classification is linked with that of the *pātras* or recipients of alms so that, for example, giving to an *uttama-pātra* entails rebirth in an *uttama-bhoga-bhūmi* or giving to a *ku-pātra* rebirth in a *ku-bhoga-bhūmi*.[4]

The inhabitants of the *uttama-*, *madhyama-*, and *jaghanya-bhoga-bhūmis* are differentiated only by the lustre of their bodies, their height, and their life-span,[5] both of these being expressed with the licence of numerical fantasy. All alike are exempt from the sufferings of disease, untimely accidents, and old age, they feel no pain, mental or physical, and there is no strife among them.[6] Born always together in couples, they attain maturity in forty-nine days[7] and they die a painless death when their children are born, the men expiring with a sneeze, the women with a yawn.[8] The former are endowed with the seventy-two arts and the latter with the sixty-four *guṇas* and both have the thirty-two *lakṣaṇas*[9] and show

[1] Śr (V) 177–82. [2] Śr (V) 183–90. [3] T (P) iii. 37.
[4] Śr (A) xi. 62–67; Śr (V) 245–8. [5] Śr (V) 258–60. [6] BhS (D) 535.
[7] Śr (A) xi. 79–82. [8] Śr (A) xi. 78. [9] Śr (V) 263.

a very slight development of the *kaṣāyas*. For this reason when they die they are reborn at once in the *deva-loka* (whilst the *devas* of course have only to expect a human or animal incarnation).[1] Throughout their long lives all their wants are supplied from ten wish-fulfilling trees (*kalpa-drumas*):[2]

(1) *madyāṅga*—supplying tasty and nutritive drinks;
(2) *tūryāṅga*—supplying musical instruments;
(3) *bhūṣaṇāṅga*—supplying ornaments such as ear-rings and diadems;
(4) *jyotir-āṅga*—supplying light more radiant than that of sun or moon;
(5) *gṛhāṅga*—supplying houses;
(6) *bhājanāṅga*—supplying plates and dishes;
(7) *dīpāṅga*—supplying illumination indoors;
(8) *vastrāṅga*—supplying clothes of silk or fine cloth;
(9) *mālāṅga*—supplying garlands of the finest flowers with the choicest perfumes;
(10) *bhojanāṅga*—supplying the fourfold aliments of the best quality.[3]

An incarnation in a *ku-bhoga-bhūmi* resulting from almsgiving to a *ku-pātra* is less desirable. The inhabitants of these regions have no clothes or ornaments or houses and live underneath the trees feeding on their leaves and flowers and sometimes eating an earth which resembles jaggery.[4] Instead of human heads they may have those of lions or elephants or other beasts; some have horns, some tails, some only one leg, and some again are devoid of speech.[5] Yet they, too, because they are lacking in *kaṣāyas*, are reborn in the *deva-loka*, becoming *vyantara* gods; as a sequel to this, however, they have a bad human incarnation.[6]

The estate of a *deva* which has been attained by long practice of asceticism and self-control in the human incarnation may yet, through the ripening of karma, bring no abiding happiness. The dwellers in heaven like those on earth are divided into castes separated by even more rigid barriers than among men. Rebirth in one of the categories of servile *devas* even though human afflictions

[1] Śr (A) xi. 72–73.
[2] Hindu mythology recognizes normally five *kalpa-drumas*. Cf. *Amara-koṣa*, i. 1, 50.
[3] Śr (V) 250–7.
[4] BhS (D) 537.
[5] Ibid. 542.
[6] Ibid. 544.

are absent will bring sorrow and vexation from envy at the sight of the more fortunate *devas*.[1]

A *jīva* who goes to the *deva-loka* comes into existence spontaneously in a perfumed *upapāda-gṛha*. He has a perfumed breath, a flawless body, and unaging youth. As he is thus born he cannot at first realize where he is, and like one awakened from sleep he imagines himself to be dreaming. Then as the *apsarases* welcome him he comprehends by *avadhi-jñāna* what has occurred. Having bathed and adorned himself he goes at once to the Jaina temple to make *pūjā* to the Jina in the same way as this is done on earth but with greater splendour. So he pursues the life of untrammelled pleasure that is the lot of the divine beings, pausing always to make the *Jina-pūjā* at the five *kalyāṇas* and in the *Nandīśvara-parvan*.[2]

It is when six months only of life as a *deva* remain to him that his great sadness comes. As he sees his clothes and ornaments becoming tarnished he realizes that the time to fall from his lofty estate has come; and he weeps to think that he must pass nine months in an abode of pus and blood—the human womb. Aware that he has no means of escape, that not even the lord of the *devas* can save him, he formulates the wish in his mind that he may be reborn as an *ekendriya*. And so even this miserable destiny may come to pass.[3]

THE ŚRĀVAKA-GUṆAS

THIS treatment of the duties of the ideal layman on the basis of a varying number of qualities characterizing the person apt to receive the Jaina creed and fulfil its teaching enjoyed considerable popularity with the later Śvetāmbaras as a means of exposition. A list of thirty-five such qualities or *śrāvaka-guṇas* universally ascribed to Hemacandra came to be preferred to all others: it is that given in a *kulaka* of ten verses at the end of the first *prakāśa* of the *Yoga-śāstra*.[4] However, at least two centuries earlier an enumeration of twenty-one *śrāvaka-guṇas* had figured in the *Dharma-ratna-*

[1] Śr (V) 191–4. [2] Śr (V) 495–508. [3] Śr (V) 195–203.

[4] YŚ i. 47–56. Windisch, in his *editio princeps* of the first four *prakāśas* of the *Yoga-śāstra*, surmised that these verses were an interpolation.

prakaraṇa[1] by Śānti Sūri and may indeed belong to an earlier writer. Vague lists of the virtues which a layman ought to possess must have long been current; they are in fact to be found in the *kathā* literature wherever the excellences of a hero are described. The canonical texts contain enumerations of abstract qualities, good or bad, which perhaps provided the original basis. It seems, however, to have been Haribhadra who first—in the *Dharma-bindu*[2]—attempted to lay down in a clear and precise fashion in *sūtra* style the principles of conduct in everyday life which would, if properly observed, make of a man a model *śrāvaka*. In his famous *kulaka* Hemacandra has versified Haribhadra's *sūtras*—or at least those which he found most apt—adding to them almost by way of afterthought a half-dozen epithets from the already current list of Śānti Sūri.

In view of the importance of numerology in Jaina writings it is perhaps worth noting that all the lists of *śrāvaka-guṇas* (except that of eleven given by the Digambara Amitagati, which will be discussed separately) are couched in multiples of seven. Thus, beside the thirty-five of Hemacandra and the twenty-one of Śānti Sūri, there are the fourteen *śrāvaka-guṇas* of Āśādhara,[3] against which it would not be unfitting to set the seven virtues of the giver (*dātṛ-guṇa*) and the seven *vyasanas* and seven *śīlas*.[4]

Though he does not use the term *śrāvaka-guṇa* Haribhadra devotes the whole of the second *adhyāya* of the *Dharma-bindu* to a detailed consideration of this subject, which he qualifies as the general (*sāmānya*) aspect of the householder's religion, the specific (*viśeṣa*) aspect being the observance of the *vratas* and of ritual practices such as *pūjā*. Hemacandra expounds his own *kulaka* in a very extensive prose commentary which serves as a quarry for later writers. The most important of these, Jinamaṇḍana belongs to the fifteenth century, but his work, a compilation from earlier sources, will be drawn on for illustration in this study.

[1] DhRP 5–7. [2] DhB i. [3] SDhA i. 11.

[4] It is curious that Mrs. Stevenson, in *The Heart of Jainism*, failed to realize that the lists of twenty-one and thirty-five both referred to the *śrāvaka-gunas*. On p. 244 she offers a translation of Hemacandra's *kulaka* under the title: 'Thirty-five rules of conduct', and on p. 224 a rather inaccurate rendering of Śānti Sūri's list, which she calls 'those twenty-one qualities which distinguish the Jaina gentleman'.

Yoga-śāstra	Dharma-bindu[1]	Dharma-ratna prakaraṇa	Dharmāmṛta
(1) Nyāya-sampanna-vibhava	nyāyopāttaṃ vittam	—	nyāyopātta-dhana
(2) Śiṣṭācāra-praśaṃsaka	siṣṭa-carita-praśaṃsana	—	—
(3) kula-śīlax-samaih sārddham anya-gotra-jaiḥ kṛtodvāha	samāna-kula-śīlādibhir a-gotra-jair vaivāhyam	— —	tad-arha-gṛhini-sthān'-ālaya
(4) pāpa-bhīru	dṛṣṭādṛṣṭa-bādhā-bhīrutā	bhīru	agha-bhī
(5) prasiddhaṃ deśācāraṃ samācaran	prasiddha-deśācāra-pālanam	—	—
(6) a-varna-vādī na kvāpi rājādiṣu viśeṣataḥ	sarveṣv a-varṇa-vāda-tyāgo viśeṣato rājādiṣu	sat-katha	sad-gir
(7) anativyakta-gupte sthāne su-prātiveśmike aneka-nirgama-dvāra-vivarjita-niketana	sthāne gṛha-karaṇam; atiprakaṭāti-guptam asthānam anucita-prātiveśyaṃ ca	su-pakṣa-yukta	tad-arha-gṛhinī-sthānālaya
(8) sad-ācāraiḥ kṛta-saṅga	saṃsargaḥ sad-ācāraiḥ	—	ārya-samiti
(9) mātā-pitroh pūjaka	mātā-pitṛ-pūjā	vinīta	yajan guṇa-gurūn
(10) upaplutaṃ sthānaṃ tyajan	upapluta-sthāna-tyāgaḥ	—	—
(11) garhite 'pravṛtta	garhitesu gāḍham apravṛttiḥ	—	—
(12) vyayam āyocitaṃ kurvan	āyocito vyayaḥ	—	—
(13) veṣaṃ vittānusārataḥ kurvan	vibhav'-ady-anurūpo veṣaḥ	—	—
(14) aṣṭabhir dhī-guṇair yukta	ūhāpohādi-yogaḥ	—	prajña
(15) dharmam anvahaṃ śṛṇvāna	pratyaham dharma-śravaṇam	—	dharma-vidhiṃ śṛṇvan
(16) ajīrṇe bhojana-tyāgin	ajirṇe 'bhojanam	—	—
(17) kāle bhoktā sātmyataḥ	sātmyataḥ kāla-bhojanam	—	yuktāhāra-vihāra
(18) anyonyāpratibandhena trivargaṃ sādhayan	anyonyānubaddha-trivarga-pratipattiḥ	—	anyonyānugunaṃ trivargaṃ bhajan
(19) yathāvad atithau sādhau dīne ca pratipatti-kṛt	devātithi-dīna-pratipattiḥ	—	—
(20) sadānabhiniviṣṭa	sarvatrānabhiniveśaḥ	madhyastha-saumya-dṛṣṭi	
(21) guṇesu pakṣa-pātin	guṇa-pakṣa-pātitā	guṇa-rāgin	

[1] Whilst the *śrāvaka-gunas* in the other texts are given as epithets the *sūtra* style of the *Dharma-bindu* of course requires nominal forms.

YOGA-ŚĀSTRA	DHARMA-BINDU	DHARMA-RATNA PRAKARAṆA	DHARMĀMṚTA
(22) adeśākalayoś caryāṃ tyajan	adeśākāla-caryā-parihāraḥ	—	—
(23) balābalaṃ janan	balābalāpekṣaṇam	—	—
(24) vṛtta-stha-jñāna-vṛddhānāṃ pūjaka	vṛtta-stha-jñāna-vṛddha-sevā	vṛddhānuga	—
(25) poṣya-poṣaka	bhartavya-bharaṇam	—	—
(26) dīrgha-darśin	—	su-dīrgha-darśin	—
(27) viśeṣa-jña	—	viśeṣa-jña	—
(28) kṛta-jña	—	kṛta-jña	kṛta-jña
(29) loka-vallabha	—	loka-priya	—
(30) sa-lajja	—	lajjālu	hrīmaya
(31) sa-daya	—	dayālu	dayālu
(32) saumya	—	prakṛti-saumya	—
(33) paropakṛti-karmaṭha	—	para-hita-kārin	—
(34) antaraṅgāri-ṣaḍ-varga-parihāra-parāyaṇa	ari-ṣaḍ-varga-tyāgaḥ	—	—
(35) vaśī-kṛtēndriya-grāma	—	—	vaśin

1. Possessed of honestly earned wealth (*nyāya-sampanna-vibhava*)

Haribhadra[1] lays down that a pious layman should exercise a profession which is beyond reproach and in accordance with family tradition, with due regard for his own substance; for wealth acquired by honest means brings absence from anxiety in this world and leads to a happy reincarnation whilst wrongly acquired wealth has dire consequences like the hook that lodges in the fish's gullet. Rectitude is the sovereign specific for amassing wealth (*arthāpty-upaniṣad*) because it helps to eliminate evil karma; though fortune may in certain circumstances be amassed by dishonesty it will only be transient. For Hemacandra[2] honestly earned wealth is money that has not been made by recourse to treason, betrayal of friends, breach of trust, theft, false witness, false weights and measures, or deceitful speech. One can enjoy it without apprehension in one's own person and give it to one's friends and kin. Jinamaṇḍana[3] says roundly that honest poverty is better than ill-gotten riches, which, according to a popular saying, will last for ten years and then vanish entirely in the eleventh. The practice of this *guṇa* excludes the pursuit of the fifteen forbidden trades and of gambling and alchemy, and implies a high ethical code in business dealings, and generosity in almsgiving and in charity to those in need.

2. Eulogistic of the conduct of the virtuous (*śiṣṭā-cāra-praśaṃsaka*)

By *śiṣṭa* Hemacandra[4] understands 'men of outstanding qualities who have been schooled by intercourse with the virtuous and the learned'. The qualities to be admired in others are courtesy, gratitude, cheerfulness in misfortune, modesty in prosperity, fidelity to tradition, and care to avoid ill repute. The essence of this *guṇa* is not to be envious of the virtues of others.

3. Wedded to a spouse of the same caste and traditions but not of the same gotra (*kula-śīla-samaiḥ sārddham anya-gotra-jaiḥ kṛtodvāha*)

Hemacandra[5] understands by *śīla* a common observance of such interdictions as those on drinking wine or eating meat. Jinamaṇ-

[1] DhB. i. 7. [2] YŚ, p. 145. [3] ŚrGuV, p. 7a.
[4] YŚ, p. 146. [5] YŚ, p. 147.

ḍana[1] offers also an alternative explanation: worship of the same *devas* and guru and performance of the same ceremonies. Municandra, the commentator of the *Dharma-bindu*,[2] infers from identity of caste and tradition that the parties to a marriage will have the same material situation, mode of dress, and language. If there are differences on these points they will not be happy together and there will be clashes between them. Where a wife, for example, belongs to a family much richer than that of her husband she will tend to be contemptuous of him. Hemacandra, Municandra, and Jinamaṇḍana all find occasion to list here the eight forms of marriage recognized in the *Manu-smṛti*, with the comment that even the four *adharmya* forms may be held to be *dharmya* when there is mutual affection between man and wife. According to Hemacandra[3] there are four ways of guarding women: having wives of good character like one's mother, not allowing them independence, assigning to them household tasks, and restricting their material possessions. If women are well guarded there will be a properly regulated home, *pūjā* and *dāna* will be rightly performed, and children will be well brought up.

4. Apprehensive of sin (*pāpa-bhīru*)

This epithet is common even in the oldest Jaina texts and corresponds to a fundamental concept of the religion. Haribhadra[4] understands by it the fear of committing offences whether overt or hidden. The former, according to Hemacandra,[5] would mean adultery, theft, whoring, dicing, and similar disastrous acts and the latter meat-eating and wine-drinking and other such vices, all of which lead to reincarnation in hell. Jinamaṇḍana[6] associates with these occasions of stumbling the twenty-two *abhakṣyas* and thirty-two *ananta-kāyas*. This *guṇa* figures also in Śānti Sūri's list.[7]

5. Following the reputable custom of the country (*prasiddhaṃ deśācāraṃ samācaran*)

Hemacandra[3] understands by *deśācāra* the customs prevailing in a particular area in regard to food, clothes, and other aspects of everyday life; if these were not observed unfortunate consequences

[1] ŚrGuV, p. 13*b*. [2] DhB i. 17. [3] YŚ, p. 148.
[4] DhB i. 16. [5] YŚ, p. 148. [6] ŚGuV, p. 19*a*.
[7] DhRP 13.

might result from public hostility in the area. Jinamaṇḍana[1] goes further: he holds that whilst pursuing the *dharmācāra*, the path of religion, one should also fall in with the *lokācāra*, the usages of the world. Since the secular life must of necessity be the basis for all who, living in the world, yet obey the precepts of religion, infractions of the *lokācāra* are to be avoided.

6. Not denigrating other people, particularly rulers (*a-varṇa-vādī na kvāpī rājādiṣu viśeṣataḥ*)

Municandra[2] explains that the word 'rulers' is intended to include ministers, court chaplains, and other officials. Hemacandra[3] quotes a verse to show that *nīcair-gotra* karma is incurred by expressing contempt for others and glorifying oneself. Overt denigration, always reprehensible, is dangerous when applied to the great ones of the earth as it may result in loss of life and possessions. Relating this *guṇa* to the *satya-vrata*, Jinamaṇḍana[4] sees in it a condemnation of envy, calumny, and false accusations. It would seem to correspond to the *sat-katha* of Śānti Sūri[5] (in Āśādhara *sad-gir*). A *sat-kathā* is defined as a story which glows with truth and narrates the life of a *tīrthaṅkara* or saint.

7. Dwelling in a place which is not too exposed and not too enclosed, with good neighbours, and few exits (*anativyakte gupte sthāne su-prātiveśmike aneka-nirgama-dvāra-vivarjita-niketana*)

Haribhadra[6] lays down that a house should be built in a suitable spot, an unsuitable site being any place where the houses are too close together or too isolated or where there are undesirable neighbours. The construction of the house should be determined by favourable omens and it should not have many exits. If there were many doors ill-disposed people would be able to go in or out unobserved, so jeopardizing the security of goods and chattels and womenfolk. In other words a householder's home should be well guarded. There should be *durva* and *kuśa* grass, untainted soil, and a supply of fresh water on the site chosen. In too exposed a position it would be easy for thieves to burgle, whilst in too enclosed a position air and light could not reach it and in the event of fire it could not escape. If the neighbours were undesirable,

[1] ŚrGuV, p. 20*a*. [2] DhB i. 31. [3] YŚ, p. 148.
[4] ŚrGuV, p. 21*b*. [5] DhRP 20. [6] DhB i. 22–24.

such as gamblers, actors, or prostitutes, one's household would be corrupted by listening to their conversations and seeing their actions.[1]

8. Attached to good moral standards (*sad-ācāraiḥ kṛta-saṅga*)

This *guṇa* appears to imply no more than the avoidance of evil company. In Āśādhara's list it appears as *ārya-samiti*.

9. Honouring father and mother (*mātā-pitroḥ pūjaka*)

Noting that the word 'mother' is placed first in the compound because of the very great respect to which she is entitled, Hemacandra[2] explains that respect is to be shown to them by making obeisance at dawn, noon, and dusk, by offering them a *pūjā* of flowers and fruit of the finest colour and perfume, by giving them the best of food, clothes, and other material needs, and by seeking their consent for all affairs of importance in life. Jinamaṇḍana[3] extends the concept 'parents' to include all persons who by their age or position merit reverence. Āśādhara uses the designation *yajan guṇa-gurūn* for this *guṇa*.

10. Eschewing a place of calamity (*upaplutaṃ sthānaṃ tyajan*)

Hemacandra[2] explains that in a place of calamity, in other words a town or village where famine or disease are endemic, or where there is war between one's own sovereign and a foreign ruler, the attainment of the *tri-varga* is impossible; in fact the fund of *kāma*, *artha*, and *dharma* already acquired would be soon dissipated. As an *upapluta-sthāna* Jinamaṇḍana[4] cites also a country where there are two rulers or no ruler or where government is carried on in the name of a woman or a child.

11. Not engaging in a reprehensible occupation (*garhite 'pravṛtta*)

Hemacandra[5] explains that a practice may be deemed especially reprehensible in one country, such as agriculture in Sauvīra, or drinking alcohol in Lāṭa, or among one caste, such as the consumption of wine or the sale of sesamum or salt by brahmins, or in

[1] YŚ, p. 149. [2] YŚ, p. 150. [3] ŚrGuV, p. 30*b*.
[4] ŚrGuY, p. 31*a*. [5] YŚ, p. 151.

one family, such as drinking alcohol in the Caulūkya family. Jinamaṇḍana[1] states with more precision that caste, country, and family tradition and the age in which one lives are the criteria by which an occupation is to be judged. If, for example, a known Jaina were to take food by night he would make a mockery of his religion.

12. Spending in proportion to one's income (*vyayam āyocitaṃ kurvan*)

Spending, says Hemacandra,[2] means the apportioning of one's substance for the maintenance of one's dependants, for one's own comfort and for almsgiving, *deva-pūjā* and other purposes, and income means what one earns by trading, tilling the soil, or rearing livestock. Jinamaṇḍana[3] goes so far as to fix proportions for this division: a man of limited means should divide his income into four shares: one to form a reserve capital, one to be put back into his business, one to be spent for religious purposes and for his own luxuries, and one to be used to provide for his dependants. A rich man, however, could well set aside more than half his income for the *dharma* and lead a life of frugality on earth.[4] In any event the layman's duty is fulfilled by wise spending since miserliness merely results in the accumulation of wealth to the detriment of one's dependants and one's own self. As Hemacandra[2] points out, if a man is unwilling to spend enough to maintain himself in good health he may be incapacited by sickness from conducting his affairs.

13. Dressing in accordance with one's income (*veṣaṃ vittānusārataḥ kurvan*)

Hemacandra[5] explains that the scope here is in fact rather wider than the appellation suggests. If a man does not wear clothes and ornaments suitable to his income, age, social condition, country, and caste, he is liable to become a laughing-stock. This *guṇa* is closely linked with the preceding one, as a man who out of miserliness will not spend his money will also dress in rags, and so, failing to obtain the esteem of his fellow citizens, will be no credit to the

[1] ŚrGuV, p. 32*a*. [2] YŚ, p. 151. [3] ŚrGuV, p. 34*b*.

[4] A division of property in rather different percentages is suggested by Devasena (see BhS(D) 578–80).

[5] YŚ, p. 152.

Jaina creed. Jinamaṇḍana[1] adds that people should not wear torn or soiled clothes; for going to the temple they should choose their best apparel whilst avoiding all ostentation.

14. Endowed with the eight kinds of intelligence (*aṣṭabhir dhī-guṇair yukta*)

These are generally in Jaina works enumerated as follows:

(1) desire to listen (*śuśrūṣā*);
(2) listening (*śravaṇa*);
(3) grasping (*grahaṇa*);
(4) memorizing (*dhāraṇā*);
(5) general knowledge (*ūha*);[2]
(6) specialized knowledge (*apoha*);[2]
(7) knowledge of the substance (*artha-vijñāna*);
(8) knowledge of the essence (*tattva-vijñāna*).

To this *guṇa* corresponds presumably the *prajña* of Āśādhara.

15. Listening every day to the sacred doctrine (*dharmam anvahaṃ śṛṇvāna*)

Weariness of spirit is removed, says Hemacandra,[3] by listening every day to the sacred doctrine. It is because of its importance to the religious life that mere listening (*śravaṇa*) is classed as one of the *dhī-guṇas*.

16. Not eating on a full stomach (*ajīrṇe bhojana-tyāgin*)

All diseases, according to Hemacandra,[3] have their origin in an accumulation of undigested matter in the intestines resulting from eating on a full stomach. This habit is therefore to be avoided in order to maintain the body in health and fitness for the duties of the religious life.

17. Eating at the right time according to a dietary régime (*kāle bhoktā sātmyataḥ*)

Food is to be eaten when one is hungry—in moderation and without gluttony—for an excess of food only provokes vomiting

[1] ŚrGuV, p. 36*b*.
[2] *Ūha* and *apoha* are, of course, terms of logic and Hemacandra admits another interpretation of them in this sense. For a discussion of their meaning see Stcherbatskoi in *Museon*, v. 165–7.
[3] YŚ, p. 153.

and diarrhoea. On the other hand to go without food when one is hungry only results in lassitude and aversion to nourishment. The food and drink consumed should be those to which one's organism is accustomed since childhood and the view should never be taken that a healthy man can digest anything. Gluttony is senseless since the pleasure of taste is only momentary and all food is the same in flavour once it has passed down the throat.[1] The right time for eating is neither the night, the early morning, nor the late evening. A pious man should first ensure that his dependants, servants, and livestock have been fed and then dine himself according to the resources of his kitchen.

18. Fulfilling the threefold aim of life without excluding any of its elements (*anyonya-pratibandhena trivargaṃ sādhayan*)

Hemacandra[2] comments at considerable length on the *trivarga* without which life is no more real than that of the smelter's bellows which breathes but does not live. To live only for the pleasures of the senses to the exclusion of *artha* and *dharma* or to live only for money to the exclusion of *kāma* and *dharma* lead to endless misfortunes whilst the practice of *dharma* to the complete neglect of *artha* and *kāma* is proper for ascetics but not for householders. *Artha* and *kāma* devoid of *dharma* lead to great miseries in the cycle of transmigration, *dharma* and *kāma* without *artha* result in a heavy burden of debt, and *dharma* and *artha* without *kāma* are tantamount to a rejection of the layman's estate.

19. Diligent in succouring the ascetics, the righteous, and the needy (*yathāvad atithau sādhau dīne ca pratipatti-kṛt*)

This implies the offering with due courtesy of food and drink and other gifts in almsgiving to monks (*pātra-dāna*) and in charity to those in affliction (*karuṇā-dāna*).

20. Always devoid of evil motives (*sadānabhiniviṣṭa*)

An *abhiniveśa* is characteristic only of the mean-minded and its absence is one of the five *guṇas* of the third *bhāva-śrāvaka*.[3]

[1] YŚ, p. 154. [2] YŚ, p. 155. [3] DhRP 45.

21. FAVOURABLY INCLINED TO VIRTUES (*guṇesu pakṣa-pātin*)

By *guṇa* here Hemacandra[1] understands benevolence, generosity, readiness to help, patience, and the habit of using courteous and friendly language as well as acts of kindness, as the seed of religious merit is thereby nurtured into growth. This entry on Hemacandra's list has clearly been borrowed from the *guṇa-rāgin* of Śānti Sūri.[2]

22. AVOIDING ACTION WHICH IS INAPPROPRIATE TO TIME AND PLACE (*adeśākālayoś caryāṃ tyajan*)

Hemacandra[1] explains that anyone who engages in an action at a forbidden time or place will certainly be the victim of some calamity from kings, thieves, or others.

23. AWARE OF ONE'S OWN STRENGTH AND WEAKNESSES (*balābalaṃ jānan*)

No undertaking can succeed unless one knows the strength and weakness both of oneself and of others as far as these depend on time and place and circumstances. Like the preceding *guṇa* this belongs to the realm of *nīti*.[1]

24. VENERATING PERSONS OF HIGH MORALITY AND DISCERNMENT (*vṛtta-stha-jñāna-vṛddhānāṃ pūjaka*)

According to Hemacandra[1] *vṛddha* is here to be understood in the sense of old, not in years, but in the faculty of discerning between what should be avoided and what should be approved and in the practice of virtue. Respect expressed by making the *añjali*, rising and offering a seat should be accorded them because they abound in good counsel. The same *guṇa* figures in Śānti Sūri's list as *vṛddhānuga*.[3]

25. SUPPORTING ONE'S DEPENDANTS (*poṣya-poṣaka*)

Municandra[4] explains that the dependants include father and mother, wife and children, and, when the head of the household is rich, any childless sister or aged relative and any friend who has fallen into poverty. It is clear that Haribhadra was here thinking also of servants and retainers for in succeeding *sūtras*[5] he

[1] YŚ, p. 157. [2] DhRP 19. [3] DhRP 24.
[4] DhB 37. [5] DhB 38–41.

prescribes that a servant should be given suitable work, carefully supervised in his occupations, and protected from misfortune; if he has to be admonished, care should be had for his self-respect. Jinamaṇḍana[1] elaborates a fourfold division of *poṣya*: relatives, divinities, preceptors, and oneself; the relatives must be maintained because otherwise they might be reduced to thieving or vagabondage, thereby bringing discredit on the family.

26. Far-sighted (*dīrgha-darśin*)

The activities of a far-sighted man are described as leading to much profit with little effort, and are widely lauded. This *guṇa* belongs also to Śānti Sūri.[2]

27. Discriminating (*viśeṣa-jña*)

This for Hemacandra[3] means knowing the difference between what belongs to others and what belongs to oneself, between what is to be done and what is not to be done: a man without discrimination would be indistinguishable from an animal. With this *guṇa*, says Śānti Sūri,[4] a man is exempt from the prejudices that stem from love and hate.

28. Grateful (*kṛta-jña*)

Śānti Sūri,[5] too, gives this *guṇa*; he insists particularly on gratitude to the preceptor for the supreme benefit of the sacred doctrine. Jinamaṇḍana[6] classifies all human beings into those very many who are devoid of gratitude (*kṛta-ghna*), those, still numerous, who are grateful for kindness received (*kṛta-jña*), those few who are ready to do a favour in return for a favour (*pratyupakāraka*), and those very few who are ready to do a kindness (*niṣkāraṇopakāraka*) without receiving anything in return.

29. Well-liked (*loka-vallabha*)

For Hemacandra[3] this means a man who is well-liked by respectable people: if his character and behaviour do not make him popular he may arouse antipathies which will prevent others from finding the path of enlightenment. Śānti Sūri[7] holds that he should be conspicuous for almsgiving and virtuous conduct and should avoid everything that is contrary to this world or to the next.

[1] ŚrGuV, p. 58*a*. [2] DhRP 22. [3] YŚ, p. 158.
[4] DhRP 23. [5] DhRP 26. [6] ŚrGuV, p. 62*b*.
[7] DhRP 11.

30. Actuated by a sense of shame (*sa-lajja*)

This *guṇa* again belongs also to Śānti Sūri.[1] It implies that a man's sense of shame forbids him to commit sinful acts: he will abide by the *dharma* cost what it may.

31. Compassionate (*sa-daya*)

This *guṇa*, again common to Śānti Sūri,[2] is of the very essence of Jainism and needs no comment.

32. Gentle in disposition (*saumya*)

This evidently implies that because of his gentle disposition a man may be easily propitiated whilst a man of a different disposition will alienate friends and relations. Because of his gentleness, too, he will eschew cruel occupations. Śānti Sūri[3] gives this *guṇa* as *prakṛti-saumya*.

33. Ready to render service to others (*paropakṛti-karmaṭha*)

This *guṇa* seems to correspond to two entries in Śānti Sūri's list: *para-hita-kārin* and *su-dākṣiṇya*.[4]

34. Intent on avoiding the six adversaries of the soul (*antaraṅgāri-ṣaḍ-varga-parihāra-parāyaṇa*)

The six enemies are lust (*kāma*), anger (*krodha*), greed (*lobha*), pride (*māna*), vainglory (*mada*), and malicious pleasure (*harṣa*).[5] Pride means the rejection of salutary advice through arrogance, particularly the refusal to hear the sacred doctrine; vainglory implies pride in one's own family, or personal beauty, or strength, or knowledge; and malicious pleasure lies in causing unnecessary pain to others or in addiction to such vices as hunting.[6]

35. Victorious over the organs of sense (*vaśī-kṛte-ndriya-grāma*)

Victory over the senses is described as nobler than victory in battle. This *guṇa* figures in Āśādhara's list as *vaśin*.

Some of the *śrāvaka-guṇas* of Śānti Sūri were shown against

[1] DhRP 16. [2] DhRP 17. [3] DhRP 10. [4] DhRP 15, 27.

[5] With the omission of *mada* these correspond to the 'five fires' *pañcāgni* mentioned by Somadeva (Handiqui, p. 288).

[6] YŚ, p. 160.

those of Hemacandra, to which they correspond. Here is the full list:

(1) *akṣudra*—not mean-minded or concerned with trivialities;

(2) *rūpavat*—physically well-proportioned. This is understood to mean 'not defective in any of the five senses, of stout bodily constitution, and of sound *aṅgas* and *upāṅgas*'. (The *aṅgas* are eight in number: the head, chest, back, belly, arms and legs, the *upāṅgas* being the fingers, toes, &c.). The explanation of this *guṇa* has caused some difficulty[1] to the commentators, who point out that there have also been good Jainas of misshapen body. It has doubtless been included in the list in imitation of the conventional descriptions of the *Tīrthaṅkara*, who is of surpassing beauty of form. A good physical build is also linked with the capacity to perform feats of asceticism;

(3) *prakṛti-saumya*—naturally gentle in disposition and therefore not apt to bear rancour;

(4) *loka-priya*—well-liked because one is generous, courteous, and well-behaved;

(5) *akrūra*—not cruel or evilly disposed;

(6) *bhīru*—apprehensive of sin;

(7) *aśaṭha*—not deceitful, but reliable;

(8) *su-dākṣiṇya*—ready to lay aside one's own business in order to render service to others;

(9) *lajjālu*—actuated by a sense of shame so that one avoids evil actions;

(10) *dayālu*—compassionate;

(11) *madhyastha-saumya-dṛṣṭi*—of serene and unprejudiced outlook;

(12) *guṇa-rāgin*—favourably inclined to virtues;

(13) *sat-katha*—avoiding unprofitable speech, or, more specifically, the *vi-kathās*. The word *sat* is to be understood as having the significance which attaches to the word *satya* in the interpretation of the *satya-vrata*;

(14) *su-pakṣa-yukta*—having a proper ambience. In other words one's family and household should be favourably disposed towards the *dharma*; otherwise it will not be properly carried out;

[1] DhRP 9.

(15) *su-dīrgha-darśin*—far-sighted so that one undertakes actions which result in good, not harm;
(16) *viśeṣa-jña*—discriminating;
(17) *vṛddhānuga*—following the decisions of men with ripened minds, because old men do not engage in sinful activity;
(18) *vinīta*—possessed of *vinaya*, i.e. offering respect to all those to whom it is due;
(19) *kṛta-jña*—grateful;
(20) *para-hitārtha-kārin*—devoted to the welfare of others. The possessor of this *guṇa* is to be distinguished from the *su-dākṣiṇya*, who helps when his help is sought, by his readiness to go out of his way to assist others, and to put them on the right path even if he is not asked;
(21) *labdha-lakṣa*—having achieved one's goal, i.e. understanding the whole *dharma*.

As has been mentioned elsewhere the *śrāvaka* is classified by the categories of *nāma*, *sthāpanā*, *dravya*, and *bhāva*. Now Śānti Sūri does not confine himself to the discussion of the twenty-one *guṇas* but deals more extensively with the *bhāva-śrāvaka*, who is said to be of six types, each of these being distinguished by various qualities which in fact amount to additional *śrāvaka-guṇas*, though the term *guṇa* is only assigned to a few of them. Here is the full classification:

1. *kṛta-vrata-karman*—who carries out the vows:[1]
   (i) listening with *vinaya* to the exposition of the *vratas* by an authoritative teacher;
   (ii) comprehending the *vratas* with their *bhaṅgas* and *aticāras*;
   (iii) accepting the *vratas*;
   (iv) zealously observing the *vratas* even in adversity.

2. *śīlavat*—who is possessed of virtues (*śīla*):[2]
   (i) frequenting the temple;
   (ii) avoiding entry into other buildings or houses without due cause;
   (iii) always soberly dressed;
   (iv) not speaking under the stress of emotion;

[1] DhRP 34–36. [2] DhRP 37–1.

(v) avoiding foolish amusements, which are a form of *anartha-daṇḍa*;
(vi) conducting one's business in a polite fashion (not using harsh words such as *dāsī-putra* 'son of a bitch').

3. *guṇavat*—who is possessed of good qualities (*guṇa*):[1]

(i) always zealous in *svādhyāya*;
(ii) always zealous in the performance of the daily duties;
(iii) always zealous in *vinaya*;
(vi) devoid of evil prejudices (*abhiniveśa*) in all activities;
(v) having faith in the Jaina doctrine.

4. *ṛju-vyavahārin*—who acts uprightly:[2]

(i) speaking in accordance with the facts;
(ii) acting without guile;
(iii) pointing out misfortunes which may ensue from a course of action. (There is some uncertainty here: this is also explained as 'pointing out proper ways of acting, i.e. those taken from textbooks of *artha* and *dharma* but not of *kāma*'.)
(iv) being genuinely friendly.

5. *guru-śuśrūṣā*—who is obedient to the guru:[3]

(i) serving the guru by making *pratikramaṇa* and preventing hindrance to meditation;
(ii) stimulating others to do likewise by praising the guru;
(iii) providing herbs and medicaments for the guru;
(iv) revering the guru.

6. *pravacana-kuśala*—who is expert in the sacred lore:[4]

(i) proficient in the recitation of the *sūtras*;
(ii) proficient in the meaning of the *sūtras*;
(iii) proficient in the general rules (*utsarga*);
(iv) proficient in the special rules (*apavāda*);
(v) proficient in intention;
(vi) proficient in practical application.

Śānti Sūri further describes seventeen characteristics (styled *guṇas* or *lakṣaṇas*[5]) of the *bhāva-śrāvaka* which again may be

[1] DhRP 42–46. [2] DhRP 47–48. [3] DhRP 49–51.
[4] DhRP 52–55. [5] DhRP 56–77.

assimilated to the *śrāvaka-guṇas*. They are classified under the following heads:

(1) *strī*—he knows the wiles of women;
(2) *indriya*—he keeps a tight rein on the horses of the senses;
(3) *artha*—he realizes that material wealth is transient;
(4) *saṃsāra*—he comprehends the insubstantial nature of the visible world, a place of woe;
(5) *viṣaya*—he is averse to the poison of the senses;
(6) *ārambha*—he seeks to avoid harmful activity;
(7) *gṛha*—he esteems the household life a bondage;
(8) *darśana*—he maintains right belief;
(9) *gaḍḍarika-pravāha*—he avoids the unreflecting, sheep-like actions of the vulgar herd;
(10) *āgama-pravṛtti*—he carries out the *āvaśyakas* and other Jaina duties;
(11) *dānādi-pravartana*—he practises the fourfold *dharma* to the best of his ability;
(12) *vihrīka*—he is not ashamed of performing religious duties;
(13) *arakta-dṛṣṭi*—he is devoid of desire or of distaste for material things;
(14) *madhyastha*—he always takes an objective view;
(15) *asambaddha*—he is not fettered by the spirit of acquisitiveness;
(16) *parārtha-kāmopabhogin*—he continues to enjoy the pleasures of the world only out of consideration for others;
(17) *gṛha-vāsa*—he remains in the lay estate but with the idea always in mind 'Today or tomorrow I will abandon it', like a harlot who is thinking of changing her lover; it is as if he already belonged somewhere else.

The enumerations of Śānti Sūri add nothing new to the content of the *śrāvakācāra*; they are made up of vague moral qualities interspersed with reaffirmations of certain basic precepts of Jainism and are only detailed here for the sake of completeness and because of the confusing character of certain terms employed.

It remains to see to what extent the *śrāvaka-guṇas* have found a place in the Digambara setting. As has already been noted the fourteen listed by Āśādhara represent an undisguised borrowing from Hemacandra, but a century or so earlier Amitagati[1] had

[1] Śr (A) vi. 9–11.

described the *parama-śrāvaka* in eleven epithets which he himself designated as *guṇas*. His enumeration runs as follows:

(1) devoid of lust, envy, deceit, anger, backbiting, meanness, and vainglory (*kāmāsuya-māyā-matsara-paiśunya-dainya-mada-hīna*);
(2) steadfast (*dhīra*);
(3) of contented mind (*prasanna-citta*);
(4) fair-spoken (*priyaṃvada*);
(5) tender-hearted (*vatsala*);
(6) competent (*kuśala*);
(7) skilled in discerning what is to be accepted and what eschewed (*heyādeya-paṭiṣṭa*);
(8) ready in mind to adore the guru's feet (*guru-caranārādhano-dyata-manīṣa*);
(9) having the taints on one's heart washed clean by the Jina's words (*Jina-vacana-toya-dhauta-svānta-kalaṅka*);
(10) apprehensive of the *saṃsāra* (*bhava-vibhīru*);
(11) having one's lust for sensual objects diminished (*mandī-kṛta-sakala-viṣaya-kṛta-gṛddhi*).

There is a chance mention of the *śrāvaka-guṇas* in Vasunandin[1] but whether this refers to those listed by Amitagati or to some totally different concept it is impossible to say.

THE KRIYĀS

THE word *kriyā* is vague and ambiguous and is applied in Jaina texts to practices of various kinds. Here it will be restricted to the rites which have been modelled on, and to some extent correspond to, the Hindu *saṃskāras*.[2] It is in the *Ādi-purāṇa*[3] that the first description of these is to be found though whether Jinasena himself conceived the idea of giving to his co-religionists a framework of ceremonies similar to that which ruled the lives of their Hindu neighbours or whether he merely gave form to concepts which were already current is uncertain. The starting-point for the elaboration

[1] Śr (V) 389.

[2] Glasenapp (op. cit., pp. 408–19), in discussing the *kriyās*, treated Jinasena's list rather summarily and concentrated on the *Ācāra-dinakara*, for which he accepted too early a date.

[3] MP xxxviii. 50–311.

of the *kriyās* may well have lain in the narratives of the lives of the Jinas and in the custom of commemorating the five *kalyānas* associated with each of them but Hindu or pan-Indian elements dominate those rites which deal with the lay life.[1]

Jinasena enumerates for the whole of a man's life—both as a layman and after taking the vows—a total of fifty-three *kriyās*. Now this figure has a quite special importance. The *Ratna-sāra*, an early work ascribed to Kundakunda but, probably considerably later, includes the following verse:

guṇa-vaya-tava-sama-paḍimā daṇam jala-galaṇaṃ ca aṇatthamiyaṃ
daṃsaṇa-nāṇa-cārittaṃ kiriyā tevaṇṇa sāvayā bhaṇiyā[2]

This is understood to mean that the 53 *kriyas* are made up of the 8 *mūla-guṇas*, 12 *vratas*, 12 *tapas*, *samatā*, 11 *pratimās*, 4 *dānas*, *jala-galana*, *a-rātri-bhojana*, and the *ratna-traya*. If this figure of fifty-three *kriyās*, already current, was familiar to Jinasena a deliberate or unconscious misconstruction of its meaning may have led him to give it a totally different field of application. At the same time the original sense must have been maintained in certain milieux as the verse from the *Ratna-sāra* is quoted, as late as the sixteenth century, by Rājamalla in the *Lāṭi-saṃhitā*.[3]

Like so many similar blueprints for living, the diagrammatic representation of man's progress from the cradle to the grave outlined in the *kriyās* is, of course, idealized, as the emphasis on the monkish life and on the individual's gradual rise in the spiritual hierarchy bear witness. *Dīkṣā*—the acceptance of the monk's vows—is, by a convenient fiction that goes back to the Śvetāmbara canon, assumed to be an inevitable stage in the normal human destiny. But the unreality of the overall picture does not impair the validity of Jinasena's achievement. For the first time in Jaina history the *rites de passage* are incorporated in the religious framework instead of being thrust aside as proper only for the *deśācāra*; the outline of existence is more complete, more rounded, than that offered by any previous Jaina writer.

But the price to be paid for this is a considerable one. Hindu ideas and Hindu customs make deep inroads in those Jaina circles where Jinasena is an accepted authority, that is in the tradition represented by Jinasena, Cāmuṇḍarāya, and to some extent by

[1] See P. V. Kane, op. cit., vol. ii, pt. i, pp. 188–267.

[2] *Ratna-sāra*, 153.

[3] *Lāṭi-saṃhitā*, inserted after ii. 5.

Āśādhara. But it is not the elaborate pattern of the *Ādi-purāṇa* which is to survive when the Jainas as a community finally lose access to the sources of power. It is rather in the fifteenth-century Śvetāmbara work, the *Ācāra-dinakara*, that we find a picture of the *saṃskāras* that is still recognizable, whilst the seventeenth-century Digambara *Traivarṇikācāra*, which has retained the names of Jinasena's *kriyās* (at least of those which relate to the lay life), describes in fact virtually the same rites as those given in the *Ācāra-dinakara*.

Of the fifty-three *kriyās* the majority record stages in the ascetic's progress and only the first twenty-two are germane to the present study: they are listed below together with those noted by Vardhamāna and those in fact described by Somasena:

Ādi-purāṇa	Ācāra-dinakara	Traivarṇikācāra
(1) garbhādhāna		garbhādhāna
(2) prīti		moda
(3) suprīti	garbhādhāna	
(4) dhṛti		puṃsavana
(5) moda	puṃsavana	
(6) priyodbhava (jāta-karman)	jāti-karman	śuci-karman
(7) nāma-karman		nāma-karman
(8) bahir-yāna	(suryendu-darśana) (ksīrāśana) (ṣaṣṭi)	bahir-yāna
(9) niṣadyā	śuci-karman (nāma-karaṇa)	
(10) anna-prāśana	anna-prāśana	anna-prāśana
(11) vyuṣṭi	(karṇa-vedha)	
(12) keśa-vāpa (caula-karman)	cūḍā-karaṇa	caula-karman
(13) lipi-saṃkhyāna	adhyayanārambha	lipi-saṃkhyāna (and pustaka-grahaṇa)
(14) upanīti	upanayana	upanayana
(15) vrata-caryā		vrata-caryā
(16) vratāvataraṇa	vratāropa	vratāvataraṇa
(17) vivāha	vivāha	vivāha
(18) varṇa-lābha		varṇa-lābha
(19) kula-caryā		kula-caryā
(20) gṛhīśitā		gṛhīśitā
(21) praśānti		praśānti
(22) gṛha-tyāga		gṛha-tyāga
(23) dīkṣā	(antya-saṃskāra)	dīkṣā

1. Garbhādhāna

This, as described by Jinasena,[1] is in effect a ritual coitus for the sake of begetting a son. It must take place at the *ṛtu*, that is when

[1] MP xxxviii. 69–76.

the woman has taken her purifying bath after the cessation of the catamenia. Three *cakras* are placed on the right of the Jina image, three *chattras* on the left, and three holy fires in front. Husband and wife, reciting *mantras*, carry out the *Jina-pūjā* and then make oblations to the three fires as was done, says Jinasena,[1] at the *nirvāṇa* of the Jina. They are then to copulate without passion for the sake of procreation.

The details furnished by the *Traivarṇikācāra*[2] are worth noting if only as evidence of the inroads of Hinduism during the seven centuries which separate Somasena from Jinasena. The *garbhādhāna* is envisaged—as was no doubt Jinasena's intention—as an act of religious preparation by day followed by a ritual coitus by night. Before intercourse the woman is to bathe her pudenda with the *pañca-gavya* and the man to say a prayer to the goddess of the *yoni*; and during the act he is to think on the Jina and recite the *namaskāra*. Amongst the beliefs noted are the need to light a candle —copulation in the dark causes poverty—to wear green, and to chew betel. Sexual congress during the period immediately after menstruation described as the *kāma-yajña* for laymen is not only suggested but made obligatory, since—and here the Hindu influence shows itself at its strongest—if the couple fail to approach each other during the *ṛtu* they will be submerged with the *pitṛs* in a terrible hell.

In the *Ācāra-dinakara*[3] the *garbhādhāna* is given quite a different meaning: it is a ceremony performed in the fifth month after conception to strengthen the foetus in the womb. Vardhamāna lays down that like all other *kriyās* up to and including *vivāha* it may be performed either by a Jaina brahmin or by a *kṣullaka* (here used in its modern sense of a layman in the eleventh *pratimā*) and does not require the presence of a *sādhu*.

2. Prīti

This ceremony is performed in the third month of pregnancy by brahmins who are *prīta*. The *Jina-pūjā* is to be made with *mantras*, an arch (*toraṇa*) being erected over the door and two full water vessels (*kalaśa*) placed alongside it. If the householder has the means he should arrange for the playing of drums and the sounding of bells.[4]

1 MP xxxviii. 72. 2 TrA viii. 29–51.
3 ADK, pp. 5*b*–6*a*. 4 MP xxxviii. 77–79.

The *Traivarṇikācāra* mentions the names only of this and the two following *kriyās* without giving details.

3. Suprīti

This is carried out in the fifth month by good laymen *paramopāsaka*) who are *su-prīta*. Like the *garbhādhāna* it is to take place in the presence of the fires kindled before the Jina image.[1]

4. Dhṛti

This is to be performed in the seventh month and once again by layman and in accordance with the same ritual. Its purpose is to strengthen the foetus in the womb.[2]

5. Moda

Jinasena prescribes that this ceremony is to take place a little before the completion of the ninth month, being performed by brahmins in order to fatten the foetus (*garbha-puṣṭyai*). The woman is decked in her ornaments and made to wear a *gātrikā-bandha* (apparently a girdle on which *mantras* have been written) as well as a bracelet to serve as a phylactery.[3]

The *moda* described by Somasena[4] would seem more properly to correspond to the *prīti* of Jinasena since it is performed in the third month. The woman rubs her body with oil, bathes with water, takes a fruit in her hand, and makes the *Jina-pūjā*. Then together with her husband she goes to the temple to make the eightfold *pūjā* to the *arhats*, and to the *yakṣas* and *yakṣinīs*. The man touches her and ties a *yantra* to her neck.

The ceremony, which really in time sequence corresponds to the *moda*, is, in the *Ācāra-dinakara*,[5] the *puṃsavana*, a direct borrowing from Hinduism designed essentially to ensure the birth of a son. Vardhamāna lays down that this is to be carried out in the eighth month from conception when all the pregnancy longings (*ḍohala*) have been fulfilled and the breasts are full of milk. The woman is clad in new clothes and taken outdoors by night whilst *mantras* intended to ensure an easy delivery are recited. Gifts of money and sweetmeats are distributed. On this occasion the presence of the husband is not essential. That Vardhamāna's description of this

[1] MP xxxviii. 80–81.
[2] Ibid. 82.
[3] Ibid. 83–84.
[4] TrA viii. 5–62.
[5] ADK, pp. 8*b*–9*b*.

kriyā has a connexion with the *moda* seems suggested by the epithet *tac-charīra-pūrṇī-bhāva-pramoda-rūpam* 'expressing the joy that her body is full' used in the opening sentence.

6. Priyodbhava or Jāta-karman

The details of this, the birth ceremony are, according to Jinasena,[1] too extensive to be given in his *Ādi-purāṇa* and may be found in the *Upāsakādhyayana*. The essential features are the reciting of *mantras* and meditation on the birth of the Jina.

In the *Ācāra-dinakara*[2] the main preoccupation at birth is the horoscope. Whilst the woman is in labour in the *sūtikā-gṛha* the guru should wait with the astrologer near at hand praying to the *parameṣṭhins*. The astrologer must be informed of the exact moment of birth in order to cast the horoscope. A prayer is made to the goddess Ambikā to guard the child. No largesse is to be distributed on this occasion because of the birth impurity.

Vardhamāna describes a number of ceremonies following upon the birth for which there are no parallels in the *Ādi-purāṇa*. These include the *kṣīrāśana*[3] or putting of the infant to suck, the *suryendu-darśana*[4] or solemn showing of the sun and moon to the mother and newly born child, and the *ṣaṣṭi-saṃskāra*[5] or adoration of the eight goddesses who are called 'the mothers'. When the birth pollution is at an end—its duration varies with a person's caste—mother and child and all the members of the family bathe and the purification ceremony or *śuci-karman*[6] is celebrated.

7. Nāma-karman

Twelve days after the birth at an auspicious time for parents and child a name that will prosper the family is to be conferred on the child. This is to be chosen from among the 1,008 names of the Jina by the *ghaṭa-pattra* method, that is, by drawing from a pot filled with scraps of paper on which names have been written, one name at hazard.[7]

The *Traivarṇikācāra*[8] says that this is to be performed on the twelfth, sixteenth, twentieth, or thirty-second day after birth or at the first anniversary. The father writes down the name praying to the lord of a 1,008 names and then makes an offering to the *yakṣas*.

[1] MP xxxviii. 85–86.
[2] ADK, pp. 9*b*–10*b*.
[3] ADK, p. 12*a*.
[4] ADK, pp. 11*a*–11*b*.
[5] ADK 12*b*–13*b*.
[6] ADK 14*a*–14*b*.
[7] MP xxxviii. 87–89.
[8] TrA viii. 111–25.

In the *Ācāra-dinakara*[1] the family has to assemble with the guru and astrologer on the same day as the *śuci-karman* or a day or so later. After the horoscope has been exhibited the guru whispers to an aunt the name agreed on by the family. Then after a *Jina-pūjā* at home or in the temple she makes known this name.

8. Bahir-yāna

This ceremony takes place from two to four months after birth when for the first time the child is taken outdoors by the mother or the nurse. The gifts he receives on that occasion from his kinsfolk are kept and only handed over to him when he assumes the administration of his father's estate.[2]

Somasena[3] understands by the *bahir-yāna* (performed in the first, third, or fourth month of life) the child's first visit to the temple with his parents and kinsfolk. In honour of the occasion gifts of clothing are made to the *saṅgha* and there is a general distribution of betel.

9. Niṣadyā

In this ceremony the child is seated on a specially adorned couch whilst *pūjā* is made to the Jina.[4] The name only is mentioned by Somasena.

10. Anna-prāśana

This is the weaning ceremony placed by Jinasena[5] in the seventh or eighth month and again accompanied by a *pūjā*. Somasena[6] gives the additional detail that after the *pūjā* the child is put on the father's lap and given some rice mixed with sugar, milk, and ghee to eat.

The *Ācāra-dinakara*[7] places this ceremony in the sixth month for a boy and in the fifth month for a girl. Various types of grain and fruits belonging to the region are offered in *pūjā* to the Jina. The image is then bathed with the *pañcāmṛta*, some of which is given to the child. Offerings are then set before the family divinity and the mother puts some of this consecrated food in the child's mouth.

[1] ADK 14*b*–15*b*.
[2] MP xxxviii. 90–92.
[3] TrA viii. 126–30.
[4] MP xxxviii. 93–94.
[5] Ibid. 95.
[6] TrA viii. 136–9.
[7] ADK 16*a*–16*b*.

11. Vyuṣṭi or varṣa-vardhana

This ceremony, which takes place a year later, comprises *pūjā*, distribution of largesse, and the feasting of kinsfolk.[1] It, too, receives only a bare mention in the *Traivarṇikācāra*.

12. Keśa-vāpa or Caula-karman

After the child has been sprinkled with scented water his head is shaved: whether or not a top-knot is left depends on his caste. When he has been bathed and anointed and his best ornaments put on he is made to reverence the *munis* and is given a benediction by his kinsfolk.[2]

Somasena[3] says that this *kriyā* should be performed in the first, third, fifth, or seventh year of age. If the previous *kriyās* have been neglected a penance should first be carried out. It should not be done at a time when the mother is pregnant again or else she will have a miscarriage or bring forth a still-born child.

The same limits of age are prescribed by the *Ācāra-dinakara*[4] for the *karṇa-vedha* or ear-piercing ceremony which symbolically renders the child receptive to the Jaina teaching. The *caula-karman*[5] is to follow at an unspecified date after this, a complete tonsure being prescribed for *śūdras*, and the top-knot being left in the case of the higher castes. Food, clothes, and begging-bowls are to be distributed to the monks and clothes and ornaments given to the barber.

13. Lipi-saṃkhyāna

At the age of five the child is to begin to learn to read and write and a learned layman is to be engaged as teacher.[6] Somasena[7] divides this *kriyā* into two: *lipi-saṃkhyāna* and *pustaka-grahaṇa*. The accompanying *pūjā* is directed to Sarasvatī.

14. Upanīti[8]

This, the initiation or investiture, coincides with the conferment of the vows by which a boy is dedicated to the life of a student (all he has learned hitherto is to read and write). These he must assume

[1] MP xxxviii. 96–97.
[2] Ibid. 98–101.
[3] TrA viii. 147–62.
[4] ADK, pp. 17*a*–17*b*.
[5] ADK, pp. 18*a*–18*b*.
[6] MP xxxviii. 102–3.
[7] TrA viii. 163–81.
[8] Āśādhara describes this *kriyā* in the *Sāgāra-dharmāmṛta*, giving exactly similar details (SDhA vii. 20).

in the Jaina temple after making *pūjā* at the same time that he puts on the girdle of *muñja* grass (*mauñji-bandha*). He will be wearing a top-knot, will be clad in a white loincloth and a white outer cloth, and will have no ornaments but will be given the sacred thread which is symbolic of his vows. He may take a new name suitable for this way of life. He must live by begging his food: a boy of princely family may, however, satisfy this requirement by begging food from the women's apartments of the palace; but in any event the best of what he obtains in this way must be first offered in *pūjā* to the Jina. The recommended age for this ceremony is the eighth year from conception.[1]

The *Ācāra-dinakara*[2] makes it clear that the *upanīti* is only for the higher castes; for brahmins study begins at eight, for *kṣatriyas* at ten, for *vaiśyas* at twelve, terminating in all cases at sixteen.

15. Vrata-caryā

During the period passed in study the *mauñji-bandha* in three coils about the loins stands for the *ratna-traya*, the white loincloth symbolizes the purity of the *arhats*, the *yajñopavīta* on the chest signifies the seven *parama-sthānas*, and the perfect tonsure reinforces the tonsure of mind, speech, and body. The *brahmacārin* must keep the five *aṇu-vratas*. Toothpicks, betel, and collyrium are forbidden to him and he must bathe only with water without using perfumes. He must not lie on a bed but directly on the ground, and his body must not have contact with other bodies. He must study first of all the duties of a layman and then philosophy, grammar, metrics, *artha-śāstra*, astrology, divination, and mathematics.[3]

16. Vratāvataraṇa

On the conclusion of his studies he drops the special vows but abides by the ordinary vows, observing for his life long the *mūla-guṇas*. With the permission of his guru he assumes clothes, ornaments, and garlands. Though he may abandon the vow of abstinence from luxuries he should continue to keep the vow of sexual continence until the next *kriyā*. If he belongs to a caste which lives by weapons he may retain them either for the sake of his livelihood or for outward show.[4]

[1] MP xxxviii. 104–8. [2] ADK, p. 18*b*.
[3] MP xxxviii. 109–20. [4] Ibid. 121–6.

17. VIVĀHA

With his guru's permission the young man is now able to marry a girl from a suitable family. Members of the higher castes must make *pūjā* to the Jina and perform the marriage ceremony in a holy spot before fire. For seven days after the wedding the couple should have no sexual relations; they should go away to another region, if possible to a place of pilgrimage and then return home with great pomp. At the proper time, i.e. at the *ṛtu*, they should copulate for the procreation of children.[1]

As has already been noted the oldest texts avoid all mention of marriage, and both Digambaras and Śvetāmbaras take over Hindu customs, often following local usages. In general from Hemacandra's time onwards the eight forms of marriage recognized by the Hindu *dharma-śāstras* are listed, despite the fact that some of them run counter to Jaina ethics: Āśādhara[2] in fact has bluntly characterized the *gandharva-vivāha* as a secondary manifestation of the *vyasana* of whoring. In the sphere of number magic it might not be inappropriate here to point out the significance of the number 4, or more often 8, in connexion with marriage. The ideal age of marriage is sixteen for a man, twelve for a girl, or else twenty for a man and sixteen for a girl. In the popular tales a young man, if a merchant, is usually married to eight girls at the same time, whilst kings have a harem of 16,000 wives. The *Śrāddha-guṇa-vivaraṇa*[3] records sixteen desirable characteristics in a potential wife and sixteen undesirable ones.

Certain aspects of marriage, at least from the Śvetāmbara angle, have already been noted in discussing the *śrāvaka-guṇas*. Vardhamāna adds little to these rather general considerations though he would appear to advocate pre-puberty marriage,[4] but gives a picture of the pomp of the ceremonies involved. He would regard the *prājāpatya-vivāha* as the only form of marriage both desirable and possible in the present age.

The *Traivarṇikācāra*[5] recognizes five phases in the marriage:

(i) the formal undertaking (*vāg-dāna*): the bride's father says: 'I will give my daughter'. The bridegroom's father replies: 'I accept';

[1] MP xxxviii. 127–34.
[2] SDhA iii. 23.
[3] ŚrGuV 17*a*–18*a*.
[4] ADK, p. 31*b*.
[5] TrA xi. 41–64.

(ii) the giving away (*pradāna*): the bride is given with her silken dress and ornaments after benediction by brahmins;

(iii) the choosing (*varaṇa*): the bridegroom's father tells the brahmins: 'Choose a girl for me', and they reply: 'we choose her';

(iv) the hand-clasping (*pāni-pīḍana*): the bride takes the bridegroom's hands in hers;

(v) the scattering of buds (*aṅkurāropaṇa*).

The problem of monogamy or polygamy has, as noted in discussing the *brahma-vrata*, more than once preoccupied the *ācāryas* and theoretically at least any second marriage has been held to be a form of the *para-vivāha-karaṇa aticāra* of this vow. Usages differ with locality but in general remarriage is admitted after varying intervals of time if a woman proves sterile or gives birth only to still-born children or to female children.[1] The later Digambara writers recognize the custom of the *dharma-patni* and the *bhoga-patni*, of which Rājamalla[2] gives a very clear explanation.

A wife, he says, is a woman wedded in the presence of one's kinsfolk after making *pūjā* to Jina, *śāstra*, and gurus; any other woman is only a concubine. The wife may be either a *dharma-patni*, a woman of one's own caste who collaborates in one's religious duties, or a *bhoga-patni* belonging to another caste who, apart from the fact that she is legally wedded, is indistinguishable from a concubine. It is only the former who can carry out the religious duties of the home and it is her son who will take his father's place when he retires from the world. The term *bhoga-patni* does not seem to be recorded before the *Lāṭi-saṃhitā* but the *dharma-patni* figures already in Medhāvin's *śrāvakācāra*.[3] Somasena[4] would recognize the first wife as the *dharma-patni* and the second as the *bhoga-patni* but following a local usage of the Kannada country would require a symbolic wedding to a plant (the *arka-vivāha*)[5] before any third marriage can be contracted.

18. Varṇa-lābha

In Jinasena's[6] picture the young man who has completed the *kriyā* of marriage is still dependent on his father and still living in

[1] TrA xi. 197–8.
[2] *Lāṭī-saṃhitā*, ii. 179–86.
[3] *Dharma-saṃgraha-śrāvakācāra*, ix. 207.
[4] TrA xi. 200–5.
[5] For this custom see, *inter alia*, M. N. Srinivas, *Marriage and Family in Mysore*, p. 108.
[6] MP xxxviii. 135–41.

his house. The father now, after making the *Jina-pūjā*, transfers property to his son in the presence of leading laymen as witnesses, bidding him set up house on his own.

19. Kula-caryā

This is nothing other than the family duty (*kula-dharma*) of a householder, it amounts to leading a blameless life, making *pūjā* to the Jina, and carrying out the six daily duties.[1]

20. Gṛhīśitā

If a man carries out his duties as a householder and holds firmly to the *dharma* he may attain the status of a *gṛhasthācārya* which might perhaps be translated as 'elder', and seems to imply that he is the object of special respect and that his advice is listened to. Jinasena[2] calls him a *dvija-sattama* (an excellent man of good caste), a *grāma-yati* (one who within the village enjoys the esteem given to an ascetic), or a *nistāraka* (one who helps across the ocean of the *saṃsāra*). This last term appears also in the *Sāgāra-dharmāmṛta*.[3]

21. Praśānti

The layman will now have reached the summit of the lay life and it is time for him to think of withdrawing from the world. He is gradually to transfer the burdens of active life to his son and to seek tranquillity, attaching less and less value to material things and devoting himself to meditation and fasting.[4]

22. Gṛha-tyāga

This is the effective renunciation of worldly life corresponding to the attainment of the eleventh *pratimā* and expressing itself in *sakala-datti*. According to Āśādhara[5] the layman is to summon a worthy son or other person from his *gotra* and in the presence of witnesses, who must be co-religionists belonging to his caste, say: 'My dear friend, up till now we have kept the household dispensation, but now we desire to abandon it, it is for you to take our post. A good son is ready to aid his father when he sets out to devote himself to the cultivation of his soul, any other son is but an enemy in the guise of a son. You must assume control of this property

[1] MP xxxviii. 142–3.
[2] Ibid. 144–7.
[3] SDhA ii. 56.
[4] MP xxxviii. 148–9.
[5] SDhA vii. 24–27.

and the religious duties and the dependants.' Jinasena[1] prescribes for the occasion a solemn *pūjā* after which the layman in the presence of his loved ones entrusts everything he possesses to his son, saying: 'This is our ancestral tradition which you must preserve. Our property is to be divided into three parts, one-third to be allocated for religious purposes, one-third for the upkeep of your household, and one-third for distribution among your brothers and sisters, who are to have equal shares. You, as the eldest, must be the protector of my children. Make *pūjā* to gurus and Jinas.'

23. Dīkṣā

The reception into the monastic life closes the first phase of a man's existence on earth. It should follow a period spent in the eleventh *pratimā*.

Almost all the lay *kriyās* that have been discussed are accompanied by a *Jina-pūjā* and by the recitation of appropriate *mantras*. Jinasena insists on their use and in fact the whole course of later Digambara Jainism is characterized by the importance given to the magic word. Jinasena also stresses that his descriptions represent only a brief summary of the most important features of each ceremony for which varying details have been given by writers of old. The *kriyās* continue to hold an important place in the main current of the Mūla Saṅgha for at least several centuries, for Āśādhara in the *Sāgāra-dharmāmṛta* makes a casual reference to them ('*garbhādhāna*, *prīti*, *suprīti*,' &c.) implying that they are too well known to need description and, even much later, Medhāvin mentions them with the same familiarity. Yet in the end the Digambaras—like the Śvetāmbaras, as we have seen—virtually borrow the *saṃskāras* of their Hindu neighbours.

Jinasena offers another, more general pattern for dividing all existence into seven stages to which he also applies the designation *kriyā*. Of these three apply to the human incarnation:[2]

(i) *Saj-jāti*. This implies birth in a good family, covering purity of lineage on the father's side (*kula*) and on the mother's side (*jāti*). With this advantage of birth it is easy to obtain the *ratna-traya*—right belief, right knowledge, and right conduct—symbolized by the three threads of the *yajñopavīta* conferred on the boy in the *upanīti* ceremony. The remains of the *pūjā* offering placed on him

[1] MP xxxviii. 150–6. [2] MP xxxix. 81–200.

at the same time indicate his confirmation (*sthiri-karaṇa*) in the faith. He is thereby given a new birth, not from a human womb, but from the womb of divine knowledge and is considered to be possessed of *saj-jāti*.

(ii) *Sad-gṛhitva*. In this stage he keeps to the household life and follows a licit profession. The four Jaina *āśramas* and the division into *pakṣa* (the disposition towards *ahiṃsā*), *caryā* (the undertaking not to commit *hiṃsā* for the sake of propitiating a deity or achieving a *mantra*, or in order to procure food or medicine) and *sādhana* (the purification of the soul by *sallekhanā*)[1] are described.

(iii) *Pārivrājya*. The life as a monk.

[1] Cf. SDhA i. 19–20.

APPENDIX

ATICĀRAS OF THE AHIṂSĀ-VRATA

(*a*) SIDDHASENA'S COMMENTARY ON THE TATTVĀRTHA-SŪTRA

tatra bandhanaṃ bandhaḥ saṃyamanaṃ rajju-dāmakādibhiḥ.
hananaṃ vadhaḥ—tāḍanaṃ kaśādibhiḥ.
chaviḥ—śarīram tvag vā tac-chedaḥ pāṭanaṃ dvidhā-karaṇam.
bharaṇaṃ bhāraḥ—pūraṇaṃ atīva bāḍhaṃ suṣṭhu bhāro 'tibhāras tasyāropaṇaṃ—skandha-pṛṣṭhādi-sthāpanam atibhārāropaṇam.
annam aśanādi, pānaṃ peyam udakādi tayor adānaṃ nirodhaḥ.

(*b*) PŪJYAPĀDA'S COMMENTARY ON THE TATTVĀRTHA-SŪTRA

abhimata-deśa-gati-nirodha-hetur bandhaḥ.
daṇḍa-kaśa-vetrādibhir abhighātah prāṇinām vadhaḥ, na prāṇa-vyaparopaṇam, tataḥ prāg evāsya vinivṛttatvāt.
karṇa-nāsikādīnām avayavānām apanayanam chedaḥ.
nyāyya-bhārād atirikta-vahanam atibhārāropaṇam.
gav-ādīnām kṣut-pipāsa-bādha-karaṇam anna-pāna-nirodhaḥ.

(*c*) HARIBHADRA'S COMMENTARY ON THE ĀVAŚYAKA

bandhanaṃ bandhaḥ—saṃyamanaṃ rajju-dāmanakādibhih.
hananaṃ vadhaḥ—tāḍanam kaśādibhih.
chaviḥ—śarīram tasya chedaḥ—pāṭanam karapattrādibhih.
bharaṇaṃ bhāraḥ—atīva bharaṇam atibhāraḥ prabhūtasya pūga-phalādeḥ skandha-pṛṣṭhy—ādiṣv āropaṇam ity arthaḥ.
bhaktam aśanam odanādi, pānaṃ peyam udakādi tasya ca vyavacchedaḥ-nirodho 'dānam.

(*d*) ABHAYADEVA'S COMMENTARY ON THE ŚRĀVAKA-DHARMA-PAÑCĀŚAKA

bandhaḥ—rajju-dāmanakādibhiḥ saṃyamanaṃ.
vadhah—kaśādibhir hananaṃ . . .
chavih—tvak tad-yogāc charīram api chavis tasya cchedaḥ—asi-putrikādibhiḥ pāṭanaṃ chavicchedaḥ.
bharaṇaṃ bhāraḥ—atīva bhāro 'tibhāraḥ—prabhūtasya pūga-phalāder gav-ādi-pṛṣṭhādāv ārohaṇam.
bhakta-pānayor bhojanodakayor vyavacchedo nirodho bhakta-pāna-vyavacchedaḥ evam aviśeṣena bandhādīnām akaraṇīyatayopadeśe sati priyā-putrāder vinaya-grahaṇa-roga-cikitsādy-arthānām api teṣām

vrata-mālinya-nimittatā prasajyate, tatas tat-parihārārtham āha 'krodhādi-dūṣita-manāḥ'—kopa-lobhādi-kaṣāya-kalaṅkitāntaḥkaraṇah, prāṇi-prāṇa-prahāṇa-nirapekṣa ity arthaḥ . . .

deśasya bhañjanad deśasyaiva ca pālanād aticāra-vyapadeśaḥ pravartate tad uktam.

'na marayāmīti-kṛta-vratasya . . .'

bandhādi-grahaṇasya copalakṣaṇatvān mantra-tantra-prayogādayo 'nye 'py evam atrāticāratayā dṛśyāḥ.

(*e*) Abhayadeva's commentary on the Upāsaka-daśāh

bandho dvipadādīnām rajjv-ādinā saṃyamanam.
vadho yaṣṭy-ādibhis tāḍanam.
chavicchedaḥ—śarīrāvayava-cchedaḥ.
atibhārāropaṇam—tathāvidha-śakti-vikalānāṃ mahā-bhārāropaṇam.
bhakta-pāna-vyavacchedaḥ—aśana-pānīyāpradānam.
ihāyaṃ vibhāgaḥ pūjyair uktam.

'bandha-vahaṃ chavi-chedaṃ . . .' (*verse 10 of Śrāvaka-dharma-pañcāśaka quoted*) tathā.

'na marayāmīti-kṛta-vratasya . . .'

(*f*) Hemacandra's commentary on the Yoga-śāstra

bandho rajjv-ādinā go-mahiṣy-ādīnāṃ niyantraṇam, sva-putrādīnām api vinaya-grahaṇārthaṃ kriyate, ataḥ 'krodhād' ity uktam, krodhāt prabala-kaṣāyodayād yo bandhaḥ sa prathamo 'ticāraḥ.

chaviḥ śarīram tvag vā tasyāḥ chedo dvaidhī-karaṇam, sa ca pāda-valmīkopahata-pādasya putrāder api kriyate . . .

adhikasya voḍhum aśakyasya bhārasyāropaṇam go-karabha-rāsabha-manuṣyādeḥ skandhe pṛṣṭhe śirasi vā vāhanāyādhiropaṇam . . .

prahāro laguḍādina tāḍanam krodhād eva . . .

annādi-rodho bhojana-pānāder niṣedhaḥ krodhād eva . . .

(*g*) Devendra's commentary on the Śrāddha-dina-kṛtya

bandho rajjv-ādibhiḥ saṃyamanam.
vadho dvipadādīnām nirdaya-tāḍanam.
chavi-cchedaḥ karṇādi-karttanam.
atibhāraḥ śakty-anapekṣaṃ guru-bhārāropaṇam.
bhakta-pāna-vyavacchedaḥ-anna-pāna-nirodhaḥ.

(*h*) Āśādhara's commentary on the Sāgāra-dharmāmṛta

bandho rajjv-ādinā go-manuṣyādīnāṃ niyantraṇam, sa ca putrādīnām api vinaya-grahaṇārthaṃ vidhīyate.

vadho daṇḍa-kaśādy-abhighātah.
chedaḥ karṇa-nāsikādīnām avayavānām apanayanam.
atibhārādhiropaṇam nyāyya-bhārād atiriktasya voḍhum aśakyasya bhārasyāropaṇam vṛṣabhādīnām pṛṣṭha-skandhādau vāhanopādhiropaṇam.
bhukti-nirodho 'nna-pānādi-niṣedhaḥ, tīkṣṇa-kṣudhādi-pīḍitaḥ prāṇī mriyata ity annadi-nirodho na kasyāpi kartavyaḥ.

ATICĀRAS OF THE SATYA-VRATA

(*a*) SIDDHASENA'S COMMENTARY ON THE TATTVĀRTHA-SŪTRA

nyasyate—niksipyata iti nyāsaḥ—rūpakādy-arpaṇam tasyāpahāraḥ—apalāpaḥ yo 'tra dravyāpahāraḥ parasva-svīkaraṇa-lakṣaṇaḥ sa na vivakṣitah, tasyādattādāna-viṣayatvāt, yat tatra vacanam apalāpakaṃ yena kāraṇa-bhūtena nyāso 'pahriyate apalapyate tad vacanam nyāsāpahāraḥ...
rahaḥ—ekāntas tatra bhavaṃ rahasyaṃ rahasyenābhyākhyānam abhiśaṃsanam asad-adhyāropaṇam rahasyābhyākhyānam . . .
rahasyena karmaṇā 'bhyākhyānaṃ strī-puṃsayoḥ paraspareṇeti pratārana-dvārena—yadi vṛddhā strī tatas tasyai kathayati 'ayam tava bhartā kumāryām ati-prasaktaḥ' atha taruṇīṃ tata evam āha 'ayaṃ te bhartā prauḍha-ceṣṭitāyāṃ madhyama-vayasi yositi prasaktas' tathā 'yam khara-kāmo mṛdu-kāma' iti vā parihasati...
ākāro 'ṅguli-hasta-bhrū-netra-kriyā-śiraḥ-kampādir aneka-rūpaḥ paraśarīra-vartī, tena tādṛśā ākāreṇa sahāvinā-bhūto yo mantro gūḍhaḥ parābhiprāyas tam upalabhya sahākāraṃ mantram asūyayāviṣkaroty eṣa sākāra-mantra-bhedaḥ prakāśanam . . .
etad uktam bhavati—anadhikṛta-sannidhau ceṣṭā-viśeṣaiḥ svākūta-prakāśanam ākāraḥ tam eva spaṣṭataram udāharati—paiśunyam guhya-mantra-bhedaś ceti . . . mantraṇaṃ mantro gupta-bhāṣaṇaṃ rājādi-kārya-sambandhas tasya bhedaḥ prakhyāpanam . . .
kūṭam asad-bhūtam likhyata iti lekhaḥ karaṇaṃ kriyā kūṭa-lekha-kriyā anya-mudrākṣara-bimba-svarūpa-lekha-karaṇam . . .
mithyopadeśaḥ—asad-upadeśaḥ pareṇānyasyātisandhānaṃ svayaṃ vā 'tisandhānam anyasya . . .
pramattasya vacanaṃ para-pīḍā-jananaṃ 'vāhyantāṃ kharoṣṭrāḥ, hanyantāṃ dasyava' iti.

(*c*) HARIBHADRA'S COMMENTARY ON THE ĀVAŚYAKA

sahasā—anālocya abhyākhyānaṃ sahasābhyākhyānam abhiśaṃsanam asad-adhyāropaṇaṃ tad yathā 'cauras tvaṃ paradāriko' vety-ādi.
rahaḥ—ekāntas tatra bhavaṃ rahasyaṃ tena tasmin vā abhyākhyānam, etad uktaṃ bhavati—ekānte mantrayamāṇān vakti—ete hīdam cedam ca rājāpakāritvādi mantrayanti.

sva-dāre mantra-bhedaḥ sva-dāra-mantra-bhedaḥ—sva-dara-mantra-prakāśanam sva-kalatra-viśrabdha-viśiṣṭāvasthā-mantritānya kathanam ity arthaḥ.

kūṭam asad-bhūtam likhyata iti lekhaḥ tasya karaṇam kriyā kūṭa-lekhā-kriyā—kūṭa-lekha-karaṇam, anya-mudrāksara-bimba-svarūpa-lekha-karaṇam ity arthaḥ...

nyasyate—nikṣipyata iti nyāsaḥ—rūpyakādy-arpaṇaṃ tasyāpaharaṇam nyāsāpaharaḥ.

(*d*) Abhayadeva's commentary on the Śrāvaka-dharma-pañcāśaka

sahasā analocyābhyākhyānam asad-doṣādhyāropaṇaṃ yathā 'cauras tvaṃ pāradāriko' vety-ādi rahasā ekāntena hetunābhyākhyānam, etad uktaṃ bhavati—rahasi mantrayamāṇān abhidhatte—ete hidam cedam ca rāja-viruddhādikaṃ mantrayate.

sva-dāra-mantra-bhedaṃ—sva-kalatra-viśrabdha-bhāṣitānya-kathanam, dāra-grahanam ceha mitrādy-upalakṣaṇārtham...

mṛṣā—alīka-vadana-viṣaya upadeśo yasya sa tathā tad bhāvas tattā tām mṛṣopadeśatām athavā mṛṣopadeśa eva mṛṣopadeśakaḥ, idam evam caivaṃ ca brūhīty-ādikam asatyābhidhāna-śikṣaṇam atas tam.

kuṭa-lekhasya—aṣad-bhūtārtha-sūcakākṣara-lekhanasya karaṇam—vidhānam kūṭa-lekha-karaṇam.

'sahas'-abbhakkhāṇ'-āi jāṇanto jai karejja to bhaṅgo
jai puṇa 'ṇābhog'-āihiṃto to hoi aiyāro'.

(*e*) Abhayadeva's commentary on the Upāsaka-daśāḥ

sahasā anālocyābhyākhyānam asad-doṣādhyāropaṇam sahasābhyākhyānam yathā 'cauras tvam' ity-ādi... raha ekāntas tena hetunābhyākhyānam raho 'bhyākhyānam, etad uktaṃ bhavati rahasi mantrayamāṇānām, vakti 'ete hīdam cedam ca rājāpakārādi mantrayante' iti...

sva-dāra-sambandhino mantrasya viśrambha-jalpasya bhedaḥ prakāśanam sva-dāra-mantra-bhedaḥ ... mṛṣopadeśaḥ pareṣām asatyopadeśaḥ...

kūṭa-lekha-karaṇam asad-bhūtārthasya lekhasya vidhānam.

(*f*) Hemacandra's commentary on the Yoga-śāstra

sahasā anālocyābhyākhyānam asad-doṣādhyāropaṇaṃ yathā 'cauras tvaṃ pāradāriko' vety-ādi.

anye tu sahasābhyākhyāna-sthāne rahasyābhyākhyānaṃ paṭhanti, vyācakṣate ca—raha ekāntas tatra bhavaṃ rahasyaṃ rahasyenābhyākhyānam abhiśaṃsanam asad-adhyāropaṇam rahasyābhyākhyānam yathā—yadi vṛddha-strī tatas tasyai kathayati 'ayam tava bhartā tarunyām atiprasaktaḥ' atha taruṇī tata evam āha 'ayam te bhartā prauḍha-ceṣṭitāyām madhyama-vayasi yoṣiti prasaktaḥ', tathā 'yam khara-kāmo mṛdu-kāma' iti vā parihasati ...

'sahas'-abbhakkhān'-āi ... ' (*verse as above quoted*)

guhyam gūhanīyam na sarvasmai yat kathanīyaṃ rājādi-kārya-sambaddham.

tasyānadhikṛtenaivākāreṅgitādibhir jñātvānyasmai prakāśanaṃ guhya-bhāṣaṇam yathā 'ete hīdam idaṃ ca rājā-viruddhādikam mantrayante, athavā guhya-bhāṣaṇam paiśunyam ...

viśvastā viśvāsam upagatā ye mitra-kalatrādayas teṣām mantro mantraṇam tasya bhedaḥ prakāśanam, guhya-bhāṣaṇe guhyam ākārādinā vijñāyānadhikṛta eva guhyam iha tu svayaṃ mantrayitvaiva mantram bhinattīty anayor bhedaḥ ...

mithyopadeśo 'sad-upadeśaḥ, pratipanna-satya-vratasya hi para-pīḍā-karaṃ vacanam asatyam eva tataḥ pramādāt para-pīḍā-karaṇe upadeśe aticāro yathā 'vāhyantāṃ kharoṣṭrādayo hanyantāṃ dasyava' iti ...

kūṭam asad-bhūtaṃ tasya lekho lekhanaṃ kūṭa-lekhaḥ-anya-svarūpākṣara-mudrā-karaṇam ...

(*g*) Devendra's commentary on the Śrāddha-dina-kṛtya

sahasā—anālocyābhyākhyānam asad-doṣādhiropaṇam 'cauro 'yam' ity-ādy-abhidhānam sahasābhyākhyānam.

rahasi—ekānte mantrayamāṇān vīkṣya idaṃ cedaṃ rāja-viruddhādikam ete mantrayante ity-ādy-abhyākhyānan raho 'bhyākhyānam.

sva-dārāṇām viśuddha-bhāṣitasyānyasmai kathanaṃ sva-dāra-mantra-bhedaḥ.

ajñāta-mantrauṣadhādy-upadeśanam mṛṣopadeśaḥ.

anya-mudrākṣara-bimbādinā kūṭasyārthasya lekhanaṃ kūṭa-lekhaḥ.

(*h*) Āśādhara's commentary on the Sāgāra-dharmāmṛta

mithyādik—mithyopadeśaḥ, abhyudaya-niḥśreyasārthesu kriyā-viśeṣeṣv anyasyānyathā pravartanam pareṇa sandehāpannena pṛṣṭhe 'jñānādinānyathā kathanam ity arthaḥ, athavā pratipanna-satya-vratasya para-pīḍā-karaṃ vacanam asatyam eva tataḥ pramādāt para-pīḍā-karaṇe upadeśe aticāro yathā 'vāhyantāṃ kharoṣṭrādayo hanyantāṃ dasyava iti niṣprayojanaṃ vacanam.

raho-'bhyākhyā rahasy ekānte strī-pumbhyām anuṣṭhitasya kriyā-viśeṣasyābhyākhyā prakāśanam yayā dampatyor anyasya vā puṃsaḥ striyā vā rāga-prakarṣa utpadyate.

mantra-bhedaḥ—aṅga-vikāra-bhrūkṣepādibhiḥ parābhiprāyaṃ jñātvā-suyādinā tat-prakaṭanaṃ viśvasita-mitrādibhir vā ātmanā saha mantritasya lajjādi-karasyārthasya prakāśanam.

kūṭa-lekha-kriyā—anyenānuktam anuṣṭhitaṃ ca yet kiṃcit tasya para-prayoga-vaśād evaṃ tenoktam anuṣṭhitaṃ ceti vañcanā-nimittaṃ lekhanam, anya-sarūpākṣara-mudrā-karaṇam ity anye.

nyāsāpahāraḥ—nyastasya nikṣiptasya hiraṇyādi-dravyasya aṃśam ekam aṃśaṃ vismartur vismaraṇa-śīlasya nikśeptur anujñā.

ATICĀRAS OF THE BHOGOPABHOGA-VRATA

(*a*) Siddhasena's commentary on the Tattvārtha-sūtra

cittaṃ cetano saṃjñānam upayogo 'vadhānam iti paryāyāḥ . . .

sacitta āhāro vā yasya sacittam āhārayatīti vā sacittāhāraḥ, mūla-kandalī-kandārdrakādi-sādhāraṇa-vanaspati-pratyeka-taru-śarīrāṇi tad abhyavahāraḥ, pṛthvy-ādi-kāyānāṃ vā sacittānām . . .

sacittena sambaddhaṃ karkaṭika-bīja-kaulikā-kulasya pakva-badarodumbarāmra-phalādi bhakṣayataḥ sacitta-sambaddhāhāratvam . . .

sacittena sammiśrāhāraḥ puṣpa-phala-vrīhi-tilānāṃ vyatimiśra-modakādi-khādyasya vā kunthu-pipilikādi-sūkṣma-jantu-vyatimiśrasyābhyavahāraḥ—abhiṣavāhāra iti, surā-sauvīraka-māṃ-saprakara-parṇaky-ādy-aneka-dravya-saṅghāta-niṣpannaḥ surā-sīdhu-madhu-vārādir abhivṛṣya-vṛkba-dravyopayogo vā.

duṣpakvāhāraḥ—duṣpakvam manda-pakvam abhinna-taṇḍula-phala-loṣṭa-yava-godhūma-sthūla-maṇḍaka-kaṇḍukādi tasyābhyavahāra aihika-pratyavāya-kāri yāvatā vāṃśena sacetanas tāvatā para-lokam apy upahanti.

(*c*) Haribhadra's commentary on the Āvaśyaka

sacittaṃ cetanā saṃjñānam upayogo 'padhānam iti paryāyāḥ.

sacitto vā āhāro yasya sacittam āhārayati iti vā, mūla-kandalī-kandakārdrakādi-sādhāraṇa-pratyeka-taru-śarīrāṇi sacittāni sacittaṃ pṛthvy-ādy āhārayatīti bhāvanā.

sacitta-pratibaddhāhāro yathā vṛkṣe pratibaddho gundādi pakva-phalāni vā.

apakvauṣadha-bhakṣaṇatvam idaṃ pratītam (sacitta-sammiśrāhāra iti vā pāṭhāntaraṃ sacittena sammiśra āhāraḥ sacitta-sammiśrāhāraḥ, vally-ādi puṣpādi vā sammiśraṃ).

duṣpakvauṣadhi-bhakṣaṇata duṣpakvaḥ—asvinnā ity arthaḥ tad-bhakṣaṇatā.

tucchauṣadhi-bhakṣaṇatā tucchā hi asārā mudga-phalī-prabhṛtayaḥ, atra hi mahatī virādhanā alpā ca tuṣṭiḥ, bahvibhir apy aihiko 'py apāyaḥ sambhāvyate.

(*d*) Abhayadeva's commentary on the Śrāvaka-dharma-pañcāśaka

sacittaṃ sacetanaṃ kandādi iha ca sarvatra nivṛtti-viṣayī-kṛta-pravṛttāv apy aticārābhidhānaṃ vrata-sāpekṣasyānābhogātikramādi-nibandhana-pravṛttyā draṣṭavyam, anyathā bhaṅga eva syāt, atas tannivṛtti-viṣayī-kṛtaṃ bhakṣayatayā varjayatīti yogaḥ.

pratibaddhaṃ—sambaddhaṃ sacitta-vṛkṣeṣu gundādi pakva-phalādi vā, tad-bhakṣaṇaṃ hi sāvadyāhāra-varjakasya sāvadyāhāra-pravṛtti-rūpatvād anābhogādināticāraḥ, anyathāsthikam tyakṣyāmi, tasyaiva sacetanatvāt, kaṭāham tu bhakṣayiṣyāmi tasyācetanatvāt, iti buddhyā pakvaṃ kharjūrādi-phalam mukhe prakṣipataḥ sacitta-varjakasya sacitta-pratibaddhāhāro 'ticāraḥ.

'apaula'—apakvam agninā asaṃskṛtaṃ.

'dupaola'—duṣpakvam ardha-svinnaṃ.

tuccham—niḥsāraṃ...

ādyāv aticārau sacetana-kanda-phalādi-viṣayau itare tu śāly-oṣadhi-viṣayaḥ.

(*e*) Abhayadeva's commentary on the Upāsaka-daśāḥ

sacittāhāraḥ pṛthvy-ap-kāya-vanaspati-jīva-śarīrāṇāṃ sacetanānām abhyavaharaṇam...

sacitta-pratibaddhāhāraḥ—sacitte vṛkṣādau pratibaddhasya gundāder abhyavaharaṇam.

athavā sacitte 'sthike pratibaddhaṃ yat pakvaṃ acetanaṃ kharjūra-phalādi tasya 'sāsthikasya kaṭāham acetanaṃ bhakṣayiṣyāmītarat parihariṣyāmi' iti bhāvanayā mukha-kṣepaṇam...

apakvauṣadhiḥ—apakvāyā agnināsaṃskṛtāyā oṣadheḥ śāly-ādi-kāyā bhakṣaṇatā bhojanam...

duṣpakvauṣadhiḥ—duḥpakva asvinnā oṣadhayas tad bhakṣaṇatā, aticāratā cāsya pakva-buddhyā bhakṣayataḥ...

tucchauṣadhiḥ—tuccha asārā oṣadhayo 'niṣpanna-mudga-phalī-prabhṛtayaḥ, tad-bhakṣaṇe hi mahatī virādhanā svalpā ca tat-kārya-tṛptiḥ.

(*f*) Hemacandra's commentary on the Yoga-śāstra

sacittaḥ kanda-mūla-phalādih pṛthivī-kāyādir vā.

iha ca nivṛtti-viṣayī-kṛta-pravṛttau bhaṅga-sad-bhāve 'py aticārābhidhānam vrata-sāpekṣasyānābhogātikramādinā pravṛttau draṣṭavyam.

tena sacittena sambaddhaḥ pratibaddhaḥ sacitta-sambaddhaḥ, sacetana-vṛkṣādinā sambaddho gundādiḥ pakva-phalādir vā, sacittāntarbījaḥ kharjūrāmrādiḥ, tad-āhāro hi sacittāhāra-varjakasyānābhogādinā sāvadyāhāra-pravṛtti-rūpatvād aticāraḥ, athavā bījaṃ tyakṣyāmi tasyaiva sacetanatvāt kaṭāhaṃ tu bhakṣayiṣyāmi tasyācetanatvād iti buddhyā pakvaṃ kharjūrādi-phalaṃ mukhe prakṣipataḥ sacitta-varjakasya sacitta-pratibaddhāhāraḥ.

sacittena miśraḥ śabalaḥ, aharah sammiśrāhāraḥ, yathā ārdraka-dāḍima-bīja-kulikā-cirbhaṭikādi-miśraḥ pūraṇādiḥ, tila-miśro yava-dhānādir vā . . .

abhiṣavo 'neka-dravya-sandhāna-niṣpannaḥ surā-sauvīrakādiḥ, maṃsa-prakāra-khaṇḍādir vā surā-madhv-ādy-abhiṣyandi-vṛṣya-dravyo-payogo vā . . .

duṣpakvo manda-pakvaḥ sa cāsāv āhāraś ca duṣpakvāhāraḥ, sa cārdha-svinna-pṛthuka-taṇḍula-yava-godhūma-sthūla-maṇḍaka-karkaṭaka-phalādir aihika-pratyavāya-kārī yāvatā cāṃśena sacetanas tāvatā para-lokam apy upahanti . . .

kecit tv apakvāhāram apy aticāratvena varṇayanti, apakvam cāgninā yad asaṃskṛtam tucchauṣadhi-bhakṣaṇam api kecid aticāram āhuḥ, tucchauṣadhayaś ca mudgādi-komala-śimbī-rūpāḥ . . .

(*g*) Devendra's commentary on the Śrāddha-dina-kṛtya

kṛta-sacitta-pratyākhyānasya kṛta-tat-parināmasya vā sacittam atiriktam anābhogādinā abhyavahārataḥ sacittāhāro 'ticāraḥ.

evaṃ vṛkṣa-stha-gundādi rājādanādi vā sāsthikaṃ phalam mukhe prakṣipataḥ sacitta-pratibadhāhāraḥ.

evam apakvasya—agninā asaṃskṛtasyāparinata-kaṇikkāder bhakṣayato 'pakvauṣadhi-bhakṣaṇatā.

evam duṣpakvasya— pṛthukāder duṣpakvauṣadhi-bhakṣaṇatā.

tuccha—atṛpti-hetutvād asāra oṣadhyāḥ komala-mudga-siñjādika bha-kṣayatās tucchauṣadhi-bhakṣaṇatā.

(*h*) Āśādhara's commentary on the Sāgāra-dharmā-mṛta

tatra sacittaṃ cetanāvad dravyaṃ harita-kāyam, apakvaṃ karvaṭy-ādi, trasa-bahu-ghātety-ādinā niṣiddhe 'py atra pravṛttau bhaṅga sadbhāve 'py aticārābhidhānaṃ vrata-sāpekṣasyāpranidhānātikra-mādinā pravṛttau draṣṭavyam.

tena sambaddhaṃ sacittenopaśliṣṭaṃ sacetana-vṛkṣādinā sambaddhaṃ gondādikam pakva-phalādikaṃ sacittāntarbījaṃ kharjūrāmrādikaṃ, tad-āhāro hi sacittāhāra-varjakasyānābhogādinā sāvadyāhāra-pravṛtti-rūpatvād aticāraḥ, athavā bījaṃ tyakṣyāmi tasyaiva sacetanatvāt kaṭāhaṃ tu bhakṣayiṣyāmi tasyācetanatvād iti buddhyā pakvaṃ kharjūrādi-phalaṃ mukhe prakṣipataḥ sacitta-varjakasya sacitta-pratibaddhāhāraḥ.

sammiśraṃ tena sacittena vyatikīrnaṃ vibhaktam aśakyam sūkṣma-jantukam ity arthaḥ athavā sacitta-śabalaṃ tat-sammiśraṃ yathā ardraka-dāḍima-bīja-cirbhaṭikādi-miśram pūraṇādikaṃ, tila-miśram yava-dhanādikam.

duṣpakvaṃ santas tandula-bhāvena atikledanena vā duṣṭam pakvaṃ manda-pakvaṃ vā duṣpakvam tac cārddha-svinnam pṛthuka-tandula-yava-godhūma-sthūla-maṇḍaka-phalādikam āma-doṣāvahatvenaihika-pratyavāya-kāraṇam.

abhiṣavaṃ sauvīrādi-dravaṃ vā vṛṣyaṃ vā.